A Crisis of Community

A Crisis of Community

The Trials and
Transformation of a
New England Town,
1815–1848

MARY BABSON FUHRER

The University of
North Carolina Press
Chapel Hill

*This book was published with the assistance of
the Anniversary Endowment Fund and the Authors Fund
of the University of North Carolina Press.*

Set in Charter and Birch

The paper in this book meets the guidelines for permanence and
durability of the Committee on Production Guidelines for
Book Longevity of the Council on Library Resources.

The University of North Carolina Press has been
a member of the Green Press Initiative since 2003.

Library of Congress Cataloging-in-Publication Data
Fuhrer, Mary Babson.
A crisis of community : the trials and transformation of
a New England town, 1815–1848 / Mary Babson Fuhrer.
pages cm
Includes bibliographical references and index.
ISBN 978-1-4696-1286-7 (hardback)
ISBN 978-1-4696-2992-6 (pbk.)
1. Boylston (Mass.)—History—19th century. 2. Boylston (Mass.)—
Social conditions—19th century. 3. Community life—Massachusetts—
Boylston. 4. Social change—Massachusetts—Boylston.
5. White, Mary Avery, 1778–1860. 6. White family. I. Title.
F74.B56F85 2014
974.4′3—dc23   2013032613

IN MEMORY OF WILLIAM BABSON,

who told me about the peepers,

and

IN HONOR OF HELEN BABSON,

who told me,

"Don't write so that you

can be understood,

but so that you

cannot be misunderstood"

CONTENTS

ILLUSTRATIONS

ACKNOWLEDGMENTS

My acquaintance with Mary White began fifteen years ago, when Jack Larkin introduced me to her diaries and her family's letters. Jack and other Old Sturbridge Village people, especially Ed Hood, Tom Kelleher, Frank White, and Jeannette Robichaud, were unfailingly generous in sharing Mary's world with me. Soon after I met Mary, I visited the folks at the Boylston Historical Society, and they became not only my greatest resource but my dear friends. It is only because of the extraordinary job Bill DuPuis, Fred Brown, Judy Haynes, and the rest of the BHS folks have done in collecting and preserving Boylston's past that this story could be told.

As all historians know, the best people in the world are the archivists who help us mine their collections. I am particularly grateful to the fine staffs at the Massachusetts Historical Society, the American Antiquarian Society, the Massachusetts Archives, the New England Historic and Genealogical Society, the Massachusetts State House Library, Historic New England, Boston Public Library Special Collections, University of Delaware Special Collections, Brown University's Hay Library, and the Worcester County Registry of Deeds and Probate Records. I am also grateful to the keepers of alumni records at Harvard University, Williams College, Wheaton College, and Andover Academy.

Local historical society archives are priceless resources in this sort of small-town research, and I am grateful to the dedicated and enthusiastic folks at the West Boylston Historical Society, New Ipswich Historical Society, Ashland Historical Society, and Northborough Historical Society. I am also grateful for the patient assistance of town clerks in Boylston, West Boylston, and Ashland; the public libraries of these towns; and the church administrators at the First Congregational Churches in Boylston and West Boylston. In addition, several individuals generously lent private resources that were very helpful: Diana Smith shared her research on Boylston antislavery petitions from the National Archives, Vernon Woodworth and Molly Scott Evans shared the manuscript of their ancestor Avery White, and Linda Branniff shared priceless local history resources from Aaron White Jr.'s adopted hometown.

Several scholars have generously provided access to their research as well as their time and advice. Brian Donahue of Brandeis, who read a draft of the manuscript, has been a long-time generous resource on historical land use and ecology in Massachusetts. Phil Lampi of the American Antiquarian Society assisted me with "America Votes," his extraordinary database of early national election returns. Ben Friedman of Harvard University shared his curriculum and readings on religion and economy in American history. John Brooke of Ohio State provided guidance on reconstructing and interpreting Worcester County voter affiliations. Bob Gross of the University of Connecticut has been exceptionally generous, sharing draft material on his upcoming book, *The World of the Transcendentalists*; references to his earlier work; and feedback on my work.

Several associations provided research and publication assistance. Old Sturbridge Village got me started on this quest with its research fellowship. The Massachusetts Foundation for the Humanities and the Bay State Historical League provided research and publication fellowships. Peter Benes and the Dublin Seminar supported the publication of two articles that formed part of the background for two chapters.

Mark Simpson-Vos, Paula Wald, and Liz Gray of the University of North Carolina Press have been ever patient with my endless questions and generous with their guidance.

Primary thanks go to my mentors, Jeff Bolster and Bill Harris. They guided, counseled, cheered, consoled, advised, and endlessly read wordy drafts, usually managing to tell me what it was I was trying to say, but ever so gently! They are both scholars and gentlemen, and I am proud to be able to call them my friends. I also benefited from the support and friendship of academics Jess Lepler and Lige Gould, who read drafts of this project.

I am ever so grateful for the support and encouragement of dear friends Joanne Myers and Ellen Rothman. They made me believe I could do this. Thanks also to my Small Group, especially my cheerleaders, Earl and Ellen.

Finally, this book is a family affair. My children, Margaret, John, and Jeffrey, transcribed diaries, entered scads of data, provided tech support, and endured endless dinner-table discussions of the "other Mary." My husband, Jeff, supported my musings, read and reflected on every chapter, shared his wisdom and insights, and gave unconditional support. He asked the critical "So what?" questions when I rambled on, he focused my fuzzy ideas, he cheered my good ones, and when I doubted, he made me laugh! I am forever grateful.

A Crisis of Community

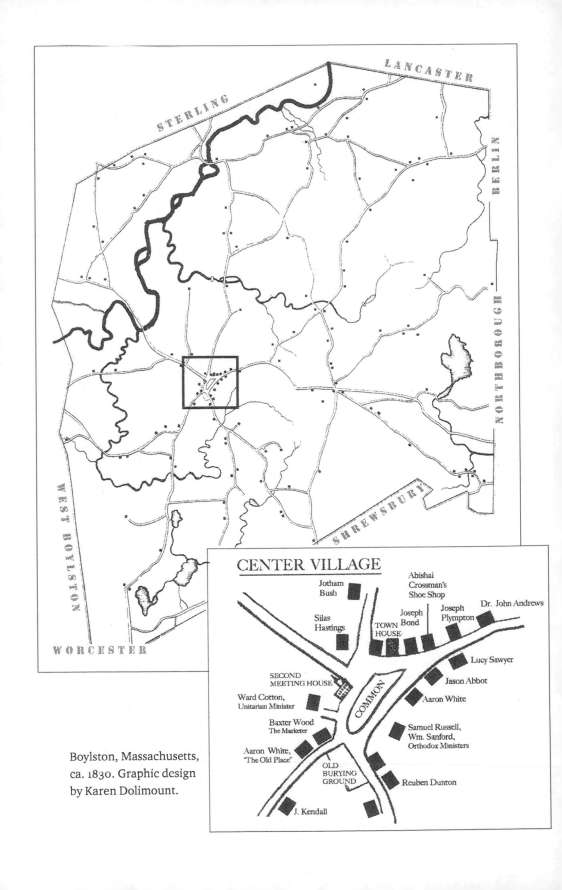

STERLING

LANCASTER

BERLIN

NORTHBOROUGH

WEST BOYLSTON

SHREWSBURY

WORCESTER

CENTER VILLAGE

Jotham Bush

Abishai Crossman's Shoe Shop

Silas Hastings

TOWN HOUSE

Joseph Bond

Joseph Plympton

Dr. John Andrews

Lucy Sawyer

Jason Abbot

SECOND MEETING HOUSE

COMMON

Aaron White

Ward Cotton, Unitarian Minister

Baxter Wood The Marketer

Samuel Russell, Wm. Sanford, Orthodox Ministers

Aaron White, "The Old Place"

OLD BURYING GROUND

Reuben Dunton

J. Kendall

Boylston, Massachusetts,
ca. 1830. Graphic design
by Karen Dolimount.

This Wilderness World

When a heavy-laden ox team lumbered into Boylston in the spring of 1842, there were many who believed it was hauling 1,000 pounds of trouble. The wagon drew up in the barnyard of Capt. John Howe—possibly the most cantankerous man in this rural village—to deliver its load: a newly cast steeple bell. Howe had engineered this moment, and he was exultant. As townsmen gingerly raised the bell upon timbers to transport it to the new town hall, the clapper swung clear. The deep tone of the bell rang out resoundingly, heralding its arrival. For some in this central Massachusetts village, it was a peal of victory; for others, it tolled alarm and dismay.[1]

Bells had long ordered community in rural New England. Before the advent of household clocks and pocket watches, the meetinghouse bell marked the passage of time, sounding the noon and 9:00 P.M. hours. All who lived within the sound of the great bell heard its call to worship and town meeting. It was the bell that alerted townsfolk to their neighbor's distress or sounded the alarm when fire threatened or danger approached. Its deep tones tolled the death of neighbors, in numbered strokes that called out the gender and age of the deceased and so announced who was no longer of this world. In times of war, the town bell was often hidden to prevent foes from seizing this symbol of communal authority. Summoning townsfolk to shared duties, joys, and griefs, the town bell was a sonorous artifact of community order.[2]

Yet *this* bell did not signify order: it heralded strife. Captain Howe's faction had encountered fierce resistance in its battle to bring the bell to town. The opposition protested: the town already had a bell. It hung in the steeple of the old meetinghouse on the common, and it had rung out its calls to community for years. By the mid-1820s, though, that community—like so many others across Massachusetts—had splintered, and now competing factions battled for control of building, bell, and the authority they embodied.

Captain Howe's party of discontents fought for more than a decade to ring that bell. Year after year, in town meeting debates that exhibited "great warmth," Howe's liberal faction put forward motions to allow their ringer to sound the hours. But their chosen man found the opposition barred his way and "refuse[d] him liberty to enter the Meeting House and ring said bell."[3] (Surrounding towns had similar contests; nearby Harvard voted to remove the rope from its bell to silence the strife.) Finally, Howe's faction petitioned the town to purchase a *second* bell to hang in the new town hall adjacent to the meetinghouse. This was the bell that rang out in Howe's barnyard, its discordant racket giving voice to community conflict. We can imagine folk all around town, long accustomed to the pitch and timbre of the old bell, pausing in their daily chores to note this unfamiliar sound and to reflect on what new community—or communities—it summoned.

Dueling bells were not a welcome sound to local farm wife Mary White. She was all too aware of the uncivil contests that disturbed the peace of her little town. The years between 1815 and 1848 were a time of unremitting turmoil in many New England towns, evidence of profoundly unsettling change. In essence, rural folk wrangled over how their lately won liberty should be lived out, and they could not, would not, agree. Though Mary prayed that "these divisions soon terminate & these people be *of one heart & one mind*," her prayers could not knit her fractious community together again.[4]

The town had changed. In the short space of a generation, townsfolk had created too many battling sects, parties, societies, classes, and identities to be served by a single bell. When Captain Howe's bell rang out in his barnyard, some heard it announcing a new declaration of individual independence: liberation from the bonds of custom, consensus, obligation, deference, and dependence that had shaped life in New England's rural towns for generations. Others, such as Mary White, heard Howe's bell toll the passing of common cause, shared faith, neighborly relations, and civic unity. For these, Howe's bell rang out an alarm, for they feared that disorder, incivility, partisanism, and uncompromising self-interest threatened the very survival of the Republic of Liberty. The dueling bells of Boylston echoed on town commons across the Commonwealth.

THIS IS A STORY about how big changes happened in a small community. We often discuss change as the product of forces that carry us along as if on a rising tide or a cresting wave. But in this tale of three decades in one rural town we can observe the process intimately, and we can see that this is at best an incomplete explanation. Powerful external influences such as the expansion of the market, advances in technology, and the rise of national political parties did indeed penetrate the Massachusetts countryside during this era, bringing unprecedented opportunities and challenges. But these exogenous forces were mediated through the choices and actions of individuals, people driven by internal motivations. People participated actively and often passionately in reshaping their lives. In the process, they adopted new ways of interacting with and thinking about their world.

These are big claims, but we make them for a small place and a bounded period of time so that we can observe choices and consequences firsthand. The story plays out over one generation, three decades renowned for their sweeping national transformations. The setting is a small farm town in central Massachusetts where we can come to know characters personally. Boylston was a community of a mere 800 souls in 1820, an uncomplicated agrarian town. Unlike neighboring villages, the town had no great river running through it, no rushing water to power mills, no turnpike or canal to bring trade or foreigners. Yet in the span of thirty years, this unremarkable farm community was, as Mary White often said, "up and doing," making choices that transformed daily life. As might be expected when some chose to break with customary behaviors and belonging, it was an uneasy, contested transition, marked by the spasms of controversy and conflict that provide our plot.

For much of this story we are indebted to a dedicated diary keeper, farm wife Mary White, who took up her pen at her marriage in 1798 and did not lay it down again until her death sixty-two years later.[5] Her jottings of daily chores, household happenings, neighborly visits, and divine Providences eventually filled ten leather-bound volumes with closely written scrawl (and barely a mark of punctuation). The cyclical routines of Mary's daily life formed the stable warp of her diary record. Interwoven with that warp was an unexpected weft: unending incidents of personal, family, and social strife.

Mary and her farmer/shopkeeper husband, Aaron, were ideally situated to bear witness to this extraordinary scene. As newlyweds, they settled in the center village of Boylston. For the next half century, they and their ten children lived, quite literally, at the crossroads of community. Their sturdy farmhouse, a one-time village tavern, stood between the meetinghouse and the burying ground; their parlor overlooked the town common. Around 1820 the prosperous couple moved up in the world, to the top of the common, to an updated Federalist mansion house at the crest of the village green. Here they expected to preside in genteel prominence over their peaceful, well-ordered village. It was not to be. Instead, Squire and Mrs. White spent the next twenty-five years fomenting, resisting, creating, and lamenting change.

Fortunately for us the White family chronicled their times. Like their mother, the children kept journals, wrote family letters, and kept account of their material debts and spiritual trespasses. The squire, a longtime town clerk, kept town meeting minutes, while Mary recorded the notes of local women's societies. Neighbors also kept family records; officers of civic associations documented their efforts; and dedicated townsmen cataloged their work for church and public committees. The youth kept school copybooks and created friendship books to share with their classmates and soulmates.[6] This frenetic personal writing and the literary documenting of private and public life is itself a sign of the times.[7] It is also the source of clues to their unsettled state. Each example reveals sometimes humorous, sometimes curious, often affecting details of troubled community and personal relationships. Assembled, they create a picture of a town convulsed. These were years, as townsfolk later remembered ruefully, when "the most malignant passions of our depraved natures raged."[8]

As our story emerges from these sources, we see a community in flux. Change was everywhere—not just in the world around the townsfolk, but in the relationships between them and in the hearts and minds within them. At the turn of the nineteenth century, much of rural Massachusetts shared a common identity rooted in family farming, town membership, and spiritual fellowship. Over the next decades many, like the Whites, responded to a spirit of the age, in part a product of recent revolution and new beginnings that reflected both the hopes and fears of a young nation in the process of self-creation. It was a spirit of improvement, a striving to "improve the opportunity," as Mary White so often urged her children. We can witness this striving reshaping the local community as people acted to convert, reform, refine, and perfect self, community, and republic. They also, however, shared a fear that should they not respond to the urgent imperative to refine and reform, the consequences—both personal and national—would be apocalyptic.[9] Urgency to improve powered local change.

They were to discover, however, that they differed on what made for improvement. As some worked to transform faith and farming, temperance and textbooks, politics and private schools, others resolutely resisted. Most troublesome was a generational divide, as offspring increasingly chose a future beyond the farm. There was conflict even within the hearts of individuals: youth struggled to discern their own path to self-mastery and salva-

Aaron White Sr. and Mary Avery White, tinted daguerreotype, ca. 1841.
Courtesy of the Boylston Historical Society.

tion, while elders wrestled with lost security and authority. The 1830s was an especially anxious decade for the White family and their townsfolk: disaffection of the young, discord in the church, an economic crisis, divisive reforms, and partisan political turmoil left many fearing for the survival of social order. And in some ways, they were right: old patterns of relationship and habits of thought were becoming obsolete. As each strove to improve the opportunity as he or she saw fit, individuals shed their shared identity for diverse and particular goals, bringing conflict and contest wrenchingly to the fore.

The story of these decades has been told before—but as a national story. These were the years of the nation's coming-of-age, an era of revolutions that propelled the country from a traditional agrarian republic to an expansive and market-oriented democracy. Scholars have presented these changes as grand syntheses of overarching processes.[10] Yet the movements, forces, and national consequences they discuss were actually taking place in a thousand particular places. When we study Boylston's microcosm, it becomes clear that important changes emanated from within, from emerging ideas of individual potential and responsibility. Mary and her neighbors asserted an unprecedented degree of personal autonomy and individual liberty. Their actions—associating, reforming, converting, instituting, innovating—remade community by radically transforming the way individuals related to each other on a face-to-face, day-to-day basis. Within the microcosm of one rural village, with its petty disputes, family heartaches, factional squabbles, and neighborly scandals, we witness choices and actions that reveal this new world in the making. This is the story of that contentious creation.

FOR THOSE WHO CAME OF AGE in the early nineteenth century, it must have seemed as if the world had accelerated in its motion. All was a whirl of dizzying change. For a century past, reason had been challenging custom; now, it transcended.[11] Between 1815 and 1848, much of the nation experienced phenomenal advances in technology, communication, transportation, and markets as well as transformative reorganization of religion, reform, education, and political enterprise. Innovations came so fast and furiously that Mary White called this new-made place "a wilderness world" in which she could find "no abiding place."

Worcester County in central Massachusetts experienced most of the revolutions that have defined this era, which makes it an excellent laboratory for studying change. Everyday folk across the county greatly expanded their commercial participation, evidence of the much-touted Market Revolution.[12] The market for farm products in the Worcester countryside burgeoned. Facing new opportunities—and new challenges—Massachusetts farmers altered their primary objective from family provisioning to more profit-oriented strategies that would produce cash as well as consumables.[13] Their motivations for that shift are varied, but the consequences were dramatic for family and community relationships.

During these same years, the Industrial Revolution took root in the rocky soil of Worcester County. The same hilly terrain that had challenged farmers produced tumbling streams to power early mills. Manufactories in towns around Boylston were soon turning out wire, nails, clocks, combs, carpet, cloth, chairs, pianos and other commodities.[14] Many rural sons and daughters willingly embraced this alternative to the hot, heavy labor of tilling the soil, an alternative that included cash wages and a chance for independence from the demands of the family farm. It also introduced them to a world their elders did not know—a world of machines, of clocks and time discipline, of standardization and efficiency—a nonagrarian world.[15]

The mass-produced goods from Worcester County factories changed life for the better for those who could afford them, spawning new aspirations for gentility and refinement.[16] Boylston's better sort upgraded their parlors with wallpaper, sets of painted chairs, clocks and looking glasses, carpets and curtains, and pianos from those local factories. They remodeled their houses, tidied their village centers, added fences and ornamental trees, and embraced the romantic ideal of a tamed pastoral landscape.[17] For some, these new goods made work easier and leisure more enjoyable. While the middling folk aped gentry standards, more humble neighbors, once proudly independent yeomen, found themselves belittled as bumpkins.[18]

The market, industrial, and consumer revolutions in antebellum Worcester County would not have been possible without extraordinary advances in the movement of people, goods, and ideas. Between 1790 and 1820, the people of Massachusetts exhibited, as one observer noted in 1839, a passion for building roads.[19] At the turn of the nineteenth century, a trip from Boylston to Boston was a two-day ordeal over poor roads; by 1825, a regular stage delivered Boylstonians to the city in about six hours. Less than a decade later, locals could take the railway cars from neighboring Shrewsbury for a two-hour trip to Boston. During the same decade, the Blackstone Canal provided a water route south to Providence and the Atlantic. New routes were arteries not just for commerce; they also brought new ideas and tales of opportunity in a wider world. These dramatic improvements in transportation launched a communication revolution, as the flow of ideas "liberated people from the weight of local tyrannies."[20]

One of those local tyrannies had been Boylston's Federalist gentry, with their nearly exclusive access to higher education and cosmopolitan connections. As their power was diluted, the town also experienced the transformative effects of yet another innovation: the rise of popular party politics.[21] During the 1820s and 1830s, the town evolved from a once-solid Federalist consensus to a two- and three-party town. Boylstonians debated whether this rise of parties and factions was progress toward popular democratic expression or descent into chaotic self-interest. They debated with passionate urgency, as each side advanced its own view of what liberty meant and how independence should play out in daily life. How should they deal with social distinction, with elite privilege and corporate concentrations of power? Were the Founders' words mere rhetoric, or were they meant to give birth to a world of egalitarian self-reliance and individualism?

Such questions engendered an era of revolutionary but contentious social idealism, as reformers debated how to perfect their society. The nation was young, and its distinctive forms of social organization and behavior were evolving. With one foot still grounded in an authoritarian past, they were poised to step into a democratic future. But which way to go? The possibilities looking forward were both exhilarating and terrifying. What would provide order in a truly free society? Rural Massachusetts had its prophets of social design. Local societies and associations sprang up to promote the improving—and regulating—benefits of reading clubs, public lectures, charitable work, and social reform.[22] Some reformers envisioned an enlightened remaking of society led by the educated elite; others imagined each individual intelligently and independently making his or her own choices. Whatever their intentions, reformers' work riled those who did not want to be reformed. It also heightened awareness of social difference among those who were *not* of the improving sort.

Perhaps the most powerful agent for change in this era was not something new at all, but the revival of something ancient. The decades of 1815 to 1840 were the height of the Second Great Awakening, and the religious sentiments of some locals were most powerfully roused. Revivalism and social tumult have often gone hand-in-hand.[23] It was religion—with issues of faith and conscience that could not bear compromise—that first opened the door to dissent and discord. When Massachusetts disestablished its state church in 1833, denominations were forced to compete for members, a battle that renewed religious fervor but also sparked passionate debate and discord. Worshippers would never again, as Mary futilely prayed, be of one heart and one mind.

And if all that were not enough, locals were worried about their children. It was not just that children were leaving home—New England youth had always been on the move toward more open land. But in earlier generations, most of those who left home did *not* leave the land. In the 1820s and 1830s, the youth of rural Massachusetts increasingly headed for a clerk's desk, workshop, factory, or business establishment. Their forefathers had pursued the yeoman's ideal, the belief that a freehold farm guaranteed their security and independence and bespoke their status as free men and worthy citizens. Their sons, however, increasingly rejected that identity. They turned to the alluring opportunities of trade, manufacturing, or professions where they could exchange their rough country clothes for white collars and clean boots, their flails and dung forks for desks and counters, their country manners for urban gentility.[24] Their parents' hearts, as we will see, ached.

THESE CHANGES FOSTERED both greater choice and greater controversy. Local conflicts grew from deeper cultural transformation shaping the new nation: a growing awareness of plural interests, an increasing challenge to the notion of a single common good, and a more determined individual pursuit of happiness. Driving all was a rising belief in each individual's power—and responsibility—to improve his lot as he saw fit.

In Boylston's story, we see a people's gradual embrace of individualism, pluralism, and ambition transforming community and personal relationships. These troubled decades did not destroy community, but they remade it.[25] A community of necessity and custom became a community—or communities—of choice and interest. Neighbors and townsmen had once been united in bonds of local belonging in order to survive. From the 1820s through the 1840s, Boylstonians felt empowered to choose their own social relations. Where once identity had been centered in town belonging, now people turned inward to self-reliant or intimate connections, or outward to unions with distant strangers who shared selective causes. Relations shifted from neighbors to networks, from compulsory to voluntary, from corporate to divergent. Liberty was vested in the power to choose where and how one would belong.

The seeds of these revolutionary transformations were present in Boylston from its settlement, carried west with settlers who prized their individual English rights, nurtured by the opportunities of frontier development, and taking root during the years of revolutionary rhetoric. But they were suppressed by a powerfully traditional social order that kept a gentry elite firmly in charge, by a monolithic state church, and by the relatively isolated and locally interdependent nature of agrarian life. For decades after 1775, despite growing internal stresses, Boylston remained an orderly town, a community that continued to conceive of identity—ideally—as a facet of local belonging to a larger group. The fracture of the church opened the gates to a flood of suppressed attitudes and choices. People began to change the way they behaved. They challenged the social order and the established elites, flouted norms, formed cliques, expanded their connections to the larger world, redefined success, pursued improvements that laid bare the growing distinctions in wealth and cultural identity within town. They did so with passion and commitment, driven by faith, principles, ideals, ambition—and a yearning for security and control. They engendered pride and self-reliance, new bonds of affection and shared interests; they also engendered jealousy, resentment, competition, exclusivity, and conflict.

If many of their battles seem familiar, it is because the issues they encountered as growing pains for the republic endure for societies that struggle to balance communitarian and individual identity. What role should religious belief play in a pluralist community? What obligations does the individual owe to community and society? What obligations does society owe its poor, sick, and dependent? How do we deal with growing inequalities in wealth? Should there be limits to privilege and power—whether vested in wealth, social status, political parties, or corporations—in a free society? In essence, how can individual ambitions and social responsibilities be reconciled? Boylston's story is about the enduring tension between communal belonging and self-possession.

IN THE CHAPTERS that follow we will first explore life in revolutionary and early republic Boylston and see how the pressures that would eventually topple the social order were percolating. We will then move forward in time to the tumultuous years of 1815 to 1848, when restraints gave way and the people of rural Massachusetts actively remade their world. We will see how they responded to "the times," as contemporaries often called this period of dramatic social change, but also how they were energized by powerful internal energies. We will find these changes contested in Mary White's parlor and Aaron's barnyard, in neighbor Crossman's shoe shop and Mr. Flagg's hayfield, on the floor of town meeting and in the vestry of the church, wherever new behaviors clashed with old customs. Mary White might wish that her family and townsfolk be of one mind, but that bell had tolled.

CHAPTER ONE

Sowing

Shortly after the Revolution, Goodwife Goodenow dreamed of buried treasure in a Boylston grove. Her townsmen, on hearing her tale, assembled a party one moonlit night. Stealing off to the grove, they invoked a spell with the aid of an open Bible, a rusty sword, the blood of a pure white dove, and a pledge of silence. Then they dug. When they hit on metal, one of the clandestine crew cried out, "We've got it now!" But his utterance, they say, broke the spell, and the pot of treasure sank from sight.[1]

It is a wonderful tale, full of magical folk belief, local shenanigans, and the power of fate to deprive us of riches. It is also part of rural New England's rich genre of buried-treasure stories from the early republic. Perhaps these stories speak to the frustrations of rural yeomen who had dreamed of prosperity in their new nation of liberty and yet struggled with debt and shackles.[2] To be sure, they seem to reflect ambivalence about prosperity and security, where it comes from and how it disappears. For generations rural New Englanders had sought and found treasure by digging in the good earth, not for pots of gold but for reliable crops of corn and rye. They had fought a revolution to secure that treasure—the independence of land-owning families in self-governing towns and covenanted churches. They had been moved by expansive promises of liberty and prosperity. Now there seemed to be a new alchemy at work. Sometimes they struck gold; sometimes their riches mysteriously vanished, or worse—beguiling promises of security morphed into new forms of dependence on inscrutable external powers. Was it all smoke and mirrors? How were they to turn dreams of liberty and prosperity into reality?

The generation that came of age following the Revolution faced numerous challenges, not the least of which was defining the liberty they had won.[3] The Revolution suggested that old restraints would be thrown off: the crown would no longer appoint governors or judges, control markets, establish religion, or bestow aristocratic privilege. What would this freedom mean in day-to-day life? How would people order their world, conduct daily business, constrain evil? On the one hand, new opportunities and choices seemed possible; on the other, familiar customs and social relations still ordered daily life. For a generation, Mary White's neighbors lived uncertainly between two worlds, one in which the shared goal of family farming bound them in collective enterprise, and one in which each embraced the freedom to pursue his or her own treasure.

We must do some digging of our own to unearth the daily life of Mary's townsfolk in the early years of the republic. Their world was not like ours. Settled in the first half of the eighteenth century, early Boylston was shaped by the customs and practices of its English forebears, by the rigors and reforms of Puritanism, and by the challenges of surviving life in and on a new land. Above all, it was a world where self was defined in relation to others, in terms of belonging. People understood family, church, and town not as a voluntary collection of individuals, but as a single organism, a corporate or bodily whole. The performance of any part of that body directly affected the well-being of the whole; injury to any member injured the body; disease in any part infected the rest. When the organism was well regulated, all members had their proper place and function, and authority descended from the head to the extremities.

We will call this understanding of their world, this sense of belonging to and depending upon community as if it were a single organism, a *corporate* (literally, *of one body*) mentality. The corporate community was a creation of necessity and custom, defined by shared needs and imposed norms. It was not romantic—it circumscribed creativity, difference, and individual choice—but it did provide a meaning-giving bulwark against unpredictable fate and unfathomable Providence.[4]

Though early Boylstonians were conditioned to live corporately, there were other aspects of their heritage that strained against submitting to the will of the whole. Along with Protestantism, their forefathers carried to the New World animating ideas about private property, individual striving, expansive opportunity, and personal liberties.[5] This dalliance with liberal ideas was subtly reinforced through their connections to empire: a growing transatlantic trade, an aping admiration of British gentility and distinction, and a shared, evolving debate over constituted authority.[6]

Individualism had local roots as well. Competition was a persistent undercurrent in this family-farm culture, for each family needed to find land for growing sons. Owning private property—and always needing more—fed an acquisitiveness that strained the gears of corporate commonweal. Moreover, New England's farm towns struggled to achieve consensus: most town histories are riddled with squabbles over the placement of meetinghouse or schoolhouse, spats over assigned church seating, and feuds over fences. No romantic pastoral havens, New England's farm towns had always endured undercurrents of self-assertion. The experience of revolution stirred up more trouble: talk of popular authority and individual rights threatened established social order with a perfect storm of egalitarian liberalism.

The generation of New Englanders that inherited the Revolution, then, had a tall order. They continued to embrace ideals that they only imperfectly realized and that were being increasingly challenged. They inherited a world of corporate community, yet wrestled with conflicting goals of commonweal and private interest, neighborly cooperation and competitive self-interest, consensus and free thought, deference to authority and a burly individualism. They respected their traditions, yet yearned to realize their dreams.

For a time, though, individual pursuits were constrained in Mary's community, as we will see, by customary need for cooperation in farming, limited markets, waning Puritan ideals, and the power of the New England town. Despite undercurrents of liberal individualism, local folk before their time of turmoil shared an identity: they *belonged*, and their local membership provided meaning and security, if not a pot of gold.

WHAT WAS IT LIKE to live in a world of intense belonging? Life was experienced in and through relation to others: as sibling, cousin, neighbor, debtor, hired help, schoolmate, church communicant. One gave birth, mastered her alphabet, hayed his field, raised a barn, cleared roads after a snowstorm, sat up with a sick neighbor, drank at the tavern, confessed his sins, and was laid out for burial with those to whom one belonged. Identity itself was wrapped up in membership and belonging. Coming of age was not so much a matter of individuation—of defining the essential nature of self versus other—but of becoming a useful member of family and community, of being fully incorporated into the whole.[7]

This corporate belonging persisted because it worked. It fulfilled the physical and psychological needs of a relatively isolated people who had to produce most of what they needed and who had to accomplish this while living at the mercy of weather, famine, pestilence, and fate. They had to pull together to survive. *Family farms* efficiently organized labor and distributed resources across the dependent and independent stages of life. *Neighbors* redistributed goods, labor, and support in times of excess and shortfall, sickness and health, mirth and grief. The *town* supported its own and protected common interests against claims by outsiders. The *church* provided moral order and a covenant relationship to bind members in mutual discipline, as well as the emotional, psychological, and spiritual support to deal with the inexplicable.[8] Owning a place in a farm-family household, a neighborhood community, the town, and the covenanted church provided essential safety, security, and identity.[9]

None of these memberships was an association of choice.[10] The corporate status of most rural New Englanders was determined by their birth and the location of their farmstead, by divine providence, or in some cases by the decision of the community; participation in these relationships was not voluntary. Family structure was patriarchal: children were obliged to labor for and obey their fathers until they were ready to marry and leave home.[11] Neighborliness—especially assisting in times of need or lending in times of scarcity—was an expected norm, and scoffers risked "rough music"—crude customs of public ridicule intended to humiliate norm-flouters.[12] There was but one church in town—the orthodox Congregational—which all were taxed to support. Those who wished to baptize their children or to share in communion had to submit themselves to church discipline. All men who met the requirements for town membership were warned to attend town meeting and were required to train with the militia, serve on the highway crews, turn out to clear paths and break roads after winter snows, support the schools, and share responsibility for the town's destitute. *Belonging* meant that one was a member, but also a possession: each individual was properly a *belonging of* the community, like it or not.

The corporate nature of this rural society did not preclude individual striving. But personal ambition was supposedly channeled to serve family, religious, and civic goals.[13] In fact, concerted striving on the part of all family members was needed to accumulate resources for the next generation's security.[14] Mary and Aaron White urged their children to "improve the opportunity," by which they meant to pursue their vocation with faithful diligence and accumulate the capital essential for family well-being. There were limits to the acceptable pursuit of profit: to a degree, the ancient moral economy—in which the community enforced fair distribution of essential resources—was still in force.[15] In the 1790s, some local farmers trekked their surplus oats and rye to market; in 1797, however, tanner Simon Davis noted that Independence Day was marked with a "great cry for bread," a traditional bread riot, where the hungry protested the export of essential grains to market.[16]

We will consider evidence of membership in early Boylston's families and farms, neighborhoods, congregation and town, drawing particularly on the diary records of two families: the prosperous White family of center village and the middling family of tanner and entrepreneur Simon Davis, from the western section of town.[17] It is important to get to know this world, because its collapse and disintegration is revealed in the conflicted and tumultuous decades of the 1820s and 1830s.

Farm-Family Household

The preservation of the family—and its farm—was all.[18] Kinship was the strongest social bond, as it had been with Boylstonians' ancestors in early modern England.[19] Most Worcester County couples of this era hoped to begin housekeeping in their own home, however humble, soon after marriage. But these were not merely relations of affection; along with housekeeping, almost universally, went farm keeping. The farmer and his wife were an economic partnership, with the farmer producing the raw materials that his wife turned into household necessities. To produce efficiently on their acres they needed the unpaid labor of their children, and so most rural families were large. Mary White's eventual family of ten children was not unusual.

Family was broadly construed. When a woman spoke of her family, she included all those who lived under her roof, over whom she was mistress and for whom she had responsibility.[20] Over the course of her lifetime, Mary White's family included her children, her widowed mother, two orphaned nieces, visiting in-laws, siblings, nieces and nephews, grandchildren, live-in hired help, a poor boy who was a ward of the town, and a clerk in her husband's store, among others. Neighborhood women "lived in" while tailoring a suit; men boarded while completing handiwork or teaching at the local school; children from the outer districts lodged while attending a writing, singing, or dame school in the center of town. In 1800, the average household in Boylston sheltered eight people; Mary's often had twelve or more.[21]

These families were elastic, expanding to include those whose help was needed—or who needed help—and shrinking as children were sent to relatives or neighbors for work or socializing. This sending out and taking in started early. When Persis Davis was unable to suckle her newborn, the infant was quickly shuttled off to his Uncle Jabez's household, where he lived for the next six weeks. Mary White noted that her four-year-old son, "my little Avery," was very glad to see her when she visited her parents in Holden, where he had been staying for several weeks in March 1805. Mary's young sons were often absent for three or more months, staying with grandparents, aunts, and uncles; meanwhile, their place was taken by Aaron and Mary's grown siblings, whose assistance in the house, shop, tavern, and farm was essential to a couple whose children were not old enough to work. "Hardly a week passed," Mary's son later remembered, "that some one did not go to Holden [where Mary's parents lived], from our house, or some one come from Holden to visit us."[22] Such comings and goings knit extended kin together.

Those who came to live in the White or Davis households were fully incorporated into the family. Master and mistress provided for their physical, social, and spiritual needs; in return, those who "lived in" were expected to submit themselves to family discipline.[23] When twenty-year-old Lucretia Collier came to work for Mary from January to August 1807, she was treated like a daughter; Mary sewed her gowns, sent her to singing school, noted her visits to neighbors and her attendance at church. To Mary, her live-in female help were more than employees: through the course of her diary she referred to these women as people who "assist me," "work with me," or "live with me." When they later wed, moved away, or died, she remembered them as those dear to her, who had "lived in my family."

Such close bonds with extended family and non-kin were possible in part because nearly everyone incorporated into family was already familiar. If they had not themselves been known by the family from birth, they were likely known by someone the family had known from birth, hailed from nearby, and shared the experience of life on the land in central Massachusetts. These were not strangers that Mary took in, boarded and fed, schooled and nursed. As their familiarity eased their incorporation into family, the Whites' live-in help joined the family on visits to neighbors, at social events, and in church; they, in turn, were expected to fulfill family obligations for social visiting and sitting up with the sick.

It was on the male head of household—the patriarch—that the duty and power of family government lay. The power of fathers to regulate their family was fundamental to their understanding of proper order; town interfered with family only in cases where the father lost his ability to support his charges or failed to keep them in good order.[24] Establishing his own farm household secured a man's self-mastery; it also secured his mastery over all those who depended on him.[25] In the journal that Aaron Jr. kept while at Harvard in 1817, he referred to his father as "honored," "revered," and "virtuous"; his greatest anxiety came at the thought of disappointing his father's expectations. Simon Davis, on the other hand, complained in his journal that his young apprentices challenged his authority in the household by their levity. A serious and deeply pious man, Davis exercised his paternal responsibility by letting them know that they were "too much inclined to levity and disrelish a serious life," that he was "disagreeably affected with their indecent levity," or that he found their frolicking "extremely foolish and wicked."[26]

As patriarchs, Simon Davis and Aaron White headed an economic entity. Their farms were little manufactories, and husband and wife directed a varied workforce through the multiple stages of turning raw materials into the family food, clothing, and other essentials. From childhood to seniority, each family member was incorporated into some stage of farm production, giving each a sense of belonging and of contributing to the family's well-being.[27] No man could run a farm alone, for, as one historian has said, "individual family members could not survive apart from the cooperative activity of the corporate whole."[28]

The farmhouse of the average local household at the turn of the century was small, crowded with people, sparse in furnishings, and designed for functionality. Its aesthetic, such as it was, was based on practicality. Worcester County's early farmhouses were built for shelter and production with little regard for personal privacy or decorative taste. They grew haphazardly, with rooms added and sheds or outbuildings moved and attached as needed. To our eye, the grounds would have appeared unkempt, with woodpiles here and dung piles there, outbuildings and tools plunked where needed, poultry and pigs roaming free. It was not that they lacked a sense of spatial order, but rather that their sense was shaped by usefulness. The typical farmhouse at the turn of the century was a rustic, unpainted, low-lying, single-story, post-and-beam structure, with one or two rooms below and a chamber or loft above.[29] The tavern-house that prosperous Aaron White purchased for his bride in 1798—considered capacious at the time—was a 1760s hall-and-parlor structure, probably with two large eighteen-by-eighteen-foot rooms on the first floor, one serving as the tavern and the other as the family's parlor; a large kitchen to the rear; and two or three chambers above for sleeping, storage, and lodging travelers.[30]

The material possessions that filled these compact dwellings were, by today's standards, few. Distinctions of wealth could be found mostly *outside*— in the form of land and livestock. Inside, beyond clothing, there was not a great deal to distinguish the wealthiest from the middling, or the middling from the modest.[31] The tools of production—cookware and washtubs, textile tools and dairy utensils—mingled with essential bedding, a worktable or storage chest, household linens, preserved foods, and farm tools. This simplicity and relative equity of home and goods at the turn of the century was an important strand in the social fabric. As these folk entered each other's garden gates or kitchen doors, they were not confronted with stark reminders of economic difference. Wealthy or middling, even to some degree poor, shared the same basic aesthetic of practicality. Most had the same essential tools for sleeping, eating, and working their farms, and not a great deal more. Shared goods, shared goals, shared lives twined locals in a familiar, familial braid.

Family Farm

In 1831, a Boylston esquire reflected on the town's history and character: "This," he wrote, "is almost exclusively an agricultural town. . . . The capital of the citizens is invested in the solid ground, and they draw on a friend, who from time immemorial has never failed to answer all just demands."[32] Farming was not a profession; it was a common identity. The same cyclical patterns of farm work regulated all lives. All shared the customary wisdom of their ancestors' husbandry; all feared the same uncontrollable foes of drought or deluge, killing frost, blight or famine; and all drew from tilling their land a shared sense of purpose and self-worth.

And so, all would have understood the significance of the anticipated event Mary White recorded in her diary each spring, between late March and early April: "Frogs peeped." As the warming temperatures turned snow-melt to chilly spring pools and frozen farm lanes to mud, the peeper frogs predictably broke into their chorus and signaled the start of another farm year. Mary noted the season's advance: "fruit trees bloomed," "hay got into barn," "geese flew," "men sledded wood." In New and Old England's farm villages for time beyond memory the seasons of work turned with the constellations in a steady, familiar progression. In December, as Taurus the Bull rose overhead, farmers hitched their oxen to sleds to draw logs from their woodlots; as Ursa Major roused from her hibernation above each March, Mary awaited the spring peepers' awakening.

The seasons of cultivation shaped intimate life as well. Mary White documented the seasonality of illness, with the dying times in March, when respiratory illnesses felled those confined to winter living quarters, and then again in July and August, at the peak of heavy shared-harvest labor, when dysentery-related disorders did their worst. Sociability, too, followed the farm seasons, as Simon Davis noted leisurely winter evenings crowded with company.[33] Life and death found their echo and explanation in the seasonal cycle: birth, growth, and mortality, like planting, cultivation, and harvest, could be followed by resurrection as surely as life returned when the frogs peeped.[34]

The common experience of farm life—shared work, wisdom, goals, and meaning—was buttressed by an ancient agrarian ethos and more recent political and social ideas. Farming was *good* work: the plowman's toil was productive, nurturing, honest, lacking in artifice, ennobling to the character of the tiller.[35] The freehold farmer who could supply his family's needs was truly independent, for he could live unconstrained by landlords or creditors. As a result, men did not seek just to farm; they sought to *own* a farm. Ownership of a farm was a publicly visible sign of full manhood and self-determination.[36] This ideal, inherited from late medieval England, was strengthened by eighteenth-century republicanism, which considered landholding and the disinterested independence it bestowed to be essential to a virtuous citizenry. Jefferson's vision of protecting the republic from tyranny by vesting authority in a democracy of small farmers kept the agrarian ideal very much alive well into the early 1800s.[37]

In early Boylston, then, all men either were farmers or hoped to become farmers. Happily, most men owned land or expected to.[38] Those young men without hope of inheritance were striving to set aside enough to secure a "competence" or "comfortable subsistence" (sufficient land to supply a family's needs). Simon Davis, for example, began married life with little capital. He worked at an unrelenting pace for the next fifteen years. He drove his neighbors' cattle to the Boston market and put his profits into a tannery on a single acre of land. Gradually he took on apprentices and expanded his works to include a cooper's shop; eventually he created an integrated enterprise, purchasing local cattle, slaughtering and barreling beef to ship to Boston for export, tanning the hides, and making shoes from the leather. Yet in 1806, despite the profitability of his growing business, Davis sold the tannery and cooperage. With the proceeds, he purchased a farm—and his independent yeoman status. Davis's experience was not uncommon. His townsman Ezekiel Peirce, who came of age in the first decade of the century, "was a blacksmith by occupation who worked at this until he had secured a competence, after which he owned one of the best farms in West Boylston."[39]

For a Worcester County farm to provide most of what the family needed, it had to include a rather precise calculus of land types. Ideally, it would have a *houselot* (shelter for humans and animals); *orchard* (fruit, cider, vinegar); *tillage* (grains and flax); *pasture* (grazing for livestock); *meadow* (hay for winter feeding of domestic animals); and *woodlot* for fuel. Once a man secured these plots, he had to deal with the second challenge: farming them sustainably so that the land maintained its fertility for the next generation. Farmers knew they had to balance nutrient inputs and outtakes. Tillage needed manure from cows; cows needed pasture and meadow hay; although pasture, properly managed, would be partially fertilized by animal droppings, meadows needed a yearly renewal of nutrients. This happened naturally when meadows along rivers, streams, and low-lying wetlands were fertilized with rich sediment during spring flooding. The long-term fertility of the whole system was dependent on this annual renewal: the floods fed the meadows; the meadow fed the cattle; the cattle fed the tillage; the tillage fed the humans.[40] Local farmers ideally strove to acquire approximately sixty acres per household—of the right type and in the proper proportions—to provide most of the family's needs and to maintain fertility over the generations.[41]

Evidence from late eighteenth-century Boylston reveals that *on average* farmers did own enough of each type of land to provide their families while maintaining soil fertility.[42] However, few farmers held just the right proportion of each type of resource. By trading their surpluses with each other to cover their deficits, farm families successfully redistributed and balanced resources across the community. The system also bound the community together in a tight web of neighborly obligations; everyone at some point was in debt to someone else.[43] With this communal swapping, most local farmers around 1800 produced more than enough to provision their families.[44] From tilled acres they harvested corn, oats, rye, and barley; from grazing land they drew dairy, meat, hides, and wool; from their barnyard, pork, fowl, eggs, and feathers; from their orchards, fruit and cider; from their dooryard gardens, green and root vegetables; from their woodlots, timber and fuel. Neighborly swapping linked farm to farm, and all to the land.

The work of wresting these essentials from the land ordered time and organized daily life. Mary White's diary recorded the cyclical chores. These same tasks were being performed in every household, uniting the farm community in common labor. The new year began with mud and muck, as Aaron fertilized the tillage with winter's farmyard refuse. In April he plowed; in May he planted; in June he weeded the garden and hoed his tillage. In July began the hot, heavy work of haying, and, in August, extra hands joined in the back-breaking work of the "dog days": reaping, threshing, winnowing, and milling grains. September brought apple picking and cider season, while corn harvest and husking continued through October. By November, with the root plants, squash, and potatoes in the cellar, Aaron called in the local butcher to slaughter his hogs and surplus cattle. In the deep winter months Aaron and his help went to the woodlot to fell and chop the next year's fuel. Then Aaron balanced accounts with neighbors for swapped labor and goods, visited, and waited for the frogs to peep. Most farmers learned these tasks following behind their fathers from early childhood; the traditional wisdom and lore of farming valued the knowledge that came from experience.

Relying on traditional farm practices united Mary's townsfolk across generation and social order. Men did what their neighbors did—and what their fathers had done—in approximately the same way and with the same tools that their ancestors had used for generations. However, in the early republic there were signs that these unifying practices were about to change. Members of Worcester County's gentry elite gathered to form an agricultural society dedicated to the promotion of "scientific" farming. They invested in innovative methods, machines, and cross-breeds. They aimed to liberate agriculture from lore and custom—and backbreaking labor—by rational improvements. Aaron White and his gentry neighbors Esquire Longley, Colonel Gibbs, Benjamin Houghton, and John Howe would all become active (sometimes prize-winning) members.[45] Scientific farming, as we will see, created distinctions based on resources and learning that would come to trouble the town's ideal of unity.

Mary and her townswomen followed the same calendar, but with tasks related to their gender.[46] When frogs peeped, calving would soon follow, and as cows came into milk the churning commenced. Mary devoted late spring to a thorough house cleaning, whitewashing walls to remove winter soot, laundering winter woolens. When the heat of summer made churning difficult, women turned their hands to cheese making. The hay and grain harvest, for which extra hired hands came to lodge, brought heavy laundry. In early autumn, Mary began turning apples into "sauce" and vinegar, fruits and berries into preserves, and putting up cucumbers, peppers, and other garden vegetables. She usually recorded, "finished making my [apple] sauce" just in time to mince meat for winter pies and turn the freshly slaughtered pig into sausages, soap, and candles. This annual cycle was overlaid on a weekly pattern of laundry, baking, and cleaning, a daily cycle of meal preparation, and the constant, unremitting task of turning flax and wool into thread and yarn, yarn into stockings, and cloth into clothing.[47] Both Aaron White and Simon Davis understood that their wives' work was essential to the family's economic well-being. Simon remembered that his first wife, though often an invalid, "was posses'd of superior ideas of economy in the management of her domestic affairs. Altho' her feeble body could not at all endure hard labor yet her prudence, her integrity, and her attentions to those things within her sphere contributed much to my prosperity."[48]

Mary's most critical responsibility, however, was not production, but reproduction. She bore a child approximately every two years for nearly a quarter century, producing the labor to run her husband's farm. Most neighboring wives did the same. Yet these children were both boon and burden: their labor powered the family farm, but they would eventually need farms of their own, and in the years of Boylston's turmoil, this need would reach a crisis of limits.

If a farmer did not have enough acres for his sons, he was faced with the challenge, common to farm families across eastern Massachusetts, of accumulating capital to purchase land or settle sons in crafts or professions. Aaron White, for example, owned a generous hundred acres, but he also produced seven sons. His strategy for providing for them was not uncommon for those with resources: he planned to send the eldest to university, set one or two up in professions, and accumulate farmland for the remainder. Over the course of the next twenty years, Aaron worked as a farmer, kept a tavern, ran a country store, marketed rural produce in Boston, lent money at interest, and took advantage of every opportunity that came his way to accumulate the capital he needed to buy land. In time, he became a wealthy man; his calculated striving doubled his farm holdings. Other local farmers also worked to produce a marketable surplus above their consumption needs, sent their teenage boys out to labor as hired hands and their daughters to work as helps, and took up craft work to supplement their farm products.

This need to accumulate capital to buy more land was no doubt one of the motivations behind early nineteenth-century striving in rural Massachusetts. Most local farmers had the resources to produce at least a small surplus of beef and grain, and there were some local markets for these goods. The most common trader was one's neighbor.[49] Aaron White's country store provided another outlet for local trade. White kept accounts with most of his neighbors, who came to him with farm produce and took away imported goods that Aaron trucked in from Boston every other month. White then either retraded this surplus produce to other locals, used it in his household, or took it to market in Boston. His store account book from 1802–4 shows that he most frequently gave credits to local farm families for butter, beef, lamb, boards, and farm work; in exchange, he provided rum, sugar, salt, spices, coffee, tea, salted fish, fabrics, and sewing notions.[50] Mary produced candles, butter, and perhaps linen thread specifically to sell in her husband's store. At the turn of the century, Boylston's largest surplus product was beef cattle, supported by the town's many acres of fertile pasture and rich intervale hay.[51]

Despite the difficulty of travel, by the turn of the century some locals were trekking a load of surplus rye meal over frozen roads to Boston, enticed by the promise of $1.25 per bushel, cash; others walked their surplus beef cattle to market.[52] Barrels of country cider slaked city thirst.[53] Others sent occasional surplus to Boston with shopkeeper White. Aaron's son Thomas remembered accompanying his father on these exciting two-day wagon excursions, made once every two months when he was a small boy in the first decade of the nineteenth century.[54] Mary prepared fowl and butter for these trips, while Aaron slaughtered an occasional pig or calf specifically for the market. So, while local farmers produced primarily for family consumption, they relied on intermittent surplus marketing—in the neighborhood, at the town store, or occasionally to coastal markets—to gain the credits and cash needed to make up their farms' deficiencies and to accumulate capital for building their sons' estates. There was always an underlying current of competition in New England's farm communities, for everyone needed land and more land to provide a competence and independent status for growing families, and resources were finite. This form of individual striving, even though devoted to family support, focused effort on private interest and personal gain, and existed in tension with the communal norm, always under the surface, but constrained by custom. In the decades to come, ambition would be unloosed.

Neighborhood

The limit of Aaron White's farm was marked by stone walls, but the little community of neighborhood had no such clear boundaries. Those who lived "nigh" to the Whites—minister Reverend Cotton, Colonel Bush and Deacon White, shoemaker Abishai Crossman and blacksmith Jason Abbot, their wives and their children—were constantly in Aaron's fields and barnyards, in Mary's kitchen and dooryard, at their front gate, their table, and their bedsides. Aaron and Mary, their kin, help, and children, likewise were often on the farms and in the homes of their neighbors, lending, assisting, and gadding. Household extended outward and blended into the little community of neighborhood.

Jason and Mary Abbot were the same age as Aaron and Mary White; both

Marys were daughters of local ministers; both had married and settled just at the turn of the century. The Abbots lived at the top of the common, close by the White homestead. Their children were about the same ages and attended the one-room center school together. In late December 1805, Mary Abbot brought her six-month-old son for an evening visit; though home was just up the hill, the infant and mother "tarried all night." A few weeks later, Mary White went to nurse the little boy, who was dangerously sick of a fever (he survived). Both Captain Abbot and Aaron White served as town officers and hosted committee meetings. They changed work, as they called their intermittent labor sharing, as well: in March 1806, Captain Abbot carried Aaron's pork to be turned to bacon at Esquire Beaman's; shortly afterward, Aaron sent his hired help to do Captain Abbot's stint on the road crew. The two Marys went together to hear their children examined at the end of the winter school session. And they played: in the winter of 1807, Mary noted a dance at Captain Abbot's, a frolic for young company, a "sley ride visit to Capt. Abbot's [with] supper in company of the neighbors," and frequent visits to the Abbots' to make music. In February 1807, Mary again went to nurse Jason Abbot's little boy, as the two-year-old endured a week of spasms and fits. When the child died, Mary White laid him out for burial and comforted her grieving friend. Six months later, she was likely present as she noted, "Capt. Abbot's [second] son born today."[55] In such a pedestrian world, one's neighbors enjoyed a special relationship based on proximity: they were the first available to lend aid in times of want, support in times of trial, and entertainment anytime. To willingly engage in these reciprocal obligations and social connections—to be neighborly—was a long-observed social norm.[56]

As early settler families planted children on nearby farms, and as these families intermarried, kin became neighbors and neighbors became kin.[57] The resulting cousinhood of dense family relationships sometimes layered kinship obligations on top of neighborly ones. But even when kinship was not present, clustered homes developed an identity and sense of shared interests based on their location—near a bridge, a mill, a road crossing—or their belonging to a school or highway district. Most neighborly ties, however, were based on the constant need to share resources and the obligations created by such give-and-take.

In a cash-poor society, farmers did not purchase what they needed from their neighbors, but borrowed on an informal, long-term credit system. Eventually, when the neighbor needed something in return, an off-setting exchange would take place. Mary's diary doubled as an accounting for such exchanges, with regular entries such as "Mr. Andrews in here in the morning and got potatoes to plant"; two months later, Mary went to Mrs. Andrews's to borrow a pair of wool cards (for combing wool fibers). Most rural folk recorded the cash value of these multiple exchanges in account books and periodically reckoned to see what was due to whom. In most cases the resulting balance was merely carried forward. Neighbors lived alternately as each others' debtors and creditors, always aware that their well-being depended on maintaining the goodwill of those on whom they depended for exchange.[58] Settling was a type of social ritual, a negotiation that fostered reconciliation on several levels and reestablished social equilibrium.[59] The account-book system "was at the center of a distinct culture. It generated its own values of cooperation, of work-swapping, of household integrity and family advancement, that were to be influential throughout the early period of capitalistic development."[60]

Farmers and their wives were also dependent on their neighbors for many of the everyday tools of husbandry and housewifery. More prosperous than most, Mary's household was well outfitted with the tools of production, though even she needed to borrow Mrs. Andrews's wool cards. Neighborhood women called upon Mary to borrow her churn, cheese tubs, cots, and textile utensils. Up to 1800, about a third of local households lacked churns and spinning wheels at a time when almost all of them produced their own butter and linen thread, requiring many to borrow on a regular basis.[61] In January 1807, a stream of men came through Aaron's barnyard, asking to use his scales to weigh their freshly slaughtered pork before sending it to market. Such daily borrowings, along with endless loans of a "horse to Shrewsbury—bad traveling"—or a cart or wagon to haul goods, an ox team to plow, or even the plow itself, were precisely recorded in cash value and bound neighbors to each other.

Neighbors were most dependent on each other, however, for their—and their animals'—labor. Farm labor needs fluctuated across the seasons and the lifecycle. Farmers met their intermittent shortage of hands by bringing in a neighbor for a half day or a day's work. When Aaron White's sons were too young to work, he frequently called in his neighbors to assist in peak seasons. Mary's diary is filled with the details of such obligations: neighbors with six teams of oxen to sled wood home from the woodlot, "Mr. Temple butchering," "Old Mr. Partridge husking corn," and a whole family of Andrews at harvest, the men reaping, the boys carting grains to the mill, and Polly Andrews helping with the extra wash. In return, the Whites gave pork or beef, a pair of shoes, or simply credited their neighborly account against future claims. Mary, who was skilled at both spinning and weaving, for years had no daughters old enough to assist her; she turned to her neighbors. In addition to her hired girl who hatchelled and spun her flax, Mary had several local women assist in spinning linen, wool, and cotton yarns and in weaving cloth. Some of the work that Aaron requested of his neighbors required skills he did not have, such as plastering walls, laying stone, and burning out his chimney. Mary called in a neighbor skilled in tailoring to assist her with cutting jackets and gowns. Such borrowing and lending of skills and labor was a deeply ingrained social habit that forged neighbors into an organic whole.[62] Simon Davis acknowledged gratefully that "Wm. Harthon been a good neighbor to me in many respects (but there some times appears to be vagaries in his brain rather extravagant)."[63] Mary grieved at the death of Mr. Goodenow: "We have lost in him a great neighbor and a useful member of society."[64]

Not all neighborly debts were recorded in account books. In a world with "scenes of calamitous providences," as Simon Davis termed them—accidents, illness, and sudden death—neighborliness meant meeting need whenever it occurred. These acts were considered deposits into the bank of goodwill, for one never knew when he or she might need to make a withdrawal.

These acts drew neighbors deeply into each others' intimate lives. Giving birth was a social rite that included a host of female neighbors as attendants.[65] Simon Davis's wife gave birth unexpectedly, while he was still out calling in the neighbors, so she was attended only by his sister and young Esther May, the hired help. Davis returned to find the two girls "in a fit of laughter, who had been shocked with fear." He then gratefully recorded that the experienced Mrs. May soon arrived, and was being "*very neighborly*. Think myself under special obligation to gratitude for the favor constantly bestowed upon me. All from the great source of Being—tho' many from my fellow creatures as instruments by which he works."[66] Mary recorded numerous instances of going to visit and nurse the sick, or spending the night sitting up and "watching" with sick neighbors. Sometimes she sent her hired girls to fulfill this neighborly duty. In May 1806, her own little boy Avery was dangerously ill, and neighbor Mary Bush came repeatedly to spend the night at the boy's side.

Neighbors were present for birthing and nursing, for wedding and for burying. Mary recorded the doleful incident of the death of her neighbor's young son; she spent the whole of the next day at their house making mourning, as she termed it, which would have included washing and preparing the boy's body for laying out and burial. When Simon Davis's beloved little boy

Ezra died in his arms after an excruciating illness, the grief-stricken father reported, "Neighbors kindly come in to our assistance yesterday & today . . . large funeral."[67] When twenty-year-old Aaron Flagg died, his neighbors provided his final essentials: shroud by Eunice Andrews, coffin by Daniel Hartshorn, and grave by Moody Wright.[68]

Some neighborly assistance mixed goodwill and fun. A young Simon Davis seemed much given to attending his neighbors' house-raisings. These events drew large crowds, a goodly supply of rum, and a festive atmosphere. In June and July 1796, Davis attended three such community socials, some lasting several days; that fall, frame raisings give way to husking bees. Mary recorded quilting gatherings for women and berry picking or fishing excursions for youth. These shared tasks blurred the boundaries of work and leisure, obligation and socializing, knitting together community.

Some neighborly activities were purely social occasions—sleigh rides and dances, frolics and walking out. The most frequent neighborly interaction, for both Mary White and Simon Davis, was visiting. The somewhat-retiring Davis recorded with seeming regret that his home in the evenings was frequently "crowded with company." On a typical evening in January 1807, Mary and Aaron ate supper with some of the neighbors. After the meal, they returned to their own home, where Colonel Bush, Mrs. Bush, and the minister, Mr. Cotton, joined them for conversation. Often, evening visits included music, and Mary enjoyed listening to singing at the Abbots, sometimes with the accompaniment of Mr. Crossman's violin, or perhaps the voices of the musical Houghton family. Mary kept a running tally of every visit she received and every one she paid. Such neighborly socializing was expected, in fact, was obligatory. Mary and Aaron's firstborn son recalled later that there was friction between his father and himself because the youth would *not* visit the neighbors.[69] These visits, of course, were not always convivial —Simon Davis noted disapprovingly when socializing was marred with arguments, where men were "chased with words . . . more nise [noise] than wise." The reserved Mary rarely reported disturbances, but noted approvingly when she had an "agreeable interview." The expectation that neighbors would socialize—constantly—was deeply ingrained.[70]

Boylston resident Tamar Farlin, who migrated to Ohio in 1815, wrote a letter to a former neighbor that serves as an elegant testimony to the emotional power of neighborly connections. Her sister, Lucy, begged to be remembered to Mrs. Partridge. "She says she longs to have you for a neighbor again. When she wishes to speak highly in praise of any friend, she says, 'She is almost as good a woman as Mrs. Partridge.'" Tamar asked to be "remem-

bered to her old friends and neighbors and pray[ed] that she may one day
see them again."[71] When Mary White wished to praise the exemplary life
of a valued friend, she declared her simply "a good neighbor and a useful
woman."

The farming families and neighbors of early republic Massachusetts lived
(as Thoreau would later complain) *thickly*, each dependent, each bound,
each belonging.[72] This dominant ideal was not romantic; it was simply essential for subsisting comfortably in their rural agrarian world. Sometimes
these bonds might seem like shackles, chaining the free-spirited individual
to corporate norms and expectations. But most would still ask, "Who could
live alone and independent? . . . Who but some disgusted hermit or half-
crazy enthusiast will say to society, I have no need of thee; I am under no
obligation to my fellow men?"[73] Exigency and ideal worked together to bind
the people of early Boylston in corporate community. If the ideal was never
completely realized, yet living thickly remained the norm.

But, as the first decades of the nineteenth century progressed, some grew
increasingly disgruntled with their close-knit ties to kith, kin, and countryside. They began to murmur that "we stumble over each other" and to seek
distance. Mary's firstborn son, Aaron Jr., who came of age in 1820, grew up
resisting communal bonds. He did not *want* to belong. He did not want to visit
neighbors; he did not want to follow his father; he did not want to farm. His
resistance, as we will see, caused friction and eventually conflict as his family
and neighbors struggled to comprehend this new ideal of individualism.

Congregation

The farm folk of early New England lived in a world of fate and providences.
The supernatural was a real and present agent, the presumed author of all
that was beyond their power to control or comprehend. Many mingled Christianity with ancient folk belief. They attended to the alignment of the stars
and to the appearance of such wonders as rainbows and lightning, comets
and earthquakes as signs of God's power to influence or transcend the laws
of nature. Mastering the lore of wonders could bring unnatural gifts, protection, or good fortune (even pots of gold); ignoring them could bring misfortune. Mary's minister father divined for water.[74] Goodwives, when called
upon to treat bodily ailments, consulted almanacs to determine on the influence of the moon or constellations. Locals superstitiously avoided a stretch
of woodland where, they feared, malicious spirits dwelled.

The deeply devout, such as Mary White or Simon Davis, saw the hand of God in both favors and dispensations. Thus, for Mary, the sudden death of a neighbor was an admonishment to "improve the time." When the horse broke into a run and upset the chaise, Mary's life was "in immediate danger, but the Lord interposed," thus "animating" her to "be prepared to meet death." When the family was visited with two kind providences in one day—little Thomas recovered from dysentery and the men got the hay in before the rain—Mary poured out her gratitude to a kind and interposing God. The total eclipse of the sun in June 1806, during which "the stars twinkled at noon day," caused Mary to marvel, "Wonderful are the changes of nature, but more astonishing are the wonders of redeeming love."[75] Simon Davis, deeply grieving the death of his little son, found consolation in the "comfortable reflection that he has passed all the storms and temptations of an evil world. . . . [H]ow inconceivably delightsome that idea of beholding him safely arriv'd on the opposite shores of immortal Felicity." As Simon declared, in the face of iniquity and trials, "there is a just GOD who rules the world and directs our destiny."[76]

Mary and Simon were Calvinists. They believed that humankind was lost in original sin, profoundly and irreconcilably alienated from God, and powerless to change that fate. Yet God, in his mercy, reached across the void and entered into relationship with his chosen ones; they, in turn, owed him their faithful love and obedience. This covenant—saving relationship with God in exchange for submission to divine will—was the *only* safe and secure ground; those in covenant with God had assurance of everlasting life in paradise.[77]

But for New England's Puritans the covenant was not an individual relationship between a believer and his God so much as a corporate relation between God and his chosen people. Salvation came through belonging to this people; expulsion from the body of the saved was akin to damnation. Thus Mary and her Calvinist neighbors understood the covenant on one level as a binding relationship between God and his people, and on another level as a binding relationship *between* the saints on earth. As a covenant people, individuals relinquished aspects of individual will in joining themselves to the body of believers; they agreed to submit to the godly laws and communal discipline for their own well-being and for the good of the whole community.[78] Covenanters submitted to communal discipline and gained the assurance of supportive relationship—belonging—to the greater body of the saints.[79]

Mary's congregation descended from a gathering of forty-five men and women from Shrewsbury's North Parish who covenanted together—wrote out and signed the terms of their relationship—in 1742.[80] Each man or woman who desired to join in full relationship with the congregation had to publicly declare his agreement with all covenant articles and submit to a communal moral code, ensuring consensus and conformity. Congregations had great power over who could enter into this relationship with them, as all proposed memberships were put to a congregational vote.[81] Though Molly Whittemore "made Christian satisfaction for the sin of fornication," the church deferred her membership for further consideration. Those who were either not at peace with some member of the congregation or known to be in a state of sin had to make public confession to return to full communion. Those who moved and wished to transfer their covenant relationship to another church needed a letter of dismissal, which the church occasionally refused or deferred if the member had been lax in attending to church discipline.[82]

Church members enforced this discipline. If any member broke covenant, the church used persuasion, negotiation, and arbitration to bring about repentance and reconciliation.[83] Within months of its formation, the congregation called Elisha Maynard forward to answer to complaints that "our said brother was guilty at the house of Mr. John Bouker on Saturday evening 13 of October last of sinful wrathful conversation, very abusive treatment of several of his neibours there present & strong [—] of drunkenness." When Maynard refused to appear and make satisfaction, the congregation barred him from communion. Eventually a penitent Maynard submitted a written confession of having acted "contrary to the Gospel and the Holy Religion." He humbly asked "the forgiveness of this Ch[urc]h for my having thus offended it and desire that you would restore me to . . . fellowship."[84]

Maynard's penitent confession was essential to restoring him to the body of the covenant. Discord in any part corrupted the whole; unity and unanimity were essential to corporate health. Offenders had to atone so community could be, literally, at one. It was, of course, only an ideal; the records of the North Parish show members called forward to answer to "breaches of covenant . . . worthy of censure."[85] Simon Davis, who attended the West Parish, noted that three members of the parish who objected to the choice of the new minister "busy themselves sowing the seed of discord among the People."[86] A month later the parish was once again agitated, finding "Isaac Smith 2nd to be much offended on acc't of R. Dunsmoor's bass viol which was yesterday introduced in public worship."[87] "Not so much love & good will between all the members of this Society as I wish for." Yet in each case, the church worked through committees and emissaries to restore the relationship. As Simon Davis noted, as the church was one body, it should be of one mind.[88]

The social order of the community was visible in the physical structure of the meetinghouse. The capacious wooden building dominated the northwest end of the common. Seating in the square box pews was assigned, with deference to age and social distinction.[89] Souls might be equal in the sight of God, but the Almighty in his wisdom had established good order in this world by arranging his people in ranks, "as in all times some may be rich, some poore, some high and eminent in power and dignities, others mean and in subjection."[90] The high and eminent were to rule as his magistrates, while the meaner sort were to submit to this authority. From the gallery above the main floor of the meetinghouse, one could see the social order of the town manifested in the distance each family was placed from the pulpit.

The chief magistrate was the minister. His power in community derived not just from the social dignity appointed a man of learning with a Harvard degree. He also administered church discipline. He held the power of ministerial censure, of withholding communion, of excommunication; he could humiliate the proud and debase an individual's standing in community.[91] He was the father of his people, and in this patriarchal society, the body of the people were to defer to the head. His high pulpit, with a set of stairs leading to an elevated lectern, signified his position. Though Simon Davis might be privately critical of some sermons, he considered those who spoke openly and disparagingly about the minister to be afflicted with "evil spirits," "bent on interrupting the peace of the society."[92]

From his perch on high, the minister gave two lengthy sermons each Sabbath, morning and afternoon. Mary's children remembered that it was the custom for ministers to intone their delivery, which must have made poor entertainment for the young; not surprisingly, Mary's diary, in addition to noting the biblical text and substance of the sermon, also included occasional references to the troublesome behavior of her children. Children of pious parents found the Sabbath order extended to their homes, with no secular reading or conversation allowed. Mary's son remembered that, as his grandmother served tea one Sunday, a young friend asked how tea kettles were made. "She replied that they were not made on Sundays, which was all the light he received on the subject."[93]

The Revolution briefly but significantly upset Boylston's established order as the body unnaturally turned against the head. The people were decidedly patriotic, voting total abstinence of dutied tea and pledging that "they would be ever ready to do all in their power to preserve their just rights and privileges."[94] But a few were strongly suspected of too much loyalty to the crown, and among them was the minister. Reverend Morse repeatedly used his pulpit to preach obedience to royal authority. Parishioners finally rebelled. First a parish committee and then an ecclesiastical council were called to arbitrate. Reverend Morse refused to budge, and finally the parish, convinced that they and their minister could never be of one mind, voted to dissolve the pastoral relation. When Morse refused to recognize the authority of this decision, the congregation "voted that he should no longer enter the pulpit as their minister and stationed guards at the pulpit stairs to see that he did not."[95] In the end, townsmen disarmed the inveterate Royalist and confined him to his farm for the duration of the war.[96] The parish believed it had no recourse with their obstinate minister but to sever relations with this festering member, lest he despoil the whole.

Severing the head to save the body was a shocking challenge to hierarchal authority, and the move no doubt reverberated deeply in Boylston; succeeding ministers and local gentry acted quickly to reassert proper order in the chaotic years after the Revolution. By 1793, a flourishing town decided to make the new order physically manifest in a fine new meetinghouse. Again they encountered difficulties. The majority wanted the structure located on the current town common, but a large minority clustered in the flourishing western region of town protested that it should be moved closer to them. After many attempts at negotiation, the town called in delegates from neighboring towns to arbitrate, who ruled that the location of the proposed structure should not be changed. Simon Davis, who hailed from the west, noted bitterly in his journal when he first heard the bell on the new meetinghouse sound. "Have paid towards it about two dollars. . . . [C]ertain designing individuals conceived it good policy in the Town to pick the pockets of those who had no part or lot with them while it was in their power. . . . A considerable part of this is paid for by those who live from near 3 to 5 miles from it. Of what service can it be struck, when it can be heard seldom if then by accident or particular attention?"[97] Resentment would simmer until those in the west, of their own resources, built a meetinghouse and secured permission to establish a separate parish.

But the most troubling issue challenging the unity of Boylston's church, and the one that would eventually give spark to the tinder of strife, was a problem of church belonging. It is difficult to overstate how much belonging to the body of the church shaped life. Yet, though everyone who lived within the town's border belonged to the *parish* and had to pay for the support of minister and meetinghouse, not everyone was admitted to membership in the church, allowed to own the covenant and share in communion and fellowship. For some, such as Simon Davis, this was a matter of choice, for despite his deep piety, he could not bring himself to agree with the church's stand on infant baptism. Thus he attended and supported, but did not belong to, the church; his children were not baptized, nor did he take communion. Others in town chose not to participate at all but were still assessed for the ministerial tax.[98] Thus, in one town with one church (there were no dissenting sects in early Boylston) there were three levels of belonging— those in full membership, those who attended but were not members, and the unchurched.

The issue of church belonging was vexed locally by an unfortunate pattern of alternating inclusively minded ministers with those who favored exclusivity. Gaining, then losing, the benefits of membership made some parishioners increasingly resentful. Rev. Ebenezer Morse (pastorate from 1742 to 1774) was an "Old Light" Calvinist, who allowed entrance to all who could prove correct theological belief, and to children of the same (the Half-Way Covenant).[99] For more than thirty years, then, the people enjoyed a relatively open and inclusive church. Morse's successor, however, Rev. Eleazar Fairbanks, was a "New Light" Calvinist, who imposed a much more rigorous standard for church admission: candidates had to prove that they had had a profound emotional conversion. In exchange for ritual and ceremony Fairbanks demanded a new standard of moral purity.[100] Fairbanks was not alone in his efforts; all around Worcester County a new generation of clergy, supported by gentry concerned with restoring order and regularity in the wake of revolutionary chaos, began reforming lax standards and reasserting discipline.[101] Fairbanks immediately set about rewriting the covenant to reflect New Light intensity, updating church music, and—most critically— revoking the Half-Way Covenant.[102] Local gentry approved of their New Light minister, with his claims that none should rise to places of honor but those who had proven their merit, and saw his efforts as validating their social and political ideals with religious authority.[103] Order, however, came at a cost: the redisciplined church was now highly exclusive, and many, unable to meet the new standards, found themselves outside the circle of belonging.

When Fairbanks retired at the end of the eighteenth century, the parish chose as their new minister the Rev. Ward Cotton, who attempted to reconcile his congregation through liberal admission and by avoiding theological niceties. But his compromises satisfied no one: the former elect disapproved of their church's inclusiveness as spiritually derelict; the liberal majority resented what they took to be a self-righteous cabal, seeking to control from within. Increasingly, opposed interests challenged the ideal of organic unity and corporate belonging, and conflict silently smoldered under a facade of unanimity.

Town

From the vistas of the hill north of Deacon Andrews's house in the town's northeast corner, the town appeared a haphazard and loosely connected collection of farms. Strung out across the countryside, homesteads and fields—all privately held property—were scattered where soils would suit.[104] Neighborhoods clustered where families and resources drew people together, but no larger community identity was visible in the landscape. It was visible, however, around the town common. Here the townsfolk had built the commonly owned artifacts of public welfare: the meetinghouse with its noon house and horse sheds, a powder house for the town's "warlike stores," a stone-walled pound for wandering livestock, the town stocks, a schoolhouse, the burying ground, and an open field for militia training and communal gatherings. These were not truly public buildings and spaces, for their use and benefit was restricted only to those who belonged to the town. The New England common, owned by all *members* for the good of the *whole body*, "objectified traditional corporate effort and control."[105]

Town membership in early Boylston was by permission only, and gaining admission—or settlement, as it was called—in closed New England towns had historically been challenging.[106] But those who secured membership *belonged*; Mary White would identify strangers by indicating, for example, "He *belongs to* Bolton."[107] It was a critical distinction. Belonging carried the right to support in times of need, but it also carried obligations. Most critically, in the interest of maintaining a consensual community, members were expected to submit their will to that of the body of freeholders. In the early republic, submission seemed a reasonable—in fact, customary—price to pay for inclusive fellowship.

Town, like congregation, was modeled on covenant. Massachusetts settlers had established communities based on a social compact by which, as the Massachusetts Constitution later codified, "the whole people covenants with each citizen and each citizen with the whole people, that all shall be governed by certain laws for the common good."[108] The critical elements of town government by covenant were, first, that the people promised to engage in mutual relationships with reciprocal obligations for each others' well-being; second, that all agreed to obey the decisions of the community and submit to their communal enforcement; and third, that the goal was to promote the common good.[109] Signed in the presence of God, covenants added a sacred cast to town belonging. In this spirit, towns held great power to control individual behavior.

If one was not born into town membership, it was no simple matter to join. Because the townsfolk were responsible for supporting their own poor, they allowed newcomers to settle only if they came with resources and reputations to ensure they would not become dependent. Itinerant poor were undesirables who could be inhospitably "warned out," or sent back to the town of their birth, where they belonged.[110] Those who were allowed to settle were expected to take up the obligations of town membership. They also were sometimes required to submit to intrusive town management of their households.[111] In return, they reaped the benefits of *belonging*: social order, pooled effort, the rights of the commons, and the assurance of communal welfare in times of need.

Those who belonged to Boylston at the turn of the century had much in common. About half of all those eligible to vote had been born in town, and the rest hailed from surrounding towns.[112] Most of the native-born were descendants of original settler families, and almost all could trace their ancestors to the Great Migration of 1620–40. Boylston was a young town, with more than half the population under the age of majority.[113] Land was the most valuable asset, and though the distribution of wealth in Boylston at the turn of the century was not so equal as on the frontier, it was far more equal than in more established areas.[114] And most men owned their land unencumbered by major debt. Those who had debts owed them mostly to their neighbors, and it was rare for any man to lose his farm to insolvency.[115]

Several times a year, primarily at the annual March meeting and again in the fall, the town met to determine how it would attend to its communal obligations. Not everyone who belonged had a right to participate in setting the ordinances by which they would be governed. Only males over the age of twenty-one with at least $200 of property and one year's residence—the truly independent—were called to appear. About two-thirds of the grown men in town met these requirements, and almost all obeyed the summons to do their civic duty.[116] Each eligible resident at town meeting could speak his mind and cast his vote, making town meeting in some ways a democracy of freeholders. However, not all voices carried the same weight.

Leadership of these meetings was usually voted to an older, established man who commanded the respect and deference of the community.[117] Throughout the early republic, Mary's neighbors chose their principal town officers from a small coterie of the wealthiest landowners, including her husband, Aaron, and his friend and neighbor, Jotham Bush.[118] These were the town's squires, those select few who could—and did—term themselves "gentlemen" on official documents. The squirearchy acted as a local aristocracy, though they exercised power not absolutely but with the assent and deference of freeholders. And their power was circumscribed by an obligation: it must be exercised in the common good. With privilege came public duty, with power, dedication to public service.[119] The twenty-five years that Aaron White devoted to endless town committees, town clerk recordkeeping, and selectman's service were both an honor and a burden of his station.

Townsmen relied on their wealthier residents in part because of traditional patterns of deference and in part because of the belief that men of property were also men of learning, wisdom, and disinterested virtue. They expected that their squires, bearing a larger share of the tax burden, would be vested in the town's general well-being—and in fiscal restraint. Their voices carried greater weight, and as voting was by voice or show of hands, there was incentive to follow their lead. After all, these same men were the justices of the peace who resolved local disputes, the administrators of most of their neighbors' estates, the ones yeomen turned to when they needed to borrow money or petition the legislature.

Through their union of wealth and office, New England's squires "became a personal symbol of authority, a key link between the local community and the world," and yet parochial to the core. They consciously "projected themselves as leaders of a corporate community, a homogenous, organic whole."[120] They often imprinted this authority on the landscape by building impressive houses, such as Colonel Bush's fine brick home overlooking the town common, deemed "one of the best in Worcester County."[121] They acted out their authority on the local stage by presiding over public ceremonies, advocating for the town in disputes with neighboring towns or before the legislature, and in promoting local improvement.[122]

It was these local squires who stepped forward to reassert order and control in the wake of revolutionary turmoil. Landed gentry faced multiple threats in that chaotic time: the egalitarian rhetoric of revolution challenged old norms of privilege and deference; revolutionary emphasis on liberty and active citizenship empowered the common man to change his lot; and religious awakening elevated individual conscience over obedience and submission. Gentry feared the potential of radicalized masses to reduce a fragile new nation to chaotic disorder. Any who doubted the threat need only look to the French Revolution. New England's squires asserted that for the sake of stability, a natural aristocracy of landed, educated men—that is, themselves—should continue leadership in the new republic as they had in the old provincial government, and they actively sought ways to advance their social leadership.[123]

Some gentry joined together in private societies to improve the cultural offerings of their rural communities. Thus, in March 1792, a group in Boylston's center village founded a private "Social Library," with 386 volumes to circulate among members.[124] All over Worcester County such private groups of gentry highlighted their separate—and elevated—fraternal status by founding exclusive improving societies. They were overwhelmingly among the wealthiest, most educated, professional men—civil officers, doctors, lawyers, and orthodox ministers.[125] Their activity fortified the connection between privilege, leadership, and improvement. Perhaps more critically, it introduced the idea that the well-being of the community, once the responsibility of the town, could be pursued by private groups of individuals. They "could claim the mantle of the commonwealth tradition," while also realizing social elevation and, ultimately, private profits.[126] For the present, yeomen accepted the dominance of this social elite. But as resentments grew, its days were numbered.

Town meeting rules were based on the expectation that townsfolk would achieve consensus on most issues. If disagreements arose, Mary's neighbors laid the matter open for discussion. But if no clear "sense of the meeting" emerged or if the item proved to be contentious, the town would appoint a committee—usually of respected gentlemen such as Aaron White—to investigate the matter and to report back to the next meeting with a proposed resolution. The meeting almost always deferred to the squire's judgment in such arbitrations. If, however, "after much debate and many trials at different times," an issue was still contentious, the town usually voted to pass over the article or, if conversation became heated, to dissolve the meeting, to preserve the peace.

Each year, town meeting had to decide how to provide for schools, roads, and the town's poor. The town's farmers were parsimonious providers of public services. Their five one-room schoolhouses were in session for only two brief terms a year, while a master tried to keep order and dispense knowledge to eighty or more youngsters of all ages.[127] Expectations were low: as long as a child learned to read the Bible, write well enough to sign a deed or will, and figure sums sufficiently to keep his accounts, most parents were satisfied. Parents were not required to send their children to school in Massachusetts until 1852, so attendance was sporadic. Discipline was left to the discretion of the hired schoolmaster, and cases of burly older boys amusing themselves at the master's expense were legendary. So, too, were cases where strapping young schoolmasters buttressed their authority with the whip.[128]

Nor did the town spend significant time or resources maintaining public roads. Though every man was responsible for repairing and regrading the road in his neighborhood district, most Worcester County roads at the beginning of the nineteenth century were dismally ill kept, little more than broad paths cleared of trees and stumps, studded with rocks and roots, rutted with the passing of hooves and feet, carts and wagons.[129] Travel along the town's three main roads and numerous cart paths was easy only when the snow, hard packed by ox teams, enameled the uneven surface with a smooth track for sleighs and sleds. But most traffic went on foot or by horseback, so improved roads were not a priority to those who knew they would have to pay for them in hard-to-find cash.

One inescapable responsibility was providing for the town's destitute. Widows, orphans, and elderly infirm whose families could not care for them—if they *belonged* to the town—became public charges. Each year at town meeting, taxpayers put these souls up for auction, settling them with whoever agreed to charge the town the least for their care. Such support grudgingly fulfilled the civic obligation of membership in a covenanted community.

Town meeting and election days provided regular excuses for socializing as a community. The common on March meeting day was a fairground crowded with vendors, while the country store and tavern did a hearty business.[130] The evening was marked by frolics. Simon Davis noted an August town meeting in 1796, followed by a "Frolic at R. Keyes"; the following year, Davis reported, "All hands [hired help] at March meeting," though adding with disapproval, "Boys [his apprentices] had an entertainment in my new shop in evening—Not agreeable to me."[131] Mary's children remembered tales of "Election to Perfection," a celebration with a parade, speeches, and festivities so exciting that they marked notches on a stick to count down the days to its arrival.[132]

BOYLSTON'S POLITICAL ORDER was briefly turned topsy-turvy in the years immediately surrounding the Revolution. After unseating their minister, the town's farmers flirted briefly with a democratic insurgency in the 1780s, as economic hard times following the war threatened them with the loss of their freehold farms.[133] In 1786, when farmer Daniel Shays of western Massachusetts led a popular uprising against the heavy taxation championed by eastern merchants, one Shaysite supporter urged the "good people of boylstoin as this is perelous times and blood Shed and prisoners made by tirants who are a fighting . . . to advance their Intrest wich will Destroy the good people of this Land—we that Stile our Selves Rigelators [Regulators] think it is our Duty to Stand for our lives and for our familys and for our Intrest wich will be taken from us if we Dont Defend them. Therefore . . . fly to our asistance as Soon as posable in this Just and Rightous Cause."[134] In the end, Boylstonians did not fly to Shays's assistance—in fact, they sent a small contingent of men to help suppress the rebellion—yet they were clearly sympathetic.[135] The townsmen may well have understood the Shaysite call as a customary demand to defend the common good, by force if necessary.[136] The one Boylstonian who was indicted for sedition and fined in the Shays affair, gentleman Jonas Temple, was elected by his townsmen to the highest town office the next year.[137] Like most of the county, Boylston's citizens expressed their populist disapproval of overbearing central powers by turning the anti-Shaysite governor out of office and rejecting ratification of the Constitution.

Nevertheless, the town's populist agitators were quickly soothed or suppressed, and the old top-down social order fairly quickly turned right-side up again. Under the leadership of the gentry, a strong Federalist consensus emerged in town. For the next half century, the town would never again give majority support to a populist or Democratic candidate for governor or president.[138] After town meeting in 1799, Simon Davis noted with approval that his "town [was] happily united in political sentiments."[139]

Local Federalist gentry were able to reassert control so quickly after the Revolution in part because the town remained fundamentally corporate in sensibility, and Federalism resonated with that corporate spirit. This was an orthodox, covenanted town, unsplintered as yet by religious dissidents; Federalist politics were rooted in an ideology and language of orthodoxy and national covenant that suited them well. Federalism also, as John Brooke has said, "demanded individual responsibility for the collective welfare, [and] equated personal independence with public obligation, an equation that had a powerful resonance for those who remained committed to communitarian values."[140] Deferring leadership to a fraternal circle of orthodox gentry and clergy may have seemed like reassuring good sense in light of the revolutionary excesses of the French. In the 1790s the townsfolk renewed their church covenant, built a new meetinghouse, and tidied their graveyard, all statements and symbols of their renewed commitment to orderly, corporate community.[141]

But local Federalist elites were likely able to contain their townsmen's brief flirtation with populism and partisan conflict so readily in part because conditions in town were improving. The town experienced a small exodus of its most needy—and most ambitious—offspring in the late 1780s. This may have served as a pressure valve, removing those most likely to agitate for democratic reforms: dissent literally went away.[142] And the town was close enough to Worcester and the Post Road that by the late 1790s, a small trickle of marketing brought hopes of coming prosperity. More and more yeomen came to see their interests—growing exports from their farms and work-shops—as in tune with those of the gentry, and as a result were more will-ing to defer to gentry leadership in pursuit of their common cause.[143] When called upon to present a toast while on a market trip to Vermont, Simon Davis declared, "The state of Vermont and the Commonwealth of Massa-chusetts—their Federalism."[144] By the early 1800s, Boylstonians consistently voted nearly unanimously for Federalist governors, though unanimity, it seems, did not spark turnout; usually only a third of Boylston's eligible men bothered to show up to rubber stamp the Federalist choice.

Boylstonians' rather lackadaisical participation in national politics dur-ing the early republic era may reflect their distraction by a highly conten-tious local political struggle. The people of the western parish, led by their wealthiest and most prominent citizen, Ezra Beaman, waged a decade-long battle for independent townhood. The distance to the center meetinghouse put them at a disadvantage, they claimed, in attending town meeting and representing their interests. And therein lay a troubling issue: the people of western Boylston had come to see their interests as different from the rest of town. In their region, they claimed, lay the future of the town—the wealthi-est residents, the most fertile Nashaway River intervale land, the promise of the river's power. Their repeated petitions to the general court for incorpo-ration were resisted vigorously by center-village and eastern folk, who knew that the departure of the westerners would cost them dearly in revenue and resources. Outspoken and strong-willed Squire Beaman refused to be de-nied, stirring up discontent and agitation that disturbed the peace of the town.

After a dozen years of disruption and "chasing words," Beaman hatched a plan. The western parish would submit a new petition to the general court for an independent township, and it was rumored that if the petitioners were successful, they would then move to *annex* the eastern section to their polity, seizing control of the whole. In 1807, debate on this plan erupted in town meeting. Mary White recorded nearly weekly meetings of selectmen and others to plan offence and defense. Finally, the town gathered on March 2, 1807, for their annual meeting. As the weather was frigid, they adjourned from the chilly meetinghouse and reassembled across the green in the warmth of Abbot's tavern. Mary reported, "The people crowded into Capt. Abbot's Barroom. The floor gave way and let about 40 of them into the cellar. Some were considerably bruised. Through a kind interposition of providence there were no lives lost."

If the event proved providential to Mary, it seemed to provide an omen for the selectmen as well. The foundation of the town had given way—there was no way that they could build a consensus through arbitration or negotiation that would return unity to this divided polity. In cases of hopelessly broken covenant there was but one solution: the estranged members must be separated. In a petition to the general court drafted and delivered by Aaron White and his fellow selectmen, they conceded: "A few disaffected individuals have . . . been indefatigable in their exertions to produce the dismemberment & eventually the total ruin of the Corporation. . . . [A]lthough we have most sensibly felt the injury resulting to us from the partial dismemberment of this small but once united & flourishing Corporation, yet our peace has been so incessantly disturbed by new projects of encroachment, and we have encountered so much trouble and expense in opposing these projects that we are now fully persuaded we shall never be at rest; that our existence as a Corporation will be in perpetual jeopardy until this troublesome and offending member is totally severed from the body which it thus threatens to destroy."[145]

Most effective in bringing unity to town in the wake of the hiving of West Boylston, however, was not peace but the aspect of approaching war. Commitment to the Federalist banner—and turnout in state and national elections—soared in response to the highly unpopular Embargo of 1808 and the War of 1812. Roused with indignation over policies that Federalists believed were antithetical to local interests, nearly every eligible voter turned out in 1808 and 1812. That year, Worcester County held its version of the Hartford Convention, when Federalists suggested that secession from the union might be the best recourse to the national Democratic and prowar politics. Aaron White served as Boylston's representative.[146] His teenage son noted in his diary, "If vice should pave the way for civil discord and faction & rend the bonds of Union may Liberty with her attendants still smile on the cold mountains of New England."[147] The War of 1812 drew Mary's neighbors' attention briefly from their farm fields and meetinghouse to the national stage. But it also drew them closer together, in the perception that their regional interests were mutual and their understandings shared, their principles and piety superior to an aberrant other. It reminded them where they belonged.

Severed Bodies

But not everyone belonged, and the consequences of exclusion could be dire. In the spring of 1880 workmen repairing the foundation of the old Whitney homestead gingerly moved the massive doorstep slab. There, entombed under a shallow layer of dirt, lay the jumbled bones of what proved to be a young female, about twenty years old, who had died sometime around 1800.[148] The girl was likely Sophia Martyn Whitney, a young bride in an old family. How could she have disappeared beneath the family's door slab, unnoticed and forgotten? The problem was that Sophia did *not belong*. In both church and town, she had no membership. And being cut off from the body of the people, as Sophia Martyn Whitney discovered, could be fatal.

Sophia Whitney was one of those few who lived outside of the bulwark of social belonging, those who would not, or could not, be joined to the whole. These were people whose physical, behavioral, or moral difference made union seem repulsive and incorporation impossible. The clearest manifestation of this repudiation was the townsfolk's tendency to isolate, burlesque, or desecrate the physical bodies of those who did not belong. Debasing the body—treating it as one might treat livestock or wild creatures—confirmed and manifested Boylstonians' belief that incorporation of these outsiders would be unnatural. This either-or outcome—bodily union or bodily rejection—was the result of a society that perceived of membership in corporate terms.

Cato Bondsman lived and served as a slave in the Andrews family from his boyhood in the 1760s. He was freed after the Revolution and remained in town, heading a small family. Cato paid his taxes and sent his children to the district schools, but the family was never really part of Boylston society.[149] They were refused a pew at church until Cato petitioned the town for favor in 1798: "Whereas Providence hath placed us among you and living under a Constitution that proclaims freedom and diffuses light and knowledge . . . [we pray that you will] appoint the family and others a seat in the meeting house or build us a pew . . . that we may enjoy free and unmolested the indulgence of attending publick worship with you."[150] His townsmen dealt with the issue by building a small second gallery near the belfry, out of view of most worshippers.

Cato's son Moses worked as a farmhand. In the winter of 1810, when he was thirty, he was fatally injured while hauling wood. As the ground was frozen, his body was kept in a local barn for spring burial. In February, however, Captain Flagg was surprised to see a "wooly scalp" hanging from the wooden underpinnings of a bridge over a local brook. It was Moses Bondsman's, whose body had been anatomically dissected and then disposed of piecemeal in the brook, and finally exposed by the rising waters of the spring thaw.[151] The ghoulish event may have caused talk, but it sparked no prosecution. In fact, no perpetrator was identified for over a century and a half, when a town historian determined the suspect was likely a young doctor, recently settled in town, who left within months of the discovery.[152] The dissection and disposal of the black man's body seem to have caused little stir. He was not one of them.

Sarah Boston was one of the Hassanamisco Indians of Grafton—descendants of an early Praying Indian village. She lived an itinerant life, as did many local Indians, moving with the seasons to follow natural resources, to sell her baskets and tell fortunes, and to seek rum and hard cider offered by farmers in payment for seasonal labor. Sarah had a temporary abode in Boylston, a shanty built against a rock ledge.[153] Mary recorded buying a basket from a black woman, likely a mixed-race Native, who came through the area, possibly Sarah Boston or one of her kinswomen.[154]

Sarah Boston lived on the fringes of Yankee life. Neighbors saw Boston and her female friends as freakish creatures, "wandering about the countryside. . . . Usually all had baskets of their own make on their arms or brushes for the hearth or other household uses," a neighbor recalled. Sarah dressed as a man and did men's work in the fields. She had three children, with no known husband. Having learned Native medicinal lore from her mother, she practiced enigmatic folk cures. She enjoyed her liquor and her freedom. Sarah Boston was everything a goodwife should not be.[155]

The people ridiculed her through caricature of her physical appearance and parody of her behavior. She was described as gigantic, well over six feet tall and at least 300 pounds, with astonishing strength. Her attire was reduced to the comedic: short skirt and a jacket, men's boots and men's hat, all wrapped in a blanket "squaw fashion." The effect of her physical appearance could be terrifying, or comedic: "[A] party of young men returning from a dance . . . at which they had partaken very freely of New England rum were passing the old cemetery . . . where they suggested stopping and waking the dead. Rapping upon the gate they shouted, 'Arise ye dead and come forth to judgment.' When from a grave arose the gigantic form of Sarah, exclaiming, 'I'm coming Lord, I'm coming.'"[156]

Sarah Boston would never be part of the Boylston community. In all respects she was alien, despite being genuinely Native. Sarah Boston sent her only daughter to live with friends in Worcester, where the girl might have a better life.[157] Meanwhile, the militia played at sham Indian fighting.[158]

And then there was Sophia Martyn Whitney. Sophia was the illegitimate daughter of Mary Ball and Edward Martyn, born in 1784.[159] Martyn never married Mary Ball, nor did Ball's eventual husband, Dr. Stephen Brigham, adopt Sophia. The bastard child was likely put out to care by the town. In 1801, a seventeen-year-old Sophia Martyn married her neighbor, Shadrach Whitney, a thirty-one-year-old farmer of middling wealth. The illegitimate Sophia Martyn must not have been an accepted and integrated part of the community, for sometime in the next decade she disappeared from the homestead, and no one in the town, apparently, took any notice. It was said that she had left her husband and gone to live with family in New Hampshire.[160] Later, with no recorded death or divorce, Shadrach married a second time. In local lore, a guilty secret lay behind a curse of misery and misfortune that seemed to plague the Whitney household in ensuing years.[161] Whitney's father, once a prosperous farmer and active in town affairs, began to withdraw from society and drink heavily; he eventually lost his home, his health, and his life.

The macabre tale of the doorstep grave reveals the other side of this world of communal belonging. Membership did not extend to those who were different, unorthodox, unconventional. Those who lived outside the dense network of relationships, shared works, mutual obligations, covenant, and social norms were not enfolded in fellowship. Since Sophia Whitney, Sarah Boston, and Moses Bondsman could not be incorporated into the whole, they were severed from the body of belonging.

BUT THINGS WERE on the verge of change. Boylston, like most of rural New England, was about to experience external forces and internal drives that would ultimately break the bonds of belonging. The transformation would not be easy—change would be resisted and contested fiercely, making the decades to come the most conflicted in the town's history. The people would no longer dig together for a shared treasure. They would question—and re- ject—the very ideals of common good and corporate community. For some this would seem like a declaration of independence from communal own- ership; for others, a dangerous descent into self-serving self-centeredness. In their struggle, we will witness relationships remade: Boylstonians will redefine liberty as freedom of choice, voluntary relations, and an ethic of in- dividualism, where each pursues his own happiness, or his own pot of gold.

CHAPTER TWO

A Church Disassembled

Let us now look forward a generation. We may peer out the window of the White family's front parlor, as son William did on an April evening in 1841. The world he saw was rather different from the rustic village center of his youth. From his writing desk by the window, William could view a much-tidied common, graced with an elegant granite town house, a new Greek Revival church, and an assortment of stores offering fashionable wares. Stone walls and fences, flower gardens and hedges imposed a pleasing discipline on the village landscape. But it was an external order only; as William was about to relate, under its facade of neat regularity, Boylston was teeming with mayhem.

As he penned his letter, William gazed across the common at the old meetinghouse of his youth. For the last five years the building had been abandoned, gradually descending into a dilapidated state, an eyesore on the orderly common. Perhaps musing on the deserted meetinghouse, William wrote to his brother, "Alas the state of religion in this town is far from what it should be." But then his letter broke off, as the scene out his window drew him hurriedly away. When he returned, he explained, "Since I have commenced this letter I have been disturbed by some wicked boys (as I suppose) throwing stones at our old meeting house and its already broken windows. I went to the door and gave one screech at them and they soon scampered away into the darkness."[1]

In the generation that spanned the 1820s and 1830s, what had happened to "the state of religion in this town" that would cause the people to abandon their meetinghouse—the symbol of their unity—and that would embolden youth to desecrate its decaying shell? This is the story of a generation of religious turmoil, played out in town meetings, tavern porches, and parlors, and within the hearts of citizens.

IN KEEPING HER DIARY, Mary White was a reserved woman, which makes her animated entry in late March 1829 all the more remarkable. In an impassioned outburst (with the rare use of an exclamation point) she announced, "The parish nominations triumphant!" Mary reveled in the success of her favored candidates in the election of officers at the annual town meeting. She was not the only one so moved. Her diary and town records reveal that local party leaders schemed for days to secure victory; that a desperate attempt at unity—a proposed Union Slate of Officers—had failed when the committee assigned to come up with a balanced roster could find no middle ground; that debate had been long and angry. There had been scenes and name-calling at town meeting, with some storming out in a rage. People decried the extreme partisanship and the ways in which it deadlocked town business. The vote, when it finally came, was split, but in the end more of the positions for selectmen, clerk, constable, and assessors were won by Mary's party than her foes. The victorious faction, including the usually complaisant Mary White, were exultant.[2]

The issues that divided Mary's townsfolk and roused such passions were not about politics, economics, or social class; they were about religion. The battling parties represented different religious sects, each vying to control elected town offices. Over the past fifteen years, the town's single meetinghouse, like so many in New England, had struggled to contain two increasingly divergent camps, one theologically liberal, the other conservative. Debate over what should be included in the articles of covenant, who should be allowed to approach the communion table, and what should be preached from the pulpit provoked such violent passions that even the otherwise sedate Mary White could not restrain herself. Years later, one who witnessed the fracas remembered "the bitter animosity of the two parties" and the ugly words and actions that poisoned the town. "Hard speeches were made, reproach, accusations and criminations were uttered and reiterated. Friends became enemies, jealousies kindled in neighborhoods, and contention and strife existed in every section of town. No heart was indifferent; every man, woman and child was strongly in sympathy with one or the other of the conflicting parties, and all were prepared to employ influences which tended to secure the peculiar ends which they desired."[3]

Issues of faith and conscience—issues in which people were deeply invested and on which they felt they could not compromise—challenged and eventually destroyed the organic corporate identity of Mary's community. Religious faith legitimated oppositional behavior. For some, the depth of religious conviction made public dissent not only unavoidable but imperative, even as it undermined a shared common good. Battling sects sundered community as they contended for control of the meetinghouse, the schools, town offices, and the hearts and souls of unaligned townsfolk. In support of their cause, some created new forms of association, private and exclusive rather than collective, based on promoting not the common good but special interest. They joined forces with those beyond the borders of their town who shared their views, breaching the old localism that had once bounded community. Most powerfully, as local evangelicals proselytized their neighbors, they elevated the individual in his or her struggle to work out salvation. This regenerate soul was a powerful force: imbued with an inner authority and feeling justified in asserting righteousness, converts—and their equally impassioned liberal opponents—fought a holy war. Change began in the hearts of individuals, rippling out through families and neighborhoods, church and town, to redefine belonging and communal relationship.

Mary's triumph was short-lived. After the next year's town meeting she reported with dismay, "Quite a revolution in the officers."[4] Much worse was to follow. Within a few years, battles over belief and religious turf would destroy the ancient congregation.

The Battle Is Joined

Religious trouble trundled into town at the turn of the nineteenth century, with the arrival of an amiable young minister from Plymouth, the Rev. Ward Cotton. Most parish gentry had been pleased with the conduct of their previous minister, Eleazar Fairbanks, a strict New Light divine who had been called to reassert discipline—religious and social—in the wake of revolutionary chaos.[5] In choosing Cotton to replace Fairbanks, the orthodox gentry no doubt attended to his excellent credentials: scion of Calvinists John Cotton and Increase and Cotton Mather, raised in Plymouth, New England's oldest Calvinist settlement, and educated at Harvard. Cotton came from a family of such substantial means that his bride's rich silks and genteel ways astonished the local women.[6]

But Cotton was *not* a Calvinist. During his years at Harvard, he studied under professors who, like many of the coastal cosmopolitan elite, had become increasingly liberal in their theology. They embraced doctrines of free will, the power of reason, the innate goodness of humanity, and the unlimited potential of moral and intellectual growth to improve humankind. Quietly, they set aside Calvinist doctrines of original sin, human depravity, predestination, and the Trinity. Liberal ideas spread first among ministers, then to their congregations. One of the earliest churches to split along liberal/ orthodox lines was in Cotton's hometown of Plymouth.

Yet Rev. Ward Cotton instituted no revolution when he first came to Boylston. He was, by the account of one who knew him well, an amiable man; "obliging in his disposition, he took pleasure in conferring favors and never sought to give unnecessary pain and trouble to those around him."[7] But pain and trouble were inevitable. Cotton was a liberal; he opened the doors of the church and preached a broad-minded gospel. The ideal congregation, he insisted, "must seek unity and acceptance of all brethren." Rather than insisting on purity of doctrine, they must "study to be quiet, doing their own business." Cotton particularly warned against excess of religious enthusiasm and emotional conversions. "The human feelings or passions . . . are properly the gales of life. They never ought, indeed, to assume the helm or place of the pilot; . . . the passions may be too warm; they may be raised so high, as to obscure the light of understanding and entirely prevent inquiry. . . . But religion, *founded on principle, and strengthened by habit*, will usually continue through life. A small stream of affections towards God, which runs steadily without abating, is better than a flood, which come violently for a time, and soon diminishes."[8]

On the surface, Cotton's plea for an inclusive, all-embracing gospel seems ideal for a community that valued corporate unity. In actuality, Unitarian Ward Cotton was attacking the very core of covenant conformity and exclusive corporate belonging that had long defined Boylston's church. He was preaching each individual's power to find his own path to God. Cotton rejected Calvinist dogma—rejected all doctrine—and in its place preached a benevolent God who could be known to all through the light of reason. Cotton encouraged ethical behavior shaped by individual—not corporate— conscience.[9]

In our times, such liberal ideas seem unremarkable. In 1820s rural New England, they were revolutionary, a rebellion against long-standing habits of enforced intellectual and moral consensus and group discipline.[10] One's identity, one's security, one's salvation no longer came through the body of the people, but individually and independently, through free will and unfettered reason.[11] Socially, liberals rejected a spiritual aristocracy of the elect and asserted that all were equally endowed with the power to make their own way to God.[12] And there was more: Cotton's rejection of religious enthusiasm was a specific rebuke to orthodox revivalists who required new members to give evidence of an emotionally wrenching conversion experience. To those members of the parish who had been excluded from the communion table for the past quarter century for failing to meet New Light standards, Cotton's inclusiveness was welcome.

To Mary White, one of the orthodox, it was not. Liberalism was a dagger to the heart of covenant and community. The orthodox believed that broad-minded pluralism threatened not only the faith of their fathers but also good social order. They were anxious for a return to doctrinal integrity, along with, as one scholar has said, "a strict discipline within the church, an adherence to well-defined standards and a restoration insofar as possible of a consensual, well-integrated, and ideologically homogenous community."[13] Mary prayed, "Let us be of one mind."

There was no immediate revolution, however. For fifteen years, most churchgoing townsfolk went to hear the amiable Reverend Cotton preach his two Sunday sermons on the ethical and social obligations of believers and the love of a benevolent God for all. Gradually, though, strict Calvinists began to grumble; by 1812, a small contingent withdrew and, together with disgruntled conservatives from neighboring Shrewsbury, formed a Baptist church.[14] An ecclesiastical council was called in from neighboring congregations to arbitrate, but no action was taken. One townsman later recalled, "There appears to have been no hasty and rash move by either party, tho both parties exhibited a determination that was absolutely unmovable."[15] What emerged, instead, was a decades-long contest of wits and wile for the soul of the town.

The situation was the same in many surrounding communities. The liberal faith that first surfaced around cosmopolitan Boston at the turn of the century made silent progress without causing a major backlash for some years. Most progressive-minded ministers called themselves simply liberal Christians and tried to avoid controversial issues of doctrine. Many of their parishioners adopted their viewpoint without even fully comprehending the theological rift that separated liberal and orthodox views.[16]

In the end, it was orthodox ministers who cast the first stone. For years, ministers within the Congregational association had been accustomed to regularly exchanging pulpits, preaching to each other's congregations. Around 1810, orthodox minister Jedidiah Morse of Boston began to refuse pulpit exchanges with his liberal brethren, claiming that he would not expose his congregation to heretical teachings. The issue might not have had legs, except for Morse's canny willingness to make use of a powerful new resource, inexpensively printed and widely circulated pamphlets and newspapers. These print pieces traveled along new turnpike, canal, and rail routes, carrying the controversy into the countryside.[17] In 1815, Morse published a widely circulated tract that accused the liberals of heresy in rejecting the divinity of Jesus and hypocrisy in attempting to hide their heretical beliefs behind vague sermons and doctrinal dissimulation. In response, liberals admitted that some among them found the Trinity to be unscriptural. But conservative Congregationalists, they countered, were an intolerant, exclusive, and reactionary lot whose doctrinal rigidity trampled on freedom of conscience and diverted attention from pressing social and ethical problems.[18] William Ellery Channing published a reply that set out the Unitarian ideal: the goal of Christianity should be to inspire people to live lives of Christian love; doctrinal issues such as the Trinity were of no use in reaching that goal and should not be allowed to destroy the peace of the Christian community.[19] Informed by this very public argument, Boylston's liberal and conservative believers chose sides for a long and ugly contest.

THREE CONSERVATIVE and deeply pious matrons—all close neighbors in the center of town and all named Mary—heard the message and were soon up and doing, building their ranks and damming the liberal tide. They demonstrated a remarkably passionate and urgent determination. In the autumn of 1815, Mary Bush, Mary White, and Mary Abbot gathered thirty-eight other townswomen into the parlor of Mary Bush's stately brick center-village house and formed a society. The act seems unremarkable today; in 1815 Boylston it was nearly unprecedented. The principle of voluntary association was not new; it underlay New England church covenants and town organization, and its biblical basis had recently been bolstered by Enlightenment social-contract philosophy. But voluntary association to promote special interests rather than common good—especially when undertaken by women—was a bold step for these evangelical women.

Their constitution explained their intentions. "Feeling our Obligations to improve what the great bestower of all good has placed in our power . . . to subserve the best interests of our fellow mortals . . . we resolve to form ourselves into a society." They pledged to contribute fifty cents per year for the privilege of meeting together, the receipts of which would be used to aid foreign missions.[20] In five concise articles they set out their rules for membership, electing officers, conducting meetings, raising and disbursing funds, and amending their constitution. The document was signed with the given and surnames—not the married titles—of forty-one women.

Those who embraced this plan hardly seemed like revolutionaries. On average they were middle-aged, well-to-do matrons, or the daughters or siblings of the same.[21] Their respectable position, along with their traditional female activities of shared work and socializing, hardly seemed controversial. Yet for some in the community, the formation of this new female society was deeply discomfiting. Only two of the forty-one initial members of the group were associated with those families who supported the liberal ideas of Reverend Cotton.[22] This was, in essence, a partisan society, and some in town found their work doubly troublesome: party spirit had no place in a consensual community, and women had no place in politics.

One of those most disturbed was Reverend Cotton. He knew these women supported only conservative, orthodox missionaries, and he had no desire to aid in spreading Calvinism abroad. He also knew that such a society would likely strengthen Calvinism in his own parish. Cotton saw the founding of this society as an opening tactic in a local battle for religious allegiance.

He was right. The women were canny; as soon as they had written their constitution, they addressed a polite request to their minister to give his blessing—in the form of an opening sermon—for their first annual meeting. Cotton found himself in an unenviable position. If he accepted, he would have to bless the work he opposed; if he declined, he would appear to publicly oppose pious women in their attempt to spread the gospel. He demurred, claiming that he was not available for the date they requested; they persisted, sending secretary Mary White to his study with a written request to name a date that would be convenient and instructions to wait for his reply. Perplexed, Cotton sent Mary back with an apologetic note, claiming he did not know when he might be free. Undeterred, the women then appealed to Reverend Puffer of neighboring Berlin, who obligingly agreed.

On January 8, 1816, the women "met at the house of Captain Abbot at nine o'clock in the forenoon from whence they went in procession to the meetinghouse."[23] It must have been an imposing scene: forty matrons on a mission. Reverend Puffer provided the public blessing the women had hoped for. Not only did he praise them for adding their "influence and example, prayer and substance" to this righteous cause of preaching the gospel "*to every creature*," he also defended their new voluntary association. "I am not insensible that many things are said against making these efforts." But, he acknowledged, the women were doing God's work, and the men would do well to join them. "Feeble individually, but united, they are a mighty engine for promoting truth and righteousness, peace and salvation among men."[24] The approving women published his text.

Cotton was appalled. He saw in the women's work not peace and salvation, but contention and strife. Suddenly, the busy minister found time in his schedule to sermonize the women himself. On October 1, 1816, the women again processed to the meetinghouse to hear Reverend Cotton preach on the "Causes and Effects of Female Regard to Christ." Women who love Christ, Cotton declared, are drawn to live like him, lives of love and charity. But women, he noted, can do this best in the way God has appointed, *in their homes*, setting examples of piety and promoting true religion among their families. He acknowledged that they might be moved by Christian love to perform acts of charity and spread the gospel. Why, though, must this be in foreign lands? Why not treat those poor, sick, and needy at home? They must beware, he warned, of striving to be great rather than good. Jesus himself checked the spirit of ascendancy among his disciples, urging on them a more modest and humble temper.

He did not caution them on this matter, he assured them, because he doubted their true charitable intentions. Rather, he knew they were innocent of the ways of the world and may be "unsuspicious of those who may misguide you and lead you from the paths of peace and of duty." Women of old had been misled by connivers, and in their naivety led to act "directly in opposition to Christ and his cause. You will be aware of such deception, and take heed that you fall not *undesignedly into the like errour*." Thus Cotton broached his real concern, that the society might become a vehicle of sectarian contention:

> Perhaps never, since the settlement of this country, have there been more exertions to promote the spirit of a particular party, than at the present day; and they will endeavour, no doubt, to [secure] the aid of females to prosecute their designs. To this end . . . societies have been instituted, whose professed objects externally are plausible, but whose ends and designs are to strengthen a party. To this end, pamphlets of various kinds are circulated, some of which more openly explain their designs; and others, although they often contain many things which in themselves are good, yet, to a discerning mind, their intention evidently is to prepare their readers, as fast as they can, to approve of and follow their measures. Now it is my desire—and I trust this Female Society, and this Religious Society at large, have the same feelings and wishes—I say, it is my desire that the inhabitants in this place should not be engaged in any proceeding which relates to any party measure or party business whatever.[25]

The women were not pleased. They did not appreciate being warned of spiritual pride, of overstepping their proper sphere, or of being duped in their gullibility by the nefarious designs of evil men. The sermon caused such a stir that Cotton felt obliged to publish it in his own defense, as "some observations in it were misunderstood, and consequently misrepresented."[26]

The matrons pushed forward. In the face of the minister's resistance, they paired their passion with action. The Female Society increased the frequency of meetings and began sewing items to sell to augment revenues. With some of their funds, members purchased conservative religious tracts for a lending library; some they donated to the national Home Missionary Society (for western missionaries) and the American Education Society (for the preparation of conservative ministers). By 1818 these evangelical women had founded a Sunday school, which served both to educate youth on how to read and understand the Bible (in the orthodox manner) and to create a nurturing, supportive community for its evangelical female teachers.[27] While the women grew in fellowship, those in the community who lacked the money, time, or religious sympathies to participate were excluded.

The town's orthodox women also used the conventional act of prayer in revolutionary ways. They held evening prayer meetings in each other's homes throughout the week, cultivating their private bonds of faith and fellowship. These intimate meetings, which may have satisfied their longing for a more active spiritual life than Reverend Cotton's moral and ethical sermons provided, reinforced their separate identity as an intensely personal, self-segregated society of the saved. When they heard that an evangelical pastor in Litchfield, Connecticut had begun a monthly concert of prayer— joining their brethren in England and around the world on the first Monday of each month to pray for the spread of the gospel in heathen lands—they followed suit. Through these monthly prayers they linked themselves to a powerful worldwide network of shared faith.[28] The rural women could now imagine themselves engaged in a great work with like-minded females around the globe, vastly expanding the horizons of their social identity. They used prayer to create both exclusive local and expansive global alliances. Unintentionally, their new alliances vitiated old community.

WHATEVER THE WOMEN'S PRAYERS may have done for the heathen, they did nothing to reduce tensions in town. Reverend Cotton found it increasingly difficult to hold his divided church together. By 1817, a visitor noted that religious controversy had caused so much division among the people that often there were no Sunday services in town at all.[29]

Boylston was far from the only parish with theological quarrels. Across Massachusetts, and particularly in the eastern half of the state, townsmen battled for control of the church. The intensity of the struggle forced the state to confront laws upholding the established Congregational Church through town taxes. Liberals who rejected orthodox teaching were faced with a difficult choice. Either they could remain part of the state church and submit to their adversaries—essentially being taxed without representation for the support of a minister for whom they had no sympathy—or they could withdraw and form their own society. In doing so, however, they would forfeit their sizeable investment in the communal property of the existing church: pews and furnishings, communion silver, building, bell, lands, and funds. In 1820, a liberal majority in Dedham decided to contest Congregational establishment and sued for control of the town's meetinghouse; the Supreme Judicial Court found in their favor, ruling that the property of the church belonged to the *majority* of those who paid for its support. Thus, the *parish*, or the whole society of taxpayers, was elevated over the *visible church*, or the covenanted. Quite suddenly, the theology of the public church became a matter of popular opinion, with both sides campaigning for control.

Locally, the situation deteriorated to a critical state. Despite the activity of the evangelical women, it appeared that Reverend Cotton had at least half the congregation behind him and could effectively maintain control. At the town's annual meeting in March 1825, a motion was made "to see if the town will agree to divide the use of the Meetinghouse among the different religious societies." But the town would not so agree. Soon after, the evangelical Congregationalists began to consider withdrawing and founding their own society.[30] Neither side talked any more of unity and consensus; both were determined that they could not in good conscience remain in fellowship with their opponents.

Had the Congregationalists withdrawn, tensions might have subsided. But the county association of Unitarian ministers knew that losing the town's Congregationalists would result in significant lost revenue and influence for the Unitarians who remained in the public church. Rev. Dr. Nathaniel Thayer of Lancaster devised a ploy to keep the whole of the congregation in liberal hands. In the spring of 1825, Doctor Thayer invited townsfolk to a meeting. He explained that area ministers were so concerned for "the afflicted state of this parish" that they had "advised [Cotton] to take a dismission, and had said to him, if he would not take a dismission . . . they would discard him and have no fellowship with him as a minister."[31] Thayer's goal, it appears, was to orchestrate the appointment of a new minister, still liberal, but less freighted with ill will. And so, after twenty-eight years of ministry, Reverend Cotton was dismissed.[32]

But Thayer's ploy backfired. The parish, almost equally divided between liberals and conservatives, called a young minister who appeared to represent middle ground. Rev. Samuel Russell seemed a gentle soul, "simple, unaffected, and kind," a Trinitarian but amenable to exchanging pulpits with Unitarians—considered at the time to be a sure sign of liberal leanings.[33] An examining committee of both liberal and conservative ministers approved his installation. It soon became clear that Russell, though gentle, was a gentle *Calvinist*. "In the early part of his ministry," one witness later reported, "a change was made in the Church Covenant; Articles of Faith were adopted to which all who united with the church in the future should assent, and to a great extent the policy of the church was changed [to be more conservative]."[34] The Unitarians were appalled, and, by 1827, it was they who decided to withdraw from the public church, asking Rev. Ward Cotton to lead their weekly services. "Accordingly, in this small town of 830 inhabitants, which would be only an ordinary parish for one minister, Mr. Cotton, now aided by this same Doctor [Thayer] and other individuals of the association, sustained worship in the School House for a Unitarian Society."[35] A year later, an even more liberal subset set up a Restorationist Society in town, and invited various Universalist ministers to preach to them of God's plan for including *all* in universal salvation. With Congregationalists, Baptists, Unitarians, and Universalists (the last two uniting after 1830) all competing for members, the ideal of a united, covenanted community died.[36] Or rather, it was killed, the unintended victim of a homegrown battle of unyielding religious principles.

Faith on the Fringes

The liberal Unitarians of Massachusetts have historically been identified with the seacoast's commercial, cosmopolitan elite. Unitarianism has been described as the faith of a privileged social class, deeply influenced both by Enlightenment rationalism and by its adherents' own success in a new market-oriented culture. As one historian has written, "As God seemed kindlier, the environment more manageable, and their fate more dependent on their own abilities, they could no longer see themselves as sinners helplessly dependent on the arbitrary salvation of an all-powerful God."[37] Their salvation, like the rest of their fortunes, lay in their own hands. From their vantage point as wealthy, urban civic and social leaders, they focused on ethics and philanthropy to further their work of improving humankind.[38] Congregational evangelicals, on the other hand, have been depicted as "stressed rural

Yankees . . . trying to negotiate the disruptions that the growth of market brought."[39] They have been associated with middling rural folk, or those recently relocated to the city from the farm, who resisted modern, cosmopolitan culture and "asserted the subsistence world's commitment to communal love against the market's competitive ethic."[40]

These characterizations may describe urban populations on which some of these studies are based; they do not describe the liberal/conservative camps in rural Boylston.[41] Various membership records survive for the Baptist, Unitarian, and Congregational churches in Boylston, and these records allow us to compare the social and economic characteristics of the congregations.[42] Among those identified as church members during this era, Unitarians-Universalists generally held a small majority in numbers. But it was orthodox evangelicals, not Unitarians, who were the privileged among these churchgoers. The town's Congregationalists, on average, were significantly wealthier than their Unitarian and Baptist townsmen.

Wealth at this period was still held overwhelmingly in land. That the town's Congregationalists were wealthier than their dissenting neighbors meant that they held more land. The town's larger land-owners were not resisting the market; many had been involved in marketing surpluses for several decades, and most were increasing that activity during the 1820s and 1830s. Members of this same class of larger landowners were more likely to be purchasing and displaying fashionable imported goods and urbane amenities for their upscale houses. Nearly two-thirds of the Congregationalists lived in the vicinity of the now-thriving center village, near shops, the meetinghouse, the town house, taverns, and several substantial new homes. They were creating a vibrant, more cosmopolitan community, while Unitarians were spread more evenly across the rural landscape.

In this agrarian town, the orthodox were less likely to be resisting a market ethos than attempting to shore up their leading role as privileged gentry. It was in their interest to maintain the existing social order. Exclusive church membership based on proven merit, focus on church purity, sure knowledge of doctrinal integrity based on literal scriptural interpretation, conservative resistance to heterodoxy, and fidelity to a corporate ideal all increased their sense of confidence that they were among the elect. The Unitarian-Universalists, by contrast, were not an educated, professional, cosmopolitan elite, but a wide cross-section of residents who had likely long lived on the fringes of the covenanted community. With less invested in the land they were more open to change and more willing to move to bring about that change.[43] Being among those who had not enjoyed the full privileges of corporate belonging, they were receptive to the liberal message of inclusive membership and universal salvation.[44]

The town's religious wars were ostensibly about theology, but those theologies also supported different visions of the social order. The orthodox claimed a place of religious and social privilege as the elect whose landed resources allowed them to benefit from new commercial opportunities. The Unitarian-Universalists included some well-to-do people, but many more who inhabited the outskirts—physically and economically—of the village social world, and who resented being forced to the fringes of society. In this unintended way, religion allowed the social tension from a growing disparity in wealth and opportunity a righteous outlet, as conscience legitimated conflict that might otherwise have been suppressed. Religious meetings no longer reproduced the whole of the town's social order; they magnified social difference.

Testimonies of Faith and Faction

By the late 1820s, the war between Congregationalists and Unitarians had spread throughout the Massachusetts countryside. As rift hardened into bitter divide, almost no town escaped a nasty battle for possession of the meetinghouse. Among Mary's townsfolk religious ill will spread beyond the meetinghouse, infecting families, neighbors, and town government.

Mary and Aaron White sent their firstborn son, Aaron Jr., to Harvard University in 1813, likely envisioning that the youth would follow in the footsteps of his Harvard-educated grandfather, orthodox minister Joseph Avery. But at Harvard, Aaron Jr. imbibed the liberal teaching of a now-Unitarian faculty.[45] To his mother's deep dismay, the young man rejected Calvinism. He did not return home after graduation; in 1819, after two years teaching and keeping shop in northern Vermont, he paid a brief visit to his parents, but found "My Mother . . . does not altogether approve of my religious sentiments so that my visit . . . was not a very pleasant one. . . . After mature deliberation I concluded to return to Middlebury."[46]

Religious discord soured neighborly relations as well. One who knew remembered: "Strong feelings were aroused in almost every breast, bitter animosities produced, severe invectives poured forth, and complaints of abuse and injustice uttered by both of the contending parties. Criminations and recriminations were made with great frequency and severity."[47] Social visiting had once bound the community together. Now, Mary's pattern of socializing changed. Two-thirds of the visits the family received were now from fellow

Congregationalists; most of the rest were from townsmen unaffiliated with a church. The family was even more selective in the visits they paid, nearly all of which were to fellow church folk.[48] Social visiting had once woven the town together. Now it deepened their divisions.

As we have seen, the Federalist consensus in Boylston since its incorporation had been so strong, as it was in most northern Worcester County towns, that party spirit rarely entered into town elections. Top local offices, particularly the important offices of moderator, clerk, selectmen, and assessors, had routinely been granted not according to political party, but by deference to wealth and age. Religious strife transformed that arrangement, as townsmen now competed ferociously to seat their fellow *churchmen* in positions of power.[49] Leading men from contending religious sects met in advance of each election to agree on candidates and plan strategies.[50] It was this intense partisanship that evoked Mary's uncharacteristic display of jubilance when Congregational men took the top offices in 1829.

That victory, however, came at a high cost. Tempers flared and angry recriminations were traded in the March meeting of 1829.[51] The election of the chief officers did not settle the dispute; emotions remained high. Next came the election of the school committee, a group traditionally composed of the town's most educated and chaired by the town's minister. When voters approved the orthodox Reverend Russell as the head of that committee, Capt. John Howe leapt to his feet and furiously interrupted the assembly. Howe was influential, a well-to-do citizen, descendant of early settlers, long active in town affairs. By temperament, he could be difficult; one detractor declared he was "a profane, brawling, quarrelsome man."[52] He was inclined to introduce controversial petitions to town meeting discussion and could be a fierce advocate for his cause. He had also assumed unofficial leadership of the Unitarian cause in town.[53] Now he proclaimed, "If the people have a mind to be such damned fools as to vote in for their first school committee man a liar, then let them go on!" Shock ran through the meeting at such unprecedented incivility directed at a member of the clergy. Afterward, as men gathered on the porch of the meetinghouse, several rebuked Howe, saying that he did not speak as a gentleman. Howe retorted that he did not care, that he could prove Russell a liar.[54]

Howe's outburst was only the latest in a string of verbal accusations he had made against the Congregational minister. In early 1827 at Captain Gales's store in Northborough, Stephen Flagg overheard someone ask Howe if Mr. Russell were his minister. "Not by a damned sight," he replied, declaring that he "would not have a damned fool for his minister."[55] Others heard

Howe publicly declare that Russell was a liar; one of Howe's hired help reported that Howe, "talking foolishly," had said the same at meal times.[56] Throughout 1828, Howe repeated the charge of dishonesty: at the home of Rev. George Allen of Shrewsbury, to the market man, Baxter Woods, to William Moore as he worked in his field, anywhere he could find an audience.[57] Russell attempted to meet with Howe to resolve their differences, but to no avail. Finally, after the public outburst in town meeting, the long-suffering minister filed for slander.

The situation was unprecedented. In cases of public contention, locals had always relied on committees of leading gentry or respected elders to work out reconciliation and restore peace. It had been extremely rare for townsfolk to bring suit against each other, and then only for long-term debt. That Howe would refuse arbitration and that Russell would involve the courts were unheard-of behaviors. But traditional approaches to reconciliation would not work; Howe saw himself as a crusader for principle, and Russell believed he was defending orthodoxy and clerical dignity. There could be no compromise.

The suit further agitated already-roiled waters. Lawyers for both parties canvassed the town, deposing townsfolk and stiffening necks. Mary White was among those deposed, as Reverend Russell had "lived within her family" for his first year in town. In April 1830, Mary traveled to the Worcester County House to attend the trial and to take the witness stand, along with many others from a now deeply divided community.

The story emerged. Behind the affair was not the ill-tempered Howe, but the Unitarian schemer Rev. Nathaniel Thayer. According to Thayer, when Russell had promised during his ministerial examination to exchange pulpits with liberal clergymen, Thayer invited him to do so. But Russell never called to arrange this exchange, and when Howe asked him about the matter, Russell said though the exchange had been proposed, Thayer had not yet found it convenient. When Howe reported the comment to Thayer, he declared it a lie. Howe was enraged, and Thayer saw a chance to bring down a conservative clergyman.

At the trial, Russell presented many character witnesses, and others testified to Howe's repeated slanders. Mary White herself took the stand. Howe, on the other hand, chose a simple defense. Since Russell *was* a liar, it was not technically a slander to call him one. The judge, accepting this assertion, made it the purpose of the trial to determine whether Russell had lied.

The besieged Reverend Russell maintained that he understood his discussion with Thayer as merely a proposal to exchange, and that it was the place of the older man to set a date; as Thayer had never set a date he had assumed it was not yet convenient. He pointed out that he had exchanged pulpits willingly with several other Unitarians in the interim. But Thayer was persistent, asserting that the younger man had intentionally misled people by claiming that he had proposed an exchange when he had never done so. Thayer's testimony felled Russell, as a predominantly Unitarian jury ruled that Russell *had* lied, and therefore that Howe had not slandered him by saying so. The triumphant Howe/Thayer contingent then magnified their victory by publishing and distributing an edited transcript of the trial. A humiliated Russell responded by publishing his own version, dismissing Howe as a man of little consequence, "lost to a personal sense of decency & moral worth," and likening his charges to "bar-room or grog-shop assertions." It was Thayer, Russell charged, who hoped to use the affair to destroy the fragile harmony of the conservative congregation.

The trial's conclusion brought no resolution to town strife. As one witness remembered, enmity based in religious difference continued to feed "those petty jealousies, those painful contentions, and those bitter animosities, which so marred the moral beauty of this place, and which caused so much pain without accomplishing any good."[58] Yet, unwittingly, the episode had accomplished something. By their actions in the cause of religion, battling sects brought an end to the norm of negotiated reconciliation and the ideal of consensual community. They opened the way to pluralism.

The Battle Is *Joining*

In the midst of this unholy fracas, Mary White's fervent prayers were answered: the Lord poured out his Spirit, as she said, upon the countryside. A powerful revival visited the orthodox church. One local later recalled, "Since the days of Edwards and Whitefield [the Great Awakening of the 1740s] the churches of this country have not seen and enjoyed such seasons of refreshing from the Lord as they were blessed with between the years 1826–32. . . . Many were pricked to the heart, and made to enquire, 'Men and Brethren, what shall we do?' Many were those who rejoiced in believing and during [Russell's] short ministry, one hundred and four were added to this church."[59]

The Second Great Awakening rolled through town at the height of the sectarian controversy. Since the turn of the century, New England had been experiencing spasms of emotionally intense religious fervor, in which individuals awakened to their sinfulness, struggled with despair, and then experienced a profoundly emotional and life-transforming conversion. Enthusiasm waxed and waned, rolled in waves and then receded, for a quarter of a century. Mary's town under the anti-evangelical Cotton, had been relatively untouched. But Russell's ministry coincided with the peak of a nationwide surge in revivals that climaxed in 1831. Thus, though beleaguered by his foes, Russell presided over an explosion of evangelical energy and efficacy. In fact, the stress that afflicted the established church may have aided its regeneration, as once-complacent, lukewarm worshippers were moved to commit.[60] Those who lived through it gave witness to its momentous nature. In late December 1829, Barnabas Davis noted in his diary, "There seems to be an uncommon revival of religion . . . in Boylston, as I understand. May it continue to be lasting and effectual." In the midst of Russell's trial, Davis noted, "In many places, revivals of religion. In one place in particular there were but 12 in the church 10 years ago, and now upwards of 300."[61]

The spirit did not come to town unassisted; the town's evangelicals made straight the way. The national revival of the late 1820s and 1830s was, to a degree, orchestrated by those already converted, using so-called scientific methods designed to "arrest the attention of the sinner and persuad[e] him to be reconciled to God."[62] Evangelist Charles Finney introduced new measures to awaken sinners, especially holding week-long "protracted meetings" of nonstop preaching. Different ministers took turns continuously exhorting sinners with bold and denunciatory language, calling on the unrepentant by name, urging them to come forward to the front-row "anxious seat" where they would experience the full power of his warning and plea, entreating them to public confession, submission, and commitment. Families and friends were urged to make personal entreaties to their loved ones, to bring seekers to "inquiry meetings," to share private testimony of struggle, despair, and joy, to gather in small supportive groups for prayer and nurturing fellowship. Finney suggested—to the initial consternation of some conservative Calvinist ministers—that the faithful did not have to wait on the Lord, but could through their own efforts invite divine visitation of grace.[63] One did not have to be chosen; one could choose the Lord. "Choose today," Mary urged her children, "whom you will serve."

The power of choice transformed religion. Many in town took their religious destiny into their own hands. Evangelicals such as Mary declared that the way to God was open, and it was up to each to choose to follow that path. Voluntary religious choice was utterly new, and utterly "at odds with the New England heritage of communal ideas and unity."[64]

Throughout 1828 and 1829, Mary and her fellow evangelicals worked tirelessly to awaken their friends and neighbors to the urgent need for repentance and submission to God. Mary believed that the work of conversion and reform was urgent because she believed, like many of her evangelical contemporaries, that the millennium was near. Christ held out the offer of forgiveness, but for a short time only, for soon He would return in judgment. Repeatedly she appealed to her family, "Give your heart to the Savior now while it is an accepted time. . . . [T]he longer we neglect to comply with the offer of eternal life the more we are exposed to eternal death."[65] To help others in approaching the Lord, Mary organized and attended prayer meetings for women and youth, for those in the various stages of conversion: "inquiring the way [to salvation]," "grieving [their sinfulness]," "indulging a hope [of salvation]," or "rejoicing [in salvation]." She attended "concerts of prayer," hosted Bible studies, taught Sunday school, distributed religious tracts, and talked—endlessly and constantly—of salvation. This extraordinarily passionate evangelism was a deeply personal expression of her faith as well as her fear for the fate of family and neighbors.

With the ground thus prepared, in the autumn of 1829 the evangelicals hosted a series of protracted meetings. Visiting ministers held these meetings around town, in schoolhouses and private homes, with different rooms and different meetings appointed for youth, for children, for women, for those at different stages of conversion. Mary's diary reveals that from September to December 1829, a religious meeting was held almost every day, sometimes several in a day. She prayed that "the seed sown there spring up and bear fruit to the glory of God."

Her prayers were answered; the revival yielded a rich harvest. Mary recorded joyfully the conversion of each sinner, the addition of each member to the church. In late 1829, fourteen came forward; the next year there were fifteen more. As the revival continued throughout 1831, and as the yield continued to climb, Mary exulted. "Mr. Benj'n Houghton [whose advanced age of sixty-two made his conversion somewhat unusual] and wife—he a remarkable instance of victorious grace. Well may we exclaim *what hath God wrought*? And may we be enabled to give Him all the glory of deliverance from the bondage of sin."[66]

THE POWER OF RELIGIOUS CHOICE was heady and liberating. Yet the decision to convert was not an easy one. Those seeking grace were warned repeatedly of false conversions, of the easy and misleading sense that one had done enough soul-searching or lived a righteous life when in reality the sinner still stubbornly clung to his own self-will. Spiritual pride was doubly damning as it hindered the humble submission required for true saving grace. Converts had to go before the church's examination committee, confess their sinfulness, testify to their personal experience of the redeeming love of Christ, pledge complete submission of their will to God, and dedicate their lives to his service. They joined themselves to a new community, committed themselves to a new life. They were then expected to live utterly transformed lives, giving evidence of their justification. They were to abandon their previously gay and frivolous lives and their unregenerate friends, find support and companionship among the pious, and work for the conversion of the world.[67]

This was a tall order. Undergoing religious conversion was a weighty personal decision that required rebirth as an inner-centered individual; joining a church meant choosing a new relationship of exclusive community; living as a justified person involved active commitment to changing the world. One might truly be called to "leave house or a brother or sister or father or mother or wife or children or town for Jesus' sake." What was this experience like? Who would choose to undergo such trauma, and what motivations supported such a decision? Seven of Mary's ten children underwent conversion experiences; one of them, sixth son Charles, left a journal of the experience that allows us a window to his soul.

Charles was sixteen when he left home to serve as a druggist's apprentice in Boston in 1836. During his first two years, he adjusted to city life and pleasures and spent his free time with cousins and friends from work rambling about, learning to swim, going to band concerts on the common, chasing fire engines, and reading novels of adventure and travel. His mother, sisters, and a converted brother wrote regularly urging him to join a Bible class, attend prayer meetings, and closet himself with his Bible or devotional texts. Mary wrote weekly to tell him of his friends who had converted—or worse, died unexpectedly before working out their salvation. "Do not forget the one thing needful. We are traveling to the Judgment Seat of Christ. Your Sisters are inquiring the way of Salvation." "My son, the whole period of our short lives is not too much to be dedicated to the service of God. Remember that the Saviour's now calling upon you to turn and live; before another year, yea before another week, your account may be sealed up, the judgment of the great day."[68]

In early 1840, the seeds that Mary had sown began to germinate. Charles became concerned for the state of his soul. In October and November 1839, the eighteen-year-old attended a moving series of lectures on the "The External Evidences of Christianity." After hearing a sermon on the Sixteenth

Psalm, he noted that the words "had considerable effect upon my mind. . . . May the truths which I heard this day be treasured up in my mind and at the Judgment Day I may look back upon this as the happiest day of my Life." He began to read religious books, such as Joel Hawes's *Lectures to Young Men* and Jacob Abbott's *The Young Christian*.

Although Charles was convinced of the truth of Christianity, his conversion had just begun. Was he to be counted among the saved? He had to endure several months of soul-searching angst about his ability to surrender his will totally. He struggled to discipline himself, to learn submission, self-denial, and spiritual humility. To aid in his quest, he attended a Young Men's Meeting for those wishing to learn the way to salvation and he read nightly from Christian pamphlets and texts. In January 1840, he joined a class of those preparing for admission to the church. Yet he was deeply troubled about his worthiness and the state of his soul—a state of anxiety that was a classic and necessary feature of the conversion process. Charles eased this anxiety by attending Bible classes, prayer meetings, "meetings for young men seeking religion," and "inquiry meetings." His brother Avery visited and gave Charles some passages he had written regarding religion. Brother William wrote letters urging a full surrender of the heart to God. On January 23, Charles recorded: "This night weighed the question with myself whether I would serve Christ or not. Resolved to serve Christ and let it be recorded in Heaven."

Still, his path was not easy nor his conversion complete. On good days he recorded that he "enjoyed some peace of mind, though my stubborn will not broken." On other days, however, he worried that he "did not enjoy any particular blessing from the Holy Spirit," or fretted that he was "very uncomfortable in my mind in regard to moral and religious feelings boath [*sic*]." Finally, on Sunday, March 8, he seemed to reach a turning point: "I felt this AM very distressed in my mind . . . [then] felt much better. I believe all that is wanting is to feel that Christ is my Guide and submit all unto him." On Wednesday of that week, Charles learned that his brother Davis had just made a public profession of his faith, and Charles declared himself more "resolved in my mind, more this day than for sometime before."

At this point, Charles informed his parents that he, like Davis, was "rejoicing in hope." Both Mary and Aaron expressed their joy at learning "that you have given your heart to the Lord. You will never regret that you have done it this early. . . . If you have made an entire surrender of your heart to God you will find a never failing source of happiness which the world can never give you."[69] On May 7, 1843, after a public examination before the elders,

Charles and his forty-three classmates were admitted to the Congregational Church at Essex Street. He confided to his journal: "I view this transaction as one which millions of ages hence I shall look back upon with infinite joy or regret. God grant that it shall be the former."

Charles's admission to the Essex Street Church was only the first step in his new life of righteousness. He immediately began teaching Sunday school, visiting his students at their homes, distributing religious tracts to seamen on the city docks, and evangelizing his coworkers and his boardinghouse mates. Charles had completed a rite of passage to the adult world of Christian work. Now he faced a new duty, to perfect himself in faith. Submitting to a transcendent authority, joining an exclusive community, and committing to a specialized code of behavior—the essential core of the conversion experience—all distanced Charles from the established authority, expansive community, and customary social norms of corporate New England towns. Charles's new identity set him apart.

CONVERSIONS TRANSFORMED COMMUNITY, but unevenly. Who among the townsfolk were drawn to such an experience and to such a commitment? Mary's revival culled young women and men from well-to-do local families with a close relative who was either already a member of the church or who converted with them.[70] The Second Great Awakening marked a shift in the average age of converts from their mid-twenties to their late teens, which suggests that new struggles associated with coming of age may have made youth more susceptible to the urgent proddings of evangelicals.[71] Although most studies of religious conversion are based on urban models, rural youth in New England were also encountering stresses.[72] Young rural women faced changes in household work, domestic ideals, and marriage prospects that made their futures seem unknown and insecure; young men faced new options and uncertain prospects in a changing economic world. They faced, in fact, a confusing, perhaps overwhelming array of new choices. Conversion, too, was a choice, but one that offered "at least a temporary therapy for doubt and uncertainty."[73]

As Mary White's anxious letters to Charles reveal, if this was a youth's revival, it was a maternal evangelism.[74] The majority of those converted, especially in the 1830s, were the children of orthodox Congregationalists, the offspring of those who had already owned the covenant. This was not by chance. Thirteen years before, these mothers had helped organize the Female Foreign Missionary Society. Now, in June 1828, Mary White, together with a few other evangelical females, gathered at the home of Mary Abbot and founded a Maternal Association.[75] The ladies met monthly for prayer and support on how best to raise Christian children. We can picture them gathered in Mary's parlor, exchanging advice, discussing sermons on prodigal youth, reading aloud together such books as the Rev. John S. C. Abbott's new bestseller, *The Mother at Home*. This contemporary classic on "maternal duties, familiarly described," explained, in its preface, "The religious sentiments inculcated in this book are those usually denominated *evangelical*. We have proceeded upon the principle that here is the commencement of eternal existence, and that the great object of education is to prepare the child for its heavenly home."[76] The member list for this association does not survive, but if it reflected the membership of the orthodox church or the converted, we can assume that they were well-to-do, comfortable matrons, with the time and resources (not to mention sufficient parlor chairs) to devote to this cause. They also were those most likely to have children facing new opportunities and challenging choices that might take them far beyond the bounds of their parents' traditional agrarian society. Prayer was the parents' best hope of protecting their offspring, and eternal reunion their consolation for earthly separation. As Mary fervently prayed, "May all my dear children be made heirs of a heavenly inheritance." "We may separate a little while, but we shall soon meet again where adieus and farewells are a sound unknown."[77]

What did conversion do to the convert? Most notably, undergoing conversion focused the mind's eye inward. Self-searching and introspection were essential to arriving at conviction of sin, and self-loathing and despair were an inevitable stage in the process of conversion. Mary's diary records the angst of some of those who struggled with a feeling of unworthiness, who "did not enjoy their minds," who grieved their sinfulness, who despaired of reaching salvation. Mention of suicide in and around town rose significantly in the peak years of the revival; between 1828 and 1839, seven people took their own lives, and five of those deaths occurred during the critical 1830 to 1832 period.[78] This was not an outlier; suicide rates rose throughout the early republic.[79] In Concord, Massachusetts, there were twelve recorded suicides in the first half of the century, five of them during the peak years of Awakening fervor. For one thirty-one-year-old female, the cause of suicide was "supposed to be in religious melancholy and despair, by reason of false and distracted notions of God and his decrees."[80] After intemperance, religious enthusiasm was one of the leading attributed causes of insanity.[81]

Those who successfully endured conversion found that their new life in faith required an ongoing commitment to soul-searching. Converts were expected to spend significant time closeted in prayer, building a personal relationship with their Savior.[82] They were also to examine themselves on a daily basis, to judge of their usefulness and faithfulness to Christ.

Such habits of introspection reshaped the emotional landscape. Evangelical Congregationalists focused on the *personal*—personal experience of emotional conversion, personal salvation, personal devotions, personal belief. Lost was an earlier focus on the corporate nature of salvation under covenant relations. Moreover, the intense focus on individual volition—the power of voluntary religious choice—in both accepting offered mercy and in evangelizing others redirected thought from community to individual. As Donald Kraybill, scholar of Amish culture has written, evangelical revivals "accent the individual rather than the community as the center of redemptive activity."[83] By contrast, the Amish he studied reject evangelical Christianity and its focus on individual belief, subjective experience, and emotionalism, which, they argue, undermine their traditional communalism. The evangelical revivals of the 1820s and 1830s elevated the individual at the expense of the mutually dependent covenanted community. It promoted a voluntary religious choice that was "at odds with the New England heritage of communal ideals and corporate unity."[84]

Evangelicalism did not eliminate collective effort; it reorganized it. Mary's converts broke away from the greater community, but committed themselves to an intense new community of faith. Members shared their personal relationship with God and each other in prayer, worship, communion, moral discipline, and support through the trials of daily life. This new grouping also enjoyed a fresh ordering. Evangelical Christianity had radically democratic potential. Hierarchy was replaced with equality before God, an egalitarian communion of saints. Critically, though, this was a private and exclusive equality.[85]

Evangelicalism also gave pious and respectable matrons such as Mary White, Mary Abbot, and Mary Bush an unconventional public role as activists. Evangelical womanhood provided an alternative to popular models of female behavior, which tended to focus on either farm-household domestic obligations or on Victorian ladyhood, a life of gay and leisured consumption. Evangelical womanhood called for useful, active, purposeful, and socially engaged labor outside the home.[86] Mary was not seeking power in the public sphere; she and her colleagues were careful to secure ministerial support, to ally their reform efforts with the church, and to limit their activities to traditional women's behavior such as meeting together for prayer, reading, social support, sewing, and education. Yet, in the name of orthodox religion, they performed socially unorthodox work. In the name of God they devised an empowering mission, allowing them to take initiative and do what the men in their community could or would not do.[87]

The evangelical doctrine of sanctification called on reborn Christians to purify themselves and perfect the world.[88] Chief among their obligations was to spread the gospel. "May we be faithful to those with whom we exert an influence," Mary declared, "in bringing them to accept of offered mercy. . . . May we be up and doing with our might whatever of duty our hands find to do knowing that in due time we shall reap if we faint not."[89] Mary's evangelical women were up and doing. In addition to their earlier associations, they now added a female reading society, a women's auxiliary to the American Tract Society, an Education Society, a group to support Sabbatarianism, and a Moral Reform Society.[90] In doing so they learned and practiced organizational skills and worldly behaviors that, had they not been working for God, they might not have dared to attempt. Mary noted four cases of young townswomen, including her own daughter, who made the commitment to serve as missionaries in Africa, among the American Indians, or on the western frontier. Their faith empowered them to live boldly.[91]

Evangelical life provided rural women with something else: female companions with whom they could form a supportive subset of community. Through their trials—the angst of conversion, worries for their children's salvation, responsibilities in religious associations—evangelical women formed close support networks. They met frequently in intimate groups for prayer and sharing. Mary reported meetings that were "solemn," "interesting," and deeply moving times of close fellowship, when "considerable feeling manifested," "each member made a statement of their own feelings," and "each one stating we trust the true state of feeling which each felt at this time."[92] Choosing to associate intimately and intensely with a small subset of community created unusually strong bonds; it also created social barriers. Shared faith trumped sharing across family and neighborhood, and the myriad new religious associations created new choices for belonging—and *not* belonging. "Our society" no longer referred to those within the borders of town, but only to those within the voluntary gatherings of church and association.

If the interactions of the evangelical sisterhood were intense, they were also extensive—evangelical women found a new family of spiritual kin spread across the nation and around the globe. Sister associations in other towns and parent associations in cosmopolitan centers of Boston, New York, London, and beyond exchanged visits, news, and letters of support.

Improved roads, regular stage schedules, canal boats, and the coming of the railroad made it easier to maintain these global connections. Imagine Mary's world expanding as she listened to graphic personal testimony from evangelicals recently returned from missions to Bombay, South Africa, or Korea or among African Bushmen or Hopi Indians. She expanded her connections closer to home, too, as she entertained agents from the national organizations of the Home Missionary Bible Society (Cincinnati), American Peace Society (New York), American Education Society (Boston), and American Sabbath School Union (nationwide). She traveled to Worcester and Boston to attend anniversary meetings of these associations; she exchanged correspondence with a missionary to the Choctaw; she prepared women to go among the Seneca and Tuscarora of western New York and the Cherokee of Indiana; she read newspapers and tracts from Boston, New York, and further afield. Mary now lived in an international commonwealth of those who shared her convictions, a commonwealth that excluded those of dissimilar beliefs. These wide-ranging associations provided a new model of civic organization. It was a model at odds with corporate community.

A House Divided

The revival that swelled the numbers of Mary's Congregational Church happened just as the Unitarian-Trinitarian controversy peaked. That the mild-mannered Reverend Russell was successfully filling pews and swelling Congregationalist membership numbers was not lost on disgruntled Unitarian-Universalists. The cantankerous John Howe focused the anger of religiously liberal townsfolk on the clergyman, but even as they won the battle in Worcester Courthouse they were steadily losing ground in the meetinghouse. The humiliation of the trial defeated Russell, who requested dismission and was gone within a year; in fact, some claim that the trial broke his health and led to his early death two years later.[93] But the Unitarians discovered that the new converts he had recruited did not fade away with him, and events were about to make those new members critical.

In 1833, Massachusetts officially separated church and state, ending mandatory financial support of religion. From now on, church support was to be purely voluntary. At the time of separation, Boylston Congregationalists held possession of the meetinghouse and church assets; they also had, as a result of the revival, a small plurality in numbers.[94] The division of church assets among those who had been former members escalated the hostility between the opposing religious camps.

In 1834, both congregations attempted to start anew. In February, the town's Unitarians received a charter of incorporation from the general court.[95] The Congregationalists, who had ordained a new and strictly orthodox minister to replace Russell, also had a "solemn renewal of our covenant" in the spring of 1834.[96] Rev. William Sanford, "an independent and fearless preacher, never hesitating to utter what he believed to be the truth," immediately set about reforming, disciplining, and strengthening his church.[97]

Upon his arrival Sanford found, by his own account, "a town torn in fragments by dissension . . . [with] warring elements, which were raging through the town."[98] With their slight plurality in numbers, the Congregationalists held onto the meetinghouse, but the Unitarians began to agitate in town meeting for their share of the church's assets. They hired legal counsel to sue for their rights to the pews, the bell, the stove, the communion service, the church furniture, even the stones in the foundation.[99] The prickly Captain Howe authored town meeting motions to dispossess the Congregationalists of joint church property.[100] Sanford realized that he would have no peace as long as his church kept possession of the building. He later confessed, "The church and the society felt deeply sensible of the evils connected with their house of worship. It was owned in part by persons who did not sympathize nor worship with them, who declined occupying their pews, and were thus deprived of the use of the property which they had vested in the house. The house itself was therefore a cause of division in the town, and tended to perpetuate the contentions which existed in this place."[101] The Congregationalists abandoned the property, though not their claim to it. They moved across the common, where they built a new meetinghouse furnished with new pews, new communion service, new Bible—with nothing to remind them of their previous affiliation.

Even so, the situation was not resolved. For six years the two parties engaged in suits and countersuits over ownership of the old meetinghouse. Strained feelings once again divided town meeting. In 1839, a motion was made that "a Committee of seven persons *from each of the different religious societies* be chosen" to select a Union Ticket of town officers, but the motion failed. Partisans then quarreled over whether the warrant for town meeting should be posted on the old meetinghouse, the new one, or on the door of Unitarian Eli Lamson's store.[102] Captain Howe sued for Unitarian ownership of the town common, attempting to make the very symbol of corporate belonging into private property. Finally, in the 1840s, the abandoned and dilapidated structure was disassembled, and its parts—pews, timbers, glass, even fieldstones in the foundation—were removed and sold to people in the community.[103] The proceeds were divvied among those who had originally owned pews in the earlier meetinghouse. "And thus," Sanford reported, "one fruitful source of controversy in the town was taken away."[104] By thus literally deconstructing this symbol of their earlier covenanted community, the townsfolk acknowledged the end of religious unanimity. The people could worship in harmony only when they abandoned worshipping as a community.

AND THAT IS HOW, on an April evening in 1841, William White came to witness wicked boys desecrating the old meetinghouse. It is an arresting image: the looming old clapboard structure, abandoned and soon to be dismantled, being gleefully attacked by youth who had no memory of the time when it stood for the monolithic power of a state church, a Standing Order, and corporate worship. In the course of the religious feud, enough stones had been hurled to fell the ideal of unity. In the name of conscience, Mary's townsfolk embraced pluralism. Shockwaves would ripple outward, ultimately affecting every aspect of life in town.

Many of the consequences of this struggle were unintended and ironic. The Unitarians under Cotton argued strenuously against divisions, yet ultimately found that peace could be found only in separation. The Congregationalists found that maintaining purity of doctrine and exclusive standards of membership in a newly competitive religious scene would require them to go out on the highways and byways to actively recruit sinners. In their work to promote conservative Christian values, the town's evangelical women moved unintentionally toward radically new models of womanhood. Youth, as well, found empowerment in Christian submission, for in attending only to the authority of God, they could defy all others.

Most powerfully, the very process of conversion—of surrendering utterly to God—transformed the individual psyche. It nurtured in the regenerate a powerful new inner focus and promoted self-motivated individualism. Religion became a private affair, a voluntary matter of conscience and personal choice. As converts turned to the work of evangelism, they found themselves repeatedly called upon to exercise self-reliance and act as independent moral agents. Religion proved a destabilizing force, rupturing traditional social order in the name of faith and conscience. But by fostering responsible personal control and individual accountability it also provided a psychic basis for a newly democratized social order.[105] The romantic, individualistic ethic fostered by revivalism transformed society, both feeding on and nurturing idealism, a belief in the possibility of transformation, and individual self-determination.

In 1852, a quarter century after the intense religious strife, Reverend Sanford commented on the extraordinary changes in town in the thirty years since his coming. The forests, he commented, had disappeared; there were new buildings, new roads. But most extraordinary was the change in the state of religion. When he came, there had been "bitter animosities" and "warring elements"; now, he asked, "where will you find a town in which there is, at this time, more good feeling among the inhabitants? There are now, as there were formerly, diverse views . . . yet there is no contention—I think no unkind and hostile party feelings. Each claims for himself, and is willing to grant to others, perfect toleration."[106] The religious wars had transformed the soul of the town.

CHAPTER THREE

Economic Choice and Consequences

On a promising April morning in 1839, with "the mercury nearly at summer heat," Aaron White and fifteen-year-old son Francis went on an excursion. The ground was warming—just three days earlier the frogs had peeped—and Aaron had been busy preparing his tillage fields for planting. Now he and young Francis headed to the shire town of Worcester to purchase a new-fangled farm tool, one that Squire Ward of neighboring Shrewsbury had been trying. It promised to transform springtime planting rituals. The trip was a success; father and son came home with a cultivator.

What a marvel! Introduced by local plow manufacturer Joel Nourse only two years earlier, this cultivator offered sets of cast-iron teeth in the shape of horses' hooves that stirred, pulverized, and aerated as they were drawn through the soil.[1] With a cultivator—one of many new cast-iron tools that were changing the nature of local farming—Aaron could expend less labor and achieve a better result. As enterprising Worcester County smithies turned out these new farming implements, farmers no longer had to constantly call upon their neighbors to get their ground turned or their crops in. Improved plows and cultivators, scythes and reapers produced better yields; they also produced disruptions in customary relations.[2]

Francis was likely excited by the new tool—the very next morning he and hired hand Abel were out putting it to the test. Abel Brigham was a local youth, the twenty-four-year-old son of a neighboring farmer, whom Aaron had hired as an extra hand for the season. Francis was delighted that his father had taken on Abel, and likely equally delighted by the new labor-saving cultivator, for both brought him a little closer to his own goal. He wanted to leave the land, to go away to the city. But Francis was disappointed; to his brother he confessed, "I have thought of coming to Boston with Mr. Rice [the marketer] a great many [sic] but I have not yet had a chance. . . . I have been expecting to go to Worcester this good while but in the summer and fall Father wanted me to work with Abel and I could not go."[3]

Aaron wanted to improve the cultivation of his acres. Francis wanted to cultivate something other than his father's land. He wanted to follow his brothers to school, to clerkships, to commerce, and to urban culture. He wanted to cultivate himself.

Francis was not alone in his desires. The local exodus of local sons who came of age after 1815 was common. Farmers' boys began to rethink their assumptions about livelihood, and some found that their dreams were no longer rooted in local land. In part this shift was inevitable as the maturing town ran out of room for new farms for offspring. But young men were also responding to changes in the broader world that created new opportunities and unleashed new desires and ambitions. They now wanted more than their daily bread, whether that be a "stuffed sophy," a starched white collar, or an enterprising mission to improve mankind. These varied ambitions combined to persuade many to consider new ways to go about improving their prospects. In changing their relationship to the land, Mary's sons and neighbors reshaped the physical and emotional landscape of their community.

Though the story of the transformation of rural Massachusetts has been told before, here we will consider how individual decisions and aspirations regarding livelihood altered community and personal relations.[4] The economic evolution of a town is at heart a story of changed relationships. Family labor, neighborly dependence, reliance on the land, deference to customary wisdom, a familiar and homogeneous local culture, shared commitment to an assumed common good: these essential relations of agrarian community had defined New England villages. Now these relations were being recast—often unintentionally—as some sought new paths to *improvement*. These changes were for the most part matters of individual choice, made by those pursuing what they believed to be rational, efficient, productive paths to a better life. For many, those choices led to market surpluses that they were able to apply toward education, more commodious and healthful homes, more comfortable and abundant clothing, and a better standard of living. For others, choices led to dependence and distress. New opportunities and challenges of the market flowed like a current into town, but Mary's children and neighbors rowed along (and sometimes against) that current, navigating their way toward their goals.

"Almost Exclusively an Agricultural Town"

To be sure, Boylston remained almost exclusively a farming town. While other Worcester County towns developed teeming mill villages or bustling commercial centers, most of Mary's townsmen continued to follow the plow. This was not by choice: Boylston's farming fate was the consequence of geography and history. The town had always been hilly and remote. The terrain might have supported mills had not the 1808 annexation of West Boylston robbed the mother town of its river, the main source of its waterpower. As a result, as Matthew Davenport recorded in 1831, "the local situation being such as to afford little encouragement for the mercantile or mechanical business . . . [t]his is almost exclusively an agricultural town."[5] There were no manufactures except for a brick-making site and a comb shop, and "there are at present but one saw-mill and two grist mills."[6] Of "mechanics," he noted, there were but a few wheelwrights, blacksmiths, and six or seven shoemakers, with small artisan shops that required little capital.[7] As late as the 1880s, Davenport's comments were echoed by townsmen who called it "essentially an agricultural town . . . offer[ing] but little opportunity for manufacturing or other industries."[8]

Even without waterpower, Boylston might have developed as a commercial and artisan center, as did other central Worcester County towns.[9] Neighboring Shrewsbury and Worcester became regional centers of trade and craft as farmers from outlying areas brought their goods to be marketed and artisans brought wares to be shipped along the post and canal routes. But in losing the river, the town also lost the convenient valley route for commercial traffic. Post roads, turnpikes, and railroads all bypassed little Boylston. To the end of his life, Aaron White lobbied unsuccessfully for a stage route to run through the village center.[10]

And so Boylstonians farmed. And they continued to produce primarily to provide for the family's own needs. Mary White's diary reveals just how diverse their farm produce remained throughout the first half of the century. Their cattle provided all of the family's milk, butter, and cheese, along with a yearly allotment of beef and veal. An annual litter of piglets yielded their pork, ham, sausages, and lard. In 1837, daughter Caroline reported to her brother "We have supported eleven old hens this winter and to their shame be it recorded, they have not laid an egg apiece since last Sept. though lately they have been cackling and scraiking great pretensions and fair promises but nothing more."[11] (We can assume the hens eventually provided either eggs—or flesh and feathers!) Mary always noted with relief when the grains were in the barn, the root vegetables in the cellar, and the vegetables from her kitchen garden put up for winter.[12] Her daughters often helped turn their orchard's fruit and berries into sauce and vinegar, preserves, and pies. The winter slaughter busied the women with salting meat and stuffing sausages, trying lard, making soap and candles sufficient for the coming year. Mary was thankful when the shed had been filled with split logs for winter fires. Throughout nearly a half century of profitable farming, Aaron and Mary continued to produce most of the family's food and fuel. Other local accounts reveal the same broad production of household needs.[13]

In some ways, then, continuity marked these decades. There were few without connection to the land, and so customary rhythms of agricultural life endured. A degree of neighborly interdependence also persisted. Through midcentury some of Mary's neighbors kept old-style daybooks of neighborly trades instead of double-entry accounts of business transactions, and they continued to trade primarily with longtime neighbors.[14] They continued their rituals of reckoning. The old system endured in part because it worked—it efficiently redistributed resources without resort to scarce cash. But it was also cultural, reflecting deeply held values of trust and reciprocity that persisted among some longtime farmers.

To say that Mary's town remained exclusively agricultural, that its farmers continued to produce primarily to meet family consumption, that neighborly values and mutual dependence persisted, is not to say that the town did not change. It did; all of these ideals were under increasing strain during the second quarter of the nineteenth century. The town's economic transition was gradual, the result of many small decisions—like buying a cultivator—to alter customary ways. Competency gave way only slowly to competition and a cash-based economy as farmers gradually entered the market, seeking ways to provide for their needs and pursue their desires.[15] Some of their choices led to prosperity, some to calamity; many led to change.

Crises, Opportunities, and Desires

By 1820, Boylston was full. The town could not support any more family farms on the old, sustainable, sixty-acre plan. Most children in this era grew up knowing they would have to go elsewhere. There was nothing unique about the town's plight. Young frontier communities had traditionally had high birth rates and, at first, abundant acres to absorb their offspring. But by the fourth generation, or one hundred years after settlement, most towns could support no more traditional family-sized sixty-acre farms.[16] This age-old problem had been gradually creeping from the coast to the hills of Worcester County and beyond, a geographically and temporally rolling demographic crisis. As farmers discovered, the crisis meant that their own farms had to produce more, for now they needed not just daily bread, but cash to purchase land elsewhere.

Even those favored sons who inherited the homestead were finding that they were less likely to receive their father's whole farm. During the critical years of the 1820s and 1830s, fathers and probate judges, aware that there was no equitable way to preserve the farm intact, increasingly divided estates between all offspring; any son who hoped to remain on the homestead had to buy back parcels from his siblings.[17] Many were forced to borrow or take mortgages to reassemble the subdivided farm. And so it happened that some of the town's land-rich farmers were, in actuality, heavily burdened with debt. The sale of an estate for debt—once unheard of—became more common.[18] To cover debts and raise cash for land purchases, more farmers consciously devised ways to reap more from their acres.

These farmers faced an old problem in a new time. Their internal demographic crisis coincided with the Transportation Revolution, that explosion in turnpike, canal, and railroad building that shattered Worcester County's isolation. The first era of road building began around the turn of the century, as market opportunities resulting from European wars (1793–1815) encouraged turnpike investors to improve the linkages between the hinterland and the coast. Private turnpikes battled with public post roads for the best routes, and both made dramatic inroads into the countryside. The number of stagecoaches leaving Boston more than doubled between 1825 and 1835.[19] None of these new roads came to Boylston Center, but one stopped at the town's northern border. Aaron carried his children by horse, chaise, or wagon to stage stops in neighboring villages to see them off on adventures to Boston, Providence, and points north.

The new roads made it easier for the townsfolk—and their farm goods—to go elsewhere. Sensing an opportunity, a local man, Mr. Woods, decided to become a marketer, making weekly trips to the city as a teamster middleman.[20] Now local farmers with surplus could ship even perishable goods such as butter, fruit, fresh vegetables, and just-slaughtered poultry to market.[21] And they did. A new weekly rhythm appeared in Mary's diary, as on Mondays and Tuesdays she churned, plucked, and packed produce for the

Wednesday market wagon. She did not *have* to adopt this new task; the family had survived comfortably without such marketing for a quarter century. But the Whites, like many of their neighbors, desired to "improve the opportunity" for the betterment of the family.

Such shipping, however, was still costly for large tonnage; in 1830, it was more expensive to send a ton of goods forty miles overland from Worcester to Boston than it was to ship the same amount overseas from Liverpool to Boston.[22] Then, in 1828, the opening of the Blackstone River Canal dramatically cut transportation costs, and the landlocked shire town of Worcester was proclaimed a seaport.[23] Rural county folk marveled at the manmade river and applauded the ease with which it brought imports to Worcester stores while carrying their surplus to the Atlantic. Two days after the canal opened, Mary's family went to Worcester, like tourists, to "take a sail," as Mary said, on the canal boat.[24]

The lure of city markets grew even stronger with the coming of the rails. Boston merchants were dismayed when the Erie Canal (opened 1825) diverted part of their interior trade through New York, and the canal siphoned their central Massachusetts trade south through Providence. So they built a railroad to connect the hinterlands directly to their hub. Opened in its entirety on Independence Day, 1835, the Boston & Worcester Railroad celebrated the liberty of mobility, zipping people and goods along at a staggering twenty miles per hour; freight rates dropped by two-thirds.[25] An excited Mary White reported the first time that "Francis drove Mr. White and myself to Westborough to take the railroad cars for Boston." When she returned, a week later, she noted, "We took our seats in the cars at a quarter past seven o'clock and arrived in Westborough at a quarter past nine o'clock in safety."[26]

The development of these new routes transformed the Worcester County countryside. Now that there was an affordable way for farming families to get their goods to market, the drive to improve their farms' productivity was strong. After all, that market cash could purchase acres for their sons' farms or their daughters' household furnishings. But more than goods went to market. As cities were linked to countryside, farm boys discovered a new world. New opportunities beckoned as clerks for mercantile and financial institutions. Along a central corridor of Worcester County, good roads and good waterpower created artisan and mechanic opportunities in smaller shops making boots and shoes, combs and wire, chairs and pianos, paper and textiles. To the south, in towns along the Blackstone River, the Industrial Revolution got on capitally, luring youth to work as machinists, textile operatives, and factory employees. These densely populated mill villages demanded goods and services, creating additional opportunities in retail, artisan work, and marketing farm products.

Opportunities were not limited to Worcester County. Before settling down, all of Aaron and Mary's sons traveled widely. They took stages as far as Montreal, sailed far up the Hudson River, explored western New York State on the Erie Canal, stopping in bustling Rochester and Syracuse. They took the rails to New Haven and steam packets to New York and Philadelphia, explored as far as Louisville, Kentucky, and Charleston, South Carolina, ventured up the Mississippi on paddle wheelers, and even sailed to the West Indies.

There were choices, then, for those confronting the demographic crisis. The expanded range of occupations was so dizzying for sons coming of age in the 1830s that one author was able to profit from a guidebook, *The Panorama of Professions and Trades; or Every Man's Book*, which was marketed to those who wanted to make an informed choice as to career.[27] Farming was no longer Everyman's goal. There appeared to be better ways to improve one's lot.

HAZEN'S *PANORAMA* suggested a shift in attitude regarding the venerable old livelihood of husbandry. Laboring on the land, dirtying one's hands in the earth, was no longer the most respectable means of securing a competence. For generations, wresting the family's needs from the land had defined manhood. Now young men wanted more.

Agricultural reformers and ministers might protest, lecturing about the virtue of working one's own land. They decried young loafers who pursued genteel clerkships and counter positions, affected polite airs and effete fashions, did no *real work*, and yet disdained laboring on the land. Such a lifestyle, they warned, would ultimately enervate the clerk and tie him to subservient dependence upon his employers and his mostly female customers. The only way to safeguard one's dignity and masculinity, as well as the virtue of an independent citizenry, was to return to the plow, to hard work and simple frugality. "'Stick to the farm, young men,' warned the *Cultivator* in 1854. 'You are tempted to exchange the hard work of the farm, to become a clerk in a city shop, to put off your heavy boots and frock, and be a gentleman, behind the counter!' Such a decision would be paramount to selling one's manhood for a wage, to 'learning to fetch and carry like a spaniel.'"[28] But most youth did not see it that way: in popular culture the once-esteemed yeoman was increasingly depicted as a rude country bumpkin.[29]

Many Massachusetts farm boys were becoming "impatient of hard work out of doors," as Horace Bushnell later recalled.[30] Farming *was* hard work, and those who had taken time off to do genteel desk labor were reminded of this when they returned to a stint in the fields. One young shopkeeper in the Worcester County town of Grafton wrote to his betrothed after a week spent in the field. "Last Tuesday I worked at haying all day. It was almost too much, but I made out to get through and should have [quit] in the middle of the day but did not like the [thought] of giving up, but I am done haying for this Season. . . . I have done more work for a week past at farming than I have for seven years [as a clerk's apprentice in a shop]."[31] The White sons also found it difficult to return to the fields after years of office work. Francis was still working for his father in the summer of 1840 when older brother Thomas took a break from his law practice to help with the hay harvest. "This is a busy season with us," Francis wrote to Charles. "Hay time is a hot hard labor, my busy time. . . . But Thomas helped us when he was at home and he said he would not work so hard as we had to for a fortnight for as much Salary as Van Buren has."[32] Many sons decided they could do without such hot, hard labor.

Daughters agreed. The heavy demands of women's farm labor, especially in the laundry and the dairy, could and often did break a woman's health.[33] By midcentury, reformers were acknowledging that "these burdens . . . bear so heavily upon the wives of our farmers as to constitute a great objection to the choice of agriculture as a business."[34] The *New England Farmer* lamented that most farmers' daughters would prefer "almost any settlement in town or city, to the domestic cares of the farm-house and dairy."[35] As farm wives of means absorbed new middle-class notions of female gentility, they were increasingly unwilling to take on the endless physical toil of turning harvest into food and clothing.[36]

More children might have been willing to stay had they felt that local farming offered great opportunities for *getting ahead*, but most did not believe that it did. Mary's contemporaries noted that the young people left, not just because land was in short supply, but also because they could not "advance their interest," as they said, in town.[37] The Reverend Henry Colman, a Unitarian minister and agricultural writer, lectured farmers at the 1821 Brighton Cattle Show to forsake such dreams of riches: "That farmer is prosperous who is able . . . to provide for the ordinary wants of himself and his family; to give his children a suitable education and establishment; to keep himself free from the curse of debt and mortgage; to maintain the character and assert the rights of the independent freeholder . . . to contribute something every year to the improvement of his estate, and . . . to provide against a season when . . . old age may render it necessary to repose from his labours and cares. This is all the prosperity which a reasonable farmer ought to expect or wish."[38]

But the youth *did* wish for more. Their expectations had been rising with the tide of goods and fashions flowing into Worcester County on the new roads, canals, and rails.[39] Some left to pursue these riches, but even those who stayed increasingly turned their attention to store-bought finery. By the early 1830s, Aaron White's village store had been joined by two others, all offering "the usual supplies of domestic, English, and West Indies goods," from cottons to crockery, as well as an assortment of enticing luxuries and amusements.[40]

What could not be had in the center village could be purchased on shopping trips to the closest metropolis. Squire White, as a leading citizen with contacts in Boston, Providence, and Worcester, set new standards of living. The family no longer lived in the old tavern at the foot of the common; in 1820, a prosperous Aaron White had purchased the Abbot place at the crest of the hill and completely remodeled the dwelling, creating a fine Federal facade with pleasant symmetry and elegant fan windows. Mary and Aaron redesigned the interior with a fashionable front-to-back center hall and an elegant curving stairway, flanked by east and west parlors. The old tavern had demonstrated production; the new mansion exhibited consumption. Where once Mary had put out flax to neighbors to spin and weave, she now purchased linen cloth. She still spun the woolen thread for knitting stockings, mittens, and caps, but she purchased her yard goods—some likely from local mills, and other finer pieces as imports—from Worcester stores.[41] Purchasing their cloth gave Mary and her daughters free hours, which, as we will see, allowed them to pursue personal and material refinement. Mary was also assisted in her household chores by a new cook stove, set kettle, and washing machine. Several rooms in the house were improved with heating stoves. In two short decades Mary recorded papering walls, putting up curtains and blinds, and putting down carpets and rugs. The family furnished their home with stylish upholstered furniture, mirrors, painted portraits, clocks, writing desks.[42] They asked Charles to send home from the city scented toilet waters, fine writing paper, visiting cards, silk for handkerchiefs, candied citron, hair oils, shaving soap, and other luxuries that could not be had in the hinterlands. To prepare for her marriage, daughter Eliza made shopping trips to Boston to secure fine furniture and to Worcester for fine fabrics.

The Whites and other aspiring townsfolk purchased goods because they wanted to improve their lives. In some cases, their purchases seemed to make economic sense, as inexpensive goods from a distance made it more efficient to purchase certain staples—wheat or factory cloth—than to produce them at home. In other cases, it was not thrift but pursuit of comfort, gentility, and leisure that drove their acquisitions. Newly available store-bought goods turned a hardscrabble life into a country living with more varied foods, lighter, more stylish, and more easily cleaned wardrobes, more comfortable furnishings, cleaner and better-lit homes, and labor-saving utensils. After 1820, household production in rural Massachusetts began to decline, as farmers and their wives learned to be consumers, turning to distant sources "to obtain what they ate, drank, wore, heated with, cooked on, slept in, inhabited, and generally used."[43] Their lives improved. But to buy these things, they needed cash.

For farmers in the 1820s and 1830s, then, it was becoming clear that family competence would require more than their daily bread. As old needs met new opportunities and desires, farm families experimented with new channels to what they believed was advancement. They rode the currents of the Market Revolution, but they rowed as well. Their decisions reshaped the social and physical landscape of the town in ways they intended, and in ways they had not intended at all.

YOUNG PEOPLE were leaving home, the most common response to the pressures of need and desire. Fully three-quarters of Boylston sons who were born between 1786 and 1825 and who survived to maturity left town.[44] The mass exodus deeply impressed contemporary observers, who spoke ruefully of offspring "abandoning the homes of their fathers," and of "the desertion of her sons and daughters . . . for more attractive pursuits elsewhere."[45]

Most did not head off to hew an independent homestead from a rugged western frontier. The majority, in fact, apparently believed they could find their heart's desire not far from their own backyards. Well over half of local sons who left home went no further than another Worcester County town. Among those who ventured farther afield, a few sought the city lights of Boston, Providence, or Worcester, while another small contingent headed to rural land in western Massachusetts or northern New England.[46] Only a handful—generally the poorest—ventured as far as the mid-Atlantic, South, or West. This was a geographically limited diaspora.

Those who hoped for professional careers as lawyers, doctors, ministers, engineers, and merchants—a small fraction of the total—were predominantly the sons of gentry, though some carved out new professions on the basis of aptitude rather than assets.[47] Usually, the demands of their professions took them to metropolitan centers. Those who left home to pursue farming—about a third of the total—were also, on average, the sons of *wealthy* townsmen, and the great majority of them purchased well-developed farms in other *local* towns.[48]

But the majority of sons who left home did not or could not pursue such options. Instead, they mostly found jobs in Worcester County factories, artisan shops, or the trades.[49] The poorest overwhelmingly left for other Worcester County towns, likely selling their labor and hoping for better. Middling and poorer sons chose local manufacturing and artisan work *in lieu of* western migration to undeveloped frontier land. In short, most sons chose to leave home *and* to leave the land, abandoning their father's yeoman identity.

The exodus of the town's youth, whether as families or young singles, was wrenching to those longstanding relationships of kin and neighbor that provided support and fellowship in their small agrarian world. It also brought family heartache and a sense of rejection. Aaron White's letters to his sons poignantly reveal his inner struggle. Charles White loved fresh fruit, and his father knew it. When the sixteen-year-old moved to Boston in 1836 to serve an apprenticeship in an apothecary shop, he left behind the family orchard of apples, peaches, pears, and cherries, vines of grapes, patches of strawberries and wild berries galore. In the city he craved the sweet goodness that had been so abundant on the old home place, and his account book included nearly daily outlays for an apple from the market carts. In his letters home he confessed "wanting fruit so much that it seemed as though [he] could eat apples core and all."[50]

His father complied, each week sending to Boston with the marketman a bucket packed with washed or mended clothes, a few baked goods, letters from home, and, almost always, apples. Aaron was glad to be able to satisfy his son's sweet tooth, but he had another motive as well. "I wanted to send you something to remind you of home."[51] He confessed that the fruit brought to mind his absent son, and he hoped that it would also make his son think of the folks on the farm. He commented frequently on luxurious yields of cherries or grapes, and promised that if "Charley" would come home he might have as much as he wished. "I have almost expected you this week, although we had not much reason to. The fact is, Charley, we have had a great supply this year of cherries and other fruit and we have thought and spoke much of you. . . . [W]e will try to keep the boys and the birds from the trees until Saturday next in the hope that you will get this in season to take the Boylston stage that day and come home. . . . So many things come to mind that I wish to say that I can say nothing as I wish and will add no more."[52] Two years later, Aaron was still using fruit to entice his son: "We have had a fine supply of cherries. I should have liked to have had your company to eat them with us."[53] "I shall try to send you this week a few apples which . . . will please you as the box contains some of your favorites." "Shall send you some of your favorite 'Peck's Pleasants' next week." "We shall always try to send you some [apples], such as we have. I rather think that any kind of fruit will taste better in Boston than it did here."[54] Charles was not lured back home. The farm was not his Eden. His father had given him the freedom to choose his life's work, and Charles had traded the farm for the counter.

Charles was not the first of White's sons to leave the farm for the city; he was the sixth. Aaron had spent years turning the capital raised from his country store and surplus from his farm into acres to settle his boys around him. In 1820, as his firstborn turned twenty-one, Aaron purchased a second farm in town, making one available for Aaron Jr. But the firstborn chose a law career and settled in Rhode Island. Aaron Sr. continued to gather up local parcels throughout the 1820s, but each son on reaching his teens chose a city profession or business. Avery apprenticed to a Boston-based West Indies merchant; Thomas followed his older brother into law with a practice in New York City; Davis opened a Dorchester tannery to provide leather for the burgeoning shoe industry; William went west as a missionary to the Indians. When Charles left home, a now-aging Aaron began to sell land that he no longer had the labor to farm. His hopes rested on young Francis. When the boy returned from visiting Charles in the city, aglow with excitement and yearning to join his brother, Aaron confessed, "I dread the thought of parting from him."[55] Aaron detained his "Frank" at home several more years, but in 1841, he let the seventeen-year-old join his brother in the Dorchester tanning business. Mother Mary wrote, "Your Father feels rather sober at the thought of parting with Francis but hopes it will be for the best. . . . But if his children must leave him, he wants to have them visit him as often as they can. He says why don't Avery come & see me, he has been a pretty good boy about coming home."[56] When Charles set up his Worcester druggist shop, his father sent him a gift: a barrel of apples.

Aaron's heartache was keen. His sons had rejected his land, his farming identity, and the companionship of his mature years. He was not alone. The decisions of youth to leave farming reduced once-authoritative patriarchs in charge of providing livelihoods to mere fathers, like Aaron, feeling heartsore and diminished.

Profiting from Higher Yields: Aaron White's Strategy

Who, then, was *staying*? During the turbulent period from 1826 to 1835, almost *all* local sons who remained did so to farm.[57] Some were men of merely moderate means, struggling to hold onto the family plot and meet their family's bare subsistence needs. But most men who remained in town were farmers of above-average means who owned or expected to own their farms.[58] Wealth was the strongest predictor of who would stay. Age was another strong predictor: if a man reached age forty and was still in town, he was likely to stay put. And those born in town were more likely to stay in town.[59] Wealth, local birth, and advanced age all provided the roots and personal investment in community that held men, forming a stable base against the parade of departing youth. It also meant that an older, wealthier, established core increasingly distinguished—and distanced—itself from poorer neighbors and laborers.[60] The town's established farmers were those more likely to pioneer new practices—new technology, rationalized methods, and marketing—that would further increase their yields and profits.

As one of these improvers, Aaron White turned his attention toward making his land produce more. He did so with the blessings of his age. Once his townsmen might have looked on such striving for gain with censure; now many were coming to believe that individual talent and genius, applied to private betterment, were essential to national progress.[61] The sum of each man's personal striving was civic prosperity, national strength, or even the hoped-for perfecting of society that would bring about the Second Coming. Self-striving, rationalized as liberal public spirit, was the mark of respectable, productive, middle-class manhood. Striving was assisted by science: improving men turned their minds to rationalizing and maximizing their resources.[62] In the White family, *improvement* was a favorite word: one must strive to realize potential, whether that be commercial, civic, or spiritual. Aaron's ambitions focused on finding new methods of farming and marketing surplus to increase his profits and better his family's life.

It would be wrong to say that in the 1820s Aaron White and his likeminded neighbors "entered" the market. Local folk, as we have seen, had always marketed their surplus, whether by swapping with neighbors, exchanging farm goods for credit at the village store, or carrying an annual load of grain to Boston. This essential exchange was, no matter how neigh-borly, in some respects commercial.[63] Historians have debated whether this trading was oriented toward family maintenance or profit seeking.[64] Aaron White would likely not have understood the distinction. He farmed primar-ily to meet his family's needs, but he also sought profits to better his family's standard of living and to provide for his children's security. Getting the most that he could from his acres was part of his obligation to *improve* his farm; it increasingly became part of his strategy to meet a rising refrain of need— and a chorus of wants.

White enthusiastically threw his lot in with those new "book farmers" (as they were derisively called by traditionalists) who experimented with novel ways to increase productivity. He was typical of improving farmers: wealth-ier, more widely read, with more contacts in cosmopolitan communities, they put their faith in science and education and eagerly adopted the sugges-tions of agricultural societies and the farm press.[65] Critically, they changed the way they thought about farm work. It was no longer merely the business of daily life; it was business. They rationalized old customs, applying sci-ence to improve methods of planting, fertilizing, crop selection, breeding livestock, organizing labor, and marketing produce.[66] They attended to their soil. They adopted new labor-saving machinery. They counted, measured, experimented, and specialized, seeking to discern and manipulate the un-derlying laws of agriculture.[67]

Not all local farmers shared White's enthusiasm for agricultural reform. One contemporary treated innovators dismissively, noting that local farm-ers for the most part "are not so much attached to agricultural societies and *book* farming as some others."[68] Practical farmers' prejudice against new methods perhaps reflected their angst at having been stripped of their status as bearers of essential folk knowledge. It may also have reflected a growing distrust of wealthy, calculating farmers whose commercial interests seemed to have little to do with the practical concerns of supplying the family larder.[69]

If Aaron White heard the sneers of some of his neighbors, he was not dissuaded. He and his family attended the Brighton and Worcester Cattle Shows each year for the latest news of advancements. He experimented with cattle breeding and was likely tickled when the *American Farmer* gave spe-cial mention to the "fine ox, grass fed, half Denton, exhibited by Mr. White of Boylston," which "showed the disposition to early maturity of native stock when it is crossed with a short-horned breed of Great Britain" at the Brigh-ton Cattle Show of 1826.[70] He rotated his tilled crops with clover hay, and used lime to increase the alkalinity of his soil.[71] He manured and mucked,

mucked and manured, season after season to improve his soil. Like other Massachusetts farmers by the 1820s, White planted potatoes, whose tolerance for acidic soils made them better yielders than most grains.[72] He experimented with hot beds to give his vegetables and strawberries an early start.[73] And he enthusiastically embraced new farm machinery. The *New England Farmer* began advertising "patent hoes and hay cutters, cast and wrought iron ploughs" by the late 1820s, and farm machinery improved dramatically in the second quarter of the nineteenth century.[74] By the 1830s, Worcester County farmers of means and mind could avail themselves of early harvesting machines, steel hayforks, horse-drawn hay rakes, and much-improved cast-iron plows, along with the cultivator that so pleased young Francis. For those like Aaron White who could afford them, these new-fangled tools promised improved productivity.[75]

White's experiments paid off. With improved soils, efficient methods, and labor-saving tools, productivity surged. From the mid-1820s on, White was consistently able to trade surpluses of poultry, butter, corn, oats, potatoes, fruit, and cider vinegar, along with several pigs, and a cow and a calf each.[76] Much of this was an extension of his earlier neighborly exchanges; in fact, many of his trades continued to be made within the community, or, in the case of fatted cows and oxen, with men in neighboring towns. By 1828, however, it is clear that White was also making regular use of the marketer, sending small quantities of surplus butter, fruit, and freshly killed pork or fowl to the Boston market on a weekly basis.[77] The timing here is critical, for in 1825 the Erie Canal flooded New England with inexpensive grain from the west. This exogenous factor allowed progressive Worcester County farmers to turn more of their tillage land to growing crops in which they had a saleable advantage. White, for example, dispatched larger quantities of oats, corn, and hay at harvest to Worcester County marketers supplying new commercial and manufacturing villages. By the 1830s, White was sending barrels of apples and cider vinegar directly to Worcester retailers.[78]

As the years passed, Aaron White's rising productivity made him a rich man, one of the wealthiest in town. He invested in banks and corporations, improved his family's standard of living, educated his children—and purchased more land to provide estates for his sons. Between 1820 and 1830, he more than doubled his holdings, buying up his neighbor's parcels as they became available. By 1835 he owned two complete farms, one of which he let out, along with the "Eager place" and the "Fuller place," upland parcels from which he harvested marketable English (planted) hay, grains, and fruit.[79]

Most farmers could not afford to augment their acres so aggressively, and the growth of some farms came at the diminution of others. White was able to accumulate land because some of his neighbors—the Eagers, the Fullers, the Houghtons—chose or were forced to sell. Decisions to buy up land produced a growing disparity in the distribution of landed wealth, straining the ideal of common interests.[80]

White's farming and marketing methods represent not a radical break with custom but a gradual intensification of it. He traded surplus, but more of it. He traded locally, but also via marketer and directly to retailers, all while continuing to farm primarily for his family's consumption. And he was not alone. Between 1800 and 1850, the town's farmers increased the number of acres devoted to tillage (saleable grains and potatoes) by a sixth and improved their tillage output by more than a quarter. More telling, their crop choices reflect changing market demands, as their production of humble rye fell by two-thirds, while their output of high-demand oats nearly tripled.[81] Men like Aaron White found ways to harvest much-needed cash from their land. And their rising farm productivity—better yields with less labor—not only improved their own standard of living; it also freed manpower and energies to fuel growth in other fields.

Yet trading at a distance was a profoundly different relationship from trading with neighbors. Aaron had been accustomed to knowing the people who consumed his farm goods, imbuing his produce with a value beyond its marketable price. Farming was *good* work because it produced life-sustaining *goods* for family and community. When he sold his crops at a distance, Aaron lost his personal connection with those who would use his produce.[82] The work of his household shifted from community sustenance to commodity production. With the intimate tie between growing and consuming broken, Aaron's relationship to his land subtly transformed. With the bond broken, the way lay open for expansion, and for exploitation.

Yielding to Higher Profits: Joseph Flagg's Strategy

Joseph Flagg was only eighteen years younger than Aaron White, but he farmed like a man of the future. Flagg was from an old Boylston family, a clan of "thrifty, enterprising" men, as one townsman later remarked. When still a young man, he inherited the lion's share of his father's large farm, along with heavy debts to his siblings.[83] Fortunately, he also inherited his father's enterprising nature, and he soon succeeded both in settling his obligations and enlarging his estate. His innovative methods of harvesting these profits, however, remade the ecological and social nature of his neighborhood.

From his farm account book (1827–46), we can glean the strategies Flagg followed to reap the most from his land. In many ways, the book shows a continuation of customary practices of family farming and neighborly trading. Entries cover the entire range of farm products—from grains, dairy, meat, and vegetables to hay, wood, and cider. His family likely consumed their share before the rest entered his account book, and the great majority of trades were local.[84] His exchanges peaked in the months of plowing, when he traded the labor of his draft animals—and his sons—for substantial credits.[85] He continued the ancient customs of keeping running accounts, with each debtor having his own page, and of allowing long-term credit, with many debtors taking years to settle their accounts.[86]

But in other ways, Flagg was enterprising indeed. He seems to have purposely planned a significant surplus in at least one crop each year, usually alternating oats, corn, and hay. He stripped his woodlots and sold off the timber. He filled his pastures with other men's cattle, charging for the service of fatting them for market, as he did for Aaron White in the summer of 1837.[87] He exploited his tillage, meadow, pasture, and woodlot in ways that maximized his cash return.[88] Flagg's book also reveals that he sought out new markets, selling directly to Worcester and Shrewsbury shopkeepers and taverners, or making market trips to burgeoning mill towns.[89] He sometimes sold whole fields of hay ("piece of grass") or lots of timber ("in the woods") directly to buyers who were responsible for harvesting; he charged an additional amount for delivering these goods to the purchaser. And he worked with marketing firms that emerged in Worcester County during the 1830s and 1840s. Firms such as Bartlett and Warren, with whom Flagg worked, simplified the process of selling farm products by combining several steps that farmers had previously arranged for separately. Bartlett and Warren bought cattle directly from Flagg, then butchered, dressed, packed, and delivered beef to market. Though they took a percentage of profit, they paid Flagg in cash, directly upon delivery of his cattle, rather than after its sale in the market. They also unraveled longtime local relationships. Marketing firms may have been efficient, but they essentially outsourced the tasks once performed by Flagg's neighborhood butcher, cooper, and marketman, freeing him from neighborly bonds.[90]

Flagg became savvy in his knowledge of markets near and far. Like most Worcester County farmers, he knew the cost of labor and varied his charge for a day's work depending upon the season, the task, and the age or skill of the man—or boy—whose labor he was providing. Like other improving farmers, he knew the going price in city markets for his commodities and adjusted his charges accordingly.[91] Flagg's price fluctuations for oats, corn, and hay also reveal his new dependence on market vicissitudes.[92] A farmer producing mostly for family needs who sold only a small surplus on the market for incidental cash would be little affected by market surges or crashes. Flagg, however, who was increasingly reliant on larger sales of a few commodities, felt his fortunes rise with the speculative fever of the early 1830s— and crash with the national economic contraction following the panic of 1837.

Joseph Flagg was surely market savvy. One entry records his personal innovation in turning resources to cash: a rent-to-own agreement for a cow! But the decisions he made to maximize short-term profits had long-term consequences for both community and ecology. His pursuit of happiness was a matter of private, not communal, well-being; ironically, he fashioned his enlarged market-oriented barn from the disassembled timbers of the old town meetinghouse.[93] More concretely, Flagg was no longer practicing sustainable farming.

Flagg discovered he could increase his immediate profits if he clear-cut his woodlots, selling the wood as timber and fuel. He could plant the newly cleared land to upland hay or grain, which would also yield saleable surpluses of corn, oats, and hay for a short while. However, without sufficient fertilizing, these fields would soon run down. For Flagg himself, this was not an issue, for ultimately he would turn the land to pasture, realizing yet more profits by fatting other men's cattle and raising some of his own to sell for beef. His arrangement with Bartlett and Warren, the beef-marketing firm, is particularly telling, for Flagg was not their debtor, but their creditor; *he* was pasturing *their* many cattle (and some sheep), stock that they had purchased from area farmers and were holding and fattening for sale during the late autumn slaughter. It did not concern Flagg that he would not have hay to feed these creatures over the winter, for they would not be wintered with him but would be returned to their owners and likely slaughtered. His land-use strategy was what one western Massachusetts contemporary called "skinning the land": "cutting off wood and timber, selling hay, and sometimes what little grain they raise, . . . 'running' [exhausting] their mowing lands and then turning them into pasturage. In short, taking all they can from the land and returning nothing."[94] Flagg's mad rush for short-term profits was not sustainable.

Gross export of nutrients in the form of timber, grain, hay, and beef brought Flagg cash, but at the cost of destroying the delicate ecological balance that had kept family farms producing a comfortable subsistence throughout the colonial era. He no longer maintained the customary ratios of tillage, pasture, fresh meadow, and woodlot needed to balance the input and outflow of nutrients. And Flagg was far from the only offender. The transformation was visible in the rapid deforestation of the countryside. In one Worcester County town, a resident estimated that land was three-quarters cleared in 1830, and nearly completely deforested by 1850.[95] Equally alarming was the degradation of pastureland. Overgrazed and underfertil-ized, pastures produced less and less edible fodder, eventually deteriorating to prickly brush, stubby with inedible juniper and cedar. In 1800, three acres of Boylston pasture would support a cow; by 1850, it took five acres.[96] Farm-ers like Flagg shifted their priorities from family sustenance and preserva-tion of the homestead to earning cash as a way to purchase their families' needs and desires. The land suffered. In 1846, Joseph Flagg sold his ances-tral farm and moved his family to fresh fields in neighboring Berlin.[97]

The coming of the railroad in 1835 assisted in the final stage of the local transition to commercial agriculture. With cheap and rapid transport, farm-ers could send perishable products to cities and mill villages. Equally impor-tant, farmers of means could purchase cheap wheat arriving by rail from the west for their own consumption, which let them plant their own tillage land to animal feed. This removed the limitation on stock keeping that had tradi-tionally come from dependence on hay as a winter feed; in addition, feeding cows corn instead of hay made them more productive milkers.[98]

Larger farmers, then, could begin to specialize in dairying. The shift was gradual, but by midcentury it is clear that a subset of local farmers was pur-posely producing surplus butter to export. The shift likely depended not just on how many cows a farmer could keep, but how many *churners*; it was his wife, daughters, and hired female help who would turn milk into money. This was not the White family's principal economic activity. Mary churned or "had butter churned" when her daughters were home from school or vis-iting, a niece came to live with the family, or when an "excellent help" (as Caroline called it) lived in. Mary might send forty pounds of butter to mar-ket one week, then none for the next few, as other needs interfered. Cumu-latively, though, by 1850 larger local farmers were producing significantly more butter for sale. Fully one-third produced 500 pounds or more per year, far in excess of family consumption.[99]

The town's more affluent farmers were also producing significant market-able surpluses of corn, oats, potatoes, and pork.[100] Like the Whites' surplus, these goods took various paths to market. If we followed these crops from the field, we would find some swapped with a neighbor, some riding to town on Baxter Wood's market cart, some carted by Joseph Flagg's sons to nearby mill villages, some sold directly to a Worcester shopkeeper. Whatever path they took, surplus farm goods paved the way to improvement.

The important qualifier was that market participation was mainly limited to *those who owned large farms*. By 1850, fewer than half the town's taxpayers owned a farm, and some of those who did manage to hold onto some land were marginal men. They farmed to survive, producing some of what they needed and trading their labor to wealthier neighbors for the rest. It is to those who sold their labor that we turn now.

"Hands" and "Helps": Working for Wages

Family had always been the primary source of farm labor in New England; one historian has called sons the northern farmer's unfree labor.[101] Certainly young Francis White felt shackled. But when a farmer could spare the labor, or when he wanted his son to accumulate cash for land, he could "give the son his time," and the young man might spend several years working out on wages for a neighbor.[102] There was no stigma attached to laboring for another man while young. It was a transitory dependency, a facet of coming of age. The ambitious sons of wealthy farmer Joseph Flagg "worked out," just as Flagg had hired the sons of other prosperous farm neighbors when his own boys were too young to work. The able-bodied son of a poor farmer was equally acceptable as contract labor. Aaron White hired sons of both poor and wealthy neighbors, usually paying them wages but sometimes crediting goods to their fathers' store accounts.

In earlier decades, as we have seen, these youthful local helps lived in and became one of the family, working alongside their employer and his sons in the field, eating at his table, sharing family beds. Their familiarity made it easy for sons of neighbors and peers to be temporarily absorbed into family. When the hired help's parents lived within the community, they provided a check on youthful exuberance and a chance for regular visits home. Working out had been a natural transitional state for youth and a familiar, tractable form of labor for farmers.[103]

Around 1830, however, the labor situation noticeably changed. The exodus of local sons left a void, and farmers struggled to find the native help they wanted. Squire White hired a succession of sons of local men through the mid-1830s, but by 1837 he was forced to scour the greater countryside for help. In mid-March, as the start of the farming season approached, Caroline confessed to her brother Charles, "He knows not what to do. . . . [H]e can hire no one for any sum."[104] Finally, just as the farm season began, White's son-in-law found a twenty-four-year-old stranger from a far-western Worcester County town. Lucius Barnes signed on for nine months, and when he left at the end of his term Aaron White was once again scrambling. He was delighted to keep Joseph Flagg's son Lincoln for two years and dismayed when Lincoln's eventual departure left him once again resorting to unfamiliar men from far away. Unable to find familiar local youth willing to work for wages, White and his neighbors were increasingly forced to turn to a new class of transients. Their dependency was neither transitory nor transitional: this was an emerging class of permanently poor, landless laborers.

The changes in White's and Flagg's hired labor represent a dramatic demographic transformation occurring during the conflicted era of the 1820s and 1830s. Three-quarters of sons were leaving town, and they were being replaced by men who were increasingly younger, increasingly poorer, and increasingly from beyond the borders of Worcester County.[105] In 1820, the majority of those who moved into Boylston were from a Worcester County town, and the rest from some other Massachusetts town. By 1850, only a handful came from a local town, while the greatest share came from a distance, often outside Massachusetts, even outside of the United States. French Canadian, English, and Irish immigrants added their accents to Yankee tones.[106]

These alien transients became a significant fraction of the local population by the 1830s, and their presence changed personal relationships. Most newcomers did not—could not—set down roots. Most stayed in town fewer than five years. They came looking for wages, hoping to accumulate enough to move on to a better position elsewhere. Their here-today-gone-tomorrow rootlessness must have been disturbing to a community accustomed to knowing their neighbors from the cradle, whose trust was based on familiarity, whose local trade and neighborly norms assumed that people would stay put. Transience upended all those assumptions.

It is hard to imagine how a close, familiar, kin-based people adapted to incorporating these strangers into their homes. They were culturally unfamiliar, to be sure. Mary fretted about the rise of Catholicism as Irish Catholics began to appear in town as hired helps and domestics in 1835.[107] Within a year, she was praying for protection from Romanism, fearing "the Roman Catholics, that their influence may not destroy our liberties and bring down upon us the judgments of heaven."[108] Worried about what she viewed as a frightening increase in the incidence of crime, she reported each robbery and assault in neighboring towns. In 1837, a stranger attempted to break into the White family house at night, scaling a ladder to a second-story window. (His attempt was foiled by Caroline, who, writing a letter by candlelight, saw the intruder and sounded an alarm.) Mary reported the incident in detail and prayed, "May the Lord protect us in our state."[109] She also reported that Aaron's horse was stolen, her brother-in-law's barn was destroyed by arson, and a robbery took place at midday in nearby Hubbardston and "the robber escaped, the man robbed injured but not mortally." The perils of engaging with strangers was brought home when a visiting preacher, feted when he took the pulpit on an April Sunday in 1830, was exposed two weeks later as a prison escapee.[110]

Nonnative hired helpers were deemed less reliable and less productive.[111] They had no parents or extended kin nearby to enforce parental authority, no local roots to bind them. It was not uncommon for dissatisfied foreign help simply to leave, abandoning their contracts for better situations elsewhere. Caroline White wrote apologetically to her brother Charles that their cousin would not be able to make a promised visit to Boston in the late 1830s "because his father's hired men have taken French leave in the night."[112] Mr. Ward of neighboring Shrewsbury regretted the loss of his good native hired hand to the West, and complained of the poor work habits of immigrant workers after 1840. "As he is Irish, I must take Irish pay [that is, nothing] for the balance."[113] Tension rose between farmers and their help when differing work traditions and expectations collided. Increasingly, the poorest in town were also the most alien, straining local ability—and inclination—to care for the needy. Locals suspected that these newcomers were a strange, unworthy, and untrustworthy lot.

And yet if farmers were to have help at all, they had to hire—and board—these culturally alien newcomers; by 1850, both Mary White and Joseph Flagg's heir had Irish domestics in their kitchen, Irish hands in their barns. Their high turnover rate meant that these foreigners were moving in and out of local homes on a regular basis. Mary and her neighbors confronted new issues of difference and otherness—at the dinner table.

Eventually, Worcester County farmers chose to turn to day help rather than season-long labor. Day laborers had always been a part of the workforce, as peak work periods required extra hands. White hired extra day hands for haying in July, reaping and threshing in August, and getting his wood in from the woodlot in the winter. He also hired by the job for specialized work, such as butchering, laying stone, or carpentry. Most of these day helps were near neighbors, and many of them were poorer men who sold their labor to fill out what their undersized farms could not provide.[114] Son Francis was thrilled when his father hired three extra men for the harvest; daughter Caroline was not, as their presence greatly increased her laundry and kitchen work. (And, to her annoyance, they brought bedbugs, a secret she told brother Charles not to share for the shame it would bring on her housekeeping!)

In time, though, as local contract labor became scarce, Mary recorded poor local men doing day work for Aaron with increasing frequency. Abishai Crossman came to hay and plant, Joseph Eager to butcher hogs, Abel Farwell to chop wood, Benjamin Sawtell to husk and thresh. All were local, all were poor. Some, with modest holdings and artisan skills, worked to supplement their meager subsistence. Others, like Benjamin Sawtell, were propertyless; they rented houses and sold their labor to wealthier farmers to survive. As a study of neighboring Shrewsbury has shown, the increased use of day labor subtly changed the nature of exchange relationships that had long marked traditional agrarian communities. These were no longer exchanges of equality or reciprocity. Wealthy farmers needed only labor, and the poor day laborers had nothing to give *but* labor. This was no changing of works; poorer farmers had slipped from independent yeomen to dependent laborers.[115] Nor were they, like the struggling Benjamin Sawtell, whose wages from Joseph Flagg barely covered his rent and charges for family necessities, likely to advance. By midcentury, opportunities to rise through farm labor were virtually nil in Worcester County towns.[116]

Mary White found it even more difficult to find female domestic help. In 1834, after her daughter and adopted niece both married and moved away, Mary went in search of a girl to assist her in her housework. She tried to engage Maria Curtis of Shrewsbury, but Maria declined. She took in an orphan girl named Nancy Fielding, but found her unsuitable. For two years she and her daughters searched fruitlessly in the neighborhood, finally securing a girl, Mary Giles from Essex County, who was known to a neighbor. Mary Giles stayed for less than a year before leaving for a better housekeeping offer elsewhere. In 1839, Mary sent her son Thomas out to scour the countryside "in pursuit of a girl to do house work." He located a Miss Whitaker from another Worcester County town and engaged her on trial. After only a month, however, Lucinda Whitaker decided she would prefer to work in a factory. In 1841, Mary was delighted to retain her townswoman Clarissa Osgood, but after a year, Clarissa left, as she had decided not to go out to work. Local women increasingly chose options other than working in another woman's house.

Mary's problem was shared by farmwives throughout the area.[117] Part of the problem was emerging urban and middle-class ideas of female domesticity, which elevated nurturing and moral cultivation while demoting domestic *work*, an ideal that simply was unfeasible on the farm. Part of the problem lay in the accurate perception of women's farm work as strenuous and wearing. Young farmwomen who once went out to work for their neighbors now had more attractive options. Girls could—and did—choose to work in urban households, to go to nearby factories, to teach, or to work at several different forms of outwork.[118]

For example, while Mary anxiously pursued female household help, her able-bodied adult daughters pursued their own options. Before her marriage, Elizabeth went to New Haven for a year to live with and work for a family her parents knew. Daughters Mary and Caroline took turns teaching in district schools. Local female teachers earned ten dollars a month for teaching the summer term, less than half what male teachers earned, but to Caroline, who confessed to her brother that she was "poverty struck" and in need of "some honest cash," it was welcome.[119] Caroline and her sister Mary also braided straw for bonnet makers, sewed shoe uppers for local shoemakers, and fed mulberry leaves to a neighbor's hungry silkworms. Their goal was to earn cash—the stuff of their independence—in any way *but* farm work.

Though local girls left to pursue personal aspirations, their replacements arrived as the result of external factors. The rolling demographic crisis pushed poorer women with few prospects out of their own hometowns, and similarly dispossessed women from overseas arrived on their heels. Like male farmhands, live-in hired women increasingly tended to come from elsewhere—first from distant towns and eventually from Ireland—and be less culturally familiar. And, as Mary White had greater difficulty finding anyone willing to live in, she increasingly hired poor women to do tasks by the day. So Mrs. Simpson came on laundry day, Mrs. McLure came to scour and scrub, Mrs. Eager to assist with whitewashing. Like a domestic piecework system, Mary divided chores and parceled them out. She paid these women in cash.[120]

Both male and female hired help gradually became more culturally alien, poor, and transient. They were no longer included as part of the family, nor traded with as equal partners in arrangements of mutual need. Even in this utterly agrarian farm town, classes of haves and have nots, with divergent interests and a range of identities, were emerging.

Reaping the Consequences

In two feverish decades, Boylstonians reshaped relations between neighbors, between locals and strangers, between farmers and their help, between farmers and their land, and between the generations. They freed some from earlier mutual dependencies and bound others in new unequal relations of dependence. They created, and emphasized, difference and distinction. They adopted innovations in trade and technology that made them more individually independent and less personally allied with the concerns of their neighbors. They brought the world to town and ventured out to meet it. They remade the town as more heterogeneous, pluralist, and cosmopolitan, a place of diverging interests.

Decisions to move brought about the demise of the cousinhood, that broad and dense network of extended kin and interdependent neighbors. In 1800, nearly two-thirds of the town's residents represented early settler families; by 1850, those settlers' descendants had dwindled to less than a third.[121] Offspring were leaving, while the inflow of young migrants were on the whole too transient, too culturally different, and too poor to marry into established families and weave themselves into the web of extended family relationships. The familiar kith-and-kin community that had grown from generations of intermarriage and living within each other's households must have been strained by these goings and comings. Neighborly lending, swapping, and long-term credit depended on a stable, familiar network of *trustworthy* people. Increased mobility disrupted traditional agrarian interdependence and put a new premium on the value of being able to provide for oneself.

The arrival of so many unfamiliar—and dissimilar—faces meant that native people were constantly confronted with difference. Nonlocal speech, patterns of behavior, and dress might be easily absorbed in a community that was overwhelmingly native born, but as nonlocals increased, Boylstonians were forced to acknowledge that their ways were not the only ways. Immigrants brought new ideas, alien religious beliefs, and unfamiliar cultural ways.

Selective mobility also led to a community striated by age and wealth. Compared to the Revolutionary generation, fewer men owned farms, livestock, and tools, but those who did owned significantly more than their fathers had.[122] This privileged class, able to purchase or hire rather than borrow to fulfill their needs and wants, gradually weaned themselves of neighborly interdependence. Their growing concentration of wealth strained old norms of mutuality based on the understanding that every farmer needed his neighbors to survive.

And what of those small farmers and artisans who survived by trading their labor to their wealthier neighbors? Their dependence deepened. Even if their few acres allowed them to call themselves farmers, they could not produce enough to free themselves from their need for neighborly assistance. By 1850, fewer than half of those who owned Boylston farms could afford to keep their own oxen; a third of the men who died in the second quarter of the nineteenth century owned no plow.[123] The interests of the poor and wealthy farmers diverged. The poor had little to gain from plans for new and improved roads; tensions rose dramatically in town meeting as men argued over the expense of road and bridge improvements deemed vital to marketing farmers but viewed as merely an added tax burden by their poorer neighbors. In Worcester County towns, prosperous, marketing farmers lobbied for new toll roads, while their poorer neighbors protested that they were "against the general interest."[124] But in truth there no longer *was* a general interest. "Much warmth" and "considerable debate" now accompanied town meeting discussion of roads, schools, and support of the poor, as different elements contested now-conflicting interests.[125]

Opposed to both native groups were the young transients, the town's alien invaders with no roots or ties to community. Their presence changed the nature of work in the field and kitchen. The potential for conflict between employers and laborers had already escalated, as new pressures to increase surplus drove farmers to intensify work and dispense with traditional leisurely rhythms and sociable customs.[126] Improving farmers such as Aaron White abandoned cooperative practices such as exchanging work, choosing efficiency over sociability.[127] The bees and barn raisings that marked Simon Davis's year in the 1790s were absent from Mary's in the 1830s. Cultural and ethnic difference now further inhibited camaraderie and shared identity.[128] Service in another man's field or another woman's kitchen, once a reciprocal or familial relation, devolved to a wage relation, allowing both employer and worker to identify the other as other, in nature and in interest.[129] In the words of historian Robert Gross, "a calculating, even suspicious spirit dominated the relations between farmers and their help. Where once farm boys had labored for their fathers out of duty, love, and an expectation that they would inherit land of their own someday, now it was money—and money alone—that kept help working on the farm."[130] Work for cash alone, of course, also had a liberating effect on some employees, who preferred receiving wages disentangled from emotional or personal relations with employers.[131]

Cash transformed relations. It eliminated the need for an extensive network of reciprocal obligations. Cash made business impersonal. But cash was the medium of the new consumer's market, and everyone wanted it. Although it was slow to replace the traditional account-book world, cash played an increasingly important role. Mary White paid her washerwoman and scullery help in cash, relieving her of further obligations to these poorest of women. Joseph Flagg treated cash as one of his commodities, lending it at interest to family, hired help, and neighbors who needed it for shop purchases. Caroline sought not just any work, but work that would bring her some cash so she could order things from her brother's Boston shop. Her father was equally concerned about cash, as she reported to her brother, "I am as empty [headed] as father's purse always is. Just at present time he says he has not enough to make a jingle with and bank bills are not to be seen."[132] Transient hired help wanted pay in cash, as they had no intention of remaining in town long enough to collect on long-term credits. Cash was the universal solvent—eroding the account-book world, neighborly obligations, and the personal nature of worker-employee ties. "Those who gave up their accounts were freer to buy and sell where they wished; they were not bound up in a web of local history."[133] They were loosed from the web of community, freed from the body of neighborhood and town.

Disentangled from neighborhood and town, farmers found themselves increasingly entangled in the market. In some ways, commercial society compromised the very independence rural farmers had prized. Profits rose and fell with the market price of their crops, binding them more closely to the cosmopolitan world beyond their fields, and making them feel dependent on forces they could not see or know. In the second quarter of the nineteenth century, local farmers—who had always understood land as wealth—kept significantly more of their assets in paper—notes, bonds, stocks, and cash.[134] This change eroded the farmer's connection to his land as the source of his competence and independence—a relationship further compromised by the tendency of some, like Joseph Flagg, to exploit rather than steward their acres. But shifting wealth from soil to paper also exposed entrepreneurs to increased risk. Aaron White worried intensely about the safety of these investments and nagged his sons in Boston and Providence for the latest news on stocks and banking stability. In the turbulent late 1830s, he was particularly anxious.[135] Caroline wrote to Charles of their father's distress over the financial panic. "He does not sleep nights very well, or he hears the clock strike almost every hour. I have threatened to take off the striking weight some night, to see what effect that will produce."[136] Aaron White had reason to worry. He knew more farms were being sold to settle debts.[137] Two of his brothers-in-law lost their estates, and he feared for his sons' security in this newly volatile economic world.

Given the risks of market farming, the decline in the land's fertility, and the difficulty of securing labor, it is not surprising that so many sons chose to leave town. That they also chose to leave the *land*, however, was evidence of a growing generational rift. Family tensions ran high during the 1820s to 1840s, as the majority of sons rejected their father's agrarian identity. We can imagine the emotional toll on fathers such as Aaron White, who deeply valued the gentry status his landed estate conveyed, as each of his sons spurned his way of life. Numerous letters attest to Aaron's sensitivity to perceived slights or neglect from his sons. Caroline confessed to Charles, "scarcely a day passes when we are not called (I mean mother, Mary, Francis [and myself]) to render a reason [to Father] for some real or imaginary misdemeanor. We always do our best to make things smooth, but sometimes we have rather a hard task."[138] Those other fathers who watched their sons leave for Worcester County workshops, factories, and commercial trades no doubt shared his feelings of rejection and abandonment.

Parents such as the Whites must have struggled with ambivalence. They constantly impressed upon their children the urgent need to improve the opportunity, to secure their prospects, both earthly and eternal. And their children did, improving their standards of living, learning, and genteel refinement. Yet in doing so, they moved beyond their parents' world and left them—both physically and culturally—behind. To succeed in new trades and professions, children needed different assets and tutelage than their parents could provide. To thrive in their newly cosmopolitan world, children fashioned new self-made identities, with manners and presentation to signal their worth to strangers.[139]

Expansive economic changes transformed local relationships. Some, as we will see, reveled in the choices and freedoms introduced by market opportunities, cash relations, cosmopolitan diversity, and the loosening bonds of neighborly and family obligation. But for all its exuberant innovation, Boylston was also experiencing anxious insecurity. The changes some thought would bring a prosperous self-sufficiency also introduced new forms of dependence and vulnerability. Parents worried ceaselessly about children's prospects and took some small comfort in heavenly reunion and security. Mary White repeated these assurances to herself in her diary, even as her husband mourned, "Of all our ten children, not one is at home at present."[140]

In January 1837, Aaron wrote to his Charley:

We hope that you are well and are doing well, although we don't hear from you so frequently of late as we have been used to. You must not omit to send a few lines with the clothing that you send home from week to week. It gives us much pleasure to receive your letters and will be no injury to you. We don't want that you should forget your old home and its associations yet. . . . The anxiety we feel for your welfare and good conduct will be my excuse for repeating some advice & directions you have received before. . . . I don't know how you get along with your employers of late and what satisfaction you are able to give. We do hope, Charley, that you will try to do your best to keep your place and please your masters. They may yet think that you will not answer their purposes if you are not careful and dismiss you after this year. . . . Did you realise the anxious solicitude I feel for your prosperity and happiness and how short and uncertain the time is for me to do anything to promote it, you would not wonder at my writing to you in the manner I now do. . . . Your affectionate parent, Aaron White.[141]

Aaron White's mournful tone reflects his sense of loss, the absence of sons, the splintering of community, the passing of old relations. His sons did not mourn at all. They celebrated the flowering of choice, opportunity, and individualism. They cultivated self-reliance.

CHAPTER FOUR

Fields and Dreams

Aaron's children and their peers were restless, striving, self-assertive spirits. They pursued ambitions beyond their parents' imagining. This generation did not accept customary roles and hierarchies, but embraced a new age of self making. They earned, learned, purchased, invested, and cultivated their way toward their varied goals. In pursuing self-determination, they declared independence from time-honored bonds to family, neighbors, and townsmen and embraced new alliances with distant and diverse partners, parties, and sects.

But they did not do so without some ambivalence. As they left parents and past behind, many spoke with reverence of their family patriarchs, with pride of their revolutionary heritage, with nostalgia of their childhood on the farm. Others expressed deep anxiety about their ability to make their way independently in a world of cities, strangers, and inscrutable markets. There was an undercurrent of guilt and angst as some young rejected their parents' values and identities, broke the constraints of their rural communities, refused to conform to parochial norms, and asserted their right to *personal* independence. Conflict between the generations ran high, as self-assertive and striving youth faced off against parents determined to maintain control, secure the family farm, and exact the tithes of filial duty.[1]

For youth, then, this was a new era of chancy, high-stakes choices. Some embraced those choices in order to pursue their personal dreams—or escape their personal nightmares; their pursuits remade their parents' customary world. Their varied stories remind us that though change occurs through individual choices, the consequences of those choices—especially in personal relationships—are often unforeseen and unintended.

Charles White—Druggist's Apprentice

Sixteen-year-old Charles White wanted to be a druggist. In choosing to leave home for training, he faced a double challenge: coming to the city and coming of age.[2] It was a daunting challenge: in Boston, Charles faced a confounding array of new choices, and the consequences of choosing poorly could be dire.[3] Naive youth, led astray by artful predators, might succumb to gambling, addiction, and prostitution. Falling in with a bad set of peers led to profanity, blasphemy, and impiety; misuse of leisure hours squandered opportunities for improvement; social gaffes endangered one's place in the white-collar class. And a volatile business climate doomed many young men. Aaron inquired anxiously and often about his sons' prospects. Mary prayed fervently that her boys be kept on the straight path in "this pilgrimage world."

Charles's father believed he had chosen his son's placement well. Aaron White reached an agreement with William Ward, a well-established wholesale druggist on Washington Street who hailed from neighboring Shrewsbury. In Boston, druggists were high-status professionals, following only merchants, lawyers, and doctors in mean wealth.[4] Apprenticing in a large wholesale firm such as Ward's might lead to a lucrative partnership.[5] Aaron envisioned a traditional apprenticeship, with a master who gradually advanced Charles through the stages of business while overseeing the boy's present welfare and future prospects.[6]

William Ward, however, did not see himself as the boy's master. Ward felt liberated from the ancient paternal notions of a master's responsibilities: he would provide no housing, no supervision, no practical, moral, or spiritual direction. What he would provide was a wage. Though Charles's family thought of him as an apprentice, his employer thought of him as cheap labor. Cash wages freed masters from other obligations, and they increasingly withdrew both personally and residentially from shop production. Apprentices now worked out the daily routine of living and learning on their own.[7]

For Charles, the transition from rural home to urban shop was rude. He suffered the usual fate of the youngest apprentice: the hardest physical labor and the worst torments of the older boys. His elder brother William wrote words of consolation after others stole the berries that the family sent for him. William urged Charles to endure the "insolence of apprentices toward the youngest," to hold his tongue and try not to mind.[8]

But things did not go well. Charles was accustomed to the pace and rhythm of country life, where work varied by the season and tasks were frequently interrupted for socializing; his employers complained that he was slow, inexact, and careless in his work. Ward was so dissatisfied that Charles was almost let go after only three months.[9] Father advised son that he was on probation: "Be sure to have the store opened and put in order in good season. Be always at your post ready to do anything that needs to be done and be careful to have it done well. They have complained that you were deaf; convince them that you can hear and obey their orders with readiness."[10] Aaron was desperately concerned to see his son secure his place.

And, ultimately, Charles was driven to improve. He learned to adjust his manner and appearance to urban standards. He learned to think, talk, and especially to write rapidly, since, in the words of one apprentice, "the commercial world would not brook sluggishness of any kind." He practiced his penmanship in his journal and wrote to his schoolteacher sister for correction. Daily practice built speed and facility, essential for a clerk. His clear and rapid handwriting became a measure of his productivity.[11]

Charles also learned to adjust his hygiene and attire to urban norms. Discovering that bathing once a week was essential for urban gentlemen, he purchased tickets for visits to Bramin's Bath House in the warm months, supplemented by evening dips in the harbor. His parents were somewhat surprised by this new need for regular bathing and hoped that he would not bathe on the Sabbath. Charles also quickly learned that heavy boots and rough country frock were not appropriate behind the urban counter; there, he needed the clerk's emblematic dark broadcloth coat, shirt with detachable white collar to change when soiled, fine boots, and silk handkerchief.[12] His mother complied by sewing more fine shirts for him, though chiding him gently to preserve these good shirts for the counter only. After receiving a raise in his second year, he spent over a month's wages on a fine new broadcloth coat, a new hat, and shoes "both to wear at the store," a black silk neckerchief, calfskin boots, and silk gloves. Charles's manners, hygiene, and attire distinguished him as an urban clerk—and distinguished him *from* his rural family and friends.[13] He could measure his progress by the changing contents of his wardrobe.

Charles could also measure his progress by his daily work assignments. Like all apprentices, he had to start at the bottom, with dirty, heavy, strenuous, and often outdoor work.[14] He opened the store, cleaned cellars and stockrooms, made deliveries, unloaded crates at the wharves. By 1838, two years into his apprenticeship, Charles had advanced to "putting up things for orders."[15] The apothecary cut and rolled pills by hand, made plasters with a spreading iron, powdered drugs in a stone mortar, and made tinctures in glass jars. Charles learned to package essence of rose in vials or extract of butternut (a cathartic) in galley pots, conjure compounds, as when preparing nitrate of strontium for Election Day fireworks, and prepare bottled quinine extract from cinchona bark for malaria treatments.

In the third year of Charles's apprenticeship, Aaron wrote, "Your time for entering the Counting room by agreement is just at hand. Let us know what your prospect is in this respect."[16] Aaron was anxious for his son to progress from chemicals to cashbooks. The accounting clerk stood higher than the counter clerk. With ink-stained fingers these clerks presided over desks and recorded the stuff of commerce: profits. But Charles was not promoted. Instead, one of his coworkers—his employer's son—"went as clerk into the counting Room. I took his place as Foreman." It may have been nepotism that cost Charles his promotion—but it may have been his own ineptitude. He was plagued during this period by missteps and errors. Mr. Ward reproved him harshly. Charles confessed to his journal, "things went all wrong with me at the store. [Elder brother Avery] had some conversation with Mr. Ward about me. Did not speak very favorably of me."[17] Charles felt keenly the insecurity of the commercial world he had chosen.

A year later, in February 1841, Charles received devastating news: Mr. Ward intended to let him go. In Ward's view, he could hire and fire wageworkers at will, but Aaron was incensed that Ward had violated the trust of a master-apprentice agreement: "From what we can learn it seems that your present employers, after getting all they could out of you, intend to turn you adrift as we say. They have by no means fulfilled their agreement that they made when you first went to them. . . . But I fear from what I hear of their general character that they are governed in their conduct by the narrowest motives of selfishness."[18] In the next few weeks, Charles agonized, but as the date of his dismissal neared, he took a step that revealed some newfound gumption. He made arrangements with a competitor. Ward counteroffered: "came to the conclusion with my employers to stay with them six months longer at the rate of $400 a year."[19]

Charles had finally become a clerk. He would now receive not a wage but a salary, nearly doubling his previous pay. At the end of traditional apprenticeships, masters often outfitted their charges with a new suit of clothes suitable to commence business. Mr. Ward did no such thing, but Charles himself acknowledged the moment by purchasing his first full broadcloth suit, coat, pants, and vest. He would have new responsibilities and authority, and at the end of his six months, he might look forward to negotiating part proprietorship. At twenty-one years of age, Charles had sufficiently mastered his trade to anticipate becoming self-supporting.

But economic competence was only one measure of success for urban antebellum youth. Equally important was disciplined self-governance. In the city, where boys worked by the clock rather than the task, the evening's leisure hours offered dangerous enticements to unsupervised youth. Charles's family worried about how he might spend his evenings and Sabbaths.[20]

Parental warnings reflected a general anxiety about the welfare of unsupervised urban youth, a homeless and masterless class. It was not that they lacked a place to live or work but that they no longer lived or worked under family government. Living in boardinghouses and working for employers who wanted no part of paternal responsibilities, these youth socialized with other unsupervised peers. Stories of youthful dissipation were frighteningly common.[21] Caroline confided to Charles the shameful fate of a former schoolmate, who, having "violated the 7th commandment," was afflicted with a shameful sickness that cost him his fiancée, his store, his goods, his reputation, and possibly his soul. She added, "I often think, dear brother, of the many temptations to evil by which you are or may be surrounded; perhaps they exist in my imagination only, would that it might be so, but I fear otherwise."[22] In the summer of 1837, just a few blocks from Charles's store, a riot erupted between Irish immigrants and Yankee youth; the militia had to restore order. Mary wrote, "We hear that you have riotous proceedings and fires in your city. We hope that you will be kept from all bad company."[23]

Mary and Aaron tried to take comfort from reimagining Charles's boardinghouse as extended family. But it was not. Charles rented a room and took his meals in the house of a Mr. and Mrs. Jones by the wharves of Fort Hill. They were one of many working-class Boston families who boarded single youth for extra income. As Caroline said, the Whites hoped the Joneses took a "family interest" in Charles's well-being.[24] Aaron and Mary looked upon the Joneses as surrogate parents, and they sometimes sent gifts of fruit and fresh produce to Mrs. Jones as tokens of appreciation. Mary wrote, "Tell Mrs. Jones that her attentions to you I consider an equivalent to any small thing that I send to her."[25]

But boardinghouses presented a paradox in newly emerging domestic ideals. As homes, they should be refuges from the commercial world, yet boardinghouses were homes that had been commercialized.[26] Charles's relationship with the Joneses reflected the transitional—and confused—nature of a society moving away from domestic economy. Charles paid rent, but for some services, such as occasional laundering or mending, he paid in favors and gifts: sharing whortleberries and watermelon from Boylston, procuring items for the Joneses from his store, carrying a pot of beans for Mrs. Jones to the bake house. In his rural village, such exchanges would have been the stuff of domestic economy and neighborly obligation; in boardinghouses, homeless youth like Charles had to negotiate these services and determine whether to pay in kind or kindness. He had to redefine his domestic and economic relationships.

His family was also concerned about the bad influences of fellow apprentices. His mother prayed that he not be led into temptation; his father advised him to "never listen to any suggestion of your fellow apprentices or others to do anything that you think will be injurious or displeasing to [your employers]." Brother William warned of "obscene and filthy talking . . . among Journeymen and fellow Apprentices. Turn away your ears from hearing filthy stories. Avoid all licentious practices to which young men in cities are much addicted."[27] Charles learned to navigate these waters as well. In time, he developed relationships with coworkers on his own terms. A friendly rapport emerged. The other boys challenged him to learn to swim; when he failed, he reported the lost wager in his journal: an expense for treating coworkers to "boles of oysters at Holbrooks Oyster Room."[28] Soon after, they taught him to swim.

Learning how to safely navigate the waters of nontraditional relationships—to interact with his boss, landlady's family, boardinghouse mates, and coworkers—was a feat of self-determination. Charles achieved this by a conscious effort to *mold his character*. Advice writers of the age envisioned the character of youth as malleable, shaped early then fixed for a lifetime. Ministers urged city boys to take control of this formative stage by consciously developing habits of respectable middle-class behavior. Charles's own parents repeatedly echoed the refrain in their letters: "You are now forming habits and character for life."[29] This was ultimately an act of self-mastery.[30] Here was the core of true independence: developing personal resources to interact safely and profitably with strangers in an impersonal cosmopolitan world. Charles read advice manuals, attended lectures, and practiced introspection in a conscious attempt to fashion his chosen self.

In 1843 Charles bid farewell to his Boston friends and colleagues. With capital loaned by his father, the twenty-three-year-old opened his own apothecary shop and hardware store in bustling Worcester. His ad in the city directory declared, "Medicines, Paints, Oil, Dye Stuffs, Window Glass, Nails, Potash, Pear ash, Paint Brushes, etc. at No. 3 Washington Square, Worcester."[31] In his seven years of apprenticeship, he had learned new ways of relating to others: how to convey his character through dress and comportment, how to interact with strangers in unfamiliar places, how to negotiate with those of competing interests, how to develop his sense of self. His growing self-reliant worldliness was suited to the urban, commercial world he had chosen. It was a revelation to family and neighbors in his parochial hometown.

Caleb Crossman—Self-Composing

When Caleb Crossman's father, Abishai, brought his bride to Boylston from neighboring Worcester in 1794, he already had skills as a shoemaker and hopes of acquiring a small farm.[32] It was a reasonable expectation. Shoemaking was a long-established and respectable competence.[33] In rural Massachusetts, most shoemakers combined their craft with farming, working on custom orders for the local community. With a young, growing family to assist him at the workbench and on the land, Abishai Crossman likely had high hopes that he would be able to achieve independence. But it turned out to be not so easy as he had hoped. Crossman lived and worked in Boylston for more than a dozen years, fathering ten children, before he was able to purchase a humble six-acre farm just west of the center village.[34] Such a small holding likely yielded the family's vegetables, fruit, and grain, and perhaps enough pasture to graze a cow. For their other needs, Abishai had to trade shoe credits with neighboring farmers.

But it was not a bad life for young Caleb, the ninth child and last of five sons. Born in 1814, Caleb grew up in a family of low to middling means.[35] Despite their humbler status, the lives of Caleb, his siblings, and parents often intersected with those of their well-to-do neighbors. Caleb and his brothers went to the center district school with the White boys. The Crossmans were often in the White family home, barn, or fields, working, borrowing, or visiting. Mary White and her daughters sat up with Crossman family members when they were ill, or served tea to Mrs. Crossman and her daughters if they came for a visit. Aaron White liked having the Crossmans visit, as the family was musical, and he enjoyed hearing them sing or play the viol or the cello. During the 1820s, Aaron secured neighbor Crossman to conduct the singers in the church choir. Caleb evidently soaked in the White family's aura of gentility—and aspired to achieve it for himself. Doing so would utterly undo his family relations.

Caleb's shoemaker father could not offer that life. In the years of the Embargo and the War of 1812, as the demand for U.S.-produced shoes grew, new techniques of organizing production in shoemaking spread to Worcester County, following a trend that began earlier in coastal Essex County.[36] Some enterprising shoemakers with capital began to expand their business beyond local custom, to make shoes in standard sizes, and to send them by lots to city markets and country stores. To supply this larger market, the larger shoemakers began to shift their work from home to "ten-footer" shops, where they coordinated the subdivision of shoemaking into lesser-skilled tasks that they put out to neighbors, usually women. By dividing and standardizing the steps of shoemaking, they increased productivity. Crossman was no exception. Though he continued some local custom work, Crossman likely made the transition to wholesale production in 1819 as his firstborn son came of age; together they purchased a ten-footer shop in the center of Boylston for their craft.[37]

Intensifying their work, producing for wholesale, and dividing labor among the family did not threaten Crossman's competence; it likely increased the family's income. By the 1820s and 1830s in Worcester County, however, shoe "bosses"—men with the assets to purchase leather in quantity and the wherewithal to distribute finished shoes broadly—began to take over control of shoemaking. They set up central shops, each employing about forty shoemakers as outworkers. The shoemaker became a mere middleman, taking in precut lots of leather from the central shop, distributing uppers around the countryside to be sewn by farmwomen, bottoming the lots as they were returned, and delivering finished cases of shoes to the central shop, where bosses arranged for them to be shipped and sold as far afield as the slave South.

The change was effectively a demotion for Abishai Crossman. He was no longer an independent craftsman, master of a family-based business. He became a piece worker, a dependent laborer, lacking power to set prices or determine markets. And as the work was divided and deskilled, needy young men flooded the field, creating ruthless competition for old-time shoemakers. Abishai Crossman faced this plight by the 1830s. While others benefited from less expensive and more readily available shoes, he was one of those who paid the cost of the transition to more efficient production.

Soon, and perhaps as an outgrowth of these troubles, other problems beset the shoemaker. In 1828, the Congregational Church summoned Crossman to face discipline.[38] Although the charges were not specified, Abishai was known to be a hearty drinker, "no friend to temperance," as Aaron

White would later say, and the church had been moving toward temperance. Although reconciled to the church, Crossman was again in trouble with the congregation in 1830. Soon after, he left to join the more liberal Unitarians.[39] In 1834, his wife was reprimanded for her delinquency and excommunicated.[40] Crossman became increasingly obstreperous, engaging in clever forms of civil disobedience. By 1840, the shoemaker was being sued for debt.[41]

Perhaps not surprisingly, none of his sons chose to follow in the shoemaker's footsteps. Each son left by the time he came of age until, by 1835, only youngest Caleb was still at home. And Caleb, it seems, was doing everything in his power to avoid his parents' debasement. He apprenticed as a Worcester jeweler and watch repairer, and in 1836, Caroline reported to her brother that Caleb was in Worcester, "working at his trade with Mr. Fenno."[42] But within a few years—perhaps as a result of the hard times of the panic of 1837—he had returned to his father's home. He purchased his father's workshop and a small farm of thirteen acres and turned his energies to shoe work, distributing shoes on an outwork basis. He took up his father's old position leading the Congregational Church choir.[43] But this life did not suit his ambitions either. Shortly after 1840 Caleb Crossman left Boylston for good, moved to the emerging commercial center of Keene, New Hampshire, and set himself up as a "professor of music."[44]

It is possible that Crossman had training in music. In 1833 the Boston Academy of Music offered the nation's first school of music instruction, allowing students to train without having to travel to Europe. But it is more likely that in an age before professional education, Crossman relied on his native talent, his gifts on the viol, and his experience as a church choral director. Rural centers such as Keene had a strong demand for teachers of refined arts. Caleb Crossman fashioned himself as a professor, and by wit and skill, he became one. By 1855 he had gone west, first to Wisconsin, then to Ohio, married, and established himself as a credentialed professor of music at a midwestern university.[45] He had also become one of the wealthiest men with one of the finest houses in his adopted hometown.[46] He had recreated himself as a genteel man of learning and culture, repudiating his humble— or humiliating—parentage.

Crossman never returned home. In 1855, when his elderly parents were destitute and dependent on town support, the town tried to seize the shoemaker's workshop as their only asset. Caleb wrote from his home in Fond du Lac, Wisconsin, to protest—not the plight of his parents, but the ownership of the workshop. It was his, he rightly asserted, and could not be sold to support the aging couple. He permitted the produce of the plot to be used for the comfort of his *mother*, as the genteel son had long disassociated himself from his father. Beyond that he rejected traditional obligations and refused to support his aged parents, who were left to the care of the town.[47] Caleb's break with family and farm town was complete—or so it seemed.

In 1886, when the town invited all past citizens home to celebrate its centennial, Caleb sent regrets that he would miss "the glorious Centennial Birthday of my own, my native town—Boylston—name always remembered and revered."[48] There may, after all, have been some ambivalence in his self-imposed exile. He quoted the romantic Sir Walter Scott: "Breathes there a man with soul so dead, who never to himself hath said, 'This is my own, my native land!'" The poem went on to say that the wandering soul who achieved "titles, power, and pelf," but cherished not his homely roots would die "unwept, unhonour'd and unsung." At his death, Crossman's body was sent home to be buried.[49]

Cassandra Hooper—A Path of Purpose

Cassandra Hooper and her siblings—three younger sisters and a brother—were not born in Boylston, and the circumstances of their coming there are somewhat curious. It seems it was firstborn Cassandra who led the way and opened the path for her siblings and parents to follow. She was a young woman of passionate determination, and, like Charles and Caleb, she was driven to live a life that was something more than long.

Cassandra grew up on her father's farm in the Worcester County town of Oakham. There Isaac Hooper prospered, steadily adding to his family—and his acres—until he could count himself among the prosperous yeomen. Cassandra was apparently a bright and curious child, soon mastering what could be offered at her common school. Her father indulged her desire to learn, sending her to private academies where she studied under pioneering female educators. In her twenties, Cassandra's credentials caught the attention of Samuel Slater, founder of Rhode Island's cotton-mill complex, who engaged her to teach the school connected with his establishment.[50]

But while Cassandra was busy teaching—and, apparently, saving—her father was encountering difficulties. His estate dwindled until he was landless.[51] It is possible that injury or poor health had rendered him incapable of farm work. Seeking shelter, the family arrived in Boylston at the peak of the town's conflicted years, taking up residence in a simple dwelling house on a one-acre parcel next to the old burying ground in center Boylston. What is rather astonishing, however, is that the house and lot was purchased not by father Isaac, but by daughter Cassandra. The thirty-year-old teacher, identified on the deed simply as "singlewoman," was the rightful owner of her family's shelter.[52]

The children, now mostly grown, set to work supporting their parents. Sister Avis, four years younger than Cassandra, went to New Ipswich Academy for a semester with Caroline White, then taught school in Boylston.[53] Younger sisters Lydia and Eunice, in their late teens and twenties, braided straw and made straw bonnets.[54] Young Charles became a shoemaker. The family, with Cassandra essentially as its independent economic head, struggled along, among the poorer but respectable members of the community.

One of the families that welcomed the Hooper daughters warmly was the Whites. Cassandra was a committed evangelical Christian, and from her arrival in 1830 she and her sisters Avis, Lydia, and Eunice were frequent visitors to the White family parlor, while Mary and her daughters returned those visits to the Hooper's humble home. The nature of the visits is clear, as they were frequently made in company with the minister's wife and other active evangelical women.[55] Cassandra had apparently embraced evangelical Christianity before her arrival in Boylston, but her younger sister Avis was "received to our Communion" along with eight other converts in March 1834; her sister Lydia made her public confession in October the same year. Like the Crossmans, the family had fallen on hard times, but unlike the Crossmans, their behavior marked them as educated, genteel, and pious folk and secured their respectability among Boylston's better sort.

Then, with no warning or advance preparations, Mary White made a surprise announcement in her diary. At the close of the afternoon service on the Sabbath of September 2, 1832, thirty-year-old Cassandra Hooper was married to a Mr. Bliss, and the couple left almost immediately to serve as missionaries to the Seneca Indians. They would continue in that work in western New York for the rest of their lives.

The suddenness of Cassandra Bliss's change in station has an explanation. Most missionaries from New England (those sent to the Native American West as well as those who ventured overseas) went under the auspices of the American Board of Commissioners of Foreign Missions (ABCFM). Since their first emissaries set sail for Hawaii in 1812, the ABCFM had insisted almost without exception that their male missionaries be married men.[56] It was unrealistic to place an unmarried man among the unrestrained sexuality of native cultures, they reasoned, lest "the powerful law of nature" overcome his better self.[57] In addition to satisfying his sexual needs, a wife would provide domestic services, maintain the missionary's household in the midst of wilderness, and serve as a model of domestic life for heathen women. In addition, she could teach native women and children, if her domestic duties allowed. So men who aspired to missionary work, after completing a rigorous course of training that generally kept them cloistered within all-male institutions, faced an additional daunting proviso: between the time they were approved and the time their ship sailed or stage departed, they needed to secure the hand of a woman willing to leave her world behind and embark on a religious mission with a relative stranger, bound for life.[58]

The ABCFM, aware of the difficulties this created, acted as matchmaker throughout the Northeast, pairing evangelical women with missionary aspirants. The ABCFM sustained a network of contacts, "usually ministers and college teachers, who supplied a confidential listing of women who might consent to marry missionaries under the necessary circumstance, women who were 'missionary-minded' as well as being young, pious, educated, fit, and reasonably good looking."[59] There was one further qualification: most had to be ready and willing to leave immediately, perhaps forever. Barely two weeks after Cassandra's wedding, Mary noted that she had "called at Mr. Hooper's this evening & took leave of their daughter Bliss who was about to go to Cattaraugus Station [missionary village of the Seneca] with her husband to instruct the Indians. May they be instrumental of much good."[60] Six days later, requisite bride in hand, Rev. Asher Bliss was ordained a missionary by the ABCFM.[61]

While the risks of such a matrimonial contract seem extraordinary, in truth there was much to recommend the pairing. Cassandra Hooper was an intelligent, well-educated, and purposeful woman of thirty; she had attended to her family's well-being; she felt compelled to be up and doing, as Mary White so often put it, to spread the gospel. She joined herself to another New Englander of like age and education. (Asher Bliss had graduated from Amherst in the class of 1829 before entering Andover Theological Seminary, from which he graduated in the autumn of 1832.)[62] Like his wife, he shared a deep commitment to evangelical Christianity and to spreading the gospel. Both secured the independent and purpose-driven life they sought—but could achieve only together.

Cassandra and her new husband had settled among the Seneca by November that year. When they arrived, there were but two or three framed buildings on the reservation, the rest being the log and bark huts of the Seneca.[63] Here they went to housekeeping, and stayed for the next thirty years. Together they bore six children. Reverend Bliss was remembered for elevating the material as well as the spiritual condition of his charges, helping them to "build comfortable houses and barns, fences and cultivate their land, set out fruit trees, etc. . . . he effected a wonderful improvement among them in these respects."[64] (Whether the Seneca agreed that their domestication was an improvement is uncertain.) Cassandra also played a purposeful role, "a lady of fine personal traits of character, deeply beloved by her associates, and by the Indians to whom she was so long a benefactress."[65]

Cassandra's younger sister Avis, a frequent visitor to the White family home, followed her eldest sister's path. In 1837, after a semester spent at New Ipswich Academy with Caroline White, Avis returned to Boylston to wed the Rev. Gilbert Rockwood, who was then appointed missionary to the Tuscarora Indians in Niagara County, New York. On November second of that year, Mary noted in her diary, "I called at Mr. Hooper's. Took my leave of Miss Avis who was soon expecting to be married to a Mr. Rockwood and go as missionaries to the Tuscarora Mission."[66] Mary's wording yields two insights: Mr. Rockwood was unknown to the people of Boylston—and likely to Avis as well, another example of missionary matchmaking. But more important, Mary noted that *both* Avis and her husband to be were to "go as missionaries," that she, and likely Avis as well, considered the required wife to be every bit as much a missionary as the ordained husband. The Rockwoods worked among the Tuscarora for over a quarter century and all their children were born on the reservation. They were credited with bringing temperance—and Anglo ways—to the Native people they served.[67]

Despite their limited means and their circumscribed female sphere, Cassandra and Avis Hooper succeeded in blazing paths of purpose and, as Mary would say, "enlarging their sphere of usefulness."[68] In their drive to improve self and society they evinced the animating spirit of Boylston during these transformative years. Justified by faith, they pioneered a new model of female behavior: an active role in the public sphere. They also fundamentally transformed traditional family order and patriarchal authority.

Benjamin Houghton—Limits and Liabilities

Not all newly blazed paths led to dreams realized. The Houghtons were an ancient Boylston family, having arrived when the town was in its infancy. The "Houghton Place," a sprawling farm just northeast of the town center, had supported the family for three generations when Benjamin Jr. came of age in 1825. These fertile acres made the family among the wealthiest in Boylston, and Benjamin's father enjoyed the respect due a leading citizen and a venerable patriarch.[69] Benjamin would not be able to maintain his father's status.

Though established and affluent, the Houghtons were also prolific, and therein lay Benjamin Jr.'s problem. He was one of fifteen children. (Musically gifted, the Houghton children by themselves constituted a whole choir for town events.)[70] The family farm had already been divided through three generations; Benjamin Sr.'s remaining 128 acres, while generous for one estate, would barely support farms for two sons.[71]

Still, Benjamin Jr. had aspirations. In the early 1830s, he courted and successfully won the hand of Lucy Ann Brigham, Aaron White's orphaned niece and long a member of White's genteel family. Her indulgent uncle outfitted the couple with fine furniture, household goods and textiles, and silk gowns for the bride.[72] Three fine chaises escorted the bridal couple to the ancient Houghton homestead, where Benjamin ran the estate for his aging father.[73] Four years later, Benjamin moved his wife and two children to their own home on nine acres in Boylston, with a mortgage taken from his wife's doting Uncle White. There Houghton built a new house worth an impressive $800 and set to work as an independent husbandman.[74] He appeared to be on his way to realizing his aspiration of becoming a member of the improving gentry.

Two years later, in the wake of his father's death, Benjamin came into his inheritance. As was increasingly the case in now land-strapped Boylston, none of Houghton's sons inherited the family farm. Rather, the entire estate was sold and each of the heirs received a one-twelfth share of the proceeds (three siblings had predeceased their father). Benjamin's portion was a mere $245, far less than what he would have needed to buy the required acres in Boylston.[75]

The same year, Benjamin sold his own house and land. But he apparently had either amassed debts or suffered severe losses in the panic of 1837, for he was not able to acquire another farm in Boylston.[76] Instead, now landless, he began to rent farms, first from Aaron White and then from another major landholder.[77] Meanwhile, his assessed worth slipped lower and lower. We can only speculate whether his reverses were due to unfortunate investments, speculative ventures, or perhaps the strain of trying to maintain a growing family and wife in the manner in which she—and he—had been raised. A prolonged illness in 1839—possibly consumption—further reduced his resources, and the family took to binding shoes in their kitchen to earn extra cash.[78] Eventually Houghton gave up farming altogether and began producing shoes full-time, distributing uppers to be bound in the neighborhood. Like Abishai Crossman, he found himself unable to command the respect due a self-reliant yeoman.

In 1843, he again tried to gain some independence, purchasing a single acre and modest house near the center village for $400, though with the help of a $300 mortgage from a local carpenter.[79] Houghton tried to piece together a living doing carpentry and shoe work, but by 1846, he was defeated. He sold his meager holding, auctioned his household goods, packed his family into a wagon, and headed west to the Hudson River mill town of Sandy Hill. Here, he likely sought work in one of the textile mills of Mr. Edward Harris, a business associate of his wife's cousin, Aaron White Jr.[80] He wrote home wistfully, "How do you get along in Boylston? Does our religious society prosper? How do you get along with our singing at church? I feel much interested about these things and I think about them every Sabbath day. I have not sat with the singers [church choir] but once since I left Boylston. This is new times for me. The singing at Sandy Hill is pretty good, though not so good as we used to have at B. It is altogether vocal. . . . Do you have Lyceums this winter? I should like to attend them. Have you got good schools this winter? I hope you have."[81]

This experiment, however, also failed; soon, he and his family returned penniless to Boylston and again tried to find carpentry and shoe work.[82] Finally, in the early 1850s, Benjamin Houghton moved his wife and children to a boardinghouse in a nearby factory town, where the family found work as laborers in the shoe and boot industry.[83] The Houghtons were respected for their upright character and piety, but Benjamin never rose out of poverty, and Lucy Ann never recovered anything like the genteel life she had enjoyed in her uncle White's household.[84]

Benjamin Houghton's story—his progress from prosperity to penury, from independent farmer's son to dependent factory laborer—illustrates the risky nature of making a living during the volatile decades of the 1820s through 1840s. The liberty of self making came at a cost. One could strive to be his own man, but one failed on his own as well. Not all who set out on their voyage of self-determination reached their chosen destination.

Lincoln Flagg—Venturing at Home

Levi Lincoln Flagg, firstborn son of Joseph, inherited his father's enterprising nature and driving ambition. He did not inherit his father's farm, however. That he would have to earn. Born in 1818, he grew up working his father's land. By the time he was fourteen, his father was lending him out to their neighbor Mr. Brewer for plowing at one-quarter wages—payable to his father.[85] Lincoln went to the district school with the White boys, but unlike the squire's sons, he did not continue on to a local academy or a business clerkship. At the age of twenty, when Joseph Flagg gave his firstborn his freedom, Lincoln hired himself out to neighboring farmers for the sum of eight dollars a month, plus board.

Lincoln's industry soon earned him the reputation of being "a real eleven fellow."[86] In 1840, Aaron White hired him on salary, a princely sum of $160, and Lincoln moved into the White's mansion house and became one of their family.[87] The women made his meals and clothing, did his laundry, and nursed him when sick; the men shared with him in the farm work and socialized with him in their hours of leisure. He was a family favorite. Francis confessed to his older brother, "I never have found any one else with whom I have lived so long as I have with him that I got along so well as I did with him."[88] But after two years, Lincoln Flagg was ready to move on with his own plan.

That plan, as he later confessed, was simple. "I started out in life with the intention of becoming worth $100,000 and living to be 100 years old," he told an interviewer in 1907. ("'I have,' he said with a smile, 'got my $100,000, but have not lived 100 years yet.'")[89] By frugal management he saved all of his wages, with which he rented part of his father's farm on shares, "he to have one-half the profits and I the other half." By the end of the first summer he had $100 to pay his father, but Joseph told his son he could keep the money until spring. With shrewd calculation, Flagg rose early the next morning and walked twelve miles to the train in Westborough, which he took to the Brighton cattle yards. There, he remembered later, "I bought cattle and sold them for profit, and this I followed for seventeen years, walking to Westborough every week, and the least I ever made was twelve dollars in one week, and often I ran as high as $60." Within four years, he was able to purchase a Boylston farm for $2,000.[90]

But Lincoln Flagg was not content to accumulate a comfortable subsistence. He set up his own cattle-marketing firm, purchasing, butchering, and retailing at three markets in Worcester and one each in the neighboring towns of Clinton and Berlin. Dividing his time between his home farm and his livestock business, Flagg earned a reputation as a "shrewd, far-seeing businessman, although always having the reputation of being strictly honest and honorable in his dealing."[91] In later life, Flagg bought and sold real estate, investing in and eventually owning over sixty Worcester tenements and 1,000 acres of county land.[92] He became the wealthiest man in town.

His neighbors honored his achievements by choosing him to hold their highest offices, as his biographer noted, "a remarkable tribute on the part of his fellow townsmen to his ability and good judgment, such as few men in any town of the Commonwealth have ever received."[93] But what people remembered the most was his constant industry, his resourcefulness, his determined striving. When he died, his obituary announced, "Levi Lincoln Flagg Ends 87 Years Work." It seemed only death released him from the obligation to improve his opportunities.

Lincoln Flagg was no different from the White sons or Caleb Crossman in wanting more than traditional farming offered, but he achieved his goals without leaving the land. His journey was not geographical so much as mental: like Charles White or Caleb Crossman, he preferred competitive striving to communal competence. His was not a family farm, but a commercial enterprise; his local relations were not of interdependence, but of mastery. He met the opportunities of his age with ambition and zealously pursued his own good.

Caroline White—Dutiful Dreamer

Caroline White, the eighth of Aaron and Mary's offspring, was torn between two worlds. Bright and inquisitive, she actively pursued the knowledge that she believed would enlarge her mind and fit her for greater usefulness in the world. And there were things from that greater world that she wanted —both experiences and material goods—that she could achieve only if she could earn her way to independence. Yet her heart was most stubbornly rooted in her home soil; she felt deeply her obligations to serve her parents and to nurture the bonds of family ties. As her siblings one by one left to seek their fortunes, Caroline's steadfast devotion to family anchored their hearts, at least, to "the old home place." Of our six subjects, it is Caroline who most clearly demonstrates the tension between communal/familial values and individual ambition.

Caroline stayed at home partly because her parents needed her household labor. Once elder sister Elizabeth wed in 1832, Caroline had the only able set of hands available to assist her mother with the household affairs. (Sister Mary helped when she could, but she was infirm—suffering from an unspecified disorder, possibly consumption—that limited her usefulness.) Despite the family's relative gentility, the Whites were a *farm* family, and farmwomen had heavy responsibilities. Caroline's letters and Mary's diary record the yearly round of cleaning, scouring, and putting up food, along with the weekly tasks of laundry, baking, and dairying and the ceaseless, year-round work of sewing and mending the extended family's clothing. Haying season was particularly stressful, as she confessed to Charles, "Father having to take care of the old farm makes rather more work in the house. We have had three hired men a week or two past, and shall continue to have, I suppose, for some time whenever the weather is fair."[94] The live-in help particularly added to Caroline's laundry duties, making Monday wash days exhausting. Caroline excused her rambling thoughts in a letter to Charles one August evening with the simple explanation, "the reason is it is Monday evening and I feel rather tired."[95] To household duties were added neighborly obligations, as Caroline was frequently sent to take her mother's place sitting up with the sick or assisting in times of trouble. When Mr. Cotton died in November 1843, Mary noted that Caroline went to assist them, lodging two days with the family to lend support and assist with the burial.

As a single adult female, Caroline was constantly called upon to aid her married sister Elizabeth with her young family in Worcester. When young nephew Myron fell into the fire and was badly burned, Aaron wrote to Charles that they had sent Caroline to Worcester to aid the family.[96] In 1840, when her nephew "Franky" turned two, Caroline was sent to fetch the boy from his mother in Worcester and tend to him in Boylston for a month while he "unlearned some earlier habits" (weaning or toilet training).[97] Whenever Elizabeth had a baby, a sick child, a move from one house to another, or any other stressful event, Caroline was sent for—and she always complied.[98]

But Caroline had dreams of her own. She had a good mind, and she wanted to improve it. From the time she was in her early teens she managed to get away for occasional semesters at private academies. This schooling was in addition to her attendance at the center schoolhouse (when household duties permitted—she occasionally admitted to her brother that "as I have to stay at home so much, I think I shall go [to school] but little longer"), as well as private lessons from itinerant reading and writing masters.[99] And she read, voraciously.

All this learning helped Caroline form a mind of her own, and she was not afraid to express her opinions within the security of family, though she frequently qualified her forceful statements with appropriately humble comments about her general ignorance as a female. In May 1837, during the onset of the panic of 1837, Caroline explained to Charles her astute (and rather accurate) opinion on the cause of the current economic woes:

It appears to me that for a number of years past, the whole nation has been madly bent on speculating and living on credit; but credit without cash, will not stand many years, and now credit has expired, those who have lived on it, must fall. Southern planters, a year or two since, bought a vast number of slaves on credit, expecting their cotton crops would pay principal & interest for slaves, and leave a handsome fortune besides; but instead, they raised so much, that cotton fell in price, and they were left greatly in debt; so that they could not pay the northern merchants and manufacturers their dues, then they failed. Thus there was one source of the troublous times, and it has caused a most disastrous train of evils. I suppose that all might be accounted for, in a somewhat similar fashion, though Gen. Jackson and his constituents, have a great share attributed to them. . . . But I will close my long speech about that, [of] which I am very ignorant.[100]

Caroline read the city newspapers regularly and felt an attraction to the cosmopolitan world they portrayed. She romanticized life in what she called the "bustling metropolis" and tended to gently disparage the small-town world of home. As she told Charles, "the letter which I received from you . . . gratified me much, and I must say as an apology for my dull scrawls, that situated as you are, in the very focus of news, you ought to have more to amuse and interest than I, who live in such a place, that scarcely a single ray reached here straight. I am sure I have nothing to say now."[101] She loved to travel, and her parents allowed her to make rounds visiting her siblings and relatives in Boston and Roxbury, Providence, and Middlebury, Vermont.

But what did Caroline want from life? She had a soul both deeply religious and deeply romantic, and her letters occasionally reveal the yearnings of her heart:

Last night as if in preparation for the day of rest, a gentle breeze dispersed the clouds and dried from the face of the earth the excess of moisture. When the sun went down the scene was truly glorious; the clearness of its departure was beautifully displayed on all the works of nature. The different shades of the green leaves showed the character of the plants or their advancement this season, the raindrops glistened on all, the singing of the birds was rich harmony for the mind as well as ear, every thing about us was radiant with the smile of God. Oh, if the polluting waves of sin had not rolled over it, this earth would be a Paradise. To make a right improvement of these blessings which are flung around us with an unsparing hand, we must "look through nature up to nature's God." We ought to feel His presence every where and whilst we feel, let us love, & adore him. . . . Let us live soberly & gladly in this present world.[102]

How was Caroline to "make a right improvement" of her blessings? There is some suggestion that at one point she considered marriage. She was certainly engaged in following the marital prospects of others. Many of her letters lead off with announcements of who had "changed her name and station," or rumors about her siblings' potential romantic attachments, to which she always bound Charles to the *strictest secrecy* lest she be accused of gossip. In fact, Caroline did indulge in matrimonial gossip, sometimes with an edge: "Miss Sophia S. Bond came to Boylston week before last to astonish the natives (as Cousin Catharine Bent used to say). She was in company with Lambert Lamson, thus publicly announcing a matrimonial engagement with the aforesaid gentleman. As soon as the house is fitted for her reception, I expect she will consent to have the noose (or rather her heart) securely fastened around his heart or purse as it is uncertain which possessed the strongest attraction. Nancy Crossman is published to a Mr. Parker of Shirley. Your quondam friend Joshua, alias Sanford K[endall] has dissolved all intentions of partnership with Miss H.L[?] Billings, no good reason assigned. I believe he said he did not think she would wish to wait seven years, the time he expects to devote to study, but *she* did not say so."[103]

As for Caroline's own heart, there is some suggestion that at one point it was devoted to the Whites' live-in hired help, the "real eleven fellow," Levi Lincoln Flagg. The situation would have been natural, as Lincoln was a much-loved member of the family for two years when both he and Caroline were in their mid-twenties. Lincoln escorted Caroline to a neighbor's wedding and accompanied her to Doctor Andrews's, "where a company of singers met to sing."[104] Most tellingly, Francis complained to his brother that "Caroline I suppose has found some one for whom she feels a greater interest," and thus was no longer sending him her regular long missives.[105] Sadly for Caroline's hopes, another Caroline entered the picture and stole Lincoln's heart. Caroline Barnes, a young lady from neighboring Berlin, came to board with the Whites while going to school with their neighbor, Sally

Cotton.[106] The eligible young Lincoln now lived with two likely Carolines; he chose the latter. Caroline White remained single for the rest of her life.

As her siblings and friends married or moved away from Boylston, Caroline was left with two pressing concerns: how was she to "improve her sphere of usefulness" and how was she to gain some economic independence? There were things she desired—books, pens, paper, special fabrics and threads, hairbrushes, and apothecary lotions—and she was keenly aware that there were limits to how often she could apply to her father for assistance. She complained to Charles of being "poverty struck." Caroline wanted a job.

In the summer of 1838, she accepted a position as mistress of a one-room school in Worcester. It is clear from her letters to Charles that she disliked the job. She regaled Charles with humorous sketches of what she called her voluntary prison:

> The seats & desks are placed in undivided rows, which makes me a great deal of trouble, for nothing is easier for those who wish to play than to slide along a little way, as it were by the attraction of cohesion . . . ; no birch fences I have made has altogether prevented this business. Then such a mob, (for I can think of no other title just now) as I have to manage. I have had thirty-three different scholars since I commenced, but average only thirty a day. No motive I can present will make some of them study, but they are full of tricks (as we say). If they can contrive to [lure] a sheep, or a dog, into the house, they consider it a far greater exploit, than if they mastered some difficult sum in Arithmetic. Occasionally I find frogs hopping about on the floor, then again, I hear some old cat mewing in a corner. As we are situated so near the woods, we are abundantly supplied with moschetoes. One day I observed one of my largest boys very busily engaged, and having the curiosity to ascertain what it was so occupied his attention, I discovered that he had cut a hole in the top of his desk, and out of a chip, he had made a sliding lid for it; this he was filling with mutilated moschetoes. Now from the specimens I have presented you, should you think I had any one who would make any improvement? But I have some, who seem trying to gain some useful knowledge.[107]

"Moschetoes" or no, Caroline's greatest difficulty with the job was that it required her to board away from home. She confessed that had she not been able to spend Sundays with her sister Elizabeth's family in Worcester, she did not know how she would have coped.

The attraction of the job, of course, was that Caroline was paid in cash. Caroline also made some "honest cash" tending a neighbor's silkworms, braiding straw to trade for cash or credits at a West Boylston store, and binding shoes for Caleb Crossman and Benjamin Houghton. Shoe binding was a rigorous task that required the strength to work a barrel stave clamp with one's knees and strong, dexterous hands to work the leather with awl and needle. Historians have assumed that only poorer, married women, desperate to augment family income without leaving the home, did it.[108] "Poor" may have been in the mind of the binder, though, for Caroline, daughter of one of the wealthiest men in town, bound cases of shoes from 1837 through 1842. As Caroline explained to her brother, "I have been trying to find employment whereby I might earn something at home," adding that the current haying season made other work impossible.[109] For her labors, Caroline was likely paid two to six cents a pair, about half what a hired man could earn in the fields. But it was *cash*, cash that she could use for her own desires.[110]

Caroline wanted to be *useful* and to gain some economic independence, but she wanted to do so within the sphere of her family. In 1841, she asked Charles, "Is it not too bad that the customs of society forbid you and I setting up business together like [cousins] George and Avery? . . . I think too you and I should hitch horses very well. I am afraid Frank & I would have some arguments about who should hold the reins and it would not be quite so pleasant riding."[111] We cannot know if Caroline ever truly considered setting up a business, but clearly her desire to "hitch horses" with family members was genuine.

In fact, Caroline eventually assumed the role of the family teamster, hitching all her siblings together through her constant letters, visits, and family nurture. In 1846 she inherited some money of her own, granting her the degree of independence she desired. Now in her thirties, Caroline devoted herself to the care of her aging parents, and eventually her widowed mother, for the next fifteen years. She found her usefulness in her role as daughter, sister, aunt, and neighbor.[112] Her choice blended an ancient female role with a new one: weaving the threads of family affection into a new fabric of social relationship, one suitable for a highly mobile, otherwise independent generation. Caroline White was a bridge from an old world to a new. One senses time and again Caroline's ambivalent desires to cross that bridge herself.

NONE OF THESE young Boylstonians followed in his or her parents' footsteps. Some viewed their parents with nostalgic reverence while discarding their patriarchal, family-farm values. Others outright rejected—abandoned even—parents and paternal heritage, shedding the parochial world of their youth for genteel middle-class lives. Their lives reached far beyond the borders of Boylston and linked them through business, mission, or voluntary association to a wider world mostly unknown to their parents.

Navigating this wider world required these young people to master new forms of relating and to establish new sources of independence. The familiar and communal dispositions of an intensely local, kin-based, and custom-bound life on the land did not suit in their new lives. This generation had to create for themselves new identities as citizens of a less predictable, more impersonal and cosmopolitan world. They strove to survive outside the protective order of family government or master-apprentice relations; to rely not on inherited land, but on self-mastery and creative adaptation; to fashion identities based on culture and consumption, rather than on local custom and belonging; to embrace their mission to boldly go where no woman had gone before. They made a generational declaration of independence; they cultivated, as did their contemporary Emerson, self-reliance.[113]

CHAPTER FIVE

Useful Knowledge

In 1793, Boylston schoolteacher Robert Thomas turned his attention heavenward to discern how to manage his farm. He was seeking guidance, not divine but astrological. Following venerable folklore, he believed that the stars and moon influenced earthly nature; seeds sprouted more readily if planted under the pull of a full moon and tubers sank their roots deeper, faster if planted under a waning moon. The heavens told when to fell trees or peel their bark, geld horses, and breed sows.[1] Thomas gathered astrological lore, pared it with astronomical calculations of lunar phases, eclipses, and tides, and made uncannily accurate weather predictions. That year, he published the first edition of *The [Old] Farmer's Almanack*, with the pithy wit and anecdotes that have kept the work in publication to this day.[2]

Boylston's almanac publisher may appear quaintly old-fashioned, but he was actually quite progressive. To be sure, he still relied on folklore, but to a much greater degree he was urging farmers to improve custom with science. His almanac blended medieval astrology and Renaissance astronomy, but also incorporated the advances of English Enlightenment scientists. He sought the universal laws of nature and attempted to apply them to improve yields and breeds, soil and feed. And, perhaps most critically, Thomas joined those others who sought to disseminate this new knowledge through printing—not abstruse texts but an accessible vernacular literature that would lift the common man to a better plane.

Many came to share this compulsion to study, to learn, to improve during the 1820s and 1830s. The movement gained strength with the spread of publishing, private academies, and rural associations for learning. This extraordinary cultural efflorescence heralded a "village enlightenment," a time when some rural folk swept aside the rustic ways of country custom for rational investigation and sophisticated sensibilities.[3] Their belief that ordinary farmers and their families could rise through learning signified the waning of cultural authority of clerical and gentry elite: broader access to learning democratized knowledge. Learning, rather than aristocratic birth or received wisdom, could be the basis for a new social order. This was very much a part of the same desire for improvement that had ordered Boylston's town green with fences and shade trees, raised a granite Greek Revival town hall (granite being the preferred stone of neoclassical Republicans), and founded a local library.[4] The White family and their village neighbors were among the leaders of this movement.

They could not foresee how their striving would transform their community. Old hierarchies gave way. Some resisted this new learning as putting on uppity airs, while others saw it as a way to challenge established authority. Those who pursued new knowledge discovered new worlds. There was an internal world of imagination and self-reflection that grew from engagement with books. There was an intermediate world of local friends with shared sensibilities, an exclusive enterprise of ideas and affective bonds. And there was a brave new world of cosmopolitan connections, an imagined worldwide community of those who shared the same books and explored the same ideas.

Thomas was not Boylston's only innovator. In the 1820s, his neighbor David C. Murdock went into business producing and marketing some of the nation's early globes and orreries, instruments that illustrated the movements of the solar system.[5] The advance was symbolic as well as scientific: Thomas had been concerned with understanding the forces that controlled the earth beneath his feet, while Murdock was concerned with understanding—and interacting with—a much broader world. Such expansive horizons revolutionized local experience of distance and connection.[6] As we will discover, this turn to the wider world left many yearning for reassuring personal bonds to family and an intimate circle of friends. Local learning redefined belonging and refashioned relationships. And it raised a ruckus.

"Common" Schools

"I go to school and study a little and sit with Lincoln Flagg. He is a very good steady fellow to sit with. We have a pretty large school and have a good time of it and we should have more play out of doors if the snow was not so deep. We have a first rate of a master. I never went to one that I liked so well. . . . I wrote this in school midst of the noise and bustle of about eighty scholars and I would not write so well as I could in some other place but if you can read it I do not care."[7]

So sixteen-year-old Francis White wrote to his brother Charles in 1840, reporting on the winter session of Boylston's center district school. He studied a little, but amid the noise and bustle of eighty scholars—ranging in age from three to twenty-one—Francis was more concerned with having a good time. His narration calls to mind nostalgic illustrations of the rustic one-room schoolhouse, carefree barefoot boys, and the three Rs. That homey, age-of-homespun image obscures the reality: the process of getting an education was in the midst of a prolonged but profound transformation during these years. In 1831, one local squire noted approvingly that "at the present time some of the inhabitants of this town have caught the generous spirit that is now beginning to pervade this Commonwealth on the all important subject of a more general diffusion of knowledge amongst the rising generation, and it is confidently hoped that the few who are alive to this subject will infuse their own zeal into the breasts of others, till there shall be a general attention to the improvement of our district schools."[8]

This was the prevailing belief in antebellum New England: for whatever was ailing, education was the tonic. Civic leaders claimed that it was essential for the newly enfranchised to be literate, informed, and morally grounded in order to maintain a virtuous republic. Religious denominations promoted curricula and textbooks to advance biblical literacy—and sectarian interests. The region's artisans and their advocates hoped that generous access to "useful knowledge" would secure their status among the respectable and independent middle class and allow New England to avoid the class system of industrializing Old England. Social reformers hoped that immigrants could be brought into the mainstream of New England culture. "Free School" proponents believed that public education would transform a diverse people into a unified nation. Anxious parents hoped that book learning might prepare their offspring for a changing economic world. And the children of farmers who aspired to middle-class status hoped to learn their way into a world of refined sensibilities.[9] All agreed: in a time of shifting economic opportunities, fluid social structure, and unfamiliar moral terrain, customary ways and communal norms were no longer reliable guideposts. What was needed was the self-discipline of a well-stocked mind and a well-formed character. Education was the answer.

As is often the case when a community debates the best ways to socialize its children, this period of transition was marked with intense conflict. Some parents worried that too much learning would make children lazy or too proud to submit to their less-educated elders. Others jealously feared that their children would not get *enough* of this newly valuable commodity. Neighbors argued over authority, control, content, and access to learning opportunities. If education was the answer, Boylstonians still had many anxious questions: who should learn and how, how much and what, to what end? And what, indeed, might be the consequences of all this advanced education and self-improvement? Schooling became a lightning rod for contention.

MASSACHUSETTS HAD quite early on required towns to provide a schoolmaster to teach its children to read and write. The obligation applied to the town only; schooling was not compulsory until 1852, and parents sent their children—or kept them home to work—at will. Boylston, like most towns, met its obligation by keeping district schools, one-room schoolhouses serving the four corners of town and the center village. Each district school offered two terms of instruction, both tied to the labor needs of family farming. Winter term usually began after Thanksgiving, when the harvest was over, and ran for twelve weeks. The summer term began after spring planting and generally ran till haying time (early July). The curriculum focused on the vernacular skills of reading, writing, and ciphering that farm folk needed to study their Bible, transact their business, and keep their accounts. Everyone knew that the most important knowledge—how to run a farm—would be transmitted by their elders at home. Responsibility for hiring masters, stocking the schoolhouse with wood, and overseeing end-of-term examinations was vested in an elected school committee drawn from the farm community.

Late in his life, Deacon Henry Brigham recalled teaching in the center district school in the 1830s, where his average class consisted of eighty pupils, "from the little tot of four years old to the stalwart young men and ladies of twenty-one years of age."[10] The atmosphere within the schoolhouse, with so much reciting and instruction going on simultaneously, was truly one of "noise and bustle," as Francis described. One former Boylston schoolmaster wrote of the difficulties that faced even the male teachers: "The winter terms were always taught by men, and as they were attended by pupils, especially young men who had reached, and in some instances passed, the age of majority, it often required not only a great amount of tact and resolution, but of physical strength and ability on the part of the master to discipline and control the troublesome element that would sometimes manifest itself. A successful Schoolmaster of those old-time district schools was considered something of an athlete in strength and movement."[11] Caroline White, writing to her brother Charles in 1840, agreed. She reported on the trials of the district schoolmaster, a contemporary and friend of Charles's: "Mr. Sanford M. Kendall has finished school keeping for this season; he closed with very little ceremony; the majority of the inhabitants of that district were much prejudiced against him; three or four of the larger scholars were determined to be rebellious and make disturbances. After trying various methods to oust him from the schoolhouse, they hit upon one at last which proved successful; they entirely closed up the chimney and fairly smoked him out."[12]

Despite these conditions, the town's school committee in the 1820s and 1830s began to require more of their schoolmaster. It was not enough that he control his large and motley assemblage, teach each according to his or her level to read and parse, spell and write, and calculate and recite by rote. During the winter term, a few advanced pupils at the center school were to be offered Latin and French, algebra, geometry, trigonometry, and even "mental and natural philosophy." Other changes were in store, most notably in the arrival of new—and ultimately controversial—school texts.

For generations local parents had been satisfied if their children mastered the elements of the iconic *New England Primer*, a biblically based Puritan speller. The town did not provide schoolbooks, so children were accustomed to bringing whatever texts their parents might have at home. If they had none, they fashioned handmade blank books out of scrap paper into which they copied mathematical theorems and problems, grammar rules, and sample letters or lines for orthography lessons.[13] However, by the 1830s, the explosion in print offered new alternatives to humble homemade copybooks, well-worn primers, and Webster's patriotic blue-backed speller. Here was potent chemistry: new print technology mixed with varied ideas about improvement, heated to the boiling point by sectarian conflict. The result was a ruckus in the classroom.

In 1837, Phineas Ball brought to school a professionally printed copybook with exercises that promised "plain rapid writing" and "practical arithmetic as it occurs in ordinary business."[14] It was hot off the press, the latest thing in school texts. Into his copybook the fourteen-year-old Phineas copied letters and numbers and practiced writing such useful terms as "demand," "paid," his signature, and the names of friends. He sketched surveying images for rivers, roads, or lakes, and he refined his handwriting by copying set lines such as, "Vanity and presumption ruins many a promising youth," and, "Have your attention always directed to something useful."

Hidden among the commonplaces of Phineas Ball's seemingly innocuous schoolbook, however, is evidence of a simmering controversy. His teacher had set him to copy a poem called "The Housebuilder," about a man who procrastinated in building his house until death provided him a permanent "home of clay." The poem was an eighteenth-century Russian piece, known

to Phineas's schoolmaster because Boston minister John Pierpont had selected it for inclusion in his 1826 school text, *The American First Class Book.*
Pierpont had not made his selections idly, as he explained in his preface,
but had chosen works that would be approved "by those, in every part of
our country, who are attentive to the national, moral and religious sentiments contained in the books that are used by their children while learning
to read, and while their literary taste is beginning to assume something of
the character which it ever afterward retains."[15]

John Pierpont was concerned that schoolbooks reflect correct "national,
moral, and religious sentiment," but as a Boston minister in the 1820s, his
notion of moral and religious correctness was inevitably shaped by sectarian concerns. A leading Unitarian, he designed his schoolbook to counter
the biblically based, Calvinistic school texts that had long dominated school
instruction. He wished to shape Christian characters in ways "more suited
to the American Republic . . . and less obnoxious to complaint," that is, less
imbued with specifically biblical or Calvinist sentiments.[16] It is not surprising that the schoolmaster in Phineas Ball's school who chose this text was
himself selected by Lambert Lamson, a school committeeman who was also
a leading citizen of Unitarian sympathies.

Pierpont had powerful coworkers in his struggle to impose standardized
non-Calvinist texts and statewide "nonsectarian" teacher training. In 1837,
Unitarian Horace Mann was appointed the first head of a newly established
Massachusetts State Board of Education. The stated goal was to upgrade and
standardize public education, but included in that agenda was the demand
that all public education be nonsectarian, a veiled attempt to counter the
influence of Calvinism in the schools. Orthodox clergy fought this change.
In 1840, they struggled unsuccessfully to abolish the Board of Education,
fearing that the board's supposedly nondivisive, nondenominational moral
instruction would "breed Unitarians, or worse, nonbelievers."[17] (By then, at
least, the orthodox had a powerful new weapon: the 1836 *McGuffey's Eclectic
Reader,* the work of a Presbyterian minister and generously endowed with
Bible passages; it was destined to become the nation's most popular and enduring schoolbook.)

This external battle over God's place in school fed Boylston's home-grown
conflict. For years, the town had annually nominated and elected without
incident five school committeemen—one for each district—as well as three
examiners. In the sectarian conflict of the 1820s, however, little passed town
meeting without conflict. The minister, as the town's most educated citizen,
had traditionally chaired the committee to examine schools, but when Uni-

tarian Ward Cotton was dismissed in 1825, the town began a protracted battle over control of the examining and school committees. It was essentially a battle for control of moral instruction in Boylston.

Each passing year these issues and appointments became more controversial. In 1827, elections were postponed, and then an examining committee of one Unitarian, one Congregationalist, and an unaffiliated church member was elected. In 1828, Unitarian Reverend Cotton was chosen to examine, but the following year, Congregationalist Reverend Russell was elected (prompting Captain Howe's profane outburst). In 1830, the town voted to let each district choose its own school agents, but that vote was then reconsidered and overturned, a process repeated the next two years. The town tried electing school committeemen by show of hands, by ballot, and by "a union ticket from the different religious societies," but no proposal succeeded in restoring peace. For the next decade, the choice of school committee and examiners raised tensions and tried tempers at every annual town meeting.[18] Their struggle represented the greater contest over the use of the Bible, or of nonsectarian teachings, in the school. Would Phineas Ball parse, "In Adam's fall, we sinned all," or, "Hypocrisy is injurious to society generally?"[19]

These were not idle questions. Behind them lay a struggle for control and a debate over authority in the schools. Schools had always played a significant role in shaping moral values. Mann's attempt to impose uniformity and control values from without was fiercely contested. Factions in town disputed every aspect of education: lines of parsing, textbooks, who should choose schoolmasters, and how students should be examined all were debated. Evangelical orthodox Protestants saw biblically based elementary education as essential to the salvation of the nation; literacy was a tool for advancing Bible study, Sabbath schools, tract societies, and conversion. Even the most improvement-driven, striving Evangelicals hewed to scripture-based texts as the essential foundation of betterment. Unitarians resisted, seeking to open the classroom to textbooks and curricula grounded in secular concerns for ethical improvement. The battle was evidence that Boylston had lost consensus on moral authority.[20]

NOT ALL THE TENSION surrounding town schools originated in sacred concerns; Boylstonians also battled over how educational resources should be divided. In the economic turmoil of these decades, parents were concerned that their children be properly equipped for the chancy competition of a market society. Reading, writing a fine hand, and ciphering were increasingly seen as essential skills for commercial occupations. Rather quickly, the learning imparted in the noisy, bustling one-room schoolhouses became a hot commodity.

The town had traditionally allotted each district an equal share of tax revenues for schooling expenses. Each district's agent had the same funds available to hire a schoolmaster, pay his room and board, and supply firewood for the schoolhouse. In 1829, however, a year of intense local controversy, a motion was passed to alter the proportion of school money among the several districts. School agents were directed to prepare a census of scholars in their districts between the ages of four and twenty-one, so that in the future school monies could be divided according to the number of scholars. The census was duly taken, but the next year the motion to divide school funds proportionately was hotly debated. Opponents insisted that money should be divided between the districts according to what the people in that district paid in tax. The controversy continued throughout the decade, with various proposals of increasing complexity put forward. (In 1836 a motion was made that one-half of the funds should be equally divided, and one-half divided according to the number of scholars in each district. It was defeated.)

What was this battle about? For years Boylston had considered schooling a communal responsibility. All town youth, regardless of their parents' contribution in taxes, were to be allowed at least one term's schooling per year, and all households, whether they had school-age youth or not, were required to pay for support of the district schools in general.[21] This shared obligation was for the public good, intended to produce useful Christian servants. As long as family-taught skills and family-bequeathed land were the most important determinants of economic competence and social status, no one quarreled over how school funds were allotted. However, as classroom skills became more important for success in the nonfarming world, Boylston's parents became jealous of these resources. Competition emerged.

Strife over school funding is also evidence of rising tensions over an increasingly inequitable distribution of wealth in town. The problem was felt most intensely in the center district, where the White children attended school. As more stores opened around the green, and more town gentry such as Aaron White chose to build their mansion houses in the bustling center village, these families came to have, on average, more resources—and perhaps more ambitions—to lavish on their children. Soon upwardly aspiring parents from the outer districts such as Benjamin Houghton Sr. were petitioning town meeting to be allowed to have their children attend the center school, perhaps believing that study there would be more effective than among their rustic neighbors.[22] Resentment against the center district was most likely heightened in the turbulent years of 1829 and 1830, when a generous bequest funded a fine new town house in the center village, with the lower level designated as the new center district school. The rest of the town grumbled about this advantage, heaped on an already-advantaged district. At town meeting, debate erupted over a motion to provide two stoves for the building, one for the town hall and one for the school. Some protested: two stoves were too expensive! After much argument, it was voted to procure a stove for the school only, but this vote provoked such outrage it was quickly overturned. It was then voted to procure a stove for the town hall only; the center district scholars in their frigid granite schoolroom would have no stove.[23] (After a bitterly cold winter session, the town consented the following January to procure a school stove.)

Education in Massachusetts had always been an intensely local concern. The town exercised considerable authority: local men procured mostly local teachers to prepare town offspring to be useful town citizens. By the 1830s, external factors were encroaching on local concerns: the state began to take over some of the authority that had once belonged to towns alone. From 1838 on, Horace Mann's State Board of Education increasingly directed—or meddled in—the choice of textbooks, the training of teachers, and the collection of school data. Local schools were no longer wholly independent, and Boylstonians were aware that they now ran their schools in conjunction with the state. After 1838, town meeting passed school articles "agreeable to a provision contained in a section of an Act passed by the Legislature." Whether, in fact, the town was agreeable to these acts we do not know, but they were certainly aware that they were now liable to observe them.

The federal government also made its presence felt in local schools after the Surplus Distribution of 1837. Andrew Jackson's fiscal policies, and especially receipts from western land sales and tariffs, had produced an unprecedented and politically embarrassing surplus in government revenue. In April 1836, the federal government authorized a temporary distribution of the surplus revenue to the states, and in 1837 Massachusetts disbursed these funds to the towns. Many towns devoted the whole to improving local district schools; Boylston dedicated a significant portion to repairing schoolhouses, using the rest to retire town debt.[24] It was the first time Boylston had received direct government aid for education, and it must have deepened the townspeople's sense that their local common schools were no longer wholly local.

By the late 1830s, then, Boylstonians were debating new questions: What would be taught and by whom? Would all children receive a common education, or would districts be distinguished by the resources of area farmers? Who would have the authority to make decisions regarding curriculum, texts, methods, teacher qualifications, and credentials? Did the responsibility—and the power—to oversee these decisions rest with the townsfolk or the state? As Boylston contested these questions, townspeople's personal ambitions, jealousies, and varied religious views combined with external forces to reshape local schools. Competitive concerns to advance personal interest and sectarian views overwhelmed the commonness of common schools.

Improving the Opportunity to Learn

Like many of the aspiring local gentry, the White family did not limit their education to the offerings of their center district school. They were active participants in the village enlightenment. They improved every opportunity to gain useful knowledge, to form their characters through reading and discussion, to enlarge their understanding of the world as an ongoing act of *self-education.*

The breadth of their educational activities—reading; attending lectures, exhibitions, and concerts; touring institutions and museums; private tutoring—reflected the inchoate state of formal education. There was no established educational path to the professions (other than the ministry), nor any recognized form of training for most emerging trades. Accumulating generally useful knowledge was the best preparation for "achieving a broad though difficult-to-measure goal of 'rise,' 'betterment,' 'fame,' or success.'"[25] To do that, the Whites supported their children in their efforts to cobble together an education from a range of local resources.

Not all the districts' schools had their sessions at the same time, and some students—especially those whose fathers could afford extra hired help on the farm—supplemented their own district schooling by attending some weeks in the common schools of other districts. Thus, Mary White records in the early 1830s that youngsters Charles and Francis attended the south district school for a month before the winter session opened in the center district. When no district school was in session, the Whites sometimes sent their teenage children—both boys and girls—to be tutored individually. Caroline and Mary studied intermittently with a Miss Nelson. Caroline recited lessons with Reverend Sanford, and Francis spent several seasons working one-on-one in the minister's study; both were likely refining their Latin and Greek in preparation for higher studies.

In the early 1830s, when local enthusiasm for useful knowledge was rising, townsfolk began to offer private classes for those who could afford the tuition. Reverend Cotton's daughter Sally kept "Miss Cotton's School" in her father's home, which catered to the youngest students. Charles and Francis went to school with Miss Cotton in 1828 when they were six and eight years old, respectively. A decade later, Mary's four-year-old grandson Myron Conant came to live with the family while attending Miss Cotton's school.

By the late 1830s, the town supported four private schools to supplement the common-school offerings. Boylston allowed the free use of the district schoolhouses, and those parents who could afford the tuition of about $1.75 per term sent their children by the week or the term. Not all were happy with this development. A local observer noted, "One disadvantage of this system . . . of supplementing the work of the town school with a private school, was that it gave the children of wealthier and more affluent people, who were able to pay the cost of tuition for their children, an unequal and undue opportunity and advantage over the poor ones who were unable to meet the additional cost of tuition and instructions."[26] Contemporaries noted with concern that "the children of one family are often all distinguished for good scholarship, while those of another family are exceedingly deficient in this respect."[27] Tuition schools highlighted growing economic inequality.

The White children also attended—and taught—special evening classes in spelling and writing. In an age when American spellings were only beginning to become standardized (Webster's mammoth two-volume *American Dictionary of the English Language* was published in 1828), mastering genteel and correct spelling, rather than phonetic or colloquial, was a mark of learned refinement. Mary White regularly noted her children's attendance at evening spelling schools, particularly in the cold winter months. William White took the winter quarter off from his studies at Williams College in 1837 and 1838 and opened a school for training in penmanship and writing in the family home. His "classes" were likely held in one of the front rooms, with his charges seated around Mary's parlor table, practicing their cursive with William's example and corrections. His sister reported that the two-month school, whose students included his own younger brother Francis, was a success.[28] That success was due to local demand for a refined hand and a well-turned phrase.

In this dawning age of clerks and commerce, a fine hand was considered an essential skill for any properly trained professional man. In one letter, Aaron urged Charles to perfect his penmanship: "[Fine writing is essential] for a man of business, yet it may at least be said that it is highly ornamental. I have always thought that it was natural for my boys to acquire the art of handsome writing and I have no doubt that with a little attention and practice you will be able to show as fair specimens as any one of them which will be no small praise."[29] But it was not professional aspirations alone that filled the desks at William's school. Writing masters such as William were also patronized by youth of both sexes who saw a fine hand as a mark of gentility. In previous generations, only aristocratic ladies and gentlemen had the time and resources to perfect the graceful Chancery script of the Italian Renaissance. Now, the aspiring middle class in America pursued this art as proof of their own claim to gentility.

When perfected, penmanship was to be put to use for another emerging middle-class passion: letter writing. Once a pastime of nobility and scribes, letters were now self-consciously exchanged by middle-class writers as marks of their qualifications for polite society. Because the letter writers thought of their epistles as presentations of themselves, they strove to produce beauty not only of penmanship but also of expression.[30] Writing masters helped their students perfect their epistolary composition, penmanship, and spelling. The letters sent to Charles by his siblings reflect their concern with mastering this art. "I am glad to find that you express yourself so easily and there is nothing I can see in the way to your becoming a finished letter writer and that is not a contemptible attainment," wrote elder sister Elizabeth.[31] Charles's sister Mary expressed her embarrassment at her own poor letter-writing skills. "I am much obliged to you for the letter received from you though I must say the compliments it contained did more to credit your partiality than your judgment. I am altogether unused to the business (as your letter intimates and as indeed I am for I write to you as often as to any one) letter writing seems a formidable task. Though the improvement which you have made in the art since leaving home at times almost induces me to adopt your plan of practicing to see if I can attain any degree of ease in the occupation; . . . I hope you will continue to favor me with letters from you which I highly prize."[32] Sister Caroline belittled her own abilities by signing herself "Madame Mistake Blot" and "Caroline Scratcher." "Francis thinks it will be a blot on my name to send such a scribble as this but you know I have passed the reach of slander in that respect. If ever you pick this out it must be at odd intervals of leisure the ensuing season." "My letter, I think, resembles that portion of a newspaper which comes under the head of miscellaneous, where you will find wonderful discoveries. Steam boat accident, Mammoth pumpkin, and horrid murder all in a string, as if you tried to see what a jumble you could make." "I have written in great haste & nearly covered a sheet of paper with poor nonsense, which I am afraid you will never be able to read, but if you cannot, get no one to assist you nor let any one see this, if you have any compassion for the credit of your sister, Caroline." "My pen & ink have been good emblems of my brain all the way through. One is cracked halfway up the quill, the other is as thick as mud."[33]

As family and friends became more mobile, letter writing proved an essential link in the chain of childhood love and memory. A badly written letter, as much as being a disgraceful presentation of self, could also be interpreted as a lack of affection.[34] Caroline and Mary were quick to reassure their brother that the shortfall lay in their abilities, and not in their love. "Don't you sometimes feel ashamed, vexed, provoked with me, for sending you such ragged, dirty, stingy little bits of paper after you have supplied me with good paper, at a very cheap rate? Now you must not ascribe it all to my closeness that I do so, but put the best construction on it, as I do, viz, it is in good taste: it corresponds throughout, the ideas, the penmanship, & the paper. . . . [T]hese little weekly scraps I trust you always destroy as soon as you have deciphered them."[35]

MARY AND AARON WHITE also paid tuition to send their children to evening "reading schools."[36] These classes improved facility with the mechanics of reading, but more important they taught students to *engage* with their texts by writing commentaries, preparing essays to read aloud in class, and enlarging on a text by addressing questions that it raised.[37] Rural reading schools in New England's villages reflect a passionate new engagement with literacy: reading was seen as a liberating act of self making and patriotic duty of nation making. The demand was met by a surge of printed materials and the cultural organizations that promoted and consumed them in rural New England. The explosion in print culture helped democratize knowledge, which was now not only available to but also tailored to the tastes and needs of middling rural folk.[38] Aspiring parents, including successful rural farmers and merchants such as Aaron White, wanted their children to be well read. And now, there was so much more to read, and so many more people to read *with*.

The flood of print media into the countryside was praised as the way to prepare an informed citizenry of the new republic.[39] Extensive reading lifted a farmer's gaze from the earth he plowed to contemplate the heavens, stored his mind with the stuff of civilized society, linked him to his fellow countrymen in distant states, and formed his character for the challenges of self making and nation making. Of course, all that reading had other consequences as well. Widely shared print culture diminished the force of local habits and lore. It diffused local dialects and vernacular usages. It diluted customary authority.[40] It provided standardized models for taste and behavior, forged ties to distant, unfamiliar peoples, and heightened awareness of national and international events. It set the world—a newly comprehensible world displayed in David Murdock's models—in motion.

The White family believed wholeheartedly in the power of reading to form character and shape powers of independent judgment. Charles's parents and siblings urged him to devote his leisure hours to reading. Brother William instructed: "Read good books. You now probably enjoy the best opportunity to improve your mind which you will ever have. . . . Study when you read; by this I mean only that it be your aim to understand and comprehend the meaning of what you read. Do not compare your amount of knowledge by the number of pages which you turn over but by the variety and correctness of ideas with which you store your mind. Think upon what you read or hear that is important and so *make it a part of yourself*. This is the only way by which substantial advantage can be derived by reading. Your main business now is to learn, learn, learn."[41] William often repeated the advice, urging Charles to "persevere in your endeavour to acquire useful knowledge."[42] William usually focused on the practical benefits of reading for developing good habits for successful business. By attentive reading, William exhorted, Charles would build his store of useful ideas, strengthen his memory, discipline his mind, and learn attention to detail, perseverance, patience, and discernment. "I mention these things now for your improvement," William explained, "for you have just commenced your apprenticeship and the formation of habits which you will have through life."[43]

Sister Caroline also encouraged Charles to educate himself. But she was concerned less with the practical benefits of reading than with Charles's sacred duty to improve his mind that he might improve the world. "You wish to know my opinion respecting spending so much time in the cultivation of the mind. Your hours of leisure being limited, how can I best spend them? I suppose is your question. Is it right from [*sic*] me to devote that time to myself? & first I would ask, do you know of any way you could do more good with it. If so, then your present course is wrong, but remember, the soul or mind is yours to prepare for a higher, a nobler state of existence, & as the education is to commence here, it is the duty of each to use all the means in their power to enlarge its capacity for knowledge and if the heart is sanctified the effort will at the same time increase the usefulness and happiness of the individual."[44]

The White family women were equally determined to benefit from books.

Until they were married, daughter Elizabeth and niece Lucy Ann faithfully attended the "Reading Society." This female society met once a month to read aloud from a library of books they had jointly acquired; while they listened to and discussed the books, they sewed items to donate to charity.[45] We can imagine the young women, seated in painted parlor chairs as they read aloud and reflected, serious or sociable. Similar female reading societies —like modern book clubs—were springing up in other rural communities.

Elizabeth and Lucy Ann's reading society was likely patterned after the earlier Congregational women's society, in which women listened to biblical and devotional works while sewing for charity. But the latter-day reading society was different in several respects. If it was like its sister societies in other towns, it addressed secular as well as sacred texts, works of history, biography, travel literature, tales, and sketches. This reading was an act not of passive consumption but of active engagement. These women were encouraged, as scholar Mary Kelley has shown, to explore the ideas and "try on the personae they encountered in their texts, sample perspectives of authors and fellow readers and measure the relevance for their lives." In the process, they engaged in self-formation: having been exposed to a range of possibilities, they were able to choose their own "distinctive personality, a particular address to the world, a way of acting and thinking."[46] The young ladies' reading society, then, used books not only to gain useful knowledge and to discipline character but also to develop personal identity.

Despite their focus on the individual, these reading societies had a collective and expansive effect. These women forged a common intellectual world. They were a reading *community*. This subset of the town's females now shared cultural references and experiences that separated them from the rest of Boylston's women. Their reading habit gave them the freedom to choose where and from whom they would acquire their knowledge. Local esquires were no longer "the information gatekeepers for their neighbors."[47] Reading women could now draw directly from the source, a heady intoxicating draught.

ONE EDUCATIONAL INSTITUTION in Boylston during the 1830s was intended to embrace the entire community. The lyceum, a series of public lectures and debates, drew crowds throughout the 1830s to hear local men of repute speak on topics of useful knowledge. Lyceum lectures began first in Britain to elevate working-class men; they were introduced in the United States in 1826 in the nearby Worcester County town of Millbury, when Yale geologist Josiah Holbrook introduced these public lecture series as a form of "mutual education." Holbrook's goal was to bring scientific knowledge and other useful topics to mechanics and farmers, both to make them better in their occupations and to help them achieve independence and uplift in a socially mobile democracy.[48] Holbrook found Worcester County to be a fertile ground for sowing useful knowledge, and soon his idea of self-education through public lectures germinated in villages across the county.[49] By 1829 the Boston Mechanics' Lyceum was providing a series of self-help lectures, a library, and periodicals for eager learners. Lectures were open to all who could pay the minimal fee, and organizers adopted an ecumenical approach to encourage attendance by the whole community. Lyceum lectures in the 1830s were "free from the taint of violent proposals, free from the worrisome suggestions of agitators. . . . [They were] to be preserved untarnished from contact with sectarian and political and minority struggles."[50]

In Boylston, as in most towns in the 1830s, a local squire, lawyer, professor, or clergyman usually delivered the lyceum lecture. Most of the presenters listed in Mary's diary were men from Boylston or surrounding communities who were known to her. They delivered lectures on chemistry, electricity, Galvinism, phrenology, the wonders of microscopes, and—by far the most popular topic—astronomy. They also entertained their audiences with travel tales, such as a presentation on "Hindoo manners and customs, displaying paintings representing scenes and things in India."[51] Winter was Boylston's lyceum season, when evening lectures were delivered on neutral ground: in schoolhouses or in the town hall, but never in the meetinghouse.

It had been the goal of the lyceum's founders to unify and democratize the community by transcending social and sectarian divisions and making knowledge "readily accessible to the common man."[52] Did lyceum lectures have this effect in Boylston? Through the 1830s, it does appear that local lecture topics avoided controversial issues, providing one of the few social rituals in which diverse Boylston audiences could come together in peace. However, in evading controversial issues, the lyceum promoted the idea that it was acceptable to agree to disagree. For the purpose of civil discourse, people checked their partisan, sectarian, and political views at the door, essentially abandoning the town's ancient goal of consensus. Democratizing knowledge was also problematic. The lectures made general useful knowledge available to those who would attend. But who attended? In Boylston, our only record is from Mary's diary, who indicated that the *young* people in her family, and their socioeconomic peers, regularly attended the lyceum.[53] The same was true in other towns. Lyceum audiences in New England were young (mostly in their twenties or thirties), native born, from the middling classes, with strong personal, social, and cultural aspirations to rise. Farmers were underrepresented.[54] Perhaps, then, these lectures did not serve to democratize Boylston's increasingly diverse population, but to foster a collective cultural consciousness of one aspiring subset of the population. This self-selected set learned to distinguish themselves from the common population of farmers by cultivating knowledge rather than acres. They represented a new class, a middle class, with its own code of village respectability and refinement, transcending the rustic vernacular culture of the countryside. As they distinguished themselves in learning, they distinguished themselves from the unlearned.

The opportunities for extramural education in the 1830s were clearly plentiful, if not equally enjoyed. Those Boylstonians who invested time and money in private lessons, writing schools, reading societies, and lyceum lectures were responding to a variety of external forces, including newly available print culture, improved communications, market opportunities, and nation-making. But when we examine the choices made in Boylston, it is clear that this drive also came from within, from both a religious and a social imperative to awaken the soul, enlighten the mind, refine the character, and perfect society. In this quest, they created an elite subset of community, those who could read and write their way to betterment. And here lay yet another motivation to learning. As social order based on commonality and gentry leadership disintegrated, they constructed a new order based on the acquired attributes of knowledge and cultural refinement. Conforming to this code of behavior signaled respectability.[55] Learning was a form of self-improvement that elevated them morally and religiously, but also socially. The *better sort* were those with well-stored minds, tasteful sensibilities, genteel behavior and appearance; the *meaner sort* were those who were unable or unwilling to improve themselves, married to older vernacular patterns of unsophisticated communal sociability.

Private Academies

The town's most prosperous and aspiring families were not satisfied with local educational resources. Beginning in the early nineteenth century, a subset of local families began to patronize private rural academies.[56] One Boylstonian later recalled, "In the earlier New England times no higher schooling was supported by many of the towns other than the district schools, and if a pupil desired to obtain a higher education than the district school offered, or prepare for college entrance, it was necessary to supplement his district school education by attendance at an incorporated academy, of which there were many scattered throughout the county towns. A pupil who had attended academy was thought to possess a superior education."[57] For families like the Whites, such superior education improved prospects for advancement in a changing world. But for other rural folk, private academies jeopardized the very fabric of traditional family and community life by encouraging pride and privilege, competition and ambition, aversion to manual labor, separation from family and neighbors, and disrespect for parental authority. As one historian notes, "The entire spirit of the [private] schools ran counter to forms of established and still-vital family cohesion and [neighborly] mutuality."[58] They were, in short, a menace to customary relations and, not surprisingly, a source of conflict.

Between 1790 and 1830 private academies sprang up across the New England countryside. In the absence of public high schools, they would remain the primary source of rural higher education for a century.[59] The earliest were intended primarily to prepare youth for the ministry, imparting the ancient languages, literature, theology, and natural sciences needed for college admission while ostensibly promoting piety, religion, and morality.[60] In the early republic, however, rural gentry began to send more of their sons—including those with no clerical intentions whatsoever—off to academies. They reasoned that liberal studies would make liberal men, fitting the best and brightest for leadership. Some civic leaders hoped that rural academies would stimulate higher culture in the rustic countryside and elevate national over parochial identities. Mercantile associations, meanwhile, hoped that rural academies might offer the practical preparation rising youth would need to build a strong commercial base in the new nation.[61] Founders' goals—pious, patriotic, and practical—appealed to prosperous rural folk.

What did rural fathers get for their tuition? The broad curricula of these new schools reflected their broad goals, including ancient and modern languages, the arts of writing and speaking, logic, philosophy, theology, history and politics, mathematics, and the natural sciences. To this was added such practical instruction as penmanship, spelling, composition, elocution, bookkeeping, and teaching methods, and such ornamental arts as music, drawing, and calisthenics.[62] Students would emerge, it was hoped, with a democratized gentility: godly, sage, polished, and proficient, the hope of the new republic.

Some rural folk were not so sure. All this education took a father's workforce away from the fields. Some fretted that too much time spent with books was enervating, leading to physical debility or even insanity. Critics wondered aloud why farm children needed so much more learning than their parents and worried that all that study might make them "too inflated with a very little learning to return to the labor of the field."[63] All this learning made children more likely to question the customary knowledge their parents had garnered from experience, or to resist traditional devotion to farm and family order.

Others questioned whether these private institutions were not in fact privileging some above others, a serious concern in a young republic supposedly devoted to rooting out nefarious aristocratic practices. Private academies were publicly chartered corporations, and their charters were granted originally in the expectation that they would provide a *public good* by training ministers and increasing learning, virtue, and piety. As their purpose shifted, however, to providing those with the resources entrée to exclusive opportunities and positions of power, opponents began to argue that this was not public good, but private interest.[64]

And then there was the sin of pride. Traditional town schools kept order and prompted learning by the rod. Private academies introduced a new form of motivation: exciting individual students to excel. Schoolmasters spoke of emulation, of imitating the best qualities of admired model citizens, and they aroused this desire through competitions to demonstrate accomplishment and win distinction. Supporters praised emulation as positively superior to corporal punishment. But doubters protested that one could be distinguished only by being *better than* his peers, and that such competitive rivalry stirred prideful ambition. Academic exhibitions fostered, they complained, a self-promoting striving that ran counter to Calvinist submission and corporate well-being.[65] They did not serve the local community's common good. Exhibitions caused heated controversy in rural villages as zealous opponents resisted what they saw as "the works of the Devil."[66]

Aaron White may have shared these concerns. But ultimately he decided the advantages in opportunity overrode any threat to community and family. He gave his children the opportunity, should they so choose, to augment their piety, gentility, and useful knowledge at an academy. All but one of his ten children so chose; six sons and three daughters attended nine different rural academies in eastern and central Massachusetts, New Hampshire, and Vermont.[67]

Not one graduated. In this, they were typical of most academy students. Attendance was intermittent. Most rural youth spent only a term or two at private schools, as family resources and labor needs allowed.[68] Francis wrote Charles that he hoped one summer to go to Andover, but their father did not think he could spare him. The White children seem to have taken turns, with no more than two in private schools in any semester. Nor, if they returned to school, did they necessarily return to the same academy. Almost all attended a semester or two at several different academies, interspersed with periods at home at the district schools or studying with a private tutor. Their placement in class was determined by examination; Caroline, after spending a semester at Middlebury Seminary in 1831, another at New Ispwich Academy in 1837, and intervening years at district schools, reciting with Reverend Sanford, or taking private classes in writing and spelling, entered Norton Academy in 1840 as a member of the "Junior Class."

Failing to graduate was not, in fact, a failure at all. The goal was not to be credentialed, as there were no standard credentials for most professions at this time. It was to augment one's store of general knowledge, shape one's character, form one's habits for a successful life, learn practical skills, and acquire respectability, none of which required a diploma. In fact, despite their extensive preparation, only two of Aaron's children went on to college.[69] For the others, though, as for most students, the goal was to gather neither a degree nor professional training but to "improve the season well," as mother Mary prayed when Francis left for school, that "it may be well with him in time and eternity."[70]

The classmates that the White children met when they went away to school were, for the most part, much like themselves. During the years that Mary and Caroline attended New Ipswich Academy, seven other Boylston females accompanied them; all were from gentry families.[71] In this they fit the profile of rural academy students during this period: mostly from rural towns and overwhelmingly from the middling classes of property-owning farmers or proprietors who relied on their own household labor.[72] These youth, by garnering education and the means of employment, were in the act of crossing the bridge that divided the rural yeomanry from the urban middle class. Though it was their family's farm that allowed them the luxury of attending academy, in the future it would be their own education, acquired skills, and industry that would secure their place in a more cosmopolitan world. By bringing these youth together, indeed, rural academies were fostering the values of a rural middle class. Simultaneously, they created a rural lower class of those who did not share their values and accomplishments.

Many rural academies were coeducational, and the early nineteenth century saw additional founding of female seminaries and academies. As a result, before 1850, more females than males received the benefits of attending a rural academy.[73] The literature of the time is brimming with complaints about fashionable female boarding schools. *Godey's Ladies Book* (May 1850) tells the tale of poor Mr. McArthur, who placed his motherless daughters in a fancy boarding school. "They entered good-natured, unaffectedly sprightly girls; they emerged, after three years of seclusion, fashionable young ladies." Although they could sing high notes and crochet fancy purses, they had no practical skills whatsoever, and had even developed a strong aversion to work.[74] Such depictions reflect rural fears that academy education spoiled offspring for productive farm work. In fact, most of these girls were not simply being "finished." Many female academies in the early republic had curricula virtually identical in core academic subjects to their male counterparts.[75]

Caroline certainly found academic challenge in her junior class curriculum at Norton Female Seminary. Norton had been established in 1834 under the direction of Mary Lyon, who later founded what would become Mt. Holyoke College. Lyon created a program equal to that offered in men's *colleges*. When Caroline attended with the nineteen members of the junior class in 1839, she and her classmates could choose from offerings in English grammar, algebra, astronomy, natural philosophy, Euclid's geometry, human physiology, botany, chemistry, intellectual philosophy, philosophy of natural history, outline of geology, ecclesiastical history, rhetoric, logic, natural theology, moral philosophy, evidences of Christianity, and analogy of revealed religion to the constitution and course of nature. (For an additional fee, she could also study piano.)[76]

Caroline's letters leave no doubt: she *loved* learning, and she did not think of her studies as "ornamental." These courses were *useful*, to be sure, in qualifying her for employment as a teacher (and all the White daughters served terms as district school mistresses between and during their studies). But their avowed purpose (and possibly the reason behind Aaron White's willingness to pay more than fifty dollars for a term's tuition and board) was to refine her powers of judgment and moral reasoning, the essence of genteel sensibility and respectable character. Whether Aaron intended it or not, Caroline's education was also equipping her to "stand and speak," to know her mind, to master the persuasive art of self-presentation, and to fit herself with the "values and vocabularies" of civic society that she might be prepared to assume active citizenship, should she have the chance.[77]

Study at a private academy undoubtedly distinguished these scholars from their peers at the common school; Matthew Davenport boasted in 1831 of the considerable number of students who had enjoyed a term at a private academy since the turn of the century. Striving for betterment created classes of the educated and the uneducated; the one White family son who chose not to attend academy later regretted the decision and felt self-conscious that, as he said, he "had no learning."[78] There is no evidence of open hostility to private education in Boylston. There is, however, evidence that some youth whose families could well afford the tuition rejected the time and expense involved and chose instead to bank on entrepreneurial drive and personal industry. Charles and Francis's friends Lincoln Flagg and Homer Ball never advanced higher than the district school. Neither chose to invest capital in tuition but instead took their savings and launched their own—eventually highly successful—businesses. Were they, like Davis White, self-conscious that they had no learning? Or did they resent the assumed superiority of those who did?

WHETHER OR NOT intermittent terms of private schooling introduced distinction or discord in Boylston, they definitely increased angst over separations and the fragility of human ties. The practice of sending children away for a term or two meant frequent leave-takings. Students experienced broken ties not only to those at home, but also to those with whom they had bonded for an intense semester and then were called upon to leave, perhaps forever. Mindy Lamson, a Boylston contemporary of Caroline, kept a "friendship book" in the mid-1830s while a student at Bolton Academy. These hand-sewn paper books, intended to record the sentiments of friends, were growing in popularity in rural New England. Mindy recorded poems, prayers, and notes from both her Boylston friends and her fellow scholars. They wrote of partings, of fragile ties, of bonds they hoped would endure, of fear that they would be forgotten, and of death. Page after page reflects their angst in the face of transience and loss: "My friend farewell I will you tell, That you and I must part, You go away and here I stay, But still we're joined in heart." Another pleaded, " Go lovely youth over distant hills, Some friend more blest than I to find, And when the evening dew distills, Gently call past scenes to mind. Thy joys, thy sorrows here to share, Such[?] can never be my lot, But grant dear one my fervent prayer, Forget me not, forget me not!" In the very center of her book, Mindy recorded her own reflections in the form of a poem she copied from the *Rural Repository*, "Broken Ties."

> The broken ties of happier days
> How often do they seem
> To come before our mental gaze
> Like a remembered dream:

Around us each dissevered chain
In sparkling ruin lies
And earthly hand can never again
Unite those broken ties.
The parents of our infant home
The kindred that we loved
Far from our arms perchance may roam
To distant scenes removed.
Or we have watched their parting breath
And closed their weary eyes
And sighed to think how sadly death
Can sever human ties.
The friends, the loved ones of our youth
Those too are gone or changed
Or worse than all their love and truth
Are darkened and estranged.[79]

Mindy's poem ends with the admonition to set aside these transient and untrustworthy earthly bonds, "And trust to holyer ties."

Increased leave-takings profoundly affected the White family. In earlier times, filial duty and land-based dependence bound children to their parents, and generational interdependence provided a degree of permanence. As children increasingly left home at younger ages, families—or at least the White family—worried intensely about maintaining family ties. To replace earlier bonds of obligation and dependence, they cultivated bonds of affection through regular exchange of visits, ritual reunions—especially at Thanksgiving—and constant intercourse through letters.

Aaron especially was sensitive about his children's faithful performance of regular filial visits. He liked his house full of family; when his children went away to school or apprenticeships he mourned their absence. He confessed to Charles, "Your brothers and sisters are now all absent excepting Mary, so that our family is very small." When Mary left to take her turn at the academy, Caroline noted, "Father is sitting alone this evening and rather low-spirited and wishes to know what I am about. I must go."[80] To assuage his loneliness, Aaron placed great importance on his children's regular visits. "We hope that Davis will find it convenient to visit us soon as your Father feels rather lonely." "William has been a pleasant companion to us in our winter evenings." "We have had a pleasant visit from Thomas. . . . We had a very pleasant visit from Avery Independence Day. We love to have our Children come and see us when they can." "Davis made us a very pleasant visit last week. Elizabeth is now with us. . . . We hope you will be able to visit us soon. Thomas we expect to see next week."[81] Each son had his regularly appointed "season" for visiting, and Aaron was keenly disappointed when anything delayed or prevented their return home. "Charley," he wrote, "we should be very glad to see you. I believe that your brothers have all been at home since you were here and some of them repeatedly. Hoping to see you here before a great while, I will trouble you with nothing further."[82]

Thanksgiving in New England by the 1820s and 1830s took on special importance as a ritualized family reunion, long before it was officially declared a national holiday during the Civil War. Mary noted each year whether her whole family was present, and remembered the absent in prayer. For Aaron, the return of his offspring at Thanksgiving was an assurance that "the tender cord of affection which binds us together" was not "relaxing its hold, as we have seen in many instances."[83] Caroline worked to orchestrate full family attendance at the ritual reunion. "I have been pondering in my mind lately, what you said about visiting home at [Thanksgiving]. I have come to the conclusion that you had better come. For one great object of our annually meeting together at that time is to preserve ever warm, those kindly feelings of love towards one another, that absence is apt to cool."[84] "I was in hopes there would have been made an extra exertion on the part of each member of our family to meet together once more at the approaching festival. I am now afraid that there will be one or more delinquent members but I hope not."[85] "Is Avery calculating to come home at Thanksgiving? I hope every one will come, for I think we shall never meet again this side of eternity."[86]

When family did not visit, a faithful exchange of letters or mementos served as reassurance of their continued affections. William praised his brother Charles: "Your conduct and deportment have been such since you left the paternal roof as has tended to keep alive an affectionate remembrance of you. On about every shelf we can see some memento of your filial regard: these are valued not so much for their intrinsic worth as expressions of your attachment to those with whom you are allied by the ties of paternal and brotherly affections."[87] Sister Elizabeth, on the other hand, scolded Charles for his neglect, and suggested his family affections were cooling. "I have heard from you indirectly several times. . . . But all this is not equal to receiving a direct personal communication from you. I certainly have no reason to suspect your lack of affection yet it is pleasant to be occasionally assured of it. . . . Is it not time for you to come home again? Recollect I had no visit from you when you were at home last, and please make up the deficiency if our lives are spared when you come."[88] William also reprimanded Charles for lax correspondence and suggested his brother perhaps had lost interest in his family ties: "I am not a little surprised that you do not write to me, after I have written to you so many letters. . . . Suppose that you should enter into some mechanical shop and find one of your brothers apparently busily engaged in some interesting employment and you should attempt to converse with him . . . but instead of answering your questions, he should say nothing to you and treat you with entire indifference. Would you not think him to be rather impolite and wanting in respect for you?"[89] When Francis went away to school at Philips Academy in Andover, he interpreted a decline in letters from home—caused by family sickness—to the home folks' having "lost part of their attachment for me. . . . One good effect the folks noticing me no more has upon me is that it weans me from home."[90]

No one was more sensitive to the perception of neglect and weakening family bonds than father Aaron. His letters repeatedly expressed his continued warmth of feeling for absent family members. If he did not receive the same in reply, he felt the slight was evidence of lost regard. He profusely thanked Charles for his letters, "as they evince that there is at least one who retains an affection remembrance of the home of his childhood and the associations therewith connected." Then he went on to indict Charles's brothers: "We have not heard from Thomas since he wrote to us a day or two after his arrival in safety at New York. That letter has been replied to. We understood that Avery was in these parts last week and hoped that he would have called to see us but in this we were disappointed. . . . Aaron who you will recollect is a little more than half the distance from us that you are has not thought it worth his while to visit his aged parents since you saw him here last Thanksgiving. He has however written to us *once*."[91]

Aaron's need for assurance of his children's love and their remembrance of home reflected his anxiety over the new economy of relationships. Children, neighbors, and friends were no longer anchored in the local community or bound together by ties of mutual need, deferential authority, or communal norms. What did it mean to *belong* where one had not *been* for a *long* time? In this newly mobile world, attachments had to be cultivated with expressions of affection and assurances of faithful remembrance. Belonging was no longer ascribed, but cultivated.

Aaron's commitment to his children's education and professional preparation increased their frequent leave-taking; the price he paid, beyond tuition and foregone labor, was the anxious fear that they would never return. Anxiety, conflict, and an escalation in difference accompanied changes in the way young people acquired an education. Partisans struggled for control over texts, teachers, and curricula in the common schools. Districts competed for funds. Locals resisted state intervention. Less affluent parents resented the supplemental classes and resources that privileged the children of their more affluent neighbors. The advanced learning of academy students set them apart from their former peers; it also elevated them above and beyond the practical wisdom of their parents. Their social experience with private-school companions helped to solidify a new sense of middle-class status, distinguished from their more rustic neighbors at home. Meanwhile, their habits of reading broadly to develop independent judgment strained old communal reliance on shared social norms. Self-cultivation is inherently a self-centered process that stresses individuality and difference. As the White children followed admonitions to "read, read, read," took in lyceum lectures, and ventured off to distant academies, they absorbed ideas that linked them to the cosmopolitan world beyond the boundaries of their hometown. All those literate Yankees were "particularly susceptible to cultural transformation."[92] Ultimately, their schooling would not only make them ready for a new world, but also bring the new world home.

But for Boylston's globally literate, independent-minded, cultured youth, where was home? All their learning had shrunk the globe to a size that, like David Murdock's manufactured orbs and spheres, allowed them to "belong to" a wider world. But was home, the rural village of Boylston, a place of earth and almanacs, still a place where they belonged? Self-formed youth were vulnerable: no longer at one with community or family, they risked the angst of real or imagined leave-takings among those most dear.

CHAPTER SIX

Re-Forming Community

The people had gone mad. Or so it must have seemed to any Boylston farmer who happened to travel through the neighboring town of Harvard in the spring of 1843. Passing the tillage fields of Fruitlands, a utopian community of Transcendentalist philosophers, he would have seen men pulling their plows by hand so as not to exploit the labor of their oxen. Down the road, Shakers were also in their fields, ecstatically sowing spiritual seeds of love from virtual baskets of mercy. One farmer was determinedly chopping down his productive apple orchard to purge his land of alcoholic cider. Meanwhile, local Millerites, perched in trees or gathered in tabernacle tents, were earnestly awaiting the end of the world.

Harvard was a locus for quixotic zeal, but Boylston was not immune to reforming enthusiasms. Some locals formed groups to promote moral uplift, regardless of whether their neighbors desired uplifting. Some withdrew into private circles for mutual—but exclusive—enlightenment. Some rejected the community's traditional family-based welfare, choosing instead new progressive but impersonal institutions. Other Boylstonians embraced new standards of decorum that challenged local norms and constrained customary behaviors. This passion for improving energized—and polarized— the community. Men refused to shop where the storekeeper did not share their social views, children formed musical bands to march through town and trumpet their causes, women assailed their neighbors with controversial petitions, the uncouth lampooned the reformed in comic parody. And anywhere—in parlor and tavern, town meeting and country store—folks came upon one another, they argued over what was proper, healthful, righteous, or just.

Boylston's battles reflected the contentious spirit of an age of reform. Social improvement, much like personal improvement, was an earnest imperative of the age, an obligation both secular and religious, shared by urban and rural, rich and poor.[1] It grew in part from the possibilities and demands of nation-making: these inchoate United States offered the opportunity to redesign social life, a utopian's dream. But how could new order arise in a land of liberty and democracy, where each individual was supposedly free to choose his or her own way? The answer, they determined, lay in collective *voluntary* efforts to bring about individual and community discipline. Old-fashioned communal compulsion was out; persuasion, conversion, and rational ordering were in. Private societies and public institutions sprouted across the countryside as individuals willingly joined ranks to *re-form* their world by tempering behavior and eliminating the sources of disorder, suffering, and vice.[2]

This fount of reforming energy was fed by several sources. A rising faith in rational solutions to social problems made use of the latest advances of science, technology, and commerce. Progressives sought to identify and eliminate the underlying *causes* of disorder through organized benevolence and professional institutions. Those aware that the eyes of the world were still on this unproven national experiment were keen to prove the benefits of democratic social order. From a different spring gushed religious zeal and the confidence that the new nation was that promised land where sin could be eradicated, society perfected, and the way made straight for Christ's millennial return. But amid all this optimism, there was also angst. Reformers were driven by an awareness that the old social order—one of fixed status, hierarchy, and tradition—was rapidly crumbling. If they did not act to bring about a new order, the young nation might succumb to unchecked interests, self-indulgence, and vulgarity. Such a failure risked national downfall, or worse, divine retribution in the approaching end-times. Historians have long debated whether antebellum reform was an expression of optimism or fear: it was both. The combined hope and fear of the age produced the organizational energy that drove reforms.[3] And it produced conflict over what was betterment and how it should be achieved. So Boylston discovered.

As we have seen, it was people like Aaron White and his Federalist gentry peers who first proposed private associations and corporations for improvement, based on English models. White and his friends had no intention of toppling established order and collective local control with their voluntary impulse; they meant to reassert gentry-led authority in the wake of Revolutionary disorder. But things did not turn out quite as they had intended. In the generation following the Revolution, Federalist and clerical authority waned. At the same time, mobility, market practices, and private ambitions weakened traditional community norms that had provided order and controlled social behavior locally. As the new century opened, customary relationships of rural life seemed in disarray, and many were troubled with uncertainties. Would democracy promote freedom and virtue or anarchy and lawlessness? Would the new growth of trade and commercialism bring a rising standard of living or selfish acquisitiveness? Would the disestablishment of churches promote freedom of conscience or a descent into atheism? Were new family roles, growing cities, and the rise of industry signs of progress or harbingers of disorder and degeneracy? If freedom meant throwing off imposed order, how could they still safeguard morality and preserve virtue in their new republic? The voluntary association—private clubs or societies for promoting improvement or special interest—seemed to offer a way for Boylston's everyday folk to freely join their hands to the work of watching and warding and refining and bettering village life.

The problem was that Yankees—and Boylstonians were no exception—perceived betterment differently. Reformers created conflict because they worked to change behavior without community consensus. The town had long relied on local customs of communal honoring or shaming, elevating or ostracizing for enforcing behavioral norms. Boylston's reformers embraced the provocative idea that the authority—and duty—to control behavior lay not with the consensual community but with the individual, and that individuals could magnify their effectiveness through associations of like-minded citizens. In their efforts to improve society, they most certainly remade community, splintering it into groups that promoted rival understandings of common good. To one like Mary, who prayed earnestly that her townsfolk might be of one mind, Boylston's struggles to define proper mothering, diet, drink, sexual behavior, or care of the poor, sick, calamity struck, and insane could drive one to wits' end.

IT WAS PEOPLE LIKE Mary White who transformed behavior in New England's villages. Ideas might infiltrate the countryside from without, spread by newspapers, tracts, and pamphlets, through networks of lecturers traveling along new turnpikes and rails, through the correspondence of new national associations with local members.[4] But the real work was homegrown. Members of local societies spearheaded membership drives, hosted lecturers, distributed print materials, circulated petitions, coordinated propaganda and fundraising events, and endlessly badgered their neighbors. Mary and her friends created the social capital famously described by Tocqueville by joining together to work for betterment.[5]

The 800 souls of Boylston supported an extraordinary range of reforms in these decades. The town was a hive, abuzz with societies for this and that. Boylston's evangelical women, in particular, organized feverishly to meet each perceived opportunity to convert or redeem. Mary White attended local meetings of the Ladies' Benevolent Society (for local charitable aid), Foreign Missionary Society, Tract Society (for the distribution of Bibles and religious tracts), Sabbath School Union (for literacy and Bible study), Maternal Association (for supporting Christian parenting), and Moral Reform Society (to redeem prostitutes). She attended lectures in neighboring towns for the Home Missionary Society (for frontier and Native American evangelization) and Education Society (for ministerial training). These groups worked to transform souls; working *for* these groups transformed the reformers. They became crusaders and comrades.

Efforts to improve souls and society were not limited to evangelicals. The town's Temperance Society drew support from respectable citizens of various denominations. The Female Antislavery Society also drew from a diverse group of townswomen. Neighboring Worcester drew Boylstonians to societies dedicated to peace, women's rights, and efforts to reform treatment of prisoners and the mentally ill.

Though some voluntary associations bridged sectarian or partisan divides, they were not a force for town unity. Voluntary societies were, in essence, lobbying organizations. Their members identified a social condition that was not to their liking and banded together to bring about changes to suit their particular principles, religious beliefs, or behavioral norms. Though supporters came from both orthodox and liberal religious traditions, from Whig and Democrat political parties, they did not represent a communal consensus. Others in town resisted their attempts to impose new codes of behavior, especially those that replaced traditional communal sociability with respectable restraint and sober self-control. As an examination of temperance reform shows, the rise of reform societies splintered community and re-formed personal relationships in Boylston.

An Intemperate Ruckus

In the middle of harvest season in 1838, Mary White confided doleful news to her diary: "We heard of a murder committed in [neighboring] Holden by John L. Davis on the person of Mr. Edwards. Davis supposed to be in a fit of intoxication. When shall our land be freed of the sin of drunkenness and its appalling effects?"[6] Her prayer was a commonplace of the temperance movement. Reformers cast their battle with the bottle as another national war for independence from an oppressive despot. Temperance reformers appropriated the Fourth of July, hosting alcohol-free picnics to celebrate their "dry oaths," sign pledges, and preach about how strong drink *enslaved* its users and threatened the security of the nation. They spoke of imprisoned souls chained to Demon Rum, and read a modified Declaration of Independence, in which Prince Alcohol replaced King George. True liberty required wresting control not only from external tyrants, but from internal appetites and sinful passions. Freedom lay in self-control. Alcohol threatened this autonomy, and so was an enemy of personal—and national—independence.[7]

It had not always been so. At the turn of the nineteenth century, rum had been the most common, and most profitable, item of trade in Aaron White's store.[8] Business in Simon Davis's store leapt dramatically when he was licensed to sell liquor, for there was plentiful custom for rum.[9] People were used to punctuating their day with breaks for rum and rest. It was expected that the gears of farm work would be lubricated with rum. Serving drink was a social obligation in entertaining neighbors. The town's major civic observances—town meeting, Election Day, Fourth of July, and the Taking of Cornwallis (October 19)—were all celebrated with drink. Americans in 1825 drank on average seven gallons of alcohol a year—more than three times that consumed by twentieth-century Americans. Socially important, drink was rarely condemned.[10]

By 1830, however, attitudes toward ardent spirits had begun to change.[11] As with many of the controversies that roiled Boylston during this period, the push to limit drink arose first as a sectarian, evangelical issue. In the mid-1820s, orthodox preachers began to assert that the use of hard spirits was a sin. Lyman Beecher identified alcohol as a moral pollutant that led to other sins (profanity, promiscuity, violence) and their social consequences (poverty, deserted families, crime, broken health, and insanity). In 1826, Beecher, along with other orthodox ministers and laymen, founded the American Temperance Society (ATS) in Boston. Having identified alcohol as a sinful toxin—the Holy Spirit would not enter the soul of the inebriate—they called for the converted to immediately renounce the sin of drink. Adopting the strategies and methods of contemporary evangelical revivalists, the ATS sponsored agents to travel New England spreading the word and recruiting converts to pledge abstinence from strong drink.[12]

Wherever they lectured, evangelical temperance agents attempted to set up the moral machines of their movement: local temperance societies. Agents enlisted the town's orthodox minister, delivered lectures on the sinfulness of alcohol, and called on the faithful to pledge immediate renunciation of hard spirits. Then they called on prominent men in town to organize a local society. Community leaders were expected to use the combined power of moral argument and social influence to persuade fellow churchmen to add their names to the society list. As new signers were initiated at monthly meetings, the movement grew.[13]

So it happened in Boylston. Gathering in the center schoolhouse on a September evening in 1830, the Temperance Society received members and elected officers.[14] Among the earliest local converts were prominent young Congregationalist men from the respected Moore, Temple, Bush, and Houghton families. The society held regular meetings, subscribed to temperance publications, and canvassed the town seeking pledges to abstain from ardent spirits. Members emphasized the need to publicly sign the pledge. Mary urged Charles: "I did not think to request if you have a convenient opportunity to sign the temperance pledge. I have seen Mr. George Allen [her cousin] since I saw you and he thinks that every temperate person ought to, on account of the influence he may have upon others."[15]

From its inception, Boylston's Temperance Society subtly reshaped the structure and bounds of community. Membership itself redefined civic belonging. Tocqueville argued that America's many voluntary societies bonded individuals to collective society.[16] But voluntary societies were not the same as corporate community. Members were a people set apart from community. Voluntary associations such as Boylston's Temperance Society had two contrasting goals: first, empowering individuals to resist the norms of their immediate corporate community, and second, bonding them in fraternity, a subset of like-minded souls. Members turned their attention inward, to personal will, and outward, to the support of association. Both trumped traditional corporate community norms.

Despite the sectarian strife of the time, evangelical temperance advocates in town did not limit their outreach to church members. The town's orthodox minister gave his antidrink addresses on neutral ground—the town hall or schoolhouses, rather than the Congregational meetinghouse—in an effort to reach beyond his denomination. The respectable churched of all denominations shared an interest in limiting vice, and evangelicals were not opposed to recruiting Unitarians. Mary, returning from one such talk, declared it "a Noble and animated discourse."[17] This opened a new approach to association: universal accord was not essential to cooperation; it was possible to associate by interest on some matters while disagreeing on others. Unanimity was no longer possible in a pluralist society, but alliance was.

Boylston's temperance advocates did not struggle alone. State and national umbrella organizations provided guidance on composing society constitutions, circulating pledges, and organizing locally. Their publications provided the verbiage for debate. Traveling agents, especially, linked distant communities to the greater movement and opened the town to happenings beyond its borders. Mary White recorded visits from temperance agents, seeking support or delivering lectures. The minister traveled to speak on temperance elsewhere, and received other speakers in return. The society sent delegates to local and state conventions.[18]

Though Boylston's temperance effort may have been ecumenical and expansive, it was also divisive. Resistance and contention were particularly apparent within the membership of the Congregational Church when, in the autumn of 1832, the newly ordained Rev. William Sanford persuaded his flock to embrace total abstinence for all new members and church discipline for those who violated this principle.[19] The vote was supposedly unanimous, but the sentiment was not. Struggling shoemaker Abishai Crossman, who (as we shall see) enjoyed his drink, soon transferred his membership to the more open-minded Unitarians. Young Abel Dakin, serving at the time as Joseph Flagg's hired help, was called before the church in October 1833 to answer to "the charge of drunkenness and profanity." As he failed to appear, and the charges were "substantiated to the satisfaction of all present," young Dakin was excommunicated.[20] This dramatic action did not sit well with his father, the elderly, respected, and well-to-do farmer David Dakin. Shortly thereafter, the elder Dakin moved his entire family from the land they had farmed for generations and relocated in neighboring Worcester. Although we cannot be certain that his removal was the result of hard feelings over his son's excommunication, when he asked the church for a letter of dismission (to present for membership in his new church in Worcester), his former congregants demurred; they ultimately granted a *qualified* recommendation only, suggesting that ill will still plagued their relationship.[21] Controversy would escalate as the movement grew.

By the mid-1830s, the temperance movement had matured. A new organization, the Massachusetts Temperance Union (MTU), now insisted on a "long pledge" binding one to *total* abstinence rather than mere moderation in the use of spirits.[22] Temperance had also spread well beyond evangelical Christians to become a social movement for self- and national improvement. Reformers discovered that they could cast a larger net by praising personal respectability and national interest than by damning sinfulness.

Tying temperance to respectability was a powerful tactic. In a mobile and rapidly evolving social world, influence and prestige were no longer inherited with the paternal estate; they had to be earned through proper behavior. To be respectable (that is, to be self-supporting, to exhibit self-control, to behave with propriety, to present oneself with decorum) was now considered essential for success. Strong drink derailed this quest. Ultimately, it threatened the survival of the nation. Mary noted temperance lectures that focused particularly on the deleterious effect of drink on "our national prosperity."[23] When she "overtook a young man in a wagon appearing like a dead man under the influence of rum," she prayed, "May this pestilence be cleansed from our land!"[24] For their own good and for the good of the nation, reformers argued, *all* men should strive for respectability through temperance.

Who responded to this rhetoric? Unfortunately, the Temperance Society records for Boylston do not survive. However, one study of those who embraced the cause in Massachusetts between 1826 and 1840 show they were not solely the elite. They were on average slightly wealthier and more likely to own property than those who eschewed temperance. They were also more likely to be churched (of any denomination) and more likely to be involved in other reform causes (though not necessarily more likely to hold political office). They appear to have been those young men who sought material and spiritual betterment, attracted by rhetoric of self- and social improvement, of respectability and influence.[25]

A study of young men's powerful recollections of signing the pledge, based on autobiographies from this period, suggests that temperance gave them a sense of individual control, of personal power to define themselves and demonstrate self-mastery. The drama of decision making was a test of self-determination: the young were challenged to control the temptation to self-indulgence; by doing so they could demonstrate the independence of self-government.[26] The act of signing the pledge, then, defined a young man as an individual; it also united him to a new community of the respectable.

Temperance came to dominate town life. By the early 1830s, Boylston had seen such innovations as the temperance wedding, where the customary flow of wine was replaced with coffee.[27] People subscribed to temperance periodicals, went to temperance lectures in town, and traveled to temperance conventions in Worcester. Men and women, including Mary's single daughters and their friends, made circuits around town collecting temperance pledges. Youth were recruited to sign the pledge, after hearing addresses specifically directed to them. Boylston's children were formed into a musical band—"the little Cold Water Army" as Mary called it—that played for temperance processions.[28] One anthem written for such young recruits included the declaration:

> This youthful band
> Do with our hand
> The pledge now sign—
> To drink no Wine,
> Nor Brandy red to
> Turn the head,
> Nor whiskey hot
> That makes the sot,
> Nor fiery Rum
> To turn our home
> Into a hell
> Where none can dwell. . . .
> So here we pledge perpetual hate
> To all that can Intoxicate.[29]

If they followed fashion, they were adorned with satin bows as temperance badges, emblems of their pledge. On the Fourth of July, temperance advocates in Boylston hosted an alternative picnic, as Mary noted with approval: "PicNic [*sic*] temperance celebration. Met at the Town Hall & formed a procession & cold water army & met in the grove near Mr. Fawcett's where addresses were made. Mr. Sanford opened the meeting with prayer, Rev. Mr. Blair, Baptist minister at Worcester & Doctor Bates, son of Northboro made an interesting address. May the Lord grant success to the cause of Temperance in this place."[30] Mary noted the "fine table of refreshments [was] prepared, handsomely decorated with evergreens & flowers."[31] Mary's temperance celebration competed with the usual rambunctious Fourth of July festivities.

Many temperance activities in Boylston, however, did *not* raise festive goodwill. Pro and anti sentiment ran hot and sometimes turned violent.[32] Mary noted several instances in which antitemperance advocates tried to interrupt temperance activities, with disturbances made by "lads and young men" from the neighboring manufacturing village of West Boylston.[33] A contemporary observer in the neighboring town of Sturbridge remembered: "Nothing ever caused the excitement that the temperance cause did from 1836 to 1844. It struck the town hard; it made its mark, and drew a line, for it went through both political parties, through the church and many family circles. He who was not for was against, and it carried out to the letter. The storekeeper who sold rum could not sell molasses or codfish to a temperance man."[34]

It was one thing to encourage people not to drink; it was another thing to demonize those who did. In the mid-1830s, the MTU began to focus attention on two classes of miscreants: drunkards and those who sold liquor to them. Drunkards were an easy target; they had long been classed among the fallen. But tavern keepers, shopkeepers, and merchants who sold spirits were usually among the town's most respected citizens.[35] Mary White's son Aaron Jr. made no friends in his adopted hometown of Woonsocket, Rhode Island, when he repeatedly brought complaints and indictments against shop- and innkeepers "for selling strong liquors without a license."[36] What began as mere hectoring of sellers escalated to judgmental attacks.[37] Evangelical temperance advocates accused those who sold liquor of carrying on—and profiting from—an evil traffic that led their neighbors to damnation. That they were men of standing and likely to wield influence made their sin even more grievous. The Unitarian Horace Mann attempted a more rational approach, arguing that it was in the retailers' self-interest to ban liquor sales, as drink made farmers unproductive and so reduced what they could afford to spend.[38] Many shopkeepers, however, aware that spirits remained their most profitable commodity, were not impressed.

For the Whites, the issue was personal. Aaron White owned the most established store in Boylston, and the first to go dry. In 1831, a local noted that the town had "three stores, in two of which are found the usual supplies of domestic, English, and West Indies goods; the other is upon the plan of *total abstinence* in the sale of ardent spirits."[39] This was Aaron White's center-village store. We do not know if the savvy retailer abandoned liquor sales willingly or only after a marital struggle. Contemporary temperance provided plentiful arguments for persuading liquor sellers to give up their traffic. The ATS literature warned sellers to desist, for "in no other way can they escape the guilt of being accessory to the making of drunkards, and the danger, in the day of retribution of being partakers in their plagues."[40] We do not know if Mary used these arguments on Aaron. We do know that the decision was costly, for Aaron lost not just sales, but custom, as those who did not share his moralizing stance could take their business to Bond's store or Hastings's tavern.

The family issue was not resolved when Aaron gave up the sale of liquor. Their son Avery was a West India merchant, and he did a substantial business in rum. The matter was deeply troubling to his mother. Mary's letters to Avery do not survive, so we do not know what powers of persuasion she exerted. The thorny issue of his continuing liquor sales was finally resolved in February 1838, when Mary wrote to Charles, "I rejoice to hear that Avery is likely to be liberated from the sad traffic of rum selling."[41]

But the family was not done with the contentious issue of liquor sales. In 1841, an aging Aaron sold his store to the family's good friend and neighbor, Dr. John Andrews. To Mary's dismay, the doctor decided to stock his shelves with spirits. William wrote to his brother, "Intemperance, that woeful bane of all human happiness and peace, is I fear on the increase here at present. Mr. Andrews keeps liquors in his bar and one and another are seen to go in there and take the intoxicating cup. I saw the effect almost as soon as I arrived in town."[42] The issue of liquor sales vexed relations between husband and wife, parents and son, and neighbors.

It was difficult for temperance advocates to vilify and reduce to disrespectability such established gentlemen as the rum sellers Avery White and Dr. John Andrews. By the mid-1830s, the MTU had decided to shift tactics from moral persuasion to political and legal restraint. In Massachusetts, licenses to sell liquor were granted by appointed county commissioners. In 1835, after sustained pressure from temperance advocates, the legislature made these elected positions. The 1835 elections for commissioners came only two weeks after the change in law, too early for temperance advocates to organize themselves. However, by the next election in 1838, they were prepared.

The struggle to control county commissioners was hotly contested, and election results in Boylston reveal that feelings ran high. In 1835, turnout was low and highly lopsided. Three years later, the story was different. Those for and against campaigned ferociously, with supporters urging the need to cleanse sin, and opposition decrying rule by fanatics and ultraists.[43] In Worcester, one observer reported, "Wherever two men are seen together, the subject of conversation is temperance. In many instances they become so furious as to almost come to blows. I perceived that whoever speaks upon the subject manifests his passions at once. In this respect, the friends of temperance are as intemperate as their opponents. Everybody is getting mad."[44] For the first time, Mary White noted the meeting for election of county commissioners in her diary, revealing that high interest surrounded the event. In Boylston, turnout was double what it had been previously, and the vote was nearly evenly divided between two sets of candidates, likely pro- and antitemperance tickets.[45]

Temperance reformers continued their legal campaign, bombarding the legislature with petitions to limit or prohibit alcohol sales. In 1838, the Massachusetts legislature bent to their will, approving a law that they believed was moderate, for it merely limited rather than prohibited sales. The Fifteen Gallon Law authorized the sale of spirits only in quantities of fifteen gallons or more. The law effectively shut down all casual drinking at taverns, pubs, and country stores. It also put drink beyond the reach of all but those wealthy enough to purchase and store a large quantity.

Temperance advocates were pleased. Then they were shocked. A huge and sometimes violent backlash ensued. Active temperance supporters found their horses' tails shaved, their trees girdled, or their houses defaced. Bitter confrontation, harassment, vandalism, and physical abuse—including tarring and feathering—fell upon those who tried to enforce the law. Even mob violence was threatened.[46]

Antitemperance protesters claimed the law was an attack on liberty and equality. One observer later recalled the arguments of the protesters: "They said their liberties were in danger; their fathers had fought for liberty; and they would shoulder their muskets, and fight over the battles of freedom, before they would relinquish their right to drink when they pleased."[47] The law, they claimed, was a dangerous infringement on their personal liberties by Puritan fanatics, who soon, if not stopped, would be regulating dress and diet. One neighboring Worcester County town vehemently denounced the law as "an act of Tyranny and fitted for arbitrary abuse," a violation of "the rights of poor and middling interests."[48] Others argued that the law exceeded the state's power to regulate interstate commerce, discriminated against those who could not afford to buy fifteen gallons at a time, and—in a jab at evangelical proponents—was unscriptural.[49] Calling the law "restrictive and coercive," they positioned themselves as those with "liberal and enlarged views."[50]

Evading or flouting the law was common, especially as there was not enough manpower to enforce it. One common ploy was to buy fifteen gallons and one gill of rum on credit; after drinking the gill, the fifteen gallons were returned and the account paid.[51] Less common, but much discussed, was the exhibition of the striped pig. This rather ingenious ploy was developed to ensure that militia musters and town meeting days—long a time of rummy sociability—would not go dry. To prepare for Dedham's militia muster in September 1838, one enterprising townsman procured a license from the selectmen to present an educational exhibit on the town common. There he set up his tent and hoisted a flag with the extraordinary image of a pig with red and black stripes banding his entire body. Crowds gathered, and the curious paid a small fee to observe this rare creature. Once admitted, they saw an ordinary hog painted in stripes, but few complained, for while viewing the curiosity they were presented with a *complimentary* rum toast! As word went round, crowds grew and many were educated. And so the issue was neatly resolved, as spirits were dispensed but not sold.[52]

The striped pig became an overnight sensation. His fame traveled faster than any four-legged swine could trot. Within a week, the Boston papers spread the tale across the region; in less than a month, the striped pig was the talk of the town from Maine to New Orleans, and, according to one newspaper, by November his fame had reached the Far West and across the ocean to London.[53] Antitemperance parties called themselves the "Striped Pig Party," and their pro-temperance foes agreed that they were indeed a swinish multitude.[54] The celebrated pig "well nigh set all Boston by the ears."[55] Boston theaters competed to produce the wittiest comic operettas honoring the pig, illustrators sold farcical lithographs of the pig's exhibition, and a comic short pamphlet, "History of the Striped Pig," quickly sold out. Both pro- and antitemperance forces produced their own brief runs of Striped Pig newspapers.[56] Most popular, however, seemed to be the Striped Pig ditty, which included, among its many verses:

> The sign at the tent was Striped Pig to be seen
> The wonder of Dedham, this four-legged thing;
> A four-penny bit they paid to get in
> Which Piggy paid back in his brandy and gin. . . .
> The folks at the muster they all agreed
> That this was the pig for crossing the breed,
> For he left his mark on every biped
> That went in sober, but came out striped.[57]

Abishai Crossman decided that the people of Boylston also deserved this educational opportunity. Aaron wrote to Charles of the incident that followed:

Yesterday was our annual March Meeting. You have not forgotten the incidents of a country March Meeting. One incident however took place of rather an unusual character for to take place in the staid and sober town of Boylston. We had a regular row. The circumstances were as follows. Our old neighbor Crossman who by the way is no friend to the law of 1838 [Fifteen Gallon Law] or to any other law for the suppression of intemperance, insisted upon exhibiting the striped pig for

"The Striped Pig," sheet music cover, lithograph, 1838.
Courtesy of the American Antiquarian Society.

the good of his fellow townsmen. Not being able to find any tenement for his purpose in the neighborhood, his zeal for the publick good induced him to pitch his tent under one of the old sheds back of the old meeting house. It was not long before some boys proceeded to erect a suitable sign of invitation nigh the premises. This of course attracted attention and soon there was a gathering of youngsters to the number of many scores. When after the usual negotiations, shoutings and other concomitants of such times, means were found to upset the table and let loose the striped pig who was seen running and rooting among the stones to the no small gratification of all excepting those who had produced him for exhibition.[58]

Aaron clearly found the incident amusing; Mary did not. She recorded, "Our temperance cause injured by one man attempting to sell without a license."[59]

Perhaps it is not surprising that Abishai Crossman was Boylston's rebellious pig exhibitor. The issue of enforced sobriety was tinged with class, political, and religious frustration by those who had found the early decades of the nineteenth century to be not so free as they had once envisioned. Crossman was among those in town who had lost ground: his shoemaking craft had been deskilled and he was facing debt and destitution, he had been forced out of the church where he had once held an exalted role as musical director, his aspiring offspring rejected his rustic sociability as uncouth; now his reforming neighbors were depriving him of the time-honored indulgence of drink. He had expected the new nation to promote his independent livelihood, freedom of conscience, paternal dignity, and liberty of self-expression; instead, he felt bound and scorned.

If Crossman was an appropriate protestor, so was his choice of a pig as his coconspirator. The lowly pig had always been a poor man's friend. It cost little to keep a hog who fed on refuse or rooted in common woodlands. The poorest man with no pasture or meadow could still enjoy his pork if the town allowed pigs to run free, and even poor city folk hoped to fatten their hogs on the trash of their well-to-do neighbors.[60] Each year, however, towns voted whether to let pigs run at large, and the issue became increasingly vexed. Middling and small traditional farmers who did not embrace the scientific farming of gentry wanted to continue to allow their hogs to run and fatten at will, while larger, market-oriented farmers and refined village dwellers wanted all livestock carefully confined.[61] Boylston's more genteel folk, concerned with the attractiveness of their domestic landscapes and the integrity of their tillage, dooryards, and gardens, voted increasingly restrictive policies for their swine from the mid-1820s on.[62] To the dismay of the town's struggling poor who saw this as a denial of their traditional rights to the common, pigs were no longer allowed to run wild at any time of the year.

Crossman's choice of a protest pig served another end as well: by claiming his exhibit was educational, he lampooned the improving pretensions of his genteel neighbors (not to mention his own children). Improvement through learning, uplift by education, and respectability through refinement, as we have seen, were all the rage among a certain set. These townsfolk, along with the rest of New England's aspiring folk, had been handing over their money to view educational exhibits of all manner of traveling menagerie, art, machinery, scientific inventions, performers, and extraordinary phenomena in the hopes of acquiring useful knowledge.[63] In fact, one perennially popular exhibit was the traveling "sapient pig," who could spell, read, cast accounts, and play cards.[64] Rural folk were amazed and educated; the exhibition of the striped pig allowed rustics such as Crossman to poke fun at their knowledge. Even more satisfying to a man like Crossman would have been "La Piganino"—an image of a refined lady singing and playing a piano know as the "Hog Harmonium," the "Swineway," or the "Porko Forte."[65] The supposed instrument was a keyboard connected to live pigs of different sizes, who squealed when pricked by the keys. The ludicrous caricature of a lady of genteel taste squealing along with the hogs was no doubt a satisfying parody of uppity neighbors.

Perhaps because of this subversive undercurrent, the striped pig became an extremely popular animal. Temperance folk tried to make light of the matter by issuing their own tale of the pig's genealogy and demise. One reported that the pig had been slaughtered and provided a memorial in the form of an obituary: "Died yesterday, at the ballot-boxes, of *delirium tremens*, that wonderful beast . . . the *striped pig*! Post mortem—innerds all alcohol and rot, heart shrunken, emitted foul alcoholic order—stomach filled with excrement of paper—handbills, circulars, letters of the 'pig party.'"[66]

Antitemperance was, however, no laughing matter to reformers. In shifting their campaign from moral appeal to legal coercion, temperance supporters had unwittingly tapped into a rich vein of popular protest. The outcry was so strong that legislators considered repeal of the Fifteen Gallon Law. Temperance advocates rallied to their cause. Mary's commitment led her from religiously motivated reform to public political action. Throughout 1839, she recorded going—or sending her daughters to go—"round to the neighbors to get signatures for the female petition" against the repeal of the law. Caroline wrote to her brother: "At this particular time, you hear much said on the subject of Temperance. Petitions on both sides [of the Fifteen Gallon Law] are busily circulating in this town. I went round in the center district with one among the females; of all I asked, I met with but one refusal and she was the wife of a drunken husband, who stood in fear of his displeasure. Therefore did not dare to sign. In one place where the rum bottle stood on the table, the toddy stick in the mug on the mantle shelf, the wife readily put her name to the petition. The voice of the people I hope will decide right."[67]

Politically, the Fifteen Gallon Law backfired for temperance reformers. The coercive action caused such an outcry that both Whigs and Democrats attempted to distance themselves from what had never been a party movement. Democrats, however, were more successful in detaching themselves, as their candidate for governor, Marcus Morton, promised to sign any repeal bill presented by the legislature; his opponent, Edward Everett, had unfortunately signed the unpopular bill into law. Morton was elected. (Political cartoons portrayed Morton riding to victory on the back of a striped pig.) Although Boylston embraced Everett, it was the tightest contest the predominantly conservative town had ever witnessed for a gubernatorial election.[68]

The temperance battle in Boylston represented a last gasp of a long community tradition of imposing communal standards. Abishai Crossman's striped pig and the hotly contested Fifteen Gallon Law show the weakening of communal authority and the rising power of associations of interests. In the future, such community decisions would be made by negotiating alliances and building majorities rather than identifying a consensual common good. The issue of temperance eventually cooled as the energy in the movement shifted to reform led by and for lower-class laborers, a voluntary self-help effort that threatened few. By then, however, respectable middling sorts in Boylston, as in most of Massachusetts, had gradually embraced sobriety.[69] In 1844, the last tavern in Boylston went out of business; shortly afterward, John Gough, the nation's leading temperance speaker, settled in town.

"Like a Good Neighbor": From Communal to Market-Based Risk Management

Not all local improvement efforts were as openly controversial as temperance. Others worked more subtly and more gradually to remake personal relations.

Boylstonians had once managed life's risks collectively; the community was their bulwark against unpredictable fate and inscrutable providence. Now some improvers began to assert that there were more efficient, more effective ways to deal with misfortune, debility, or dependence. People could—and should—shape their own prospects. With progressive practices, individuals could control risk, direct prosperity, ensure health, and master vice. And if they did not, they should be referred to experts or institutions for management, treatment, discipline, or cure. Over the course of a generation, neighborly functions were specialized and institutionalized. They were also depersonalized: Boylstonians "purchased what one had previously performed."[70] They shed their collective responsibility for their neighbors' well-being.

Consider the role that insurance companies were beginning to play in rural Worcester County. The idea of attempting to manage risk was not new; from classical antiquity to medieval and Enlightenment Europe there had been burial societies, guilds, and voluntary mutual aid societies that had provided for members incapacitated by illness, old age, or death. But in colonial New England, most rural folk considered one's best insurance against the effects of illness, accident, fire, and weather to be the goodwill and obligation of townsfolk. If a man's wife died, his crop failed, or his barn burned, kith and kin came to his aid. If his children fell sick, neighbors came in to nurse them. If he lost his senses, or all his worldly goods, his townsmen took him in, for one never knew when he might be the one in need. Although some private associations formed to manage the risk of fire in densely developed wood-built cities, insurance contracts to limit exposure to risk of private property, health, or life in rural areas of New England did not become readily available until the middle third of the nineteenth century. Then, people who had once hedged against risk collectively and outside of the market began to do so within the market and individually.[71]

Early corporate insurers, mostly local, sold shares and became successful in accumulating capital, which they lent out as commercial and industrial loans and as mortgages.[72] The gains to someone such as Aaron White Sr., a prosperous man with money to invest and property to protect, were substantial. The stock shares and bonds of these new private corporations provided a novel form of investment for rural gentry. A generation earlier, a man like Aaron White would have had far fewer options for putting surplus earnings from a thriving farm to work; he would have been limited mostly to buying more land or lending locally to neighbors on long-term credit with fixed interest rates. Purchasing shares in local corporations not only increased the possibilities of multiplying wealth, it also underwrote economic development in the countryside. Aaron White was one of those who promoted the advent of rural corporations. He chose to invest heavily in insurance and bank stock, holding shares in value equal to his landed estate.[73]

These early local insurance companies offered another benefit to a man with substantial property: a way to free himself from fate. With insurance, he could rebuild after fire, survive if disabled, maintain his estate despite illness, and provide for his dependents at death. By 1830, Aaron White had arranged for fire insurance on his home, barns, and farm with policies from the recently founded Worcester Mutual Fire Insurance Company. Mary recorded traveling with him to Worcester in 1832 to collect the renewed policy.[74] She also recorded every incidence of fire in the surrounding communities—as well as the value of the loss and whether the property was insured. The key concern was no longer that Mr. Flagg's barn or the West Boylston meetinghouse or a nearby textile factory had burned, but whether the loss would be recouped. Rebuilding an insured barn differed from the neighborly barn-raising following an earlier uninsured loss.

Aaron may have freed himself from dependence on his neighbors and townsmen in the face of calamity; his poorer neighbors could not do so. The emergence of institutions for managing risk transformed one of the essential elements of Boylston's earlier community—interdependence—by freeing some while leaving others in a state of dependence that was no longer universal nor mutual. Traditional neighborly reliance became modern poor support.

Farewell to Alms

At the turn of the century, Simon Davis complained that Boylston was "burthened with poor."[75] His understanding that the poor were a local responsibility—and burden—was rooted in English tradition: each community had to support its own. The Old Poor Law of Elizabethan England made the parish responsible for the care of its destitute residents, and that legal tradition carried over to the Bay Colony.[76] Some of the earliest laws in Massachusetts reflect concern with limiting this local obligation by jealously guarding who was permitted to be legally settled in any community, and thus eligible for local aid.[77] Boylston squabbled with neighboring towns over responsibility for various poor folks right through the 1840s. But once legally settled—by birth or by ten years of tax-paying residence—those who could not support themselves became the responsibility of their townsfolk; the poor were taken into local households.[78]

Biblical strictures and aristocratic paternalism might augment town-based aid with charitable acts. Thus, in June 1836, Mary White noted in her diary that neighbors pledged money "to purchase a cow for Old Mr. Eams as his had lately died." As the weather turned bitter later that year, the minister's wife made the rounds of the neighborhood farmhouses, "collecting money for Old Mrs. Smith's cloak."[79] Both of these elderly people were experiencing temporary difficulties, for which their neighbors provided temporary assistance. Those who were utterly destitute, however, became wards of the town. These unfortunates came before town meeting to face the unhappy fate of being auctioned off to whoever would charge the least to keep them.

This auction, or vendue, as it was commonly called, occurred each March at the annual town meeting. Among the regular items of town business was an article calling on Boylstonians to "make disposal of and provision of their poor, as they shall think proper." Thus, in 1836, eighty-three-year-old David Bush, a one-time Tory whose estate had been confiscated during the Revolutionary War, was bid off to Henry Brewer for $1.04 a week. The eighty-one-year-old widow Lucy Cutting, apparently considered an easier charge, went for only ninety-nine cents a week, while Calvin Brigham would take nothing less than $1.95 a week to care for the ninety-year-old spinster Catherine Eager. Promiscuous twenty-two-year-old Relief Stone, who had compounded her father's poverty by producing a bastard son, was also on the public dole. Proud old Zachariah Sawtell came forward at the meeting and proposed that he would support himself and his seventy-something wife if the town would give him $45.00 per year. The town bickered over his request; direct relief was controversial, as some feared it encouraged idleness and corrupted character.[80] The town denied the request, then voted to reconsider, finally deciding that the proposed rate of eighty-seven cents a week for the couple was a bargain. Between 1830 and 1840, the town averaged about six destitute cases per year.[81]

Being vendued was not a fate to which any able-bodied soul would submit. Imagine the ignominy of standing up publicly while neighbors bid on your value, turning town meeting into a sort of slave auction. Then, the sold-off became utterly dependent upon his new master. The low bidder took his poor charge into his household, where he supposedly provided shelter, food, clothing, and nursing; if needed, he also secured a decent burial shroud, coffin, and someone to dig the grave, for which the town reimbursed his additional expense.[82] Though the caretakers pledged "to provide and take care of them in sickness and in health," there were no established standards, and treatment varied. The bound-out were expected to labor for the family as much as physically able. The town met the cost of providing for their poor each year through a tax on the real and personal estate of its residents, so there was incentive to accept the lowest bid and, presumably, the least care.

Who was likely to be put up for vendue? Between 1820 and 1845 in Boylston, these included several mentally incompetent people, an orphan, one unwed mother and her infant, a woman whose husband appears to have deserted her, a farmer crippled in a farm accident, the children of a destitute young widow, and assorted elderly folks who had long passed the age when they could contribute to their own upkeep.[83] Other than the unwed mother and perhaps the aging Tory, all of these were what New Englanders would have considered deserving poor: their hardship was an act of God, the result of illness, accident, infirmity, abandonment, or advanced age. (Boylston was not troubled during this period, as some urban areas claimed to be, with rising numbers of idle, unemployed, or intemperate poor—those whose poverty was the supposed result of a flawed character or sinful, irresponsible life.)[84]

And yet, though the numbers remained relatively constant, the costs for supporting the town's poor doubled between 1825 and 1840.[85] Poor relief was by far the most volatile, and usually the most burdensome, portion of the annual budget. Selectmen were proactive in restraining these expenses. They tried to foist the costs for aging Tory David Bush onto the state, claiming that since he had been stripped of his citizenship for his treason, he was technically an alien, not legally settled in Boylston. (They lost.) They sued (and were sued by) neighboring towns, trying to prove that some of their poor had legal settlements elsewhere. They tried to anticipate potential poor cases and seize assets that could be used to support that person. Thus, they took over the affairs of the blind and deranged Widow Butler, gaining guardianship of her meager estate and using it to offset her support while she was boarded out at town expense.[86] James Davenport was appointed guardian for a neighbor who risked "wasting his estate by excessive drinking" and becoming a charge on the town.[87] Yet costs continued to rise.

Though other towns frequently blamed rising poor costs during this period on intemperance and poor character, in Boylston the problem appears to be related mainly to mobility and economic instability. The great majority of those on the town dole were elderly. In the past, Boylston's farmers had often ensured their care in old age by bequeathing their home farm to one child, on condition that the elderly be cared for by the inheritor's family. But as estate division increased and fewer Boylston children remained in town, more of the town's elderly were facing their final years alone. Some found their problems compounded by the volatile new farm economy. And so the rolls of the *elderly* poor mushroomed. In 1831–32 the town supported four elderly paupers; twenty years later, that number had doubled.

During the 1820s and 1830s, social and economic changes—factors that reshaped Boylston from without—began to influence local attitudes toward the poor in their midst. Mobility fractured the cousinhood, replacing family and familiar neighbors with alien immigrants. Communication and transportation dissolved the bonds of localism. Market concerns reshaped labor relations, replacing mutual dependence with impersonal wages and contracts. Commerce and manufacturing drew people to large, central places, where unfamiliarity and transience made communal obligations obsolete. Together, these exogenous shifts strained long-time assumptions about local, mutually shared responsibility for the community's needy.

At the same time, a new belief in the power of the individual to shape his own destiny focused attention on the responsibility of the poor for their own condition. When misfortune was the result of divine providence, the poor man bore no blame for his lot. But as people came to feel responsible for creating their own successes, they were also more likely to hold paupers culpable for their failures. Conflating poverty with immorality, they often assumed idleness, dissolution, promiscuity, or poor judgment lay behind poverty. These shifts in attitude were idealistic and punitive at the same time: reformers believed that an improved social environment could eliminate poverty, and that those who could or would not provide for themselves should be compelled to enter a structured and controlled environment to correct their behavior.[88]

In the early nineteenth century, urban reformers began to propose increasing the number of workhouses or almshouses for the unemployed poor. Almshouses harkened back to ancient English traditions of providing hospitality for the worthy sufferers and punishment for morally nonconforming. New England's early urban almshouses practiced repressive benevolence, providing the bare essentials in exchange for a strict, institutionalized regimen of work.[89]

In 1820, the Massachusetts General Court appointed a committee to study poor relief around the state and to propose improvements to the poor law. The committee polled towns on their practices and issued its findings in 1821. The Quincy Report, as it was known, distinguished between the impotent, worthy poor and the culpable, able poor. It was this last that drew most of the attention of the committee, for current systems of poor relief supposedly "diminished industry" and "destroyed economical habits" by assisting the able poor in their idleness. The Quincy Report strongly recommended that each town establish a "house of industry," "in which work is provided for every degree of the ability in the pauper; and thus the able poor made to provide . . . for their own support." This system, they claimed, was not only most economical, but also more likely to promote a moral society.[90]

In the next twenty years, sixty towns built new almshouses or poor farms, while others refurbished old ones.[91] Housing the poor in neighbors' homes gave way to institutional care. There was a distinction, however, between urban workhouses, such as those established in Boston and industrial Manchester, New Hampshire, and rural poor farms. The inmates (as they were called) of rural poor farms were likely to be familiar to each other and the community, and so lived under less regimented and repressive regulations than those in impersonal urban institutions. Because they worked a *farm* in a *farming community*, they shared the same round of seasonal duties and ethic of working the land as their neighbors. Young and old, men and women, continued on the poor farm the sorts of work they had done at home, producing their own food and supporting their expenses of lodging, fuel, and clothing by sale of products from the farm, much as their neighbors were doing. Still, there was no doubt that they lived in an institution. They surrendered their independence. Being sent to "the farm" meant the end of one's personal liberty. The poor were overseen by a supervisor, assigned to and observed in their work, required to submit to house rule (particularly in regard to temperance and sexual behavior), and denied control of the products of their labor.[92] If the ethic was not so repressive as urban workhouses, it was also not so idealistic. Rural poor farms rarely strove to reform their inmates as to exact from them the labor that would pay for their upkeep. Expedience, economy, and order prevailed.[93]

The people of Boylston quarreled for years over whether to establish a poor farm. At town meeting in March 1836, a petition was presented to this end, and a committee was appointed to "look into the utility" of such an institution. Nothing came of the committee's report. However, two years later, after the financial hard times of the panic of 1837, the petition was presented again, asking for a poor farm "for the accommodation and support of the Town's Poor." The article caused so much contentious debate that the selectmen finally tabled the matter. But the issue continued to roil; in 1840, the town decided to strip the selectmen of their authority over the poor and establish "Overseers of the Poor" to attend to these duties. With their new officers in place, supporters of the poor farm tried again, and they succeeded in securing a committee "to inquire of other Towns as to the utility of a Poor Farm." The committee returned a month later, but was so divided in opinion that its members chose to report not as a body but individually. The town clerk reported: "having inquired of several Towns where they had farms for the use of the Poor, the result was found to be that there was a savings in the expenses for their support, especially where there was a large number of Paupers." Apparently moved by the prospect of tax savings, the town voted that the same men "see upon what terms they can purchase a farm and report next fall." When time came to report, however, the still-divided committee met an even more divided town, which rejected their proposal for purchase. Opponents tried to kill the proposal, but when the moderator "tried the mind of the meeting" he determined there was a majority in favor. It would be another seven years of bickering before the poor farm was finally established.[94]

What did Boylstonians find so controversial in this proposal? Andrew Ward, leading citizen of neighboring Shrewsbury, attributed opposition to a reluctance to change traditional ways: "It has been so long and so generally practiced in this part of the country, that for an individual to attempt to remedy it, is for him to set himself against thousands."[95] Poor farms also separated the poor from the rest of the community, isolating them in their house of shame. More worrisome to moral reformers, the poor farm forced the worthy and innocent poor to share their lives with such moral deviants as drunkards, the unchaste, and the idle. Some feared the expense of purchasing the farm. Others—those poor and middling farmers who bid on the poor—may have resisted losing this source of income.[96]

Those who argued *for* poor farms in rural Worcester County cited humane, moral, and practical reasons. Boylston's Capt. Jason Abbot, the man who repeatedly presented the poor-farm petitions to town meeting, had experienced vendue in his own family. When his incapacitated daughter was sold to the lowest bidder, he apparently found the process intolerable. The following year, he bid on his daughter himself; he introduced the first town poorhouse proposal soon after. The system was unquestionably humiliating. Shrewsbury's Ward criticized the practice as worse than slavery, for the humiliation of being sold was repeated annually, placing the poor ever under a new master. Daily the vendued person, "an educated and feeling person as the slave is not," was reminded of his dependence, reducing him to a state of "utter mortification."[97] Others might have argued feelingly that vendue separated families, especially in dividing widows from their young children. In 1820, for example, Mrs. Sawyer and her youngest child were put out to one family, while her four older children were put out to separate households.[98] Some apparently believed that under the poor-farm system, the overseer could prevent intemperance and cure drunkards.[99] But the main argument in Boylston—the only reason directly revealed in town documents—was economic: poor farms saved money. The Quincy Report echoed this observation, arguing that the average expense of $1.31 per head per week to board out was far more costly than an institutional approach.

Boylston's poor farm did, ultimately, save the town money. The town purchased the ninety-five-acre Whitney farm in 1846 for $2,200 and invested another $900 in livestock, farm tools, and household furnishings. After this initial investment, the annual sale of butter, eggs, lard, pork, milk, calves, hay, timber, and knitted woolen socks—all produced by the inmates and resident farmer—paid for the salary of the caretaker and his wife and the living expenses of the residents. Within five years the town had recovered its initial investment in annual savings on the poor budget.[100] Among Boylston's more enterprising and calculating farmers, such evidence of efficient economy was a compelling motivation to change old ways.

But there were nonfinancial consequences of this shift from household-based to institutional welfare. For some, it may have accelerated a decline in family authority. The average age of inmates at the farm rose from seventy-one to over eighty in the first quarter century of its existence.[101] The farm had been established in part to meet the needs of a growing number of elderly without family to care for them; its existence may have increased the number of offspring who, like the shoemaker's son Caleb Crossman, went off to make their fortune and left their aged parents—no longer the arbiters of their children's fate—to the town's care.

There were other unintended consequences. When comingled with the family, participating in the daily acts of shared family life, the poor were naturally viewed as individuals, and their care was immediate, concrete, and personal. When they were shifted to the poor farm, these relationships were lost. With the poor removed from the townsfolk's midst, it was easier for the rest of the community to treat them as abstract objects or a debased class—an item in the town budget—rather than personally, as intimately related members of a household and community.[102] Their isolation also made it easier to dismiss the poor as culpable for their own misfortunes. As Boylstonians embraced the ethic of the self-made man, with each having the potential to rise according to his industry, poverty became a mark of flawed character. Among the poor farm's earliest inmates, after all, were Abishai Crossman and his wife, those rebellious inebriates who had flouted the Fifteen Gallon Law.

The tendency to blame the poor for their plight may have reflected local angst in the face of a volatile social order. The panic of 1837 had made most area farmers aware of their vulnerability. Those who had mortgaged land faced foreclosure and the loss of their means of independence. The panic reminded farmers that they, too, could become inmates if their riches vanished in an economic downturn. If poverty could be identified with weak character and deviant behavior, then struggling farmers could reassure themselves that their own efforts at self-improvement and industry would maintain their place in society.

Establishing a pauper institution ultimately made Boylston more efficient, bureaucratic, and segregated. It also strengthened the idea that responsibility lay inward with the self, or outward with the government, rather than among neighbors. Communal care became public commission. It also brought home once again a lesson of the new nation: liberty was a right of the economically self-sufficient; dependents forfeited freedom.

Out of Mind, Out of Sight

In late August 1832, Mary noted somberly in her diary, "Mr. Jerm'h Pratt died Friday and buried from the town house where there was a prayer made. A very aged man, *non compos*." Jeremiah Pratt had been deranged, or *non compos mentis*, for at least the last fifteen years of his life when he died at age ninety-one. For all of that period, he had lived quietly within the community, bound out to the care of his neighbors. As he was not "furiously mad" and posed no threat, Jeremiah Pratt was accepted as merely another dependent member of the community who required charitable care.

Pratt's treatment reflected earlier ideas about deranged souls.[103] And derangement was, for most of the colonial era, considered a matter of the soul. "Distraction" was believed in colonial Massachusetts to be "a manifestation of a supernatural drama, with God, the devil, and the distracted person as the principal characters."[104] Such trials might be either the result of divine punishment or merely the mysterious workings of God's providence. Since the cause was supernatural, there was little hope that the distracted might be cured by human means, but also little fear that the person's deviant behavior needed to be restricted or controlled. The nature of small-town familiarity, community surveillance, and social norms made the anomalous behavior of the distracted or feeble-minded soul seem less threatening in early republic New England.[105] In their predominantly rural communities, the insane had few restrictions on their movements or behavior. Most were cared for within their families, with their degree of care dependent on family wealth. If no family support was available, the insane person became a pauper and, like Jeremiah Pratt, was boarded out in the same manner as other town dependents. The concern to the community in these cases was not their insanity but their poverty. Only in rare cases in which a distracted person appeared violent did the law allow confinement.[106]

Most cases of insanity in Boylston in the first decades of the nineteenth century fell within this framework of family- and communal-based care. One of those families that boarded Jeremiah Pratt during his long dementia was the poor but respectable couple Ebenezer and Abigail Butler. Later, the Widow Butler fell into the fire, causing burns that left her blind and precipitated her own insanity. With no family to care for her, Abigail Butler became a ward of the selectmen, who boarded her out to Otis Flagg. Relief Stone was mentally incompetent when she became pregnant out of wedlock; the town took responsibility for Relief and eventually her two children, boarding out Relief and her feeble-minded daughter while indenturing her able-bodied son.

Jeremiah Pratt, Abigail Butler, and the Stone females were deranged and dependent, but viewed as harmless; the town absorbed them into their traditional network of communal care. Mary Ann Abbot posed a somewhat different challenge. In July 1830, Mary White was called to assist her longtime neighbors, the Abbots. Mary reported that their daughter, thirty-two-year-old Mary Ann, was "very much deranged." She was suffering, apparently, from raving insanity (possibly schizophrenia), such that the family required two grown men to watch her with Mary that night. Though Mary prayed for the woman's "restoration of reason," Mrs. Abbot called in the next morning "very much alarmed at Mary Ann's situation." By the evening, Mary Ann seemed calmer, but despite the attentions of a local doctor, she was soon again wildly deranged. Her behavior was so erratic that Caroline White came to describe any irrational act as being "as crazy as Mary Ann Abbot." Her parents struggled for six months to cope with their daughter's delirium, but by the spring of 1831, they had decided to turn her over to the care of the community. Surrendering Mary Ann's only personal assets, valued at thirty-five dollars, her parents made her a ward of the selectmen.[107]

Had the town considered Mary Ann truly a danger, they could have had her confined, chained in a cell, a legal option since colonial times. But the town did not view her that way. At town meeting in 1831, Mary Ann was bid out to Mr. Robert Hudson Jr., one of the town's most established and respected citizens, who agreed to take responsibility for her care. The next year, Jason Abbot himself bid for his daughter. Soon after, her reason returned.

We know these cases of insanity because the sufferers became paupers and so entered the public records as charges to the town. Most cases of dementia, mental incompetence, and madness were cared for within the family, and so lost to history.[108] Mary White's diary, however, provides insight into the family care of her own increasingly senile mother, the Widow Avery.

Mary Avery was not a dependent, but a widow with resources. Strong minded and outspoken, the minister's widow made her own decisions before the onset of her dementia. She customarily boarded with each of her local daughters in turn, spending "a quarter"—or thirteen weeks—in residence before moving on. At times, she chose instead to board herself out in the family of Capt. John Bond, the wealthiest man in town, whose elegant mansion house crowned the hill in the center of town. By 1838, however, as the widow advanced into her eighties, her daughter began to confess to her children that their grandmother appeared "rather broken in mind," her memory failing and "her mental faculties much impaired."[109] Caroline was much more forthcoming in her letters to her brother: "I am seated in Grandmother's room . . . & she is busily preparing herself to go to rest, a business not a little formidable to a person of her fast-decaying faculties; though I must say her tongue moves with the same facility it was always remarkable for, & if her ideas seem to come at lagging distances (as they generally do) she makes up in constant repetition, so as to produce her former continuous sounds. . . . O dear what ugly blots! & Grandmother must have the credit, for she caused me to turn round suddenly by pulling my skirts."[110] Over the next two years, Grandmother Avery's dementia increased. "Grandmother is a great deal of care. Last night such a time!! About midnight she began to thump and talk or rather rave, calling for fire. She had not gone to bed for good not she. I tried to explain but to no purpose and then Mother came and finally returned to bed without doing anything to calm her. She continued to cry and scream and scold by turns calling upon somebody or everybody to come to her assistance, upon friends long since dead as if alive, and as a last resort got out of bed came to mine and then round the room crying murder murder help. Father then came and ordered her to get into bed immediately and finally succeeded with my assistance though she continued to scream for some time. Such was the scene for two hours."[111]

Grandmother Avery's dementia was a trial, but the Whites kept her within the family. As she was neither indigent nor dangerous, Mary Avery's insanity did not concern the community, except to the extent that they extended neighborly assistance and support in her care. Mary Avery died in the White family home in 1842, surrounded by attending family and assisting neighbors. Five neighborhood women came to watch her on her deathbed, and three more came to assist in preparing for burial. The community followed her funeral procession, attending in death as they had in life.

Such treatment suggests that locals continued to view madness and dementia as blameless and untreatable afflictions, to be borne with Job-like patience and general acceptance. As Gerald Grob notes, this informal, local approach to the care of the insane worked in predominantly rural communities, where society was intensely local and familiar, and "deviant behavior, unless extreme in nature, was tolerated" because it was not threatening.

In urban areas, however, these views were changing, and new ideas and practices would eventually infiltrate the town's rural borders. At the beginning of the nineteenth century, perception and treatment of the insane began to shift, for much the same reasons as treatment of the poor had changed. Some progressive intellects began to seek natural causes for what they increasingly saw as a bodily disease rather than a supernatural condition. Focusing on the behavior of the insane, some doctors identified a "breach of the natural order," where disordered or excessive behavior or emotions led to a disordered mind. This made the insane person culpable for his condition; it also suggested that a cure might be found in strictly controlling behavior and environment.[112]

Both suggestions—personal responsibility for one's condition and control of deviant behavior—found a receptive audience in early nineteenth-century Massachusetts. Social and economic changes had created a more complicated world, especially in cosmopolitan centers experiencing urbanization and an expanding market economy. Especially disorienting were immigration and movement: growing, mobile, nonnative populations displaced familiar neighbors. This complex society aroused anxiety and fears of disorder. Critics warned that deviant behavior, unchecked, threatened the social fabric of the new nation. Old systems of family government and communally enforced norms seemed insufficient to control newly threatening behavior. In response, some reformers suggested dual controls. Individuals must develop internalized controls to regulate their behavior; the government must police and control deviant behavior when individual controls failed.

Reimagining distracted souls as culpable and dangerous deviants led to a period of brutal repression in the early nineteenth century. Towns increasingly banished from their borders any person without a legal settlement who exhibited unusual behavior, including such nonviolent but obstreperous behavior as shouting and swearing.[113] The growing numbers of wandering insane were, as one contemporary remembered, "left, forlorn and friendless, to roam through the county, exposed to the insults of the thoughtless and wicked; to hunger, cold, and various calamitous and fatal accidents, a terror to female delicacy."[114] In November 1830, Mary White noted in her diary that such a "poor, crazy man" called at their house, and she had given him "supper and lodging in the barn." Those who did have legal settlement were increasingly confined, kept in chains in a private home, or locked in cells in almshouses or jails. A 1796 law had authorized local authorities to confine the furiously mad in jails, but in the first decades of the nineteenth century, rising fears of deviant social behavior led to the incarceration of even the docile insane.[115] An 1829 Massachusetts report indicated that of 289 deranged souls, two-thirds were confined, 38 of them in chains.[116] Others reported on the horrific conditions in which the confined insane were kept, often "chained in a back room without furniture, without comforts, and sometimes without a fire even in the midst of winter; some of them were confined in jails surrounded with great wretchedness."[117] It was not just urban centers that came to fear uncontrolled madness. A woman from rural New Hampshire recalled the treatment of the town's insane during her youth in the 1830s: one cold winter day, "a poor Crazy Man" who had broken his chain and escaped appeared at their door, half clothed, broken chain still hanging around his waist. He rushed in to the warmth of the fire, talking nonsense and dancing, frightening the family. "There was another Crazy Man in Town who was kept Chained in a barn. His insanity was caused by over studying in the summer. When the big barn doors were opened any one could see him as they passed by. If they stopped to look at him, he would say, "'much learning makes me mad.'"[118]

Eventually, such brutalization sparked calls for reform. Boston's liberal elite, in an act of paternal benevolence, sponsored a private hospital for the insane in 1812. But as the problem of the poor, wretched, wandering—and frightening—deranged magnified in public perception, calls for a public response grew.[119] In 1829, Horace Mann initiated a study by the Massachusetts legislature; its report on the numbers and conditions of the state's insane prompted the founding of the state's first public institution for incarcerating and treating the deranged.[120]

The Worcester Lunatic Asylum opened in 1833, with a large, impressive-looking institutional building, clearly visible from the Abbot's hilltop home in neighboring Boylston. The man chosen to lead that institution exemplified the reforming attitudes that would shape the treatment of insanity for the next several decades. Samuel B. Woodward, though an orthodox Congregationalist, was a theological liberal who rejected the depravity of mankind and embraced the idea of individual free will. The key to reform, he believed, was to help individuals learn to direct and control their will through developing conscience. In addition, Woodward believed insanity was the mind's response to a disordered environment and that the application of a scientific program of moral treatment could ameliorate suffering. The key to a cure was to create properly regulated environmental conditions, then to allow the addled person to regain mental order and develop self-control. To withdraw the afflicted from his chaotic environment and place him where he could experience the therapeutic calm and order necessary for recovery, Woodward advocated institutionalization.[121]

Woodward's reports to the legislature in the first five years of the asylum's operation reveal the social concerns and idealistic hopes that fostered institutionalization. The deranged mind had, in effect, been sickened by overexposure to modern society. Rapid change, overstimulation, the pursuit of material goals, "political strife, religious vagaries, overtrading, debt, bankruptcy, sudden reverses, disappointed hopes," and fears of the end times had disturbed the natural functioning of the mind.[122] Thus, patients were insane because they lived in a turbulent, unstable society. Though environment was critical, Woodward usually located the immediate cause of insanity in his patients' *response* to that society: excessive behaviors (intemperance, smoking, masturbation, religious fanaticism) or disappointment or fears regarding family or economic relations (disappointed love, domestic affliction, economic woes, loss or fear of loss of property). Two-thirds of his diagnoses were attributed to an individual's action or volition, rather than physical causes or any force beyond his or her control.[123] Woodward called for control of the environment to eliminate sources of overstimulation, excitement, or stress and for teaching the patient self-regulation.

On September 2, 1837, Mary White wrote in her diary, "Mary Ann Abbot's insanity appears to be returning. May the Lord in mercy avert this calamity." But the Lord did not avert the calamity, and this time, Captain Abbot and his wife, now in their mid-sixties, did not attempt to care for their daughter at home. Instead, they carried her six miles south, to the Worcester Lunatic Asylum.

The massive, multistoried brick building overshadowed most of still-parochial Worcester. Two long wings, each filled with eight-by-ten-foot chambers, flanked a four-story center hall. When Mary Ann arrived on September 8th, she was classified by type: those who were manic or furiously mad were generally separated from the merely melancholic and the quietly recovering.

Mary was diagnosed as "hemorrhagic," that is, suffering from the results of bleeding in the brain, usually resulting from an earlier, often mild injury to the head. Such bleeding, experts believed, caused profound personality changes.[124] Victims often exhibited emotional derangement, moving quickly from tears to laughter, becoming easily excitable and irritable, losing all self-reliance and self-control. Their normal character was sometimes completely reversed so that the "most kind, considerate, and gentlemanly" victim might "lose all control of himself," become subject to morbid "instincts," and commit impulsive acts of a violent, even brutal nature.[125]

Once admitted, Mary Ann followed a strict daily regimen to help her reestablish a balanced body and an ordered mind.[126] A schedule determined the time for waking, meals, working, religious worship, and recreation. Diet and hygiene were strictly prescribed, to balance stimulation and aid in general health. In addition to outdoor recreation, inmates had daily time dedicated to worthy reading and religious reflection to build moral strength. As occupational therapy was considered key to recovery, Mary Ann likely worked at some useful task for part of each day. A critical component of therapy was regular conversation with Woodward to build relationships of respect and trust and thereby strengthen self-respect and self-control. Woodward also attempted to restore bodily balances through stimulants and narcotics.[127] He believed—and advertised—that insanity, like any medical ailment, was treatable: "It is now most abundantly demonstrated, that with appropriate medical and moral treatment, insanity yields with more readiness than ordinary diseases."[128]

Unfortunately for Mary Ann, Woodward's treatment never had time to take effect. By the autumn of 1837, though the building had already been expanded, the asylum was nearly filled to capacity. Within days she was suffering from one of the curses of crowded institutional life—dysentery. On September 23, Mary White wrote, "Capt. Abbot came here this morning and informed us of the sudden death of his daughter Maryann who was insane at the hospital at Worcester. May this providence be improved by us all. The corpse brought home at night. I went to Capt. Abbot's. The family much affected. May this dispensation be sanctified to them."[129] The next day she attended Mary Ann's funeral, noting, "She was carried to the meetinghouse. Mr. Sanford delivered an address. A hymn was performed by the choir." Mary tried to "sanctify this dispensation" by using the opportunity to urge immediate conversion for her son Charles. "We are continually reminded in providence of the uncertainty of life. Mary Ann Abbot who had become insane was carried to the Hospital at Worcester died on Saturday morning of a dysentery. Her parents are deeply afflicted. She expressed a hope in Christ before her insanity came on which is a great consolation to her friends."[130]

Why did the Abbots send Mary Ann to the Worcester asylum instead of caring for her at home or within the community as they had previously? Although Boylston was undergoing some of the social flux that has been blamed for urban anxiety over deviant behavior, it is not apparent that Mary Ann's condition had created any particular anxieties during her earlier bout with insanity. She had been lodged within the community, with no mention of restraints. She clearly had periods of great agitation, followed by calm, but had she been declared furiously mad and in need of confinement, the town would have been required by law to commit her to the Worcester asylum. This was not the case; if it had been so, the town would have been responsible for the cost of her care, and the treasurer recorded no such expense. Although the record indicates that the family had the support of the court, the decision to entrust Mary Ann to the asylum was most likely made privately, by her parents, and paid for by them.[131]

If the Abbots chose to send Mary Ann to Worcester, they did not do so for reasons of economy. The cost of private admission to the hospital was high, far greater than boarding a person out within the community.[132] What seems more likely is that the proximity of the asylum had made the Abbots aware of a new approach to insanity, and held out to them the hope of improvement. Since Mary Ann's first derangement, Woodward's asylum had won a national reputation.[133] Woodward spoke glowingly of his successes, claiming a recovery rate between 82 and 91 percent and asserting, "In recent [onset] cases of insanity, under judicious treatment, as large a proportion of recoveries will take place, as from any other acute disease of equal severity."[134] Woodward's claim likely gave the Abbots hope that, by entrusting their daughter to an emerging profession with specialized knowledge, they could improve significantly on her chances for a cure.

We do not know what it was like for the Abbots to deliver their daughter into the hands of strangers. It must have been an act of faith, no doubt somewhat controversial among less progressive minds in Boylston. But their decision is evidence of a shift in authority, away from friends and neighbors, the time-honored knowledge of the local doctor, and the comfort of the minister, toward the knowledge of experts and professional institutions. Emerging faith in scientific knowledge, specialized expertise, and institutional order had penetrated even rural Boylston. It also reveals a painful irony. For even as some embraced their sense of agency (and urgency) to control and improve their world, at the same time they faced an ever more complex and unknowable world. Mary and Jason Abbot saw their daughter pass from family and communal care to an institutional setting beyond their control or even comprehension. Institutional welfare—like the complexity of the market, the mysteries of industrial machines, the schedules of railways—all incorporated rural folk into a larger, more enigmatic world.

Removing the poor and insane from community households to institutions also aided in the emergence of the private domestic household. As long as the town's dependents were absorbed within households, the boundaries between private and public were uncertain. Isolating dependents in the poorhouse and asylum, however, allowed people to think of them as *other* and to shift responsibility of their care from the personal to the public sphere. The growth of the public institutions complemented—and enabled—the growth of middle-class domestic privacy. By supplanting traditional communal interdependence and its personal obligation for communal welfare, these institutions allowed people to reimagine themselves as independent beings, bound only by the affective ties of family.

IN 1842, MARY WHITE noted a wedding in her diary. Miss Sophia Cotton, neighbor, friend, and contemporary of Mary's daughters, and a committed member of Mary's reform associations, married Mr. Nathaniel Whitney. Mary and her family did not attend the wedding, for it was held at the "community lodge" in Hopedale, Massachusetts. "Mr. Ballou," Mary noted, "married them." Sophia Cotton left Boylston to join a fledgling utopian community on a 600-acre social compound in southern Worcester County. At Hopedale, Adin Ballou and his followers hoped to separate from corrupted society and create a perfected community. Following "Practical Christianity," members would share all possessions in common while promoting pacifism, temperance, abolition, women's rights, spiritualism, and education. Sophia Cotton and her fellow seekers believed their utopia would serve as an example for others striving to utterly re-form community itself. Like utopias springing up around the region, the people at Hopedale embraced something old, now newly radical: an intensely communal life of mutual bonds and obligations.

Their neighbors might think they were crazy.

CHAPTER SEVEN

Political Principles, Partisan Passions

On a frigid day in January 1838 Mary White ventured across the common to the town hall. She braved the cold to hear Rev. Warren Burton from neighboring Worcester deliver, in her estimation, "a very interesting lecture."[1] He warmed the chilly air with a scalding scold. The people of Boylston, he warned, were being robbed of their freedom and reduced to "White Slavery!"[2] Even worse they were submitting voluntarily—even enthusiastically—to the yoke.

To what malevolent force were Mary's townsfolk surrendering? To the frenzy of party politics! Men who blindly followed the party line surrendered "their own free minds and independent, uncontrolled wills" to behind-the-scenes manipulators who orchestrated, in his words, political puppetry. Partisan passion "dethrones the free popular Will and leaves nothing but popular willingness," willingness, that is, to be directed by self-interested schemers. "What! Read only that which one set of men speak and write, think what they pretend to think, and believe just what they prescribe, and nothing else, and vote just as they dictate. . . . O there is no measuring the low servitude to which you would go down!"[3]

Burton described in vivid terms how the faithful were beguiled into exchanging independent judgment for partisan cant. He drew on popular images of enigmatic powers capable of controlling the mind or manipulating the body. Party leaders cast a *magic spell* over the faithful, conjuring images of the glorious and the nefarious. Patriotic phrases and maxims, great men's names, heroic deeds, or memorable events invoked riotous enthusiasm; slurs, notorious associations, or perfidious images summoned a frenzy of hatred and fear. Such mindless passion provided the energy for party organizers' giant political machine. Party faithful were but cogs in this machine, stimulated to action at the will of its engineers. Emotions provided the fuel for the machine, which then operated along "the wires of association," manipulated by the "pulleys" of rant and slang, harangue and press, creating movement precisely as designed—to make the machine produce votes on command. Any resistance was overcome by that most perfect lubricant, party spirit—or spirits—stimulating, intoxicating, besotting, raising men's passions and robbing them of their senses. "How you gulp down its contents with the inherent fire—and then, all beside yourself, rush blind and headlong to the polls."[4] Burton played effectively to contemporary fears of forces believed capable of enslaving free men: demons and dark arts, inscrutable machines, self-serving elites, or intoxicants that robbed one of self-control.

To drive home his metaphor, Burton conjured up "The Turk," a then-famous automaton exhibited internationally by German inventor and showman Johann Maelzel. The Turk was a life-sized, mustachioed, turban-and-gown-clad humanoid machine who challenged all comers to a game of chess. Maelzel toured the United States in the 1820s and 1830s with the Turk, along with an ingenious mechanical trumpeter, mechanized songbirds, and dancing dolls. But it was the Turk that captured the wonder of Americans; they flocked to see him.[5] In 1836, two years before Mary heard Burton speak, Edgar Allan Poe wrote an essay about the famous chess-playing humanoid, deducing that the machine did not think by itself but was controlled by a mind external to it.[6] No matter that the automaton was later revealed to be a fraud; the analogy worked wonderfully to Burton's purpose. For here was a being who appeared to act independently, but in fact was controlled by another—and for the duplicitous purposes of private gain. Such was the voting machine: "Let us see the operation from the beginning. . . . First, Demagogue, with rant-and-slang-sopped touchwords at the ear and eye; next, oil, wire, and wheel—how they play on nerve, feet, hand, thumb, and finger. Now watch! Between the tips of these [fingers] . . . a little patch of paper, marked with a few drops of cheap liquid . . . there—there! . . . Stuck out above a paltry wooden box—they open, in falls [the ballot],—wait a little and look again—Wonderful! . . . It is a President of the United States!"[7]

Mysteries, magic, machines, mind control! "Mighty Maelzel! Monarch of Mechanism as thou art, never dist thou import or invent the equal of this! Turk, Trumpeter and Rope dancer are all beaten hollow. It is well thou diedst without knowing it, or discouragement and envy would have killed thee!"[8] But the voting machine was far more dangerous than Maelzel's Turk: its mind was malevolent, its purpose pernicious. The party spirit it produced kindled "the fires of vindictiveness, which burn into and burn asunder the friendly bond of neighborhood, shrivel the "sweeties charities" of hearth and home, set brother against brother and father against son![9] The excesses of partisan machinations threatened to destroy community and nation.

Mary heard Burton lecture several times in early 1838, sending other members of her household to hear his message as well. Alarmed, she fervently prayed, "May our nation be led to feel their responsibilities to their country and God and be delivered from political bondage."[10] Yet in Boylston, the evils of partisan politics that Burton detailed—the passionate and prejudiced debate, the cult of personality, the exchange of reason for slogan and rant, rifts among neighbors and family members, uncompromising incivility, demonizing of opponents—all this was just beginning to emerge in early 1838. Partisan politics came late to Mary's town. When it came, however, it came with a vengeance. Mary's prayers that the townsfolk "be of one mind" would go unanswered; in her own family, especially, conflict burned deep.

Political Personalities, Partisan Interests

Warren Burton's fears were based on a reality: the 1820s and 1830s witnessed an extraordinary boom in popular—and highly partisan—politics across the nation. Though Federalists and Jeffersonian Democrats contended for power at the turn of the century, and New England Federalists fiercely resisted the War of 1812, rivalry faded somewhat in Worcester County following the war.[11] A single-party "Era of Good Feelings" followed in which President Monroe could assert (perhaps optimistically) the political unity of the nation. His 1817 inaugural address celebrated "the American people . . . one great family with a common interest."[12] The next decade proved, however, that the American people had many interests and were soon to separate again, like water and oil, into the contentious factions of the Second Party System.[13] It was the age of improving Whigs (National Republicans until 1833, and Whigs thereafter) and populist Democrats; it was an age of popular participation and polarization in politics.[14]

It has been said that intense party loyalty was not merely an aspect of Jacksonian-era life; it was the lens through which many viewed their world.[15] In a town not far from Boylston, one stalwart farmer commissioned an itinerant artist to paint his portrait, instructing the limner to depict him reading his newspaper—with its Democrat banner prominently displayed—proclaiming his party allegiance to all posterity.[16] Such committed partisans embraced their party's goals so passionately in part because they believed that the survival of the republic lay in the balance. But party passions were intensified by the custom of couching political issues as matters of religious or moral judgment.[17] In the midst of national transformation, each side felt a terribly urgent need to prevail, for, as one historian has written, "the character of American Society, it seemed, was about to be determined for all time to come."[18] In such a heated atmosphere, the ideal of "one great family of common interest" gave way. The caucuses, conventions, and campaigns of the Second Party System promoted competition and contest.

Who were Whigs and Democrats in this era, and what "character of American Society" was each party trying to promote?[19] In broad terms, northern Whigs believed that economic prosperity and personal morality were essential to maintaining liberty and that government had a role to play in advancing both. To that end, they generally supported the growth of financial institutions, corporations, and industries as well as schools, charities, and cultural associations that promoted economic growth, middle-class respectability, moral values, and piety. Jacksonian Democrats, the minority party in much of the North, believed that liberty was best preserved through the broad participation of common men: farmers, mechanics, and laborers whose republican simplicity would prevent moneyed interests from hijacking democracy. They decried powerful elites, monopolies, and moralizers and saw the future of the nation in protecting individual liberty and providing the opportunity for each to make his own way. "For Whigs freedom was something to be achieved; for Democrats, it was something to be preserved."[20]

And what qualities were likely to characterize the man who gravitated toward one party or the other?[21] To a degree, each region, state, even county produced its own brand of Whig or Democrat ideology, based on local conditions and personal inclination. This was certainly true in 1830s Massachusetts, where the strength and concerns of the majority Whigs undulated from the commercial seaboard to the agrarian west. In Massachusetts generally, Whigs tended to view themselves as heirs of the classical republican tradition: those who prized the ideals of a well-ordered society and believed it best administered by leading local men of property governing in the interests of the common good. However, the Massachusetts Whig elite married the ideals of the Revolutionary past with visions of a progressive future, where *improvement* promised to raise the quality of life for all and realize the dreams of an expansive liberty. They sought to reconcile virtue and commerce. To this end they embraced state support for new commercial ventures, the founding of associations and institutions for public uplift, the spread of religion, the refinement of public spaces and private manners, and—above all—the security of their property and capital.

Not all Massachusetts Whigs embraced commerce and reform goals equally. An old guard of cultural conservatives disliked reformers' moralizing enthusiasms and worried that inflexibility in these matters might offend essential trading partners—especially in the Cotton South. Their counterpart, later dubbed "Conscience Whigs," strove to perfect society. Some were evangelicals who believed that reforming sin was a religious obligation; others were social perfectionists who, while not evangelical, nevertheless felt obligated by morality and reason to address social ills. Both reforming and conservative Whigs, however, shared a desire to impose top-down order on a potentially chaotic, formless (and somewhat frightening) democracy. Rank-and-file Massachusetts Whigs likely identified with the values and aspirations of their leaders, seeking their own propertied independence, middle-class respectability, ever-improving prospects, Godly social order, and assurance of control and instituted order.[22]

Massachusetts Democrats of the 1820s and 1830s tended to be those who resisted this imposed order.[23] The rank and file in eastern and central Massachusetts represented an oppositional political culture. They were often outsiders in their communities: members of dissenting churches such as Baptists, Methodists, or Universalists; those who resented the imposition of legislated reforms such as temperance or who sought to protect their individual rights from trespass by a majority; those small-holder or non-property-holding artisans, mechanics, or laborers who did not see their interests coinciding with the propertied elite; those who felt that improvements such as turnpikes, canals, and railroads were built on their backs and paid for out of their pockets but did them little good; those who feared the power of concentrated money in the form of banks and corporations; those who believed that their Revolutionary right to self-determination was threatened by Whiggish moralizing; those who feared that their right to an equal share in government power was threatened by Whiggish dominance. They wanted small and unobtrusive government, advocating for low expenditures for road and canals, low salaries for public officials, and restraint on the aristocratic tendencies of princely Whig officials.[24] Often on the cultural periphery, Massachusetts Democrats tended to resent and resist the somewhat-homogenous Whig social core—not to mention Whig social airs.[25]

As with the Whigs, Massachusetts Democrats were of two strains. "Custom House" Democrats were a group of small businessmen and politicians who felt excluded, socially and politically, by the majority party. With bitter rancor toward the state's "aristocrats," they proclaimed themselves progressives on issues such as suffrage expansion and imprisonment for debt but avoided banking and labor issues that might threaten their own commercial interests.[26] The state's "Liberal Democrats," under the leadership of historian and statesman George Bancroft, embraced the radical promises of the Revolution. They decried exploitation of wage labor, suffrage restrictions, and threats to the liberty of common men posed by banks, paper money, and financial corporations. This group, which would become known as Loco-Focos, believed that democracy was imperiled by a growing concentration of wealth and power in the hands of a few.[27] Both Custom House and Liberal Democrats shared a distrust of the privileged elites of the business community whose greed, they claimed, threatened the independent livelihoods of farmers, laborers, and small-shop artisans.[28]

If all these strands—conservative and reforming Whigs, Custom House and Liberal Democrats—coexisted in rural Boylston, they did so quietly and peacefully for most of the years of the town's social strife. During Jackson's presidency (1828–36), Boylston produced no local party organization and no caucus, provided no delegates to county or state party conventions, hosted no bonfires or parades. No impassioned party speeches were delivered on the floor of town meeting, no evidence remains of parade floats, party picnics, or fervid electioneering. Yet party sentiment was slowly percolating. Let us see if we can discern what shaped local opinions and who embraced what political visions.

BOYLSTON REMAINED for many years an apparent oasis of political consensus and calm. Until the War of 1812, Boylstonians had been little bothered by those internal stresses that historian John Brooke has associated with the emergence of partisan conflict in Worcester County, and during the war they were solidly and passionately united behind Federalism.[29] As we have seen, prerevolutionary gentry leaders in Boylston reasserted control after the war, and the continuity of their leadership strengthened their ideal of corporate unity. No dissenting churches were founded to threaten established orthodoxy. No early factories introduced labor dissent. Evangelical activism, flourishing voluntary associations led by the gentry elite, and, most of all, rising market opportunities for yeomen farmers fed local allegiance to the established Federalist order. No doubt this was in part because Boylston remained an agrarian town where a significant number of men owned their own farms. These were the self-selected class of men who had not emigrated or sought work in nearby factories; they were rooted, relatively prosperous, self-determined men. They, like Aaron White, may well have envisioned themselves as part of the respectable middle class that had embraced the market economy and a moral code of self-discipline and piety. They saw their interests at one with the Federalist coastal commercial elite, and with their successors the National Republicans, and then with the Whigs.

In fact, from the 1820s through the mid-1830s, while Boylston raged over other issues, the political waters were not merely placid, they were positively becalmed. During the long, one-party reign of Governor Levi Lincoln Jr., political interest flagged so appreciably that in some years barely a quarter of the eligible men bothered to make their way to the polls for state elections.[30] Boylston was not alone in this; turnout for the town mirrors that of the county during this period, reflecting the general doldrums that marked state politics during this era of one-party rule. Voter interest in state elections began to rise in the mid-1830s, but, as we will see, turnout did not reach the intensity of the War of 1812 years until 1840. In elections for governor during most of the 1820s and 1830s, local men predictably cast their votes for National Republicans and their successors, the Whigs, consistently yielding majorities of three-to-one and higher.[31] The only ripple in this steady stream came in 1832 and 1833, when a small contingent backed a third-party, Anti-Masonic, candidate. But Anti-Masonry was weak in Boylston, in part because of the town's long twilight of conservative unity, and in part because there was no lodge—and no known Masons—within the community.[32] Boylston's political calm and consensus provided little opening for populist insurgents, and little personal resonance to the Anti-Masonic warning that the secret fraternity threatened independence.

The town was no more excited by national contests. In 1824 and 1828, while others fiercely debated whether John Quincy Adams or Andrew Jackson should occupy the White House, barely a third of eligible Boylstonians bothered to vote, and those that did cast their votes overwhelmingly for the conservative Adams. Half of Bolyston's men ignored the presidential elections in the 1830s as well, and fewer than a quarter of the votes cast went to Democrats Jackson and Van Buren.[33]

Boylston, then, was a solidly conservative town, yielding formidable majorities in national elections to Federalists up to 1824, then to their heirs the National Republicans, and finally, by 1834, to the Whigs. Townspeople's conservative sympathies bridged the sectarian divide; both Unitarians and Congregationalists voted Whig. Even as some southern Worcester County factory villages began to hear disgruntled voices of workers protesting abuses of power by the "oligarchy," "monied aristocracy," and "nobility of this village," agrarian Boylston appeared calmly and complacently Whiggish.[34] So strong were general conservative currents that even in neighboring West

Boylston, where several textile factories were transforming the town, results were much the same, although turnout was significantly higher.[35] For most of the 1820s and 1830s, Boylston was an insulated, conservative, backwater, one-party town.

WITH SUCH LOW TURNOUT and lopsided results, we might be tempted to think that politics played no part in Boylston's decades of strife. But there is more to the story. If we look carefully at *local* elections, if we attempt to identify *who* was voting for *whom*, revealing patterns emerge. The town was keenly political, with highly contested elections along deep fault lines. But for most of the period, interest was not vested in national political parties, nor even in statewide partisan contests. It was local issues that bedeviled Boylston, and those issues were personal and passionately debated. Mary's neighbors fought over religion and reform.

If we look at those whom Boylstonians chose to be their leading town officials—their selectmen (head municipal officers), town clerk, treasurer, and state representative, the fault lines appear. All were men in their middle to later years; all were men of prosperous estate. In this, the townsmen continued their ancient custom of deferring to their elders and betters. More notably, nearly all were National Republicans/Whigs. But this illusion of accord is shattered when we examine their religious affiliations. Here we see the contest that roiled Boylston so intensely in the 1820s and 1830s played out on the town meeting floor. From 1822 to 1824, as the religious storm brewed but before it broke, mostly Congregationalists were elected to leading positions. However, from 1825 through 1831, elections were hotly contested by religious sect. Men from "religious parties" met prior to town meeting to try to arrange their "ticket" and assure ascendance; Mary, as we saw, exulted when her churchmen emerged victorious, and decried their unseating a year later by Unitarians. Throughout this contested era, control of the board of selectman and other leading offices see-sawed between battling denominations. In addition, the average wealth of elected officials dropped, as religious views biased some men against customary deference to elite authorities. Finally, in 1832 as church disestablishment approached, the Unitarians gained decisive control—and kept it for the rest of the decade. They lost the church building, but gained the town hall. Religious issues were so intensely felt that for four years in the 1820s the town apparently could reach no compromise on a representative, and so sent no one to the general court. Finally, the year after Unitarian minister Ward Cotton was ousted from his pulpit by the minority Congregationalists, enraged Unitarians united to elect him as representative. They returned him to that post for nearly a decade. Only after 1840, as voluntary religious practice emerged, did rivalry based on religious sect finally fade.

This contest for denominational control of town politics opened fault lines and legitimated contest at the polling place. Political-party rhetoric must have seemed tame after sectarians' hot words about "liars" and "damned fools" at town meeting. Religion, with its hold on conscience and its resistance to compromise, trumped habits of deference to established authority, commitment to corporate well-being, and respect for consensus. Religious commitment sanctioned—demanded—competition and contest, a battle for ballots, a vision of the opposition as the evil other.

Analysis of state ballot questions yields a similar distinction. When Massachusetts proposed a constitutional amendment to disestablish the state church in 1820, conservative Boylston overwhelmingly rejected the article.[36] But after a decade of religious strife, when the town was again given the choice to abolish the state church in 1833, they voted to do so nearly *unanimously*.[37] The Standing Order fell.

State elections are revealing as well. From the early 1820s to the mid-1830s, as we have seen, town interest in state elections flagged, with turnout rarely reaching 50 percent. However, in the late 1830s the Fifteen Gallon Law reached into the heart of Boylston social life. Boylston's evangelical Whig temperance reformers had visibly, audibly backed the law, but other Boylstonians were not pleased to have this moral code imposed upon them. The following year, with voter turnout surging, disgruntled Boylstonians turned the Whig governor who had signed the law out of office, as a record number cast their ballot for Democratic candidate Marcus Morton.[38] The Democratic victory was an anomaly; Boylston voters had not turned pro-Democrat, but antitemperance. The next election, they returned to their Whiggish ways.

Boylstonians, it appears, did indeed care about elections—for a long time they simply did not care that much about national politics. When control of the local church or one's personal habits were at stake, Boylstonians debated, conspired, electioneered, and voted. It was not until fierce debate over religion and reform had fractured the ideal of corporate consensus, until nonpublic associations and exclusive societies had dispelled the sense of collective interest, that Boylstonians began to invest themselves in promoting partisan politics. For as corporate identity gradually eroded over the 1820s and 1830s, political identity emerged. In 1840, a genuine two-party town finally emerged.

Mobilizing the Party Faithful

As we have seen, by the late 1830s, landlessness, transience, and ethnic diversity were on the rise in Boylston, as was resistance to orthodox piety, forced behavioral reform, and privileged, exclusive societies. Across Worcester County, jealousy over social and economic difference was escalating. More and more men came to resent the so-called village nobility, as well as newly empowered corporations and institutions that might "deprive the people of their power and rightful influence in government."[39] By 1838, social discord or nascent class tensions were both reflected in and heightened by—for the first time—a significant Democratic Party base in Boylston. That year and after, the Democratic gubernatorial ticket ran a close second to the Whigs, garnering more than 40 percent of the vote.[40] Between 1838 and 1844—the height of the Second Party System—Boylston was finally a politicized town.

Active competition between opposing political parties played out on the local level through tactics of mass persuasion, many drawn directly from the earlier example of religious evangelicals.[41] After all, politicians and revivalists shared a common goal: to convert and energize those for whom participation was purely voluntary. This was about winning (or, as Burton would have said, controlling) the mind of the people. In Worcester County, party faithful issued calls for commitment through partisan newspapers, which, like the evangelical press, cast issues in urgent moral terms. Also like the evangelical press, the papers invoked an imagined community of the like-minded, united across space and distinct from the nation at large.[42] Party loyalists gathered locally to plot strategies in committees, caucuses, and campaign clubs. Locals for the first time chose delegates to regional and state conventions—another revivalist innovation—and in the process wedded small-town committeemen to the national party machine. As the election approached, party faithful put on entertaining spectacles to draw crowds to political speeches: uniformed marching clubs, brass bands and drummers, torchlight parades, bonfires, barbeques, rallies, and liberty poles. Election days were holidays celebrated with a special "election cake" (though others found free food and drink through partisan treating at the polls). Boys expressed their glee with explosive caps and fireworks. Such exploits created excitement, drew crowds, and strengthened party identity.

White family letters and diaries do give some sense of the timing and type of partisan mobilization. For the years before 1838, little is noted but the day of election itself: Mary always baked an election cake, recorded the town vote, and endured young Francis's experiments with explosive caps. In 1838, however, Mary began to note visiting speakers giving political lectures at the town hall and neighbors stopping by with various political petitions. By the end of the decade she was recording seasonal meetings of Whig and Democrat committees at town hall and the journeys of local delegates to conventions in Worcester.[43] Hired hand Lincoln Flagg went to a Loco-Foco convention in Worcester (no doubt much to the consternation of his Whig employer, Aaron White).[44] Politics also entered into family letters. Caroline, in fact, noted her weariness with political hoopla. "This day [Election Day] in your bustling metropolis, as well as in our busy corner, is considered a very important one. I do not feel near the interest in politics I did a few years since. . . . [W]ith my increase of years the increase of my acquaintance with the two opposing parties has led me to think that whatever the principles of either may be, the majority on both sides exhibit rascally conduct & when we attempt to lean on either for support, they are like broken reeds piercing us through. I will now dismiss national politics, thinking that you & I just this minute feel more interest in the affairs of church & state at home."[45]

The diary of firstborn son Aaron Jr. provides the best evidence of small-town politicking. In his adopted hometown in Woonsocket Falls, Rhode Island, he was a party regular. He participated in political meetings and caucuses, but more tellingly, he proselytized for the cause. He took walks through town, "electioneering on the way," or "preparing the minds of my friends" for town meeting, or "conversing considerable with different persons concerning the coming Congressional Elections." He began making local speeches, a performance, he noted, which was "new business to me."[46] Caroline wrote to Charles that brother Aaron had visited home after a recent trip to Worcester, where he had attended a political convention, "not as a delegate" but rather as a spy "to observe the Nakedness of the Land." (In this reference to Genesis 42:9, Caroline took the role of Joseph when he accused his brothers of having come to Egypt to scout for vulnerable defenses.) The passion Aaron Jr. felt for these activities is palpable. He rejoiced when "we are carrying all before us!" and mourned when he had to endure the gunfire, crackers, and flag waving of victorious antagonists. With intensity such as this, partisans like Aaron turned neighbors, employees, and family members into potential adversaries. Partisan rivalries were acted out in street theater, meeting halls, and parlors and at the family dinner table.

Local politicking was intense for the presidential election of 1840. Whig organizers whipped up enthusiasm or fear—Burton's magic oil—by spreading the message that the "Democratic action against the national financial system was bringing economic ruin."[47] Many in Boylston, having recently suffered through the devastating panic of 1837 and the ensuing recession, believed this message. A year before the election, Boylston Whigs organized a town Whig committee for the first time.[48] Mary noted their meetings in the months leading up to the election.[49] Boylston Whigs nominated wealthy young farmer Eli Lamson as their delegate to the Worcester County Whig convention in 1839, and sent him again, along with Esq. Nathanial Davenport, to the great Worcester Whig nominating convention in June 1840.[50] The Democrats of Boylston made use of the same tactics to mobilize the faithful and recruit converts. They founded their own town committee, matched the Whigs meeting for meeting, and sent their delegates to Worcester's Democratic convention.

To a degree it is possible to discern who in Boylston identified with the majority Whigs and who were expanding the growing ranks of Boylston's Democrats. It is by far easier to identify the town's Whigs, who as activist joiners and petitioners left a paper trail of their commitment. Identifying commitment-phobic Democrats is a challenge.[51] However, general characteristics and broad outlines emerge from the records. Boylston Whigs were on average prosperous men, more prosperous than those who did not vote the Whig line.[52] This may reflect the market interests and commercial attitudes of local Whig farmers, or a sense of frustration at being excluded from prosperity by struggling Democrat farmers and laborers. More telling is the revelation that two-thirds of all potential Democrats were unchurched, while three-quarters of all Whigs were affiliated with the town's established orthodox, Unitarian, or Baptist congregations. Once again, we see the powerful role of religion in shaping local life, this time not as sectarian strife, but as political resistance. Boylston's Democrats refused to identify with conventional religious practice or submit to evangelical pressure. Not all of Boylston's Democrats were poor or unchurched outsiders; the occasional presence among their lists of highly prosperous and active Baptists, Congregationalists, and Unitarians such as the wealthy Flagg brothers, Deacons Moore and Temple, and the much-respected Col. Gibbs, suggests that Boylston nurtured a minority of liberal free-thinkers, radical Loco-Focos. Their voices were likely an undercurrent in town discussion, sounding an alarm about concentration of power in banks and financial institutions, growing inequity in the distribution of wealth, and threats to individual rights. The White family, as we will see, would produce its own prophet of egalitarian individualism who tilted at privilege, power, and proselytizing.

State and county party organizers worked at keeping their machine in good running order. Well in advance of elections, the Whig State Central

Committee was oiling the gears, distributing instructions to town party leaders. They urged local Whig clubs to "diffuse political information" by distributing pamphlets, holding meetings, hosting speakers, and canvassing school districts, and they begged a personal guaranty that this would be done.[53] Minister's son John T. Cotton, chairman of the Town Whig Committee, gave his pledge: "We are organized for the purpose of keeping matters right in regard to the important interests of our Country at the approaching crisis; we have all the light which honest men can desire to guide us in the path of duty; & we have endeavoured to disseminate that light as far as our influence extends; we are well supplied with documents & newspapers of various kinds, wherein are set before us, in the fullest and clearest manner, the important interests at stake in the present situation of parties; & if we do not decide & act, accordingly it must be, that we 'have chosen darkness rather than light.' . . . [Y]ours in sustaining the cause of truth & righteousness in our Country."[54]

These communications politicized personal relations. Men wrote as bosom buddies to strangers, asking for their personal guarantee of fidelity; farmers entertained renowned public speakers; local men went farm to farm to "disseminate the light" to their townsfolk and strangers; villagers wrote to the county partisan newspapers. Their political passions built bonds across distance between strangers who shared their views—and walls between neighbors who did not.

The pinnacle of political excitement came with the state convention. In 1840, the year of the Log Cabin campaign, Whigs held that convention in neighboring Worcester. In a departure from previous party meetings, towns sent not just delegates but all party faithful; Worcester overflowed with a massive gathering of spirited partisans. The multiday event merged democracy and spectacle, as organizers shaped the outpouring into "A Great Meeting of the People," as the party secretary recorded. He continued: "One of the largest, most spirited and enthusiastic gatherings of the farmers, mechanics, and citizens generally which has taken place in the state," with a "triumphal march of the advance guard of the army of freemen," a parade of thousands "of all employments and occupations," witnessed by thousands more. Marchers came arranged by towns, each accompanied by musical bands, parade floats (log cabins "dressed with flags" and drawn on wagons were a popular theme), banners to represent town and trades, carriages decorated with green branches, flags, and emblems, and wagons distributing crackers and cheese. Convention day itself began with a cannon salute. "The streets resounded with the music of numerous bands, with Harrison melodies and with the continual cheers of the multitudes covering the side walks." "No description will convey an idea of the magnificence of the scene. . . . More than thirty bands of music were playing appropriate marches, more than one hundred and fifty banners were spread to be seen. The street was literally wreathed with flags. . . . [T]he windows and balconies were crowded with ladies who waved their handkerchiefs and were cheered with the waving of banners, the roll of drums, the flourish of trumpets, and gallant applause." The procession, a mile and a half long, was followed by addresses, and finally, the meeting of the delegates.[55]

The emotions stirred up by this grand event, held on Boylston's doorstep, reverberated through the town. Mary noted the "great Whig meeting" in her diary. Festivity, celebration, exciting images and stirring words, and, most of all, broad popular participation in making this memorable moment increased individual commitment to the cause. As people celebrated their solidarity, they accentuated their difference from those who did not share their political ideology. Just as Burton warned, hurrahs and harangues produced an army informed by passion, preparing to battle an evil other. Aaron Jr. referred to the opposition party not just as his foes, but as "the *wicked*," and ridiculed their electioneering as "nonsense."[56]

By 1840, Mary White knew well the intensity of emotions that lay behind these partisan loyalties. She had good reason to take fright at Warren Burton's warning of mysterious machines and potent spirits taking control of people's minds and robbing them of their senses. She had seen, as Burton had warned, how they burned "asunder the friendly bond of neighborhood," and especially shriveled the sweetest charities of hearth and home. For no two men were as politically polarized as her husband and her firstborn son.

A House Divided

Aaron Sr. and Aaron Jr. were men of strong political persuasions. Father and son were both deeply patriotic; each revered the revolutionary generation and was determined to preserve its legacy. But they disagreed on what that legacy was. The father sought an ordered republic guided into the future by leading citizens of learning, capital, and commerce; liberty would be secured by the institutions of law and commerce they founded. The son sought a democracy where each individual was free to make his own way into the future, with freedom vested in personhood, not property; liberty would be secured by destroying all institutions that abetted privilege and inequality or suppressed individual expression. The father believed he was securing the liberty won by the Founders; the son believed he was fulfilling their promises of equality. Aaron Sr. was a staunch Federalist and eventual Whig; Aaron Jr. was a radical Democrat.

Their opposing political views likely arose from differences in generation, personal experience, and individual character.[57] Aaron Sr. was born on the eve of the Revolution. He witnessed Charlestown aflame from a Roxbury hilltop as a four-year-old during the Battle of Bunker Hill; he spent his youth in a world at war.[58] He came of age when the nation was still a very fragile thing, and knew the fear and turmoil caused by insurgencies such as Shays's Rebellion and the Whiskey Rebellion. He shared the general horror at the bloody brutality and lawless mobs of the French Revolution.[59] He wholeheartedly embraced Federalist—ultimately Whiggish—order and regularity, imposed by a "natural aristocracy" of leading citizens upon those of lesser rank and understanding. His firstborn, on the other hand, inherited the orderly world his father had created, but he also inherited a sense of obligation to fulfill those revolutionary promises as yet unredeemed: equality and justice for all. He not only lacked his father's confident sense of gentry privilege, he despised it. The conditions of his coming of age made him sensitive to any form of domination and anxious about the perils of dependence. Eschewing farming, he set out on his own in an inchoate world of commercial opportunity and insecurity. He chafed at the inequities and injustices he encountered, and he embraced a radical resistance to all forces that threatened individual autonomy.

Let us consider first the father. As we have seen, Aaron Sr. understood the role he was to play in this new government: he was the local squire. His wealth and property entitled him to lead and obligated him to serve. He preserved an earlier ethic and devoted himself to overseeing the well-being of a homogenous, organically whole community. Like all good squires, he championed law and order, administered neighborhood justice, established institutions for local improvement, and dispensed parochial charity and avuncular advice.[60] He expected, in return, deference and obedience. Aaron White may have been old-fashioned in these views, but his townsmen did not appear to mind. Throughout the town's contested decades they continued to turn to him to chair committees to resolve neighborly disputes and petty misunderstandings, and he obligingly witnessed deeds and administered probate for his townsfolk.

As Federalism evolved into National Republicanism, Aaron Sr. appropriately broadened his role. He espoused a progressive community vision and played his part in promoting local improvement by joining agricultural societies, uniting with corporations, supporting the lyceum. He campaigned to bring a post office to the center village, invested in county insurance companies, and became a temperance man. In short, like most country squires in the 1830s, he supported all forms of economic and moral improvement consistent with conservative social order.[61] In the process, he amassed a fortune by taking advantage of agricultural innovations and corporate investing. He viewed the new financial institutions, like the social institutions that he helped found, as propitious, yielding regional progress along with personal profits. Good governors, good institutions, and good morals all boded well for the nation's future.

When Whiggery arrived, nearly everything about it suited the socially conservative but economically innovative squire, and he naturally assumed local leadership. In 1834, when Worcester County's Whigs signed a massive petition in support of the Second Bank of the United States, Aaron White and neighbor Col. Jotham Bush—Boylston's old-time squires—headed the Boylston contingent.[62] An irascible Democratic newspaper columnist identified White as part of a conspiracy of old-time Federalists who now controlled the Whig machine.[63]

It is tempting to assume that Aaron's orthodox faith and his earlier support of the Standing Order also inclined him toward Whiggery. But in this we must be careful. For Aaron did not share his wife's evangelical sympathies, nor, by the 1830s, did he embrace his minister's commitment to eradicating sin and perfecting society. We cannot know the secrets of his soul, but we can know that his fellow church folk—surprisingly—never nominated him to the socially important role of deacon. His wife recorded his intermittent attendance at church, rejoicing on those rare occasions when he accompanied her to all three services, but more frequently noting (no doubt wistfully) that "Mr. White tarried at home." It was likely through her insistence that he eventually gave up spirits and tobacco, but he steadfastly refused his support to Mary's more radical evangelizing and reforming. Aaron was not a Conscience Whig. He was not striving to improve his soul and his self-control; he was not striving for respectability; he was not striving to submit his will to the Almighty. Squire White no doubt felt that he was already a self-determined, eminently respectable, and moral man. His role was to lead the cultural core of mainline Protestant conservatives in his community.

By 1840, as Boylston's Whigs organized an active local committee, Aaron White and Jotham Bush were retiring from the political scene. They were old men now, and leadership was passing to the next generation: Eli Lamson, who had recently built a textile mill in northern Boylston, took the reins, assisted by the Unitarian minister's son, John Cotton, and the Congregational deacon William Moore, who was busy building a prosperous market orchard. They shared Aaron's improving spirit and entrepreneurial drive, but in other ways they were not at all his successor. These men did not see themselves as civic-minded country squires, and they assumed neither the privileges nor the obligations of squirearchy. They did not derive their status from landed estates, but from their self-made success in new ventures. They participated in politics not out of a disinterested sense of responsibility to promote the common good, but out of concern to promote economic modernization and preserve the national financial system from Democratic ruin. They held no illusions about the survival of corporate community in Boylston; they understood that plural interests had emerged, and they entered politics girded for conflict. In this changing of the guard, what Aaron had understood as republican civic service became popular politics.

NO ONE COULD HAVE BEEN more politically dissimilar from Aaron White Sr. than his firstborn. Aaron Jr. was, as we have seen, a contrary soul, resisting family pressure to submit to social norms, rejecting his mother's Calvinism, refusing to follow his father into commercial farming. He did not want to be knit together with family and neighbors; he did not want to be dependent on or submissive to the will of the community. He wanted to be "a sovereign self, free and independent—and respectful of the boundaries between itself and others."[64]

Aaron Jr. was a free-thinker, an iconoclast, determined to pilot his own ship. He suffered from occasional bouts of depression, but none so dark as the year he was forced to return to his father's house empty-handed and without prospects for self-support. He loathed that dependence. Once established on his own he reflected with deep satisfaction on his simple but self-determined life. It may have been his own struggle for independence that led him to advocate so passionately for the rights of factory workers, mechanics, and farm laborers who had been stripped of their autonomy by new labor relations. And it may have been his own sense of having struggled to resist his parents' values and expectations and the intense obligations of family that made him strike out against what he viewed as despotic practices of concentrated power.[65] Despite—or perhaps because of—his father's gentry affiliations, Aaron Jr. railed against privilege and aristocratic elitism, especially when it resulted in exclusive favors or extraordinary powers. Though he denied being a leveler, he battled privilege and monopoly wherever he perceived it. He became a warrior for personal autonomy.

Aaron White Jr., date unknown. Courtesy of the Boylston Historical Society.

Aaron Jr. identified with a subset of his generation—certain grandsons of the Revolutionary patriots—who believed that they were fulfilling the promises of the Founders. He was a college classmate of George Bancroft and contemporary of Emerson and Theodore Parker, and like them he idealized his patriot grandfather and the principles for which he fought. But these men understood those principles differently from their fathers, who had been charged with bringing order and nationhood out of revolutionary chaos. Where their fathers had focused on republican ideals of commonwealth, these men embraced democratic equality and personal autonomy. Where their fathers had believed that civic participation must be grounded in property, these sons insisted it should be grounded in (male) personhood. Where their fathers had accepted the organic rightness of social hierarchy and the need for deference, duty, and obligation, these sons took to heart the equality and autonomy of all men. In pursuit of these ideals, Aaron Jr. would fight passionately against patrician privilege and influence, business monopolies, restricted suffrage, coercive authority, curbs on personal autonomy, parental power, and domination of any sort. The most essential sovereignty, he would assert (though not so radically as his contemporary Henry Thoreau), was supreme independent authority over self. He would deny "the right of any institution—church, state, or family—to coerce the individual."[66]

Aaron Jr. became a social radical, much to his father's consternation.[67] But he did not start out that way. The son began in his father's footsteps. At college, he joined a "Washington Benevolent Society"—a Federalist political club—and prayed that "these meetings be prospered."[68] But experiences getting started in life left him disaffected with his father's world.

When Aaron Jr. graduated from Harvard in 1817, he was unsure—and deeply unsettled—about his prospects. He did *not* want to farm and agonized over what to do to secure a living. As graduation approached, he was "troubled with melancholy reflection," with "much anxiety regarding my future security" and a "head full of plans & considerations as to what I shall do when I get out of college."[69] On the eve of his graduation, he confessed his fear of being "cast upon the world" and launched "upon an ocean on whose quicksands thousands have been shipwrecked."

His first attempts at school- and shop-keeping were failures. A year after graduation, he noted fretfully, "Winter is coming and I am out of employ & what is worse, know not where to obtain any."[70] And if life did not seem precarious enough, the panic of 1819 wrought bankruptcy and fear all around him.

Aaron ultimately decided to apprentice himself to a prominent Middlebury lawyer and read for law, while teaching and doing odd jobs to support himself. But after two years, his lawyer-employer left practice, and Aaron returned—with utter dread—to Boylston and the humiliating prospect of being once again a dependent in his father's household. Thanksgiving of 1820, in his twenty-second year, he would later remember as the most miserable of his life. He left Middlebury reflecting on how much he had prized the last two years spent "under no man's guidance but my own." A week later he "was at the home of my father, without a home, without money, where to turn I knew not. Winter was coming upon me unprepared. The blast sounded shrill & bitter without which my proud & independent spirit found no refuge in the house of my father."[71] Soon after, he left Boylston for Providence, where he passed the bar and set himself up in law practice. He lived the rest of his life so as to be certain that he would never again suffer from such dependence, nor feel the sting of an insecure financial world, nor tolerate those who robbed the man of small means of his substance.

But Aaron Jr. was not done—not yet—with dreams of entrepreneurial success. In the 1820s, the young lawyer took all available avenues to prestige and position. He secured the office of postmaster of his adopted hometown of Cumberland Hill, a position that brought patronage and profits. He hatched a scheme to secure a corporate charter for a canal to link Providence to Worcester, and was hugely cast down by being beaten to the punch. Barely twenty-four years old, he sponsored and oversaw several public lotteries to raise funds for new roads and an extension of the railroad in his adopted hometown, successfully secured a bank charter for Cumberland Hill, established a temperance society, and confided to his diary about his "head full of schemes." In 1824, he came out strongly for John Quincy Adams; no wonder that when Aaron Sr. visited, he pronounced himself well pleased with his firstborn.[72]

Aaron Jr.'s political transformation may have come in 1829, when he moved to the emerging Rhode Island factory town of Woonsocket Falls. Powered by the Blackstone River, the Ballou brothers' Social Manufacturing Company had been spinning cotton thread in Woonsocket since 1810, but it expanded significantly with the opening of a second mill in 1827 and the completion of the Blackstone Canal the following year. The booming factory village offered opportunities for a young lawyer. Shortly after his arrival, he was invited to take charge of a new bank in town. As cashier and one of the directors he spent his first year hobnobbing with the textile factory owners, financiers, and other locals of established position and wealth.[73]

It was Anti-Masonry, it seems, that severed these ties and set Aaron Jr. on his radical course. He would later reflect with pride and satisfaction on his active role in "warfare against the institution of Freemasony," and the killing of "the old monster."[74] Anti-Masons believed that the secret order of Freemasons were conspiring to influence the government for private gain by using their fraternal ties in legislatures to forge monopolies, oppress labor, and subvert the rights of the people.[75] Aaron become a crusader. He attended meetings, drafted resolutions, was chosen as a delegate to Anti-Masonic conventions, served on their statewide committees, acted as state secretary of the party, published an Anti-Masonic book, and penned newspaper articles that "labored to overthrow and expose [the Masons] to the gaze and ridicule of the world."[76]

Aaron's Anti-Masonic views most likely did not sit well with his fellow bank directors. It was not uncommon for local bank directors to be Freemasons; Dexter Ballou may have been a Mason—his brother George was a lifelong and enthusiastic member of Woonsocket's own lodge. "Typically, after striving eagerly to establish banks in their town, men who would become leading Anti-masons were pushed out of positions of influence within these new institutions."[77] By 1831, Aaron was deeply and publicly involved in the Anti-Masonic Party; shortly thereafter, he either resigned or was forced out of the bank.

It was a turning point in Aaron's political evolution. From thence forward, he was deeply, adamantly opposed to banks and banking, and equally opposed to emerging Whig views of an improving *class*—the better sort—and their claims to civic leadership. He was opposed to all his father embraced.

Hard Money, Hard Feelings

By the 1830s banks were a highly politicized subject in the nation's capital, in small towns, and most certainly around the White family dinner table. Hopelessly divided on the topic, the family could not discuss banks or banking in peace. Were banks respectable institutions serving important community and national needs? Or were they "beasts of prey" out to swindle the poor farmer and artisan for the gain of a selfish, privileged few?[78] Caroline wrote to her brother Charles in May 1837 that her mild criticism of banks at home was considered heretical. "Indeed, if I happen to say a word against the 'banking citadel' it produces so much excitement, that I think they know it is rather feeble or they would not be alarmed at my weak weapons."[79] The unnamed defender of banks was their father, Aaron Sr. On the other end of the spectrum was his firstborn. While his father was defending the banking citadel at home, thirty-nine-year-old Aaron Jr. was busy discrediting banks and bankers in his Woonsocket lawyer's office. Aaron confided to his journal in the 1830s that he passed his time discussing banking "with all who visit my Office and rising up a strong feeling of indignation against the banks whenever I can. I most heartily wish that the whole were abolished."[80]

Father's and son's differing views reflected their opinions about the need for—or fear of—large central institutions that could regulate—or dictate—monetary affairs and so facilitate—or manipulate—the allocation of capital. To commercially oriented Aaron Sr. banks were a boon; to his privilege-wary son, they were a bane. A political lightning rod was the Second Bank of the United States (BUS), which since its inception in 1817 had been a partisan affair. As the nation's central bank, the BUS—with the backing of National Republicans in Congress—received a twenty-year charter to provide stable national money and credit. The BUS held the deposits of the federal government and handled its fiscal transactions; the majority of its stock, however, was held by private investors. National Republican—and later Whig—supporters argued that the bank's specie reserves would help stabilize the value of currency, regulate capital markets, and fuel economic expansion without the risk of skyrocketing inflation. Such an expansion, they insisted, would benefit not just the commercial elite, but all—including the majority of small farmers—who desired credit to pursue market opportunities.[81] The Democrats, however, were never at ease with the concentration of money and power in this one public-private institution (at the time, the largest financial corporation in existence), especially since so much of its stock was owned by a relatively small number of wealthy Whig men. Some feared what they saw as the dangerous and unconstitutional power it vested in the central government, and the threat that this power posed to state sovereignty (and not inconsequently to slavery). Populist Democratic president Andrew Jackson was profoundly antibank, proclaiming it a corrupt corporation serving the special interests of private stockholders at the expense of the citizenry. He was determined that the bank should die, and when National Republicans attempted to force an early recharter during Jackson's first term, it sparked an all-out partisan "Bank War." Jackson won reelection on his antibank rhetoric, and then "killed the Monster" by removing federal deposits. When the ensuing panic of 1837 devastated the national economy, Whigs placed the blame squarely on the Democrats' antibank policies.[82] Images of the "Hard Times" of 1837 often portrayed the recession as a partisan beast. A shocked population envisioned itself the blameless victims of malevolent forces—not the forces of their own economic speculation and unsound investments, however, but those of warring political parties, "the villains and heroes of national party politics."[83] Aaron Sr. and Aaron Jr. each believed the source of suffering lay in the other's politics.

But it was not the national bank alone that roused father-son antagonism. The two held antithetical views on the many local banks sprouting across Massachusetts at this time. These were state-chartered but privately run village banks. Father and son particularly disagreed on the merit—or menace—of the paper notes each local bank issued as a form of currency. Aaron Sr. supported these independent banks not just because he was invested in them. To him, these institutions served the public good, providing the currency and credit to lift all boats on a rising tide of prosperity.[84] If a few enterprising souls like himself who had invested their energies and resources in these new ventures realized some particular gain, it was deserved and did no harm.

These early banks were not like their savings-and-loan descendants. They have been described as private "investment clubs," whose purpose was not so much to serve the public as to enrich their shareholders.[85] In the Worcester County countryside, groups of local gentry gathered in every small town with sufficient water to power a factory formed such an investment club. They applied for a charter, founded a local bank funded by their purchase of shares, printed paper bank notes, and used this as currency to build and man new manufactories. Investors grew wealthy with the growth of the industries their banks had financed.[86] For people such as Aaron Sr., the emergence of village banks was a sign of progress, easing the inconvenience of scarce cash in the countryside, promoting economic development, and making their investors wealthy.

His son did not agree. Aaron Jr. became a crusader against proliferating private banks, and most especially against the paper notes they issued. He railed against what some saw as spurious financial instruments and shady practices that enriched wealthy Whigs at the cost of the common man. He believed banks were, as Hezekiah Niles charged during the panic of 1819, "little knots of cold-calculating individuals" who "manipulated the public trust and beggared widows and orphans."[87]

The new relations of private commercial banking, in fact, challenged traditional morality. The use of "insider networks" that privileged favored customers in making loans was a widely accepted practice but did not sit well with those who expected their public charter to bind banks to serving the common good.[88] Laborers, artisans, and petty proprietors were anxious that wealthy bankers were investing their hard-earned deposits recklessly, engaging in speculation and shady practices to boost bank profits.[89] When the same humble farmer or artisan applied for a loan, however, banks were highly selective in granting credit. Journeymen artisans found it very difficult to get loans to set up their own workshops and engage in the market. The *Evening Post* noted that "the application of the laborious mechanic is treated with contempt and rejected with disdain," while the banker's peers and family received generous credit.[90] Rural merchants who hoped for credit were subject to prying reviews of their personal character, their drinking and sexual habits, as well as their resources. The Mercantile Agency (later to become R. G. Dun) rated the credit worthiness of most of Boylston's petty proprietors, for example, cautiously; entry for a Brigham family son in August 1843 doubtfully noted that he was "not a fair character or attentive to trade. Worth nothing, not safe, is not doing right."[91] Those farmers who were able to secure mortgages discovered to their surprise that they were governed by new rules which stressed strict and unbending terms of contract, punctuality, and fines, lawsuits, and loss of property for late or missed payment, and that these new financial institutions gave no ear to traditional pleas of bad weather, pests, illness, or other common misfortunes.[92] The long-distance, impersonal, legalistic nature of new banking relations was a troubling departure for rural debtors. The risky, speculative, and anonymous nature of bank deposits was equally troubling to creditors. Farmers, artisans, and working men blamed banks for violating traditional mores, occasionally even resorting to mob violence targeting bankers personally to express their outrage.[93] These new forms of banking relations "raised questions that cut to the core of an emerging commercial society—a society where commodities, currency, reputations, and flesh-and-blood people increasingly floated free of custom, tradition, and place."[94] What Aaron Sr. saw as progress, his son saw as moral transgression.

Between father and son, as between commercial Whigs and hard-money Democrats everywhere, no aspect of the new banking relations was more controversial than paper money. Most paper money was printed not by the federal government but by each private bank. The right to issue banknotes was included in a bank's charter, and each bank designed, printed, and circulated its own currency. These highly varied slips of colorful paper were promises to pay; in theory, they could be returned to the issuing bank for their face value in gold or silver specie. Confidence that this slip of paper could be converted, like magic, into a pot of gold rested on the assumption that the bank had on reserve sufficient assets to redeem their notes for specie on demand. Banknotes entered into circulation primarily when the bank used them to pay its debtors or issue loans, and served a critical purpose in an expanding economy by providing a practical medium of exchange.[95]

The problem was that not all notes could be redeemed for face value—and some had no value at all. Banks kept increasingly smaller fractional reserves on hand, so it became crucial to know something of each bank's ability to redeem in specie before accepting its note at face value. But as the number of banks issuing notes jumped dramatically—from 200 nationally in 1815 to over 700 by 1840—it became impossible to track their individual financial status. As a result, the notes of well-known banks that were considered trustworthy tended to circulate close to par, while notes from distant, unfamiliar banks were discounted.[96] With so many notes of such differing value in circulation, it became baffling to determine the worth of the paper presented in exchange for goods or services. And those in the know profited from others' ignorance.

The recipient of an unfamiliar banknote had few options. If he were savvy, he might consult a "bank note detector"—new monthly journals that evaluated the market rates of a range of notes—before accepting the bill. Or he could accept the loss and sell his depreciated notes to money brokers, who profited from collecting devalued currency and traveling the sometimes-long distances to redeem the note at its home bank.[97] But even this form of redemption was stymied by unscrupulous financiers who purposely founded suspect banks in remote locations "for the express purpose of making it difficult, if not impossible, for the notes to be exchanged for gold and silver."[98] Even worse, some unwitting holders of notes discovered that they were worthless, either printed by a now-defunct or "broken" bank or counterfeited. Counterfeiting, either by raising the value of a genuine bill, altering the bills of defunct banks to put in the name of a solvent institution, or issuing completely spurious notes, thrived.[99] In such a climate it was not difficult for the unscrupulous to manipulate the system to their benefit, and the unwary and uninformed—usually journeymen, artisans, laborers, and small proprietors or country traders—were swindled at every turn. Some employers paid their workers the face value of notes that they had purposely collected at a depreciated rate from out-of-town or insolvent banks. When the workers tried to exchange them for goods at local stores, they found that grocers and other shopkeepers raised their prices to cover the potential loss on tainted money, as well as the inflation that accompanied a flooded currency market.[100] The distress caused by such paper money swindling was well known, and it enraged Aaron Jr.

From his position in a textile village, surrounded by factory operatives, artisans, and petty proprietors, Aaron Jr. interacted daily with those who suffered from bad paper, from tough credit, from impersonal debtor relations. As a rising lawyer active in civic affairs, he also knew the sorts of insider relations and risky profit-seeking ventures that many bank directors pursued. Having struggled himself with financial insecurity and dependence, he was furious at what he viewed as the scandalous behavior of Whig commercial elites. As his memorialist recorded, "with characteristic pertinacity, he made his practice conform to his principles, and he avoided in every possible way the use of paper money in any form, putting himself to great inconvenience for this purpose."[101] Aaron accepted only coin in payment for his legal services, and he paid his bills that way also. If forced to accept a note, he went immediately to the issuing bank to exchange for coin. His major activity on some days was making journeys around the area to "call on different Banks for specie," finding it "tough work to make them do their duty," and persisting in his demands until "they paid the bills, though very unwilling."[102] He wrote essays for local newspapers decrying banks and paper money.[103]

Aaron Jr.'s greatest fear came to pass in May 1837. A combination of global market strains, U.S. financial policies, and overheated bank-credit inflation finally gave way to a sudden contraction and sparked a panic. With creditors demanding payment in specie, overextended banks realized they would likely not be able to meet demand and suspended all payment of specie.[104] Notes could no longer be redeemed for gold or silver. The independence and security of many people were seriously compromised when left holding worthless bills.

The 1837 panic affected Aaron Sr. and Aaron Jr. quite differently. The sharp contraction of credit and failure of financial institutions was felt acutely in the rural village. Wealthier farmers like Aaron White, who had invested in shares of bank and insurance stock, feared their savings would evaporate. The father confessed to son Charles, "You know that I am considerably interested in the safety of our banking institutions which seem to be in a very precarious situation just now and what will become of my interest in them I know not but I know that there is no dependence on the stability of anything on earth and that riches make to themselves wings and fly away."[105] Aaron Jr., with his till safely stocked with coins, had no such worries. But he had fury. With their worthless paper notes, bankers were now no different from counterfeiters, he raged, and they had spread suffering and ruin among those honest folk who held their notes. He turned to the Rhode Island General Assembly to force payment and prosecution, but to his horror found that the Whig-dominated assembly intended to sanction the action of the banks by an act of legislature.[106]

The proposed act further enraged Aaron Jr. He feared the Whig legislators were complicit with the bankers and together represented the threat of unchecked power to corrupt the rights of the people. In a memorial to the General Assembly, later published as a broadside, White condemned this old foe: special privilege granted for private benefit. The banking power was an evil empire, and the legislators, he claimed, had a sacred trust to protect "hardworking honest citizens" from this despotic violation of law, trust, and honor. The law left "thousands holding [the bankers'] unredeemed promise of payment for the sweat of their brows, curtailed in the very necessaries of existence." The Whig legislature was willingly allowing an "incorporated Order of Nobility" to usurp the rights that the nation had so recently secured. If they were not destroyed, the banking class would combine to "disobey our laws," then assume law-making power and ultimately enslave the many for the benefit of the few. Aaron's accusations—corrupt aristocracies, privileged classes of nobles, tyrannical use of unchecked power—reprised revolutionary rhetoric. He was cheered by the thought that popular excitement against the banks was growing strong, adding, "I verily believe that before long Banks will disappear and the sooner the better."[107] His memorial, however, was "met with great indignation" by the Whig General Assembly and defeated.

Aaron Jr. did not give up. To remind people of the insecurity of paper money, he took some of his supply of coin and had satirical brass "so-called dollars" struck. The coin depicted a hung or "suspended" pig (a *sus pendens*, or hanging swine) and the date on which specie had been suspended. It warned all holders: "Never Keep a Paper Dollar in Your Pocket Until Tomorrow." White distributed the coins to remind people of the inherent worthlessness of paper. (Ironically, White's coins today are quite valuable.)

The gulf that separated Aaron Sr., a Whig bank investor and proponent of corporations, and Democrat Aaron Jr. with his anti-aristocratic, antimonopoly, antibank, anti-paper-money views, represented a fairly recent divide in rural Worcester County. Both sides claimed to promote the Founders' ideals of liberty. But the father believed that liberty followed prosperity, and government support of private economic development was essential to social improvement and national security. The son was a crusader for liberty based in personhood, not property or capital, and ultimately for that other promise of the Revolutionary years—equality.

Liberty, Equality, and Paternity

At the end of the 1830s, Aaron Jr. would adopt a cause that would mark him forever as a radical Democrat, the antithesis of his father's orthodox Whig mentality. He went to war—literally—to defend universal male suffrage and popular sovereignty. Defending his principles would cost Aaron Jr. his home, his law practice, and his reputation and would deeply strain relations with his family. He would declare these sacrifices necessary for "the rights of mankind."[108]

As we have seen, suffrage in Revolutionary New England was restricted to freeholders.[109] In the early nineteenth century, most states eliminated this property-holding qualification and democratized voting rights, meeting demands of former soldiers, landless immigrants, urban laborers, and a new class of shop and factory laborers for broader suffrage.[110] Massachusetts eliminated its property requirement in 1821.

Rhode Island did not. It continued to operate under its colonial charter, which required ownership of at least $134 of landed property to be admitted as a freeman of the state with voting rights. When the colony had been agricultural and maritime, this requirement was not onerous; more than three-

Aaron White Jr.'s satirical "so-called dollar," brass, ca. 1857.
Courtesy of Robert S. Koppelman, The CoinSite.

quarters of white males had been freemen in 1775. However, in the next fifty years, the state led the nation in urban, commercial, and early industrial growth, creating a large population of working men who owned no land. By 1840 the majority of white males were excluded from the franchise.[111] To make matters worse, Whiggish lawmakers refused to adjust political representation, so that rapidly growing urban and industrial centers in the northeast were significantly underrepresented compared to sparsely settled rural townships in the south and west. By the 1820s, the politically impotent began to grumble; by the 1830s they had organized to seek reforms.[112] They were joined by some commercial and professional men who protested voter fraud by large landowners who temporarily sold freeholds on Election Day to those who would vote as the landholder wished.[113]

But the reformers made no headway: power lay in the hands of the landed minority, who adamantly refused to modify suffrage or representation. They argued that the point of government was to protect property against the irresponsible landless, not to mention recent foreign and Catholic immigrants and the more deeply rooted black population.[114] Echoing John Jay, they claimed that those who owned the country ought to govern it.[115]

Tension grew during the 1830s as repeated peaceful efforts at constitutional amendment were rebuffed. From 1834 to 1838, landless agitators were joined by a small group of lawyers, including Thomas W. Dorr, to form a Constitutional Party. Their calls for moderate reform were answered by conventions, but the resulting reforms were always voted down. One contemporary noted, "the disfranchised of Rhode Island had presented themselves before the Charter Assembly, about as many times, by their petitions, as Moses and Aaron, on behalf of the Hebrews, and on a similar errand, had presented themselves before Pharaoh; they had waited many years longer than did the Hebrews, for the granting of their petitions—but the Assembly thought it 'really doubtful whether any change was actually desired, by any large number of the citizens'!"[116] Discouraged, the party disbanded after 1838, and the movement temporarily lapsed.

But Thomas Dorr was a formidable advocate. The well-educated patrician son of a Providence Whig China-trade merchant, Dorr was a lawyer who gathered around him other professionals who shared his equal-rights principles. Inspired by the insurgent populism of the 1840 Log Cabin presidential campaign, Dorr took a bold new tack: he proposed that the people themselves possessed the authority to alter or abolish existing government whenever it failed to protect their rights. The people, he insisted, had the authority to form government—without the consent of the existing powers. Dorr and his supporters embraced the newly launched Rhode Island Suffrage Association and issued a general call for an extra-legal "People's Convention" to draft a new state constitution and institute a new government, overturning the existing authority.

Dorr's call for a people's constitutional convention—outside of and unauthorized by the existing government—was based on the Founders' words ("that whenever any Form of Government becomes destructive of these ends, it is the Right of the People to alter or to abolish it, and to institute new Government"). It emulated the methods of 1787.[117] His reasoned legalism drew supporters among some professional and commercial reformers; his populist rhetoric drew supporters among the disenfranchised; and his anti-Whig stance drew the attention and support of Democrats, whose party leadership he then assumed. By the spring of 1841, the campaign had grown to an immense popular movement of mechanics, farmers, and middle-class professionals.[118]

This was a cause to which Aaron White Jr. joined himself heart and soul. He had not been part of the suffrage movement in the early 1830s, as his energies had been engaged in Anti-Masonry and antislavery. In December 1840, however, he attended his first Suffrage Association meeting in Woonsocket, and was immediately converted. Within a month, he was himself addressing Suffrage Association gatherings. In April, he participated in the 3,000-strong "Grand Free Suffrage Parade" in Providence, with its roasted ox, collations of beer, electrifying speeches, and banners proclaiming, "Virtue, Patriotism and Intelligence versus $134 worth of dirt," and "Peaceably if we can, forcibly if we must."[119] The Suffrage Association followed this extravaganza with a summer of organized parades, barbeques, and spectacles, such as the Newport gathering in May where gun- and sword-toting marchers called for a new constitution.[120] Aaron attended the "Great Suffrage meeting in Providence" on Independence Day, where "exciting speeches were delivered, badges denoting membership were worn in public, processions displaying banners and accompanied with music marched through the streets, and every artifice was used to swell their apparent numbers and terrify their opponents."[121] Aaron addressed suffrage gatherings around the state, kindling passions and mobilizing support for an extra-legal "People's Constitutional Convention" to be held in October.[122]

By his own testimony, Aaron was drawn to this battle "to defend the common right of the citizens of the United States to make their own constitution of their own free will," a natural extension of his own campaigns for personal sovereignty and self-mastery.[123] But White was no doubt also drawn to the personal character and principles of Dorr, a fellow crusader against privilege and the tyranny of "the aristocracy." Dorr, like White, had been born the grandson of a Revolutionary War patriot and the son of a prosperous merchant, and like White he had attended Harvard and become a lawyer.[124] Like White, he felt alienated from his father's material and social world of privilege. He shared with Aaron Jr. a deep and invincible faith in democratic principles, and he adopted the same liberal causes, including religious liberty, opposition to banking reform, and abolitionism. Like White, he had abandoned his father's strong Whig commitments to champion reform as an "ultra," a radical Democrat.[125] His circle included men of similar bent, such as George Bancroft, John Greenleaf Whittier, and Orestes Brownson.[126] Aaron White Jr. believed deeply and passionately in the rightness of Dorr's principles and in the virtue of his character, and would defend his friend to the death.[127] Dorr, in turn, would lean heavily on White, declaring at one point that Aaron Jr. was "a brother to him."[128]

The Suffrage Association's fevered efforts bore fruit. Dorr called for a People's Convention for October 1841. When it met, with broad representation from almost all Rhode Island towns, the elected delegates drafted a progressive constitution based on equal-rights ideology—with the glaring and costly exception of refusing the vote to black and female citizens—along with a first-ever Rhode Island Bill of Rights.[129] The People's Constitution was ratified by a majority of the state's adult white males in December, and elections for state office scheduled for April 18, 1842.

Outcry from the existing charter government—now dubbed the "Law and Order" faction—was swift and strong. They protested that the right to alter or abolish governments existed only under conditions of extreme oppression and that in other cases, the ruled must submit to the authority granted to the rulers through election.[130] Once constituted, *governments*, not the people, became sovereign, and could be altered only through legal proceduralism. Prominent Law and Order men accused the Dorrites of being "anarchists, disorganizers, infidels, incendiaries, and plunderers," lawless men bent on destroying the common good.[131] In March 1842, as elections for the new government approached, Rhode Island justice Job Durfee declared the People's Constitution illegal. The people, he avowed, were a *corporate* entity, whose sovereignty resided in their elected represented assemblies.[132] The Dorrites were a treasonous mob whose overthrow of law and order would be the end, not the beginning of, liberty.

Aaron White Jr. was one of nine Rhode Island lawyers who penned the Dorrite response, which argued the absurdity of people being able to make or amend their government only by permission of their rulers. Drawing on the precedent of the Revolution, they asserted, "At the American Revolution, the sovereign power of this State passed from the king and Parliament of England to the People of the State, not to a portion of them, but to the *whole* People, who succeeded as tenants in common to this power. . . . [Since] all power is naturally vested in and consequently derived from the people, [such power] may be reassumed by the people whenever it shall become necessary to their happiness."[133]

By April 1842, a furious cascade of events had begun, leading inexorably toward violent confrontation. As Aaron Jr. and his Dorrite compatriots approached the election of People's Government officers, family and conservative friends tried to warn them off their radical path. Thomas Dorr's parents begged him not to assume leadership of the new government.

> We beseech you, we pray you, to pause before you pass the Rubicon and become engulfed in political, criminal degradation, where our feeble prayers will not avail to save you from disgrace and ruin. We again beg, entreat and pray you to retire from the strife you are exciting, for the Law must prevail or all Government is at an end. If your heart is sensible to the parental anguish we have and now suffer, we pray our Heavenly Father will vouchsafe and awaken in you a corresponding feeling for our sufferings and influence you to renounce the course you are pursuing and restore us to a peace of mind which has for a long time been a stranger to us. May God in his infinite mercy

. . . preserve our grey hairs from that shame and disgrace which will attend you if successful in your present course and hurry us sorrowing to the grave.[134]

But Dorr ignored their entreaties. The April 18th election for Suffrage Party officers went forward, and Dorr accepted his new post as governor in the insurgent government. The next day he wrote urgently to White, begging his close associate to join him immediately in Providence to confer "on matters of the highest importance."[135] Dorr faced a serious problem, for the old charter government refused to cede power, and the new government had to decide if and how to wrest it from them. On May 3rd, Dorr, his fellow elected representatives of the People's Government, and upwards of 2,000 of their compatriots—500 of them armed—paraded through Providence and convened their General Assembly. They met—not in the State House, which they failed to claim, but in an adjacent foundry—where an armed guard patrolled during the hours of session, "escorted the 'Governor' to and from the place of the meeting, and kept watch at his house during the night."[136] Anxious foreboding hung over the city, as competing governments occupied the same city. One observer who compared the hovering threat of violence to living under a Parisian mob noted, "The agitation was at its height. Families were divided, and brothers, fathers, and sons were arrayed on opposite sides," while "shops were closed, the business at the college was suspended."[137]

After two days of high tension and citywide alarm, Dorr adjourned the meeting and traveled (or fled) to Washington and New York to gain outside support for—and prevent armed federal intervention against—his government. He wrote to Aaron that their friends in Congress "urge us to go on with one voice. . . . The movements of democracy here . . . and the general expression of public sentiment in our favor have alarmed the administration with the fear of an American War of the People against the Government."[138]

Falsely believing in his overwhelming popular support and in assurances of armed assistance from abroad, Dorr returned to Providence in mid-May in a warlike mood. Aaron Jr. argued strenuously with his governor to avoid open conflict, or to postpone it as long as possible, fearing that their many moderate middle-class supporters would desert them if faced with armed rebellion.[139] But Dorr ignored White's arguments, and in a move that Aaron later criticized as "rash and indiscreet," led a contingent of armed supporters in a botched raid on the Providence Arsenal. Dorr's own father was among those who repulsed his attack.[140] The results were disastrous, as most of the elected representatives of Dorr's government resigned in protest over such violence.[141] The opposition used the raid to incite terror in the populace, spreading rumors that Dorr intended to revisit the French Revolution's reign of terror by sacking the city, raping its women, robbing its banks, and plundering its riches.[142] Dorr fled to Aaron White's home in Woonsocket, and White then assisted him in escaping to New York City, where Aaron's brother Thomas could aid him.[143] White then returned secretly to Providence, taking back roads to avoid detection and only barely eluding an army of agents sent out to track him down.[144] At Dorr's direction, Aaron assumed control of suffrage affairs in his place, expecting to be arrested at any moment, especially after President John Tyler declared that federal troops would support the existing Law and Order government if necessary and would refuse to recognize the Dorrite constitution.[145] Mary White, deeply concerned for her son's safety, prayed anxiously, "May the Lord avert the dangers which hang around him and make the wrath of man to praise the Lord."[146]

Meanwhile, the old charter government mobilized its own reign of terror. They instituted martial law and declared that any participation in the Dorrite government was an act of treason punishable by life imprisonment. Arrests, raids and searches, interrogation, seizure of property, calumny, and intimidation were practiced to break the will of those who had supported the People's Government. Brutalized and demoralized, all but the most radical of Dorr's followers deserted the cause. Aaron White detailed these abuses to Dorr, noting that suffrage men were fired from their jobs, evicted from their dwellings, and foreclosed on by their banks, that the streets were patrolled at night by arrogant "Law and Order" hoodlums who threatened them with violence and broke into their houses at will to search for arms. "Will the people of these free United States sit quiet and see and hear of such proceedings as these without one great struggle to establish personal rights?"[147] The city, he declared, was cowed, though some parts of the country stood firm.[148] As he later testified, "It has been my chance to meet, since that period, individuals of the suffrage party suffering under all the various forms of oppression that a most inhuman persecution could devise and dare inflict. I have met them fleeing from their homes before an infuriated banditti called law-and-order soldiers. I have found them in prison and in exile, I have seen them suffering from the derangement of their business, from the loss of property, and from the loss of employment. In all these situations, I have always found them buoyed up by one common consolation: and this was, that the principle which they deemed the ark of their country's freedom, they had never surrendered."[149]

Aaron was among the few who remained faithful to his embattled leader, writing to Dorr that he must return from exile and peaceably convene the Dorrite General Assembly to ensure the government's legitimacy.[150] He suggested that Dorr convene not at Providence, where the Law and Order forces held control, but at the country village of Chepachet, where Dorrite friends had been training as militia, "and call your Military friends to the same place as I believe that in that place you could be protected."[151] He promised, "If you have any fighting to do, commit it to my hand and I give you my promise that it shall be done with the same sincerity that Sancho Panza gave his promise to Don Quixote to disenchant Dulcinea."[152] Dorr agreed. On June 25, he issued a call to arms to his followers, directing them to Chepachet. But upon his arrival the next day, he discovered fewer than 300 faithful—mostly artisans and farmers, as all elected members of the People's Legislature had deserted—gathered to defend him.[153] His father, Sullivan Dorr, visited him in tears, warning him that a large Law and Order force was coming to surround him and begging him to escape from certain sacrifice of his life.[154] Seeing the futility of his position, Thomas Dorr dismissed his military, dissolved his government, and fled.[155] Law and Order forces moved in, making mass arrests for treason. Between 100 and 200 prisoners were taken, roped together, on a forced march to prison in Providence. In a coordinated attack on Aaron's hometown of Woonsocket, sixty prisoners were taken; Aaron's home was broken into and plundered and a warrant for his arrest issued as a principal advisor to the traitor.[156]

News of the Dorr movement's collapse and mass arrests traveled north to Boylston. Aaron Sr.—like Sullivan Dorr—faced a horrible choice. His Whig principles utterly rejected his son's radical politics. Yet his son's life was in danger. For attempting to warn and save his son, the venerable Sullivan Dorr had been seized and threatened with hanging. Despite the peril, Aaron White Sr. chose blood over politics. Rushing to Woonsocket, he ran head on into Law and Order forces, who immediately arrested and imprisoned him as a close relation of one of their primary foes.[157]

Unlike Sullivan Dorr, however, Aaron Sr. never had a chance to speak with his son. Aaron Jr. was not in Rhode Island, nor would he ever return. Seeing the writing on the wall, he began "arranging my affairs" in late May, sending off his most valuable papers and library to Massachusetts. When he left his Woonsocket home immediately before Chepachet, he stripped it of most of its essentials, fully expecting that "Law and Order" would soon be visited upon it; indeed, anti-Dorrite gangs forced his doors, broke his windows, smashed chests and boxes, and made off with items.[158] One contemporary reported, "Aaron White was obliged to flee from the State. And who is Aaron White? One of the most profound lawyers in Rhode Island—the man whose Constitutional argument presented to the State Anti-Slavery Convention of 1836 has been admired by the first lawyers in the country. Aaron White, it is to be presumed, could not have failed to see and exhibit the validity of the Rhode Island Constitution. Nothing but an arrest under martial law could meet the arguments of such a man. And nothing but flight from the State could preserve his freedom. His aged father, it seems, fell into the hands of military 'law and order.'"[159]

Aaron White Sr. was apparently soon recognized as a faithful Whig and released; he was back in Boylston within a week. Aaron Jr., however, faced a difficult summer. He had information that Law and Order officials had declared Dorr and himself "first and second in iniquity," and orders were given "to make short work in our Cases."[160] Though actively hunted by lawmen from Rhode Island and Massachusetts, he escaped across state lines to the wilds of northeastern Connecticut, where a local innkeeper hid him in a secret compartment under the attic stairs for three weeks. As the hunt intensified, Aaron came to fear for the safety of the innkeeper's family, and slipped out one night to hide in a thick pine grove nearby, where the innkeeper instructed his grown daughter to bring daily meals and essentials for survival.[161] Finally, as his hunters closed in, a disguised and unshaven White stole along back roads to the capital city of Hartford, where he found audience with an old friend—the governor—who granted him asylum. With this protection, Aaron returned to tiny New Boston, a village of Thompson, and settled. His mother noted continued concerns for his safety in "his exiled condition," and prayed that he might "soon have the privilege of a free man and his foes soon be made to see the error of their ways."[162]

Aaron did not easily relinquish the cause of popular sovereignty or the fate of his friend Dorr. In exile, he wrote ceaselessly to "raise the hue and cry" in the Democratic press, helped other "appointed apostles of liberty" arrange their legal affairs, worked with his brother Thomas to secure Dorr's constitutional archives, and personally copied the ledgers of names of all those who had voted for the People's Constitution before surrendering those ledgers to Rhode Island authorities, that he might keep proof of the legitimacy of the constitution's ratification.[163]

Following the Dorrite insurgency, the Law and Order government eventually adopted a new constitution, granting most of the suffrage reforms for which Dorr had campaigned. But they did not forgive Thomas Dorr, and when he returned to the state in 1843 he was arrested, tried, and sentenced to life in prison at hard labor. At Dorr's request, Aaron White along with a group of lawyer friends continued to argue for his vindication and release and for the rightness of their popular-sovereignty doctrine.[164] They eventually took their case to the Supreme Court, where an unsympathetic Chief Justice Roger B. Taney refused to rule in favor of any action that southern slaves might interpret as justifying insurrection.[165] Dorr, his health broken by harsh prison conditions, was released in 1845, and his faithful advocate and friend Aaron White comforted him with assurances that "your acts have already given you a place in history and a character to be preserved for all time" and that when "once a man has obtained such in treasure, I know of nothing in this world that can be weighed against it."[166] In pursuing the Founders' promises, the Dorrites saw themselves as romantic republican heroes—if ultimately quixotic or tragic, nevertheless, true to conscience and principles, true to self, truly *independent*.[167] Dorr was a tragic hero, a broken man, and he died shortly afterward.

Aaron's sacrifices in pursuit of popular sovereignty speak to the passionate commitment of some men of his generation to fulfill the promises of the Revolution. Early suffrage reformers in Rhode Island had included some laborers from the "Working Men's Party," but ultimately the doggedly idealistic drive toward constitutional reform came from an organized middle class of professionals, mostly young lawyers and commercial men.[168] They believed, as Aaron White claimed, in the urgent need to "overthrow that system of Aristocracy which for so long has ruled and still continues to oppress under new forms the poor People."[169] And they believed it passionately. Aaron White Jr. confessed to a fellow Dorrite, "I have always been a friend to peace & peaceful measures, but I sometimes feel as though [the Law and Order faction] will never be made to recognize the principles of Justice & Humanity until, by the light of their blazing dwellings they read them written in the blood of their Children."[170]

AARON JR.'s savagely passionate words reveal the depth of emotions that lay behind partisan cant by 1844. Whigs and Democrats demonized each other in Boylston and beyond: Whigs believed they battled to sustain "the cause of truth & righteousness," while Democrats fought to defend "the principle of Justice and Humanity." Each saw the other as villain and threat to national survival. The polarized nature of partisan politics disrupted and remade relations between townsmen, neighbors, and kin as they came to see not just their interests but their fundamental values as opposed. It took time before we would come to see "struggle among competing groups for the control of the state as a positive virtue—indeed, as the only foundation for liberty."[171] But Mary's townsfolk and family grappled with political pluralism, as yet to understand their common ground, as yet to come to terms with accommodation and compromise. In their politicized town, Boylstonians could not, as Mary prayed, "be of one mind," for they were no longer of one body.

CHAPTER EIGHT

The Bonds of Antislavery

On a mild December afternoon in 1840, Mary White set out on foot from her center-village home. The determined sixty-two-year-old matron trod muddy roads and cart paths, uphill and down, from time to time stopping in at a farmstead. These were not social calls, or visits to the sick, or a neighborly exchange of goods. Mary was seeking signatures for a female antislavery petition. It was hard work, made more difficult by the hostile reception of those who thought women had no place meddling in politics and who would scold, "it's none of your business, gals, and you'd better go right straight home."[1] But Mary White believed that slavery was a sinful "stain on our National Character," and her evangelical conscience told her she "had a duty to perform to do away with this stain."[2] Mary's passionate commitment to conscience would carry her down an unintended path of radical activism.

Abolition shook Boylston to its core. It focused years of debate over the nature of liberty. From kitchens to fields, tap rooms to town meetings, men and women had spent the past quarter century battling bondage: to parents, neighbors, community, state church, social norms, creditors, corporations, political parties, ignorance, and vice. All of these struggles asserted the right of each individual to self-determination. As Maelzel's Turk had demonstrated, those who were not self-mastered were *slaves*. The language of enslavement had been employed to condemn any restraint on autonomy. With the rhetoric of bondage and freedom so much in play, inevitably the town came to grips with the issue of race slavery. But it came, for the most part, reluctantly. Sensing the powder-keg potential of the issue, most shied away; those that confronted it affronted the rest. The ensuing battle rent family, friends, and community, leading to consequences unforeseen and unintended. Ultimately, resistance to race slavery would become the standard around which Boylston's disparate peoples would reunite, sharing a new identity as defenders of the Republic of Liberty.

Antislavery Arrives

When Reverend and Mrs. Sanford arrived in town in 1832, they brought with them connections to an extensive network of early antislavery activists. Harriet Smith Sanford came from an evangelical and socially activist clan. Her sister Sarah Smith edited the *Moral Advocate*, a New York periodical for moral reform, worked for temperance, and was vice president of the second Antislavery Convention for American Women in 1838.[3] Sister Grace Smith Martyn was first directress of the Ladies' New York City Antislavery Society.[4] Brother-in-law Job Martyn, a Congregational minister, lectured for the antislavery cause. Through the Smith-Martyn families, Harriet had ties to male and female abolitionist leaders and agents in New York, Philadelphia, and Boston. The twenty-five-year-old minister's wife shared her family's strong antislavery convictions, and she was about to connect rural Boylston—and her neighbor Mary White—to the energies of this national network.

Her husband did his part as well. Reverend Sanford kept his new congregation mindful of the slave's plight with concerts of prayer, antislavery sermons, and pulpit sharing with itinerant antislavery agents. Mary and her family listened. In 1836, daughter Caroline wrote to her brother: "Last Friday, I enjoyed the high privilege of hearing Mr. [Henry] Stanton deliver an address. . . . I expect to hear Mr. Stanton again this afternoon and am longing for the feast."[5] Three days later, when Mary heard Stanton speak, she prayed, "May the Lord grant his blessing to the efforts they are making to abolish Slavery."[6] When Harriet's brother-in-law Rev. Job Martyn visited town, Mary reported to her son, "[Mr. Martyn] appears as interesting as ever. He has delivered one Antislavery lecture here. He thinks that the Monster Slavery has received his death wound."[7] As the new minister and his wife settled into the parsonage, Mary embraced a new friend, and a new cause.

In itself, antislavery was neither new nor radical.[8] But when William Lloyd Garrison took up the crusade with the strident Boston publication the *Liberator* in early 1830, antislavery went from genteel and moderate to fervent, uncompromising, and provocative.[9] Garrison argued that slavery was *sinful*; renunciation—that is, emancipation—must be immediate. By identifying slavery as sin, Garrison was able to enlist the activist energies and unbending conscience of evangelicals such as Mary White.[10] Antislavery organizers appropriated the language and methods of revivalism. (Nonevangelical Quaker and even Unitarian abolitionists, whose concern was more with the unethical nature of slavery, also recognized how effective revival-like methods of abolitionizing—converting others to the cause—could be.) Convinced hearers were to embrace emancipation as they did repentance, enroll in antislavery societies as they did in churches, and commit themselves to a new life of sanctification: antislavery activism. There was urgency to this work: God would take righteous vengeance on the United States if the stain of slavery were not soon expunged.

By 1836 Mary was convinced of her duty to "have something to do in the cause of freeing the slaves." [11] She was up and doing. In May that year, Harriet and Mary organized the first meeting of the Boylston Female Antislavery Society (BFASS). The two women drew on their experience with organized benevolence. They knew the first order of business was to draft a constitution, enroll members, and elect officers. Harriet and Mary framed their cause:

> Believing that the usurped dominion of one man over another is sin inasmuch as it takes from him the ownership of his own person, robs him of the right to the product of his own labour, reduces him from a person to a thing, shuts him out from the enjoyment of the means of grace, darkens the mind, and debases the intellects and sacrifices all domestic rights that it there lays in ruins the comfort and happiness of more than three million of our fellow-citizens in this land of boasted freedom—that it tramples in the dust all that is dear to women and is inconsistent with the principles of a free government as it is with the law of God—and believing it to be the duty of every one to exert their influence to effect their emancipation—therefore we the undersigned women of the town of Boylston agree to unite ourselves into a society for the purpose of more effectively exerting our influence in the behalf of the oppressed. [12]

Though Harriet and Mary conflated current political, economic, moral, and religious indictments of slavery, their primary objection was to its *sinfulness*. Yet therein lay a problem for these two orthodox Calvinists. Their condemnation could not rest on a literal, common sense reading of scripture that sanctioned slavery. They relied, instead, on what they believed to be the "essential insights" of Christianity, with profound implications. [13] In laying out the ways in which slavery violated the divine will, Harriet and Mary spoke to the radical egalitarian potential of Christianity: the equality of all souls before God. The conditions of slavery prevented the slave from knowing the path to salvation, enslaving the soul as well as the body.

Beyond sinfulness, slavery violated emerging norms of a Protestant middle class that valued self-supporting independence, respectability, and domesticity. Slavery denied the right to self-determination and economic self-mastery, the prized goals of middle-class manhood. Slavery kept its victims bound in ignorance, denying now-hallowed goals of uplift and self-improvement. In a culture that enshrined the domestic sphere as a female haven, slavery violated "all that is dear to women." Childbearing was debased as commodified reproduction; sexual abuse of female slaves by lascivious masters trampled the modesty and chastity of women; selling spouses and children away from their families destroyed domestic bonds and family stability. Antislavery women sought to protect the integrity of domestic life from all such incursions. A study of antislavery petitions from this era concludes that while men argued for public policy based on northern and southern sectional interests, "women invoke[d] the language of faith and feelings."[14] Slavery was sinful; it was also socially, economically, and politically opposed to all that middle-class American women such as Mary and Harriet cherished.[15]

Black Souls

In seeking to understand Mary and Harriet's characterization of slavery, we should ask what experience either of them had ever had of the institution, beyond the tales of fugitives and the reports of visitors to the South. Neither woman had ever traveled to the South, but Mary was old enough to remember slaves and ex-slaves personally. Mary's grandmother had requested the gift of a slave girl to serve her household as a wedding present. Dinah lived her whole life with the family, marrying a coachman and having many children, all of whom Mary's grandmother gave away when quite young. Mary's mother, when asked if Dinah felt badly about this, explained, "Oh no, she did not care any more for them than the cat when her kittens were taken from her."[16]

What assumptions did the women hold about the nature of black people? There is no doubt that both women had met and interacted with northern free blacks. During the first half of the nineteenth century, Worcester County towns averaged about 1 percent "colored" population, a category that likely included Native American and mixed-race people as well as those of African descent.[17] Though these people may have been familiar, they were nevertheless undeniably other, as poor Cato Bondsman learned when he petitioned for a pew in the meetinghouse.[18]

Black bodies were a thing of curiosity in white antebellum New England.

Northern whites attended to the physical differences of blacks, particularly with the rise of so-called racial science: the black cranium, it was theorized, housed a brain deficient in reasoning capacity but superior in musical skills.[19] Consider P. T. Barnum's first venture in profiting from curiosities: the exhibition of Joice Heth, supposedly the 161-year-old nurse of George Washington. In 1835, Barnum traveled around New England offering the chance to view this extraordinary spectacle: a wizened and withered old black woman, "the Greatest Natural and National Curiosity in the World." People—including Mary White—turned out in droves to view, touch, and comment upon what many saw as a grotesque freak of nature, a forerunner to the carnival sideshow. Barnum played upon Heth's age and patriotic ties to the Founding Father, but he was particularly successful in rousing popular interest by playing on the "otherness" of the black body. His advertisements described Heth's body in animalist terms. Many visitors agreed, describing her as physically repulsive, possessing paws or talons.[20] Upon her death in 1836, there was clamor for Heth's public autopsy, happily capitalized upon by Barnum as another spectacle of race. Blacks—like poor Moses Bondsman, the unfortunate Boylstonian whose scalp was found floating in a brook—were the most likely subjects of autopsies in this era, in part because their kin had less power to resist, but also to satisfy a white population determined to prove the scientific basis of racism. Historian Benjamin Reiss points out, "as the economy dilated and as social roles for whites grew more varied and unstable, essentialized notions of race served as ballast for anxieties about the shifting grounds of identity, status, and authenticity."[21]

How did Mary White view Joice Heth? Did she seek in Heth a reassuring affirmation of her own superior place in a shifting society? The opportunity came in September 1835, as Mary and Aaron traveled to Providence. Mary commented on viewing the Heth exhibition, "I went to see an old colored woman who was nurse to General Washington, her age 161 years. She has been totally blind for more than half a century, but retains her hearing. Repeats & sings hymns, her voice very clear. She appears very willing to leave this world as she believes she shall go to her Savior, whom she has professed to love 116 years. She is said to have led an upright & exemplary life."[22] Of far more concern to Mary than the state of Heth's body was the state of Heth's soul. We cannot know what Mary thought of the minds or bodies of blacks, but she clearly believed that their souls (slave or free) were receptive to grace.[23] In loving and being loved by the Savior, blacks were acceptable to God, and so acceptable to Mary White. Her faith led her to embrace a radical spiritual egalitarianism.

Working for the Cause

Mary and Harriet justified their antislavery work by asserting the duty of women to "exert influence." The trouble, as they were about to discover, was in finding ways to exert influence that were not offensive to their conservative fellow churchwomen. Antislavery was not popular; between 1830 and 1865 only 1 percent of American men and women were active abolitionists.[24] Those who worked publicly for the cause in the urban North risked being stoned, mobbed, or becoming the focus of violent riots.[25] Elizabeth Chace of Rhode Island later recalled that she was repaid for her antislavery work with ostracism, persecution, slander, and insult. Very few women were willing to take on such work.[26] When Harriet and Mary canvassed the women of their church, they could find only a handful brave enough to enlist. So the pair went out to the highways and byways. In a town simmering with sectarian animosity, they appealed to the women of the Unitarian Church for their sympathy. With cross-sectarian support, they recruited forty-six women to sign their new society's constitution.[27] It was an unprecedented act of alliance building, choosing to reach across a sectarian divide to form a coalition of shared interests.

Boylston's antislavery women were a diverse group, a mix of Congregationalists and Unitarians, single, married, widows, from their teens to their seventies.[28] Their residences were scattered around town, with only a small cluster in the center village. They were not generally part of Mary's regular social network. In fact, most of Mary's closest friends and most frequent household visitors were notably absent from the abolitionist ranks.[29] Two common characteristics stand out: most of these women were affluent, and most were related.[30] Affluence afforded the time and resources to devote to charitable causes. And family ties—the presence of siblings, parents, and in-laws—suggest both that families tended to take up the cause of abolitionism together and that family support was essential when embracing such an unpopular cause. Even so, few women were willing to enlist.[31] Boylston's society, then, like most rural women's antislavery groups, was a small, diverse coalition of women who shared one strong conviction.[32] As we shall see, they were not like-minded about acceptable ways to pursue their goal.

With their first members enrolled, Harriet and Mary set about the work of the society. Embracing the tactic of moral suasion, they focused their work on informing themselves and their neighbors about the sinfulness of slavery and raising money to pay traveling agents and publishers to do the same. The constitution mandated that "the time of meeting [2 pm to 5 pm] shall be spent in work for the benefit of the cause, while some one shall read books or papers calculated to enlighten and interest us in the Anti-Slavery cause." The women took a subscription to the *Emancipator*, a periodical of the New York Antislavery Society, rather than Garrison's Boston-based paper, the *Liberator*, perhaps because Harriet's sisters were involved with the former. With materials in hand, the women gathered monthly to pray, sew, and listen to readings. With donated fabric, linen thread, and yarn, they gathered in each others' parlors and knit stockings and sewed lace caps, cuffs, and aprons. This sewn work they sold locally, and in 1836, by Mary's account "the Treasurer received between 2 and 3 dollars for work done."[33]

But things were not well with the BFASS. Attendance at their sewing meetings soon fell off, as fewer and fewer women were willing to continue. Mary recorded the troubled time in the society's records, noting how support flagged and little was accomplished. In part their struggles may have been related to the panic of 1837. Fiscal insecurities may well have cost some farmers' wives the privilege of devoting time and resources to charity. But attrition was more likely the result of the society's close affiliation with the Boston Female Antislavery Society, a group whose radical tone and methods it increasingly adopted. Mary's diary and letters during these two years reveal that she and Harriet were stretching the limits of female propriety.

In abolitionizing their neighbors, Mary and Harriet politicized female benevolence. Most meetings included scripture reading, conducting business, reading and conversation on slavery, sewing, hymn singing, and a closing prayer, all traditional female benevolent activities. But into each of these tasks, they introduced a voice of protest urging social change. Their prayers became political petitions: "May [our] labors be blessed of the Lord to bring about the emancipation of the poor Negro." Their hymns became protest songs:

> I am an Abolitionist!
> I glory in the name;
> Though now by slavery's minions hissed
> and covered o'er with shame;
> It is a spell of light and power,
> The watchword of the free;
> Who spurns it in the trial hour,
> A craven soul is he.[34]

Their readings from antislavery periodicals became lessons in propaganda and persuasion. Many *Liberator* articles were directed to women's sewing groups, teaching them how to stand and speak convincingly, present and defend arguments, and develop cogent appeals to the mind and emotions of their fellow women.[35] These were lessons in advocacy and activism.

As the women of the Boylston Antislavery Society sat listening to these readings, they sewed articles for an antislavery fair, embellishing their handiwork with heart-wrenching or startling images of their slave sisters. The BFASS completed a cradle quilt and a bed quilt that "none but an Abolitionist would buy."[36] They were probably decorated with poems such as the one printed on a quilt sold at the 1837 Boston Antislavery Fair:

> Mother when around your child
> you clasp your arms in love,
> And when with grateful joy you raise
> your eyes to God above—
> Think of the *negro*-mother,
> when *her* child is torn away—
> Sold for a little slave—oh, then,
> For *that* poor mother pray![37]

Some were stamped with stenciled images of shackled slaves pleading for mercy.[38] The Boylston women recorded crafting pincushions and needle books; they may well have embellished them with the motto, "May the use of our needles *prick* the consciences of slaveholders," a popular item at the 1837 antislavery fair. Pen wipers were inscribed, "Wipe out the *blot* of slavery," while wafer boxes proclaimed, "The doom of slavery is *sealed*." If all sewing was so marked, Garrison reasoned, the subject of slavery would be always kept before the mind of the items' users.[39] Thus sewing was politicized.

Rural antislavery societies supported traveling abolition agents as they came through town. Harriet and Mary hosted these speakers, even as the tone of their addresses grew fervent and radical. First came the men, notorious souls such as Amos Dresser, the young seminarian who had been publicly whipped in Tennessee for possessing antislavery literature. Then, more shockingly, came the women. The Quaker Grimké sisters' scandalous practice of speaking in public before "promiscuous" (mixed male and female) audiences earned them the censure of orthodox clergy as immodest agents of "degeneracy and ruin."[40] In October 1837, *after* the Grimkés had been publicly censured, Mary noted: "attended in the evening lectures by the Miss Grimkes on Slavery. Very interesting lectures. May the Lord direct them in

Cradle quilt, probably Boston, 1836. Gift of Mrs. Edward M. Harris,
accession # 1923.597. Photograph by Peter Harholdt.
Courtesy of Historic New England.

all they do." The next night, she "went to Mr. Sanford's and had the pleasure of seeing the Miss Grimkes."[41]

Mary also offered hospitality to these agents, even though such courtesy often brought criticism to others.[42] Though some women had been ostracized for publicly associating with blacks, Mary provided lodging for black male abolitionist agents—and not in the barn. Mary confided to her diary, "Mr. Brown and Mr. Washington, a colored man, lodged here and went from here this morning."[43] The two had spoken in Boylston at an antislavery meeting the day before. This degree of intimacy was uncommon even among abolitionists, who often felt strongly that blacks should not be treated with familiarity. In nearby Leominster, Frances Drake was ostracized when she walked in public with the Remonds, a black abolitionist family visiting from Salem. Neighbors informed her that it was improper for her to "treat niggers so familiarly."[44] Sharing hospitality, courtesy, or even the sidewalk with black people could unleash a storm of criticism.[45] Mary set a radical example in bringing Mr. Washington under her roof and to her dinner table. Caroline advised her brother Charles, "Do treat with respect the colored person who conducts himself respectfully, let not the tincture of the skin be your standard how you shall treat a person, but their conduct."[46]

The Anti-Slavery Almanac proposed a strategy for women to use in educating their neighbors about the evils of slavery: "Let the friends of the cause in each school district start a subscription, raise what they can, purchase a library, appoint some one to act as librarian, and then draw out the books to read . . . and put into the hands of their friends and neighbors. . . . In this way, three or four abolitionists may abolitionize almost any town or village."[47] Harriet and Mary's society at various times subscribed to the *Emancipator* and the *Cradle of Liberty*, and Mary noted that she "had the privilege of reading the *Liberator*"; the society also purchased Theodore Weld's *American Slavery As It Is* and Maria Chapman's collection of antislavery readings, *The Liberty Bell*.[48] Its constitution called for directors to circulate these books. If they did, Weld's book in particular may have had a profound effect. Subtitled *The Testimony of a Thousand Witnesses*, it used documents such as advertisements for runaway slaves to describe in graphic detail the conditions of plantation life and the tortures to which slaves were subjected.

The highlight of each year was the antislavery fair and convention. These events were intended to raise money and awareness, but they inevitably raised controversy. The products of the women's sewing circles, sold at these fairs, carried their political messages back home. The women who made, priced, and marketed these goods were entering the marketplace. When fe-

male fair organizers began retailing imported antislavery wares as well, conservatives protested that fair work exceeded the bounds of female propriety
by thrusting them into the world of commercial values and competitive behaviors.[49] Mary and Harriet were not deterred. Though they felt inadequate
to the task, they appraised most fair items, occasionally leaving large items
such as quilts unpriced, as they "would not set bounds" to the generosity of
anyone who might procure such an item at the fair.[50] In 1840, Mary noted
in her diary two days spent hearing addresses at the Worcester Convention
and visiting the antislavery fair there. If neighbors censured her unmatronly
mercantile behavior, she endured it in resolute silence.

Rural female antislavery societies developed ties between large urban or
statewide organizations by their regular correspondence. Mary directed her
Boston-based son to deliver or pick up papers from "Mrs. Chapman, No. 46
Washington St., Antislavery office," referring most likely to Maria Weston
Chapman, the publicly active secretary of the Boston Female Antislavery
Society. Mary, Harriet, and neighbor Hannah Sophia Cotton wrote regularly
to the Chapman and Weston family women. Their letters were a mixture of
business, news, confessions of trials, and prayers of encouragement. Woven into them are voices of persevering determination. They decried party
feeling and declared, "We consider union strength." Mary wrote of "light
breaking in for the oppressed," while Hannah spoke of "slaves fleeing American tyranny." They assured their urban colleagues that the women of rural
Boylston were working for the deliverance of the downtrodden.[51] This exchange of sympathy, support, and advice—what the women of nearby Fitch-
burg called their "epistolary social intercourse"—created a sense of female
political community that united them with like-minded women across the
state, the nation, and even across the sea.[52] Like other rural abolitionists,
Harriet and Mary also sent notices of resolutions to antislavery newspapers,
and followed the news of other societies.[53]

ALL OF THIS WORK of the BFASS was to some degree controversial and in-
timidating to diffident members, but it was petitioning that caused the most
qualms. Signing—and certainly circulating—petitions was a political ges-
ture, a redefinition of women's relation to the state. Where once the petitions
of women to their governors had merely prayed for special favor, antislavery
petitions demanded action, asserting the will of an activist people. Female
petitioners defended their work, claiming it was a *moral duty* of women to
"supplicate for the oppressed and suffering." Harriet's sister Sarah Smith,
speaking at the Antislavery Convention of American Women in Philadelphia

in 1838, declared that such work was justified not as political action, but as "a question of justice, of humanity, of morality, of religion."[54] Woman would be less than woman if she did not plead for the slave. If she faced censure, she must endure it for the sake of the suffering: female delicacy could not be considered "while people are enslaved, degraded and dishonored."[55] Mary agreed. She and her unmarried daughters signed and circulated petitions, and Mary prayed in a letter to Mrs. Chapman that they "be made willing to be of no reputation in the cause of the oppressed."[56]

Women who circulated petitions reported being called "unwomanly" or "trollops" and threatened with violence.[57] An August 4, 1837, edition of the *Liberator* reported that petitioners were told, "My darter says that you want the niggers and whites to marry together," or, "I hope you get a nigger husband." Some refused to sign, not because they favored slavery, but because they opposed women working for political ends. Some husbands shooed petitioners away, declaring, "'Women are meddling with that that's none of their business.' Occasionally a man met them at the door and bid them 'be gone and never bring such a thing to the house again.'"[58] Maria Child called petitioning "the most odious work of all," while Harriet Hale of Providence admitted that "few are found possessing that self-denying spirit requisite to lead them from house to house to obtain signatures for a petition. This of all others is considered the most thankless and difficult field of labor. Oh for the spirit of the early martyrs which would enable us to desire the posts of greatest danger and toil."[59] Mary and Harriet took this post, using blank petitions supplied by the Boston Female Antislavery Society.[60] Between 1836 and 1842, Mary noted repeatedly carrying petitions to her neighbors or enlisting her unmarried daughters to do so.

During 1837 and 1838, the peak years of antislavery petitioning, the citizens of Boylston sent at least eight petitions to their congressman, Levi Lincoln, for presentation to Congress.[61] Harriet Sanford submitted three with the signatures of females; one was submitted by William Sanford with the signatures of males; and four were submitted by William Sanford with the signatures of males and females. Six of those petitions survive in the National Archives.[62] An analysis of the petitions reveals that antislavery likely aroused gender and family conflict.

Men and women in Boylston petitioned for the same causes: to abolish slavery and the slave trade in the District of Columbia, in the United States, or in newly admitted territories or states; to reject the annexation of Texas (a proposed slave state) to the union; and to protest the tabling of antislavery petitions by Congress. All used preprinted forms. Interestingly, the men's petitions use brief and to-the-point statements of their grievance: "Respectfully pray your honourable body to immediately abolish slavery and the slave trade in those territories where they exist." The petitions submitted by females, however, set their appeal in the context of religious justification: "The undersigned women of Boylston, Mass., deeply convinced of the sinfulness of Slavery, and keenly aggrieved by its existence in a part of our country over which Congress possess exclusive jurisdiction in all cases whatsoever, do most earnestly petition your honorable body immediately to abolish Slavery in the District of Columbia, and also to put an end to the slave trade in the United States. We also respectfully announce our intention to present the same petition yearly before your honorable body, that it may at least be a 'memorial of us' that in the holy cause of Human Freedom, 'we have done what we could.'"[63] The delicacy of wording, and the concern to cast their work as a holy cause, succeeded in Boylston, as women there were far more likely than men to sign antislavery petitions.[64] This difference may represent a *dis*inclination among Boylston's conservative Whig males to support antislavery. Records reveal little active male support for antislavery in town.[65] The local culture of abolition, it seems, was shaped by gender.

There were other revelations. Significantly more Congregationalists signed petitions than did Unitarians, but this may be related to the fact that the petitions were initiated by the Congregationalist minister and his wife and carried by Congregationalists, who may have been more likely to visit Congregationalist than Unitarian neighbors.[66] But surprisingly, unlike the membership of the BFASS, the majority of signers were unaffiliated with any church, and were drawn from all economic classes. Being poor or unchurched, apparently, was not a bar to opposing slavery on paper.

Many of the women who signed had a spouse sign as well. Many, but not all. Critically, ten women signed the petitions whose husbands most notably did *not* sign. One of those was Mary White. We can be certain that Aaron White had plentiful opportunities—and likely great family encouragement—to add his name to the enrolled, but he did not. Aaron was apparently what would come to be called a Cotton Whig: one who felt that antislavery threatened commerce between northern textile industries and southern cotton producers, and that northerners had no business interfering with the business of other states.[67] His reasons for not signing were never discussed in the diary or the family letters, but he was clearly at odds with others in his family. His wife, his three daughters, and at least two of his sons were ardent abolitionists. Tension within the household over this issue must have been palpable.

The petitions revealed other community fault lines. This was predominantly a cause of the younger generation. Although there were a handful of older signers, such as the intrepid Mary White and her friend Mary Abbot, or respected elderly gentry such as Robert Andrews and Nathaniel Goodenow, the majority were young people in their twenties and thirties.[68] This was the cause of Harriet Sanford's generation, not Mary White's. Those who had never known slavery were more likely to condemn it than those for whom it had once been normative.[69] It seems likely that the issue of slavery brought tension into family relations, as parents and children claimed opposing positions. Such was certainly the case with Aaron Sr. and his firstborn son. Aaron Jr. broke with both his father and his fellow Democrats by insisting on liberty and equality regardless of race. He attended lectures, distributed antislavery newspapers, formed a local antislavery society, read, wrote and disseminated abolition reports and books, attended antislavery conventions, advocated for the cause before the state General Assembly, and authored petitions and resolves. What pleased his mother perplexed his father.

Despite the stigma attached to the work, petitioning was effective. Congress was deluged with petitions, which both houses routinely tabled. In December 1838 Mary received a letter from the Hon. Levi Lincoln that "informed us of the neglect that our petition was treated with in Congress." That Mary White received correspondence from her congressman (the former governor of Massachusetts) suggests how petitioning, in effect, expanded notions of women's citizenship. It is not known what her husband thought of Mary's corresponding with Representative Lincoln.

There was, in fact, only one more step that this pious middle-aged matron needed to take to be classed among the most radical activist women of her time. And it is possible that Mary White took that step. On November 2, 1837, Samuel Fisher, a cabinetmaker from the neighboring town of Northborough, wrote in his journal, "Herd Mrs. White Lectu[r]e on Slaverry in Baptist meeting house in afternoon."[70] This would have been a bold move indeed. She may have been inspired by the recent public speaking tour of the audacious Grimké sisters.[71] The sisters pleaded an urgent cause that, as Mary said, required they "be of no reputation in the cause of the oppressed." If Mary was the speaker in Northborough, it is hard to imagine her mind as she faced the disapproval of her husband, the censure of her social peers, and the sneers of the majority of Boylston's male population. Was she supported by Harriet? Harriet's own sister would speak in public before a female audience the following year, and her orthodox husband would support her. But most orthodox clergy were not so accepting.

IN THE SUMMER of 1837, activist antislavery women in Massachusetts received a severe scolding from the Congregational clergy. They branded work such as Mary's "immodest," "indelicate," and "unnatural," "bringing shame and dishonor" on her sex. "We cannot but regret the mistaken conduct of those who encourage females to bear an obtrusive and ostentatious part in measures of reform, and countenance any of that sex who so far forget themselves as to itinerate in the character of public lecturers and teachers."[72]

Under such censure, most orthodox members of the BFASS fell away. A loyal remnant kept the cause alive in 1837 and 1838. Mary described these lean times: "The Society struggled for an existence. Several pieces of work were begun but none were finished. In 1838 and in the preceding year there were never members enough present to elect their officers & there were none during that year. We were this year unprofitable servants for nothing was done comparatively. 3 or 4 members kept the Society from utterly sinking in oblivion. They came to the place of meeting sometimes there would be two, sometimes three, and sometimes there would be only one present of a society of 46 members. Let it be recorded to our shame!!" In 1839, eleven determined women sewed throughout the summer; by October, they were ready to send their work to an antislavery fair. Then came disaster.

Throughout 1839 Massachusetts orthodox clergy had grown increasingly vocal in their criticism of antislavery women's activism. In response, the leadership of Boston's Female Antislavery Society—by now mostly liberal Unitarians—became vocally *anticlerical*, accusing orthodox churches of laxness on the issue of slavery. When the male Massachusetts Antislavery Society declared that women could serve as full members of their organization and elected Abby Kelley to their national business committee, Congregational clergymen withdrew in protest and formed a new organization, the American and Foreign Anti-Slavery Society. The division caused unprecedented upheaval in the cause. Minister's wives and pious orthodox women mostly withdrew their membership from societies affiliated with the "old organization" and reconstituted themselves as new societies with more modest goals of clothing and comforting fugitives. "Ultraist" women, usually anticlerical Unitarians or Quakers, held power in the old organization and continued to push for immediate abolition and for civil equality for blacks—and women. Each group continued to craft items for their major fundraisers, the antislavery fair. But now there were *two* competing Boston fairs, and much ill will.[73]

On October 16, 1839, the antislavery women of Boylston met to vote on the disposition of their handiwork: five pairs of scarlet socks, a cradle quilt, and a rather extraordinary bed quilt stitched with antislavery messages and images.[74] Harriet Sanford was absent; Mary ran the meeting. After taking a vote, she drafted the following: "Resolved that we approve the principle on which the Massachusetts Antislavery Society [the "old organization"] was formed. . . . [W]e will therefore do all in our power to sustain the October Fair." Their handiwork went to the radical, anticlerical organization. Mary, despite her orthodox background, approved the disposal.

Harriet was furious. She was determined that the Boylston women would support the new clerical organization. A chance letter between Chapman sisters reveals the intensity of conflict: "In the course of [Elizabeth Doubleday's recent] visitations she was in Boylston about the time of our fair. . . . [B]ed quilt was made up there and quite a dreadful fight they had about it. Mrs. Harriet Sanford, the orthodox minister's wife, clerical of course, was very earnest to have it go to the Boston Female [new organization], but the old organization, among whom were Miss D's relations, declared that if it were so disposed of *every stitch which they had set (and they had set a good many) should come out.* Resolution like that generally carries the day and so we got the bed quilt."[75] The quilt must have been extraordinary indeed. It was reported that William Lloyd Garrison himself purchased the item, for an unknown sum.[76] But what a scene for the staid and sober town of Boylston!

Harriet was not easily placated. When the antislavery society next met in March 1840, she entered a protest about the quilt. Rebuffed, she and eight other members withdrew and formed a new antislavery organization of conservative Congregational women.[77] Reverend Sanford supported his wife's efforts by inviting Rev. Charles T. Torrey, one of the founders of the "new organization" in Boston, to share his pulpit and recruit for Harriet's fledgling society. Mary confessed that though "Mr. Torrey has been lecturing with us in favor of the new organization. . . . I believe he has not made many proselytes."[78]

Mary was left nearly alone to carry on the older, more radical organization, along with her daughters and a few young Unitarian women. She wrote to Mrs. Chapman for support: "Our antislavery society at present are meeting with opposition from the new organization as they term themselves (our minister and his partner). . . . [M]ay we be enabled like Gideon of old with a small band to overcome a host of enemies."[79] She persevered and later reported triumphantly: "In the year 1840 . . . some were not there whom we were accustomed to see at the 1st meeting of the Society—but were our ranks thinned? No! Was there less Anti-Slavery there than in former years?

We think not! For not-withstanding the rain, there were 13 present. . . . [W]e proceeded to elect officers."[80] Rarely did Mary express such emotion in her diary; one senses that she believed the little band prevailed because, as with Gideon against the Midianites, God was with them.

Following her conscience, Mary persevered without the support of her church, against her minister's authority, and against her husband's inclination. Many of those women who pursued ultraist antislavery tactics also embraced women's rights, laying the groundwork for the women's suffrage movement, but Mary White did not. She was not a radical feminist; she was a radical evangelist. She accepted the impropriety and indignity of women working in the public sphere but believed that violating those norms was a personal sacrifice some women made that they might cleanse sin and alleviate suffering. Her wish, as she wrote to Mrs. Chapman, was "that all bitterness and denunciatory writing were laid aside and we were simulating our blessed Savior who meekly bore all injuries. I think then we should see more light breaking in for the oppressed."[81]

For several years Mary struggled to keep up the work of the "old organization." Her group sewed to support the liberal fairs, petitioned, attended lectures, and hosted radical speakers, including the notorious Abby Kelley. But in 1842 Mary's little band lost several key supporters as young women married and moved away. By July, she noted in her diary, "Went to the hall to attend Antislavery Meeting. No one present but Miss Sally Cotton."[82] In December that year she wrote her last letter to Mrs. Chapman: "Some of our most active friends have moved out of town yet there are some who continue to feel for the down trodden and oppressed. Hope that the era for their deliverance is not far distant. We send what little cash we have on hand, $3.63."[83] Then the records ceased.

Mary's passionate commitment to the oppressed, however, did not cease. The records of the new Female Benevolent Society, the conservative organization that Harriet founded during her quilt protest, list the first officers: Harriet Sanford was president, and Mary White was vice president. A careful reading of Mary's diary reveals that she attended and supported the work of *both* societies.[84] She harbored no party feeling; she let no personal resentment interfere with the important work of abolishing sin. In the "new organization," Mary sewed clothing for slaves who had escaped to Canada.[85] The ladies of the society—all members of the Congregational Church—were unhesitant in attending to this noncontroversial work; Mary's diary notes regular gatherings of twenty-five to sixty women.[86] Within several years, however, the sewing circle began to vote the avails of their labor to more general works of charity. By 1846, organized women's abolitionism in town ceased.[87]

From Moral Suasion to Politics

Still, Mary noted, the cause moved slowly forward. After several failed attempts, in February 1843 Mary's church finally resolved "that in the opinion of this church the system of American Slavery is Sin against God & man and that no possible circumstances can justify a man in knowingly holding his fellowman as property."[88] This was small progress for a woman who hoped for immediate emancipation. But there were other hopeful signs. With the decline of moral suasion as a reform tactic, Mary began to note the hopeful progress of antislavery politics.

In 1840, Boylston recorded the town's first vote for an abolitionist president. Each year Mary noted the town's slow but steady increase in support—one vote, four, eleven, then thirteen—for what she called "the Abolition Ticket." In 1845 her sons and daughters went to hear Gerrit Smith and Henry Stanton lecture for the Liberty Party in Worcester. She took note of each sermon on national leadership: "Sermon from Prov. 29c 29v. When the righteous are in authority the people rejoice but when the wicked bear the role the people mourn. May we be humbled under a sense of our sinfulness as a nation."[89] "Mr. Sanford preached . . . a call to repentance and on the import of choosing good rulers and putting away slavery from our mindset."[90]

Mary's satisfaction at the progress of the Liberty Party locally was no doubt mirrored by her husband's chagrin. Political antislavery was growing in central Worcester County by the early 1840s, particularly among religiously oriented Whigs.[91] Their conversion to the Liberty Party came at the cost of Whig votes. As West Boylston globe maker David Murdock reported to the Worcester Whig Party chairman, "the Abolition party are our most bitter opponents. This we keenly feel, for they are men that have acted with us formerly, with very few exceptions they are from the whig [sic] ranks."[92] Aaron White likely understood the radical challenge: antislavery politics posed an insurgent threat to the county's conservative political elite, especially those commercial and manufacturing-oriented gentry who were committed to a stable relationship with the South.[93] Though she could not vote, Mary could discuss—and pray: "In the evening a conversation mainly of politics. May the Lord direct the electing of this nation that slavery and oppression . . . may cease."[94] If Mary was discussing with her husband, it was likely not a "pleasant interview."

As the years progressed and the cause of emancipation did not, resignation and fear set in. Though Mary still prayed, "May the Lord direct the efforts to wipe the foul Stain of Slavery from our National Escutcheon," she worried that it was too late. Increasingly her entries turned to foreboding: "Mr. Davis delivered an Antislavery discourse. The text from Isai. 60 12v. [For the people or kingdom shall perish that does not serve you; Those nations shall be utterly destroyed.] May this nation be delivered from the sin of Slavery. May we be indeed humbled under a sum of our manifold transgressions."[95] Mary's fears echoed the apprehension of many in the 1840s that apocalypse was imminent. Increasingly she voiced fear of divine retribution in the form of a devastating war. By 1847, she prayed, "May the Lord make me humble and watchful and avert from us his judgments. May the Lord deliver us from the Horrors of [the impending Mexican] war . . . and we be humble penitent and believing Christians."[96]

And then, at least politically, it seemed that Mary's prayers for progress in the fight against slavery might be answered. Northern discontent over a broad range of perceived incursions on their rights and liberties by proslavery elements coalesced into a new movement that took the town and the county by storm. In 1848, after years of only modest growth in support for the Liberty Party candidate, nearly two-thirds of Boylstonians deserted their allegiance to the Whig and Democrat machines and cast their vote for the Free Soil candidate.[97] Turnout was high and support strong: in embracing the Free Soil Party, Boylstonians declared that they would no longer let southern slave interests violate their rights, threaten their property and their independence, and make a mockery of revolutionary ideals of liberty.[98]

To be sure, many of those votes were cast to secure the liberties not of southern slaves but of white northerners. Free Soil in Worcester County drew on many discontents. Gag rule petitioners were outraged that their political rights had been violated, calling the tabling of their petitions a threat "to the fundamental principles of republican government, to the rights of minorities, to the sovereignty of the People."[99] Sectional concerns ran high, as fears of the power of slave states grew with the admission of each new slave territory; the proposed addition of Texas, which could potentially be divvied into six new slave states, was particularly alarming. Free white laborers who dreamed of staking a claim to liberty in public frontier lands were concerned about the extension of slavery. It is telling that the Free Soil platform dropped abolitionists' rhetoric on slaves' natural rights to liberty and abandoned demands to end slavery in states where it already existed. Their primary concerns were the political rights and economic well-being of northern white men.[100] But abolitionists could take some hope from the growing political consensus in the North that the power of the South and with it the extension of slavery must be opposed.

Mary could take some hope. With Free Soilers joining cause with evangelical abolitionists, energy was finally coalescing around an agenda to curtail slavery. Their platform urged the federal government to play a more activist role in achieving these ends. If Aaron disliked his wife's radicalism, he would have been dismayed to see her two first cousins, Charles and George Allen of Worcester, taking a leading role in the Worcester County Free Soil movement. The pair's public resolve declared, "Massachusetts wears no chains and spurns all bribes. Massachusetts goes now, and will go forever, for free soil and free men, for free lips and a free press, for a free land and a free world."[101]

Within a decade, Free Soil would evolve into the Republican Party, which Boylstonians would embrace almost unanimously. In the face of war against section and slavery, the town would once again know political unity.

THE BOYLSTON Female Antislavery Society, despite its brief and contested life, had a transformative effect on several social levels. As with other associations, it introduced Mary, Harriet, and the faithful to a broad network of like-minded coworkers. Through their shared experience attending lectures and concerts of prayer, supporting fairs and conventions, subscribing to publications, circulating petitions, and sharing letters from other "friends of the oppressed," these women formed long-distance ties that stretched from Boylston to Boston, New York, Philadelphia, Oberlin, and Cincinnati. With that association came a sense of sorority. As far as we know, Mary never met the radical Maria Weston Chapman, but after years of corresponding with her, she addressed her as "My dear Mrs. Chapman," and signed her letters, "Your friend, Mary White." Antislavery work affirmed for Mary that she had a role to play in that wider world.

Antislavery also remade relationships in Boylston. Antislavery alliances transcended previous ruptures by religious sect and possibly by class, creating new social bonds based on this shared cause. When Mary and Harriet reached out to the wives and daughters of the Unitarian minister and the daughters of their old foe, Captain Howe, they also affirmed that it was possible to cooperate on some matters while disagreeing on others. They affirmed the legitimacy of dissent. While forming new relations within the community, antislavery also stressed old ones. Mary's work set her in opposition to her husband, her minister, and some of her closest friends. She accepted the necessity of difference. When people such as Mary White followed the dictates of faith and individual conscience, it was no longer possible that "all might be of one mind."

The challenge to form their own opinions and make decisions based on personal principles was transformative to Boylstonians, if unintentionally so. Expressing one's mind sometimes took courage, as William White related to his brother: "I took the stage . . . with a few passengers, one of whom . . . I had considerable pleasant conversation, finding him a good christian [*sic*] and Abolitionist. One gentleman in the stage . . . was not an Abolitionist and was quite strenuous in opposing our sentiments. But we did not cower under him, feeling that we were in N[ew] England where mob law and lynch law has not yet become the law of the people but where each man may think and speak his own sentiments without fear of tar and feathering."[102] To "think and speak his own sentiments" were actions of self-formation and self-assertion. Abolitionists such as William and his mother Mary were empowered to think independently and to act contrary to social custom by the strength of uncompromising religious conviction. For Mary to follow her convictions to their logical consequences—associating with scandalous women, housing black antislavery agents, participating in commercial ventures, persuading neighbors to sign petitions, corresponding with her senator, and speaking in public—required her to confront both patriarchy and gender norms. To carry her convictions into practice, Mary unwittingly elevated the work of self-formation and self-determination. Her passionate faith carried her forward into a new and unfamiliar realm of liberal individualism. As historian Julie Jeffrey has noted, "few abolitionists, male or female, perceived the consequences of encouraging women to use their moral influence in the cause."[103] It would be tempting to assert that Mary White was at heart a women's rights activist. That would be a mistake; Mary did not set out to secure access to power in the public sphere, and there is no indication that she valued such power. She never advocated woman suffrage. But compelled by faith and conscience, she felt keenly obliged to act powerfully and publicly.

Finally, abolition spoke to the fundamental concern of Boylston's troubled years: defining and defending the nature of personal liberty. The Revolution had promised liberty, but the meaning of that promise was not self-evident. For the past twenty-five years, the people of Boylston had been debating the meaning and limits of *personal* versus *corporate* independence. Could—

and should—individuals live truly free and be allowed to act as independent, rational, autonomous beings? Would self-determination be constrained by local custom, patriarchy, or social hierarchies? Would it succumb to sinfulness and vice? Would it be limited by one's ownership of property, or one's access to knowledge and opportunity, or the color of one's skin? Should self-advancement be checked by obligations for the welfare of neighbors? Would self-reliance be undercut by new bonds to employers, banks, associations, and corporations? Would freedom of self-expression bow to new standards of respectable behavior, discourse, and appearance? The goal of liberty was self-mastery; to be mastered by another was slavery. But not all bonds were iron chains. Boylston's antislavery effort spoke to a generation's effort to define their own liberty within the context of community and society; it reflected their growing commitment to extend that ideal of personal liberty to a more expansive republic. And behind this goal, a now diverse people united.

CONCLUSION

Reaping

In the early spring of 1843, as Mary White waited for the frogs to peep, some of her neighbors were awaiting the end of the world. For the past decade, religious prophet William Miller had been traveling the countryside, urging folk to prepare for the Second Coming. His meticulous study of the Bible convinced him that the signs of the times matched biblical prophecy and that Christ would return imminently. Miller gained a following in Worcester County. His disciples held tabernacle meetings in sprawling tents, spread his teachings, and urged their neighbors to prepare.[1] Now the date—March 21, 1843—was fast upon them. Throughout the spring, Mary reported the growing frenzy. Her children and hired help attended Millerite talks; lawyer Nathanial Davenport related "some of his visions of the second coming of Christ"; Mr. Flagg lectured on the Second Advent; and Deacon Moore conversed "on the subject of the temporal Millennium."[2] The ferment roiled Mary's church: the congregation expelled Squire Davenport and his daughters Sally, Nancy, and Caroline for embracing Miller's teachings.[3] As the date neared, Millerite believers sold or gave away their property and prepared for the end. On the fateful night, some claim the believers donned white ascension robes and assembled on hilltops to await the sound of the trumpet with outstretched arms.[4] Three members of the Flagg family were among their number.[5] But they were disappointed. Mary White noted simply, "May we all be prepared for [Christ's] appearing whether sooner or later." Shortly afterward she added, "Frogs peeped."

The Millerites were widely derided for what many dismissed as hysteria. And yet in some ways the once-familiar world of rural Worcester County may have seemed as if it *were* coming to an end by the mid-1840s. In the previous twenty-five years, dramatic changes had remade the physical and interpersonal landscape. An earlier world of parochial, customary, and familiar farming communities was giving way to more fluid and diversified towns.

Those anxious for their souls had once covenanted with the local church; now they cultivated private convictions and joined themselves to global associations of like-minded believers. Those who once learned time-honored wisdom and customary practices from their elders now pursued knowledge in books, clubs, private academies, and cosmopolitan society. Those who once turned to their neighbor's care or grandmother's remedies to ease their discomforts now sought the help of medical experts, newly published advice books, and patent medicines. The poor or incompetent were once taken in by their neighbors; now they were sent off to institutions and asylums. Those who needed credit once turned to their family or neighbor; now they relied on impersonal banks and corporate lenders. Those struck by calamity once relied on kin and neighbors for assistance; now, with the help of insurance and investments, the afflicted rebuilt and recovered on their own.

Farmers no longer followed their forefathers' ways of working the land, and the produce once bound for the family table now found its way to distant markets. Sons no longer followed their fathers behind the plow or to the ballot box. People no longer followed their leading citizens in town affairs and politics. Following in general was losing fashion. They turned from government by a so-called enlightened elite pursuing the common good to government by common men rationally pursuing their own goals. They turned inward, to self and a new private domesticity, and they turned outward, to new communities of choice and interest. They exchanged their long, generational view of family and farm for the more immediate prospects of self-improvement and personal freedom. They embraced self-definition and self-reliance, self-control and self-direction. A collective localism gave way to expansive liberal individualism. Emerson was a prophet of this individualism, yet he understood that it came at a cost. He lamented that community was now "composed of a thousand different interests, a thousand societies filled with competition, in the arts, in trade, in politics, and in private life," and "united by no common good."[6] This disunion, this disembodying of the corporate nature of earlier Boylston, liberated each to find his or her own way, and left many pursuing new forms of incorporation into something larger than self.

This transformation was not something done to people, but through them and by them, as they adjusted their relationships to suit—or create— new conditions. And they did this with a passion. They *cared*. The people of Boylston invested themselves heart and soul in their causes, animated by intense and urgent inner energies. They demonstrated the power of religious thought to motivate behavior and shape society. They also embodied the optimism of the age: fired by a new confidence in their own ability to effect change, they felt empowered—and obligated—to be up and doing. External forces created opportunities and challenges. Some responded with uncompromising faith or political principle, ambitions for betterment, determination to cultivate self, and dreams of perfecting society. Believing that they could and must change their world, they did.

This was not a sudden revolution, and the transformation could not be pegged, as William Miller had tried, to a specific date or event. It took a generation for people to process external changes and harness internal energies. It took a generation for them to adjust the way they thought about themselves and their relations to family, neighbor, community, and nation. And it was this generation of the turbulent 1820s through 1840s, when new and old understandings of relationship and belonging contended, that was so marked by conflict.

The consequences of these shifts were not always intended, and sometimes they were ironic. Aaron White did not see that his devoted work to cultivate his sons would lead to their abandoning his world of cultivation. Mary White did not imagine that her pious and evangelical work for the black slave would advance the rights of white women. Joseph Flagg did not anticipate that his use of marketmen and cash would destroy the traditional account-book culture in which he had been raised, or would draw racially and ethnically diverse laborers to town (one of whom would marry his granddaughter, much to local consternation). Each made decisions in response to evolving conditions. Some embraced pluralism, diversity, cosmopolitan connections, individualism, and self-determination; others held fast to the familiar social relations of corporate community. How one views the fomenters and the resisters depends on whether one gives higher value to cooperation and consensus or individualism and diversity.

By the Civil War, Boylston's era of conflict had passed. The war created a larger but looser sense of regional unity and commitment to liberty, while the inescapable swelling of Irish and French Canadian immigrants seeking work in neighboring mills made pluralism an inevitable part of life. In 1886, as the town celebrated its centennial, citizens looked back nostalgically at earlier decades. They remembered a peaceful age of homespun, open hearths, and barefoot boys. Returning from distant cities to celebrate the anniversary of their town, native children romanticized the virtues of their forefathers: "Good morals, industry, frugality, honesty, neighborly kindness, fidelity to marriage vows, public spirit and the fear of God were the sources of their happiness. They had pleasant gatherings and innocent hilarity, and an outflow of love to family and kin and kind, which enriched their minds. . . . [T]hey had a religion that enlightened their minds, sweetened their affections, bound them together in kindly neighborhood, and showed them the way to heaven."[7] Delivering the historical address at the centennial celebration, a speaker too young to remember the town's earlier days informed his audience that "the history of the town of Boylston during the first century of its existence was, like that of most country towns of its size and situation, quiet and uneventful."[8]

Mary White knew better. In the summer of 1840, she confessed to her diary, "Changes are continually taking place around us, showing us that here we have no abiding place. Let us live for one that shall endure."[9]

Aftermath

"Aftermath" is a wonderful farming term: it refers to that which grows after the mowing. What grew to be for those Boylstonians we have come to know?

Aaron White saw the last of his sons, Francis, depart for the city in 1842. All seven sons eventually became wealthy Victorian gentlemen of business or law—somewhere else. Charles would go on to prosperous partnership with his older brother Thomas in a lucrative sulfur-refining business in New Jersey. The two would eventually build fine estates next to each other on then-upscale Bergen Point, where they lived with their families in Victorian gentility. Young "Franky" joined brother Davis in business and, after prospering, traveled extensively in Europe, seeking sublimity in landscape and art; his wife would complain that "I hired Irish help" was sufficient explanation to leave in a suicide note. Avery and William, like their brothers, prospered in trade and retired in Victorian gentility. Daughter Mary, at the age of twenty-nine, married widowed Congregational minister Elnathan Davis, and shortly thereafter the couple went west as missionaries to the Indians. Only Caroline remained at home to nurse her father through his final illness and to console her mother when he passed away in 1846.

Aaron White Jr. marched to a different drummer. After the Dorr affair, he found comfort in his Connecticut exile. He married the innkeeper's daughter who had brought him sustenance in his woodland hideout. For his young wife, Cornelia, he built a fine home; for himself, he built a new legal practice. A year later, his joy at the arrival of his firstborn son turned to grief when the birth was shortly followed by his wife's death. Refusing to move any of her belongings, he moved into his office, and kept the house as an untouched memorial to her for the next half century. He lived simply and quietly, working for those causes he believed worthy and charging little for his efforts. He raised his son, Cornelius, as a country lad, and though he offered the boy a college education, the youth refused. Cornelius chose to spend his life in independent seclusion, quietly retiring from the world to a small subsistence farm.

Aaron Jr. spent the last twenty years of his long life traveling around the countryside, buying up by the pound old alloyed copper pennies that the government had discontinued. These he shipped to Washington to trade for new pure copper cents. When he died in 1886, the locals made a surprising discovery. Among his papers was a document indicating that they would find a treasure buried not far from his house. They dug, and were astonished to discover barrel after barrel—literally tons of coins—in treasure he had buried over the years.[10] He would not entrust his independence to institutions, but, like farmers for generations before him, and like his son after him, he trusted to the security of the good earth. At least, he likely reasoned, these barrels of coins were secure and would not "make wings and fly away," like the pot of gold when the spell was broken, or his father's banknotes when specie was suspended.

Although Aaron Jr. lived a long life in New Boston, he always remembered the Dorr affair as the most important and proudest part he had played on the stage of public life.[11] On his tombstone he had inscribed, "Here driven into exile while defending the rights of man, I found hospitality and love, a home and a sepulchre."[12] The treasure that he had buried he directed to be used to endow law libraries in every county in Connecticut, that men might know and defend their lawful rights.

The neighborly Abbots, Jason and Mary, died within days of each other while others waited for the world to end in 1843; the irascible John Howe went to rest in peace in 1845. When the poor farm opened in 1847, Abishai Crossman and his wife, Ruth, were among its first residents. As Crossman became poor and disreputable, Lincoln Flagg became wealthy and venerable. Flagg and his wife, the chosen Caroline, became social pillars of the community. They had five sons and three daughters, one of whom, Alice, married her father's hired hand, George Hazard, a black man. Reverend Sanford served his flock for twenty-one years, retiring on the eve of the Civil War, that price of slavery that Mary had so feared.

Mary White remained on the "old home place," running the farm with the assistance of hired Irish hands and her devoted daughter Caroline. In later life, she gained sainted status among her townsfolk. In 1929, the local historian lectured on the Congregational Church, in which he detailed the terms and personalities of all the ministers. Then he noted, "Time will not allow for any extended or individual notice of the men and women who have composed the laity of the church; but of the women there is at least one of whom a passing notice should be given, one, who after she became connected with the church unceasingly devoted her life to its service, and who in my early boyhood was most affectionately referred to by the then older members of the church as its 'Mother of Israel,' Mary Avery White, wife of Aaron White, Esq."[13]

Mary White died on May 26, 1860, at the age of eighty-two, on the eve of the war that would end slavery. (It would also take the life of her beloved grandson, Franky Conant.) Her last hours are recorded in an obituary published in the *Boston Recorder*:

> With more than the usual vigor had her mind shone out the past few weeks, and her bodily powers, if slightly more feeble for some days, were still so active as to give no intimation of so near a departure. Calm . . . she passed the hours of night, and to the questions of filial kindness, "Is the Saviour present with you, mother? Is his sympathy precious?" came the feeble yet assured response, "Yes." . . . With the dawn she was raised from the bed, and assisted to the chair so familiarly her own. . . . "Do you lie comfortably?" tenderly inquired the loving daughter. "Oh, yes, I lie nicely," was said calmly. The numbered minutes hastened to their close. This moment the heavy breathing was distinctly heard by the daughter, now penning a note, a few feet distant—the next, it came not—life's clock had suddenly stopped. . . . All was still. The aged saint had closed her eyes on earth, and opened them to the full glories of heaven. She touched the shore of time only to feel in the next step the firm ground of eternity.[14]

Mary left this world seeking a heavenly home where family and friends would be eternally reunited in an eternal abiding place, all would be "of one heart and one mind," and change would be no more.

Several weeks after Mary was laid to rest, the town prepared to celebrate the annual anniversary of national independence. July Fourth in 1860 was an anxious time. The survival of the nation seemed in question. Uncompromising sectional positions, complicated by racial, religious, ethnic, and class tensions, made for a conflicted union. As if to reassure, Boylston's bell-ringer rang out enthusiastic Fourth of July peals on the ancient bell atop the meetinghouse. The bell cracked and rang no more.[15]

APPENDIX A: PROSOPOGRAPHY

The "collective biography" of the town of Boylston traces all tax-paying citizens of Boylston and their families over the course of the first half of the nineteenth century. This database was used to track geographic and economic mobility of taxpayers and their families and to trace the status of subsets of the population by characteristics such as religious denomination, livelihood, etc. The database was constructed as follows:

1. From Boylston tax lists selected at five-year intervals from 1800 to 1850 (excluding 1810, for which no tax records survive), I made a composite listing of all taxable residents, with their taxable deciles over time.

2. I then expanded this list, working with Boylston vital records, to include household heads, parents, spouse(s), and children of those taxed with dates of birth and death where available. For this step, I also used family genealogies, town histories, and online genealogical resources.

3. Church affiliation was added where it could be determined.

4. "Occupation" or livelihood was added using the 1850 U.S. Population Census, town and county histories, genealogies, obituaries, probates, and court records.

5. Town of birth and geographical destination were added where they could be determined from town records, census records, town histories, and genealogical records. Note that geographical destination and occupation based on census records may be intermediate since the subject may have moved or changed profession after the census was taken.

6. Note that this tax-based biography underrepresents those highly transient young people who moved through town before coming of age. It also underrepresents those sons who left town before coming of taxable age.

The "Boylston-born cohort" prosopography is based on Boylston vital records rather than tax records. It includes every male born in Boylston between 1786 (town founding) and 1825 who survived to maturity. This should include all males who came of age during the 1820–40 study period. This database was used to compare the status of *all* Boylston-born males, including those who left town before reaching taxable age. Included in this database are parents, siblings, spouses, and offspring;

taxable Boylston decile where known; geographic destination; and occupation where known.

Primary sources used in constructing this database include the following:

Boylston and Shrewsbury Baptist Church Records, OSV

Boylston Congregational Church Collection, BHS

Boylston Tax Assessments, BHS

Boylston Unitarian Congregation Society Records,
    George Wright Collection and Hiram Harlow Collection, BHS

Boylston Vital Records, BHS

Town Meeting Minutes, Boylston Town Clerk's Record Books, BHS

Worcester County Probate Records, MA

WORC

These were supplemented by published town histories, genealogical studies, and genealogical websites.

APPENDIX B: GEOGRAPHIC MOBILITY

TABLE B-1. Geographic Destination of Boylston-Born Males by Family Wealth Deciles

Destination	All Boylston-Born Males		Family Tax Decile 1–5		Family Tax Decile 6–10	
	N	%	N	%	N	%
Boylston	64	24.9	47	25.3	17	23.9
Worcester County	108	42.0	79	42.5	29	40.8
Metro Boston	22	8.6	20	10.8	2	2.8
Western Mass.	8	3.1	7	3.8	1	1.4
Greater New England	20	7.8	15	8.1	5	7.0
West or South	15	5.8	7	3.8	8	11.3
Unknown	20	7.8	11	5.9	9	12.7
Total	257	100				

Source: Boylston-Born Cohort Database (see appendix A). The cohort includes all males born in Boylston between 1786 and 1825 who survived to maturity. Family wealth decile (1=high, 10=low) represents the father's tax decile at age fifty, based on the Boylston Tax Assessments, BHS.

TABLE B-2. Livelihood Choices, Where Known, of Sons Born in Boylston, 1786–1825

Livelihood	All Sons		Sons Who Out-Migrated	
	N	%	N	%
Farming	101	46	55	34
Rural craft	19	9	10	6
Manufacturing	41	19	35	22
Trades	32	14	30	19
Professions	29	13	28	17
Other	—	—	3	2
Total	222	101	161	100

Source: Boylston-Born Cohort Database (see appendix A). Livelihood can be established for 222 out of 292 of the Boylston-born cohort, or 76 percent. Livelihood choices of those sons who *left* Boylston can be traced for 161 of the 219 out-migrating sons, or 74 percent. Livelihoods are grouped as follows: farming (farmer, farm laborer); rural craft (smith, wright, peddler, etc.); manufacturing (shoe or boot maker, comb maker, furniture/piano maker, other small-shop worker, factory/mill employee, machinist, mechanic); trades (transport services, communication services, building, retail provisions, wholesale provisions); professions (merchant, lawyer, engineer, manufactory owner, minister, business clerk, banker, professor).

TABLE B-3. Persistence, Wealth Decile, and Average Age of Boylston-Born Males by Decade, 1820–1850

Decade	1820–30	1830–40	1840–50
Percentage of Boylston-born males who persisted	63.7	63.8	66.5
Number who persisted	72	102	109
Average wealth decile	4.86	4.83	4.94
Average age	40.7	40.2	42.7

Source: Boylston Prosopography (see appendix A).

TABLE B-4. Percent Age Distribution of Boylston Males by Decade, 1800–1840

Age	1800 N=535	1820 N=435	1830 N=415	1840 N=403
Under 10 years	30.5	29.9	25.5	25.8
10–15 years	16.6	16.1	15.5	12.8
16–25 years	18.1	17.2	21.0	20.6
26–44 years	19.8	18.6	15.3	15.2
45 years and over	15.0	18.2	22.2	25.6
Total	100	100	99.5	100

Source: 1800–1840 U.S. Population Censuses.

TABLE B-5. Wealth of Boylston Male Taxpayer In-Migrants, 1820–1850

	1820–25	1825–30	1830–35	1835–40	1840–45	1845–50
Mean decile of in-migrants	6.8	7.8	8.2	8.4	8.7	8.1
Median decile of in-migrants	8	8	10	10	10	10
Modal decile of in-migrants	10	10	10	10	10	10

Source: Boylston Prosopography (see appendix A). Wealth decile is for the later tax year in each period (e.g., for 1820–25, tax decile is for 1825).

TABLE B-6. Place of Birth of Boylston Male Taxpayer In-Migrants, 1820–1850

Place of Birth	1820–25	1825–30	1830–35	1835–40	1840–45	1845–50
Local town	41	33	34	20	21	15
Other Massachusetts town	27	28	32	33	19	25
Other New England state	—	3	3	7	4	7
Other state, Canada, England, Ireland	—	—	—	—	9	21
Unknown	32	36	32	39	47	30

Source: Boylston Prosopography (see appendix A).

APPENDIX C: AGRICULTURAL DATA

TABLE C-1. Sustainable Diversified Subsistence Farm Acreage Requirements

Land Type	Sustainable Acres	Approx. Percentage
Houselot/orchard	4	7
Tillage	6	10
Meadow	15	25
Pasture	15	25
Woodlot	20	33
Total improved	60	100

Note: To sustain a family of six to eight people, a diversified farm in Massachusetts generally included about 2–4 acres for houselot, barnyard, dooryard garden, and orchard; 6 acres for tillage; 12–15 acres each for meadow and pasture; and 20–30 acres for woodlot. These estimates are based on family consumption of grains and the manure needed to keep that tillage land fertile, along with family consumption of wood and the time needed for that wood to regrow. Thus, if a family needed approximately 50–60 bushels of grain to thrive, they would need approximately 5 acres of tillage, with an additional 0.5–1 acre for flax to provide linen. Fertilizing that tillage required the manure of roughly 0.75–1 cow per acre. These 4–6 cows would need about 2.5 acres each of pasture to graze, or 10–15 acres, increasing over time. In addition, for winter feeding each cow would need the hay from about 1.5–2 acres of meadow, increasing over time. Each household consumed on average 20–30 cords of wood per year, requiring the harvest of about 1–1.5 acres of woodlot a year. As hardwoods generally took about 20 years to regrow to a harvestable size, a sustainable woodlot needed to be 20–30 acres. The estimates used in the above calculation are based on minimum subsistence requirements for tillage, pasture, meadow, and woodland from Merchant's *Ecological Revolutions*. Sixty acres is an approximation and varied depending on soil fertility and type. For other estimations, see Kimenker, "The Concord Farmer," 140–41; Gross, "Culture and Cultivation," 44–48; and Lowell, "Remarks on the Agriculture of Massachusetts," 320–26. For minimum and average consumption requirements, see Merchant, *Ecological Revolutions*. For yields of tillage, pasture, and meadow in the late colonial and early national period in Concord, see Donahue, *Great Meadow*, 203–11. For acreage devoted to flax for linen production, see Kelsey, "Early New England Farm Crops: Flax."

TABLE C-2. Agricultural Change: Massachusetts Valuations for Boylston, 1784–1850[a]

Year	1784	1801	1831	1841	1850
Polls	188	228	193	225	239

Buildings					
Dwelling houses	87	134	123.5	129	153.5
[Work]Shops	0	2	19	60	79
Tan houses	5	1	0	0	0
Warehouses	0	0	3	3	2
Grist, fulling, saw, carding mills	7	8	8	6	3
Barns	90	121	115	126	132
Cotton manufactory					1
Land					
Tillage	574	536	561	541.5	620
Upland mowing	330	434	764	1,106	1,410
Fresh meadow	1,034	1,285	808	728	565
Pasturage	1,508	2,294	2,882	3,821	3,741
Cows that acres will feed	—	749	708	715	751
Woodland	1,923	2,486	2,472	2,664	2,604
Unimproved land	5,600	3,628	2,011	1,598	2,011
Unimprovable land	1,075	2,801	1,204	624	235
Produce					
Wheat (bushels)		98	56	151	28
Rye (bushels)		2,321	1,438	886	808
Oat (bushels)		2,333	4,581	5,486	5,997
Corn (bushels)		6,321	5,657	4,931	7,357
Barley (bushels)		125	134	70	16
Peas and beans (bushels)		79			
Hops (pounds)		0	5,200	1,000	2,200
English hay (tons)		400	656	1,004	1,261
Fresh hay (tons)		1,005	600	479	393
Cider (barrels)	1,154	1,175			
Livestock					
Horses	112	142	94	94	121
Oxen	148	214	167	157	149
Steers (neat cattle)	450	490[b]	250	204	110
Cows	378		431	413	581
Sheep and goats	444		309	184	110
Swine	228	265	179	184	37

TABLE C-2. *continued*

Year	1784	1801	1831	1841	1850
Polls	188	228	193	225	239

Other Assets					
Money at interest	0	0		0	18,920
Money on hand or deposit		9,740		0	0
Stock in trade	0	1,800		0	2,000
Ounces of silver plate	0			0	66
$ value of shares of stock		650		0	5,900

Sources: Massachusetts Valuation of 1784 for Shrewsbury, Districts 2, 3, and 4, State House Library, Boston, Mass.; 1801, 1831, and 1841 Massachusetts Valuation for Boylston, Aggregates, transcription from manuscript, OSV; 1850 U.S. Agricultural Census.
[a]No data survives for 1810 and 1820.
[b]Neat cattle and cows are listed together in 1801.

FIGURE C-3. Comparison of Flagg's Corn and Potato Prices with Rothenberg Price Index

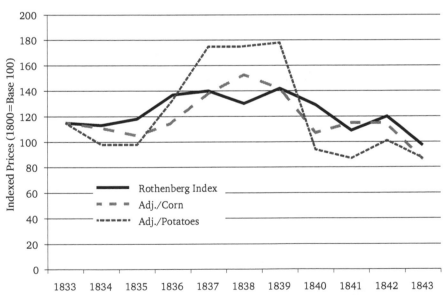

Sources: Joseph Flagg Account Book, OSV; Winifred B. Rothenberg, "A Price Index for Rural Massachusetts, 1750–1855," *Journal of Economic History* 39, no. 4 (December 1979): 975–1001.
Note: Corn is 13.9 percent and potatoes 1.2 percent of the commodities used in Rothenberg's thirteen-commodity "market basket" for her price index.

TABLE C-4. Comparison of Boylston Farms, 1784 and 1850

Land type	Sustainable Approx. Acres	Sustainable Approx. Percentage	1784 [N farms=76] Acres	1784 [N farms=76] Percentage	1850 [N farms=103] Acres	1850 [N farms=103] Percentage
Houselot/orchard	4	7	—	5.4	4	4.4
Tillage	6	10	7.6	10.2	6.0	6.6
Meadow	15	25	17.9	24	19.2	21.2
Pasture	15	25	19.8	26.5	36.3	40.0
Woodlot	20	33	25.3	33.9	25.3	27.9
Total improved	60	100	74.6	100	90.8	99.9
Total unimprovable			87.8		21.8	
Total land			162.4		112.6	

Sources: Massachusetts Valuation of 1784 for Shrewsbury, Districts 2, 3, and 4. State House Library, Boston, Mass.; 1850 U.S. Agricultural Census.

Note: A farm in 1784 was any improved land with a house, for a total of 76 farms. A farm in 1850 was determined by reporting in the 1850 U.S. Agricultural Census, for a total of 103 farms. Houselot/orchard includes acreage for yards, gardens, and orchards. It was not specified in the 1784 valuation. Many calculations of improved land from the period do not include woodland, even if it had been intensively managed as a woodlot.

TABLE C-5. Boylston Pasture and Meadow Fertility, 1801 and 1850

	1801	1850
Pasture in acres	2,294	3,741
Number of cattle pasture will keep	749	751
Acres of pasture needed per cow	3.1	5.0
Acres of fresh meadow	1,285	565
Acres of English upland meadow	434	1,410
Total meadow	1,719	1,975

Sources: 1784 Massachusetts Agricultural Valuation and 1850 U.S. Agricultural Census. The increase in upland meadow, which was not renewed by spring flooding, hastened the general decline in overall soil fertility.

TABLE C-6. 1850 Boylston Farm Surplus for Market

Product	N Farmers with Surplus	% Farmers with Surplus
Grain (corn, oats, rye)	67	65
Potatoes	100	95
Butter	93	88
Cheese	20	19
Hay	67	65
Beef cattle	40	39
Swine	53	51

Source: 1850 U.S. Agricultural Census.

Note: The farm family is assumed to be composed of six to eight people. Minimum consumption per family:

—Grains: Minimum of 30 bushels of corn, oats, and rye and an average of 50 bushels; plus, a minimum of 20 bushels and an average of 25 bushels of potatoes. See Merchant, *Ecological Revolutions*, 180; and Pruitt, "Self-Sufficiency and the Agricultural Economy of Eighteenth-Century Massachusetts," 358.

—Hay: 1.5 tons required to feed the family's minimum one milch cow. See Merchant, *Ecological Revolutions*, 178–79. Note, however, that farmers who keep more than one cow in order to market dairy and beef will not have surplus hay to market as well.

—Butter: Minimum 150 pounds, based on widow's portions estimating per person consumption of butter at 20 pounds and on a study that estimated nineteenth-century per person butter consumption peaking at 19 pounds per person. See Craig, Goodwin, and Grennes, "Effect of Mechanical Refrigeration on Nutrition," 327.

—Cheese: Minimum 200 pounds. See Shammas, "How Self-Sufficient Was Early America?" 241. Shammas estimates .5 pound per person per week, or 150 to 200 pounds per family.

—Meat: One beef cow and one to two pigs per year.

Any produce in excess of these family minimums is assumed to be available as marketable surplus. Note that this is the percentage of *farmers* (103 in 1850); only one-third of Boylston taxpayers owned farms in the 1850 census.

TABLE C-7. Improved Land and Livestock in Boylston 1784 and 1850, Distribution and Average Size of Holdings

Year	1784	1850
Number of polls	176	239
Percentage of polls with improved land	58 (N=103)	43 (N=103)
Average # improved acres held by those who own improved land	50	65
Percentage of polls with cows	56	43
Average # cows held by those who own cows	3.8	4.8
Percentage of polls with swine	51	43
Average # swine held by those who own swine	2.5	3.6

Sources: Massachusetts Valuation of 1784 for Shrewsbury, Districts 2, 3, and 4, State House Library, Boston, Mass.; 1850 U.S. Agricultural Census; 1850 U.S. Population Census.

APPENDIX D: POLITICS

TABLE D-1. Boylston Votes for Governor by Party in Percentage, 1786–1848

Year	Adult White Males Age 20+	Turn-out	Worcester County Turnout	Federalist	National Republicans	Whig
1786	175	.21	.13	100	—	—
1790	189	.24	.22	22	—	—
1796	216	.30	.28	94	—	—
1800	234	.43	.34	52	—	—
1804	233	.45	.32	86	—	—
1808	139	.94	.37	76	—	—
1812	154	.85	.45	83	—	—
1816	186	.67	.44	80	—	—
1820	198	.56	.56	83	—	—
1821	201	.55	.53	81	—	—
1822	205	.47	.52	84	—	—
1823	208	.56	.59	80	—	—
1824	211	.66	.65	—	73	—
1825	214	.30	.30	—	98	—
1826	218	.50	.34	—	96	—
1827	221	.40	.30	—	98	—
1828	224	.29	.25	—	74	—
1829	227	.26	.29	—	37	—
1830	230	.44	.40	—	63	—
1831	229	.43	.36	—	55	—
1832	227	.46	.52	—	55	—
1833	226	.51	.51	—	—	66
1834	225	.59	.53	—	—	87
1835	224	.51	.45	—	—	78
1836	223	.58	.50	—	—	65
1837	221	.57	.54	—	—	77
1838	220	.63	.61	—	—	53
1839	218	.64	.65	—	—	58
1840	217	.76	.76	—	—	65

Anti-Federalist/ Democrat-Republicans	Democrat	Anti-Masonic	Liberty	Free Soil	Scattering	Total Votes
—	—	—	—	—	—	36
78	—	—	—	—	—	45
6	—	—	—	—	—	64
48	—	—	—	—	—	100
14	—	—	—	—	—	106
24	—	—	—	—	—	131
17	—	—	—	—	—	131
20	—	—	—	—	—	125
17	—	—	—	—	—	111
19	—	—	—	—	—	111
16	—	—	—	—	—	97
20	—	—	—	—	—	117
27	—	—	—	—	—	139
—	—	—	—	—	2	65
—	—	—	—	—	4	109
—	—	—	—	—	2	89
—	26	—	—	—	—	65
—	63	—	—	—	—	58
—	37	—	—	—	—	101
—	45	—	—	—	—	99
—	24	21	—	—	—	105
—	15	19	—	—	—	115
—	12	—	—	—	1	133
—	22	—	—	—	—	114
—	35	—	—	—	—	128
—	23	—	—	—	—	126
—	36	—	—	—	11	154
—	40	—	—	—	2	139
—	34	—	1	—	—	165

Year	Adult White Males Age 20+	Turn-out	Worcester County Turnout	Federalist	National Republicans	Whig
1841	219	.68	.65	—	—	62
1842	222	.74	.68	—	—	56
1843	224	.80	.67	—	—	58
1844	226	.78	.68	—	—	62
1845	229	.61	.56	—	—	64
1846	231	.56	.52	—	—	62
1847	235	.55	.51	—	—	69
1848	237	.59	.56	—	—	38

Sources: 1786–1812 vote totals from Lampi, "First Democracy Project"; 1814–48 vote totals from Boylston Town Clerk's Record Books, BHS. Adult white males (AWM) were estimated from 1790, 1800, 1810, 1820, 1830, 1840, and 1850 U.S. Population Censuses, including all white males above the age of twenty years. As no tax or census data survive for 1786, AWM for that year is based on 25 percent of the total population, the standard proportion of polls to population. Population figure for 1786 from DuPuis, *History of Boylston, Mass., 1786-1886*, 1. For 1790, AWM was calculated by deducting 9 percent of total males sixteen and over(reflecting proportion of sixteen- to twenty-year-olds in 1800 census). For 1800, 1810, and 1820, 50 percent of the age bracket from sixteen to twenty-five was included. Years between census counts are extrapolated. Worcester County turnout from Brooke, *Heart of the Commonwealth*, appendix 1, 399–403.

Note: West Boylston separated from Boylston in 1808. AWM in 1808 is based on the population after the separation. There were two elections in 1831, when elections changed from spring to fall. This is an average of the two.

TABLE D-2. Boylston Votes for President by Party in Percentage, 1824–1848

Year	Adult White Males Turnout	National Republicans	Democrat-Republicans & Democrats	Anti-Masonic	Whig	Liberty	Free Soil
1824	.35	89	11	—	—	—	—
1828	.41	88	12	—	—	—	—
1832	.50	—	22	17	61	—	—
1836	.54	—	25	—	75	—	—
1840	.75	—	32	—	66	2	—
1844	.76	—	28	—	58	14	—
1848	.67	—	15	—	28	—	57

Source: Boylston Town Clerk's Record Books, 1815–48, BHS.

Anti-Federalist/ Democrat-Republicans	Democrat	Anti-Masonic	Liberty	Free Soil	Scattering	Total Votes
—	34	—	4	—	—	149
—	33	—	11	—	—	165
—	29	—	13	—	—	179
—	30	—	8	—	—	176
—	27	—	8	—	1	140
—	26	—	9	—	3	133
—	30	—	1	—	—	130
—	12	—		50	—	139

NOTES

Abbreviations

AAS   American Antiquarian Society, Worcester, Mass.

BHS   Boylston Historical Society, Boylston, Mass.

BPL   Rare Books and Manuscripts, Boston Public Library, Boston, Mass.

BU   Brown University, Providence, R.I.

Dorr Papers   Dorr Correspondence, Thomas Wilson Dorr Papers, 1826–45, Rider Collection, John Hay Library, Brown University, Providence, R.I.

HU   Harvard University, Cambridge, Mass.

LOC   Library of Congress, Washington, D.C.

MA   Massachusetts Archives, Boston, Mass.

MHS   Massachusetts Historical Society, Boston, Mass.

NA   National Archives, Washington, D.C.

NEHGS   New England Historic Genealogical Society, Boston, Mass.

OSV   Collections of Old Sturbridge Village, Old Sturbridge Village Research Library, Sturbridge, Mass.

UD   University of Delaware Special Collections, Newark, Del.

WC   Williams College, Williamstown, Mass.

WORC   Worcester County Registry of Deeds, Worcester, Mass.

Introduction

1. Noonan, *Educational History of Boylston*, 43; Dupuis, *History of Boylston, 1786–1886*, 52. Town meeting authorized the bell to be hung. Town Meeting Minutes, March 7, 1842, Boylston Town Clerk's Record Book, BHS.

2. McCrossen, "The Sound and Look of Time." For examples of this temporal ordering particularly after 1780, see Brooke, *Heart of the Commonwealth*, 239; Harrington, "The Village Death Bell," 142; Lubken, "Joyful Ringing, Solemn Tolling."

3. Town Meeting Minutes, Boylston Town Clerk's Record Book, May 1830, November 1835, May 1841, November 1841, February, 1843, BHS.

4. Diary of Mary White, January 20, 1828, OSV.

5. Of the original ten volumes of Mary White's diary, covering the years 1798 to 1860, six volumes survive. Three of those, for the years 1805–7, 1827–35, and 1852–55, are in the collections of UD; three other volumes, for the years 1836–52, are in the White Family Collection, OSV.

6. In addition to Mary White's diary, the other major White family primary resources

include the Journal of Samuel Charles White, 1838–44, OSV; Diary of Aaron White Jr., MHS; William J. White Collection, Archives and Special Collections, WC; Diary of Joseph Avery White, private collection of Vernon Woodworth and Molly Scott Evans of Dover, Mass.; White Family Letters, OSV; Diary of Nancy Avery White, AAS.

7. On print culture in the early national period, see Gross and Kelley, *An Extensive Republic*.

8. Sanford, *Two Sermons*, 51–52.

9. For a synthetic review of hope and fear as motivating spirits of the Jacksonian Age, see Walters, *American Reformers*, 3–19; Mintz, *Moralists and Modernizers*.

10. Recent syntheses of the Jacksonian Age include Sellers, *The Market Revolution*; Wilentz, *Rise of American Democracy*; and Daniel Walker Howe, *What Hath God Wrought*. An earlier classic is Schlesinger, *The Age of Jackson*. See also Feller, *The Jacksonian Promise*; Pessen, *Jacksonian America*; Wiebe, *Opening of American Society*.

11. This process of rationalization is one aspect of what others have called modernization. See Laslett, *The World We Have Lost*; Wiebe, *The Search for Order*; Lockridge, *New England Town*; Richard D. Brown, "Modernization and the Modern Personality"; Richard D. Brown, *Modernization*; Appleby, "Modernization Theory"; Waters, "The Traditional World of New England Peasants"; Henretta, "Families and Farms"; Jedrey, *The World of John Cleaveland*, among others.

12. On the debate over the emergence of the market in rural New England, see Kulikoff, "The Transition to Capitalism in Rural America." A market-centered interpretation of the consequences of the Market Revolution can be found in Rothenberg, *From Market-Places to a Market Economy*, as well as Daniel Walker Howe, *What Hath God Wrought*. "Moral economy" historians following a Marxian interpretation of market consequences include Merrill, "Cash Is Good to Eat"; Henretta, "Families and Farms"; and Sellers, *Market Revolution*. For other treatments of adaptation and resistance to the coming of capitalism, see essays by Thomas Dublin, David Jaffee, Gary Kulik, and Jonathan Prude in Hahn and Prude, *Countryside in the Age of Capitalist Transformation*. See also Clark, *The Roots of Rural Capitalism*.

13. See Clark, *Roots of Rural Capitalism*; Vickers, *Farmers and Fisherman*; Bushman, "Markets and Composite Farms."

14. *Documents Relative to the Manufactures in the United States* (also known as the McLane Report).

15. Thompson, *Customs in Common*, 352–403; Wallace, *Rockdale*, 124–85. For contrasting views on the perceived merits of factory work, see Dublin, *Women at Work*; and Dawley, *Class and Community*.

16. Bushman, *The Refinement of America*; Breen, *The Marketplace of Revolution*; Jaffee, *A New Nation of Goods*.

17. Joseph S. Wood, *The New England Village*, 102–34.

18. Van Tassel, "The Yeoman Becomes a Country Bumpkin." Bushman argues that the pursuit of refinement actually blurred class distinctions by elevating middling society to material equality with the gentry. Bushman, *Refinement of America*, 410–12.

19. Larkin. *Reshaping of Everyday Life*, 211.

20. Daniel Walker Howe, *What Hath God Wrought*, 237.

21. The literature on the rise of political participation in this era is vast. For classic interpretations, see Schlesinger, *Age of Jackson*; and Wilentz, *The Rise of American Democracy*.

22. For "social control" interpretations of antebellum reform, see Griffin, *Their Brothers' Keepers*; and Paul E. Johnson, *Shopkeeper's Millennium*. Analyses stressing humanitarian motives include Banner, "Religious Benevolence as Social Control"; Walters, *American Reformers*; Kohl, "The Concept of Social Control and the History of Jacksonian America"; and Mintz, *Moralists and Modernizers*.

23. For varied views on the role of religion in remaking or reinforcing social order in America, see Bushman, *From Puritan to Yankee*; Isaac, *The Transformation of Virginia*; Heyrman, *Southern Cross*; Butler, *Awash in a Sea of Faith*.

24. See Opal, *Beyond the Farm*; Luskey, "Jumping Counters in White Collars"; and Zakim, "The Business Clerk as Social Revolutionary."

25. See Tonnies, *Community and Society*, which argued that traditional community based on kinship and affective ties was destroyed by modernization and replaced by modern society, a world of impersonal and contractual associations. See also the response of Bender, *Community and Social Change in America*, which insisted that distinctive personal folk and ethnic relations persisted in urban migrations and that community and society are persistent patterns rather than evolutionary starting and ending points. This study of Boylston sees the continuation of community in both local, affective relations and in translocal ties with those distant strangers who share interests.

Chapter 1

1. See Davenport, *Brief Historical Sketch of Boylston*, 21; George L. Wright, *Names of Places*, 18.

2. Alan Taylor, "The Early Republic's Supernatural Economy"; Anthony, *Paper Money Men*, 1–21.

3. See Appleby, *Inheriting the Revolution*, esp. 1–25.

4. For studies of corporate mentality and social organization in early modern England, see Wrightson, *English Society, 1580–1680*; Laslett, *The World We Have Lost*; Stone, *The Family, Sex and Marriage in England*; and Thirsk, *The Agrarian History of England and Wales*. For traditional popular culture in premodern Britain, see Thompson, *Customs in Common*. For closed corporate community in New England, see Lockridge, *A New England Town*. For the Puritan covenant theology in New England, see Miller's *The New England Mind* and "The Marrow of Puritan Divinity," 48–98; for covenanted community, see Simpson, *Puritanism in Old and New England*. See also Weir, *Early New England*.

5. Wrightson, *English Society, 1580–1680*; Macfarlane, *The Origins of English Individualism*.

6. McCusker and Menard, *Economy of British America*; Breen, *Marketplace of Revolution*; Bushman, *Refinement of America*; Bailyn, *Ideological Origins of the American Revolution*; Armitage, *Ideological Origins of the British Empire*; Greene, *Pursuits of Happiness*; Eliga H. Gould, *The Persistence of Empire*.

7. For a modern version of this communal-centered understanding of coming of age, see Spiegel, "One Man Tackles Psychotherapy for the Amish"; Cates, "Facing Away"; Kraybill, *The*

Riddle of Amish Culture; Kraybill and Olshan, *The Amish Struggle with Modernity*; Hostetler, *Amish Society*.

8. Thomas, *Religion and the Decline of Magic*, "Prologue."

9. Darrett Rutman defines colonial New England towns as familial; neighborly and cooperative by necessity; localistic and internalized; face-to-face and familiar in scale; ordered by the predictable seasonal cycles of agrarian life. Rutman, "Assessing the Little Communities of Early America." Jack Larkin proposes household, neighborhood, and congregation as the "little communities" that structured New England life. Larkin, "Rural Life in the North," 1211. Richard Brown asserts overlapping rural membership in family, congregation, and town. Richard D. Brown, "The Emergence of Urban Society in Rural Massachusetts," 33. Christopher Clark suggests that such interdependent social relationships may provide better explanatory insights into rural life than dichotomies of market or self-sufficient economic behavior. Clark, "The View from the Farmhouse," 202.

10. Richard D. Brown, "The Emergence of Urban Society," 33–35.

11. This differs from the claims of Barry Levy but is supported by the evidence in Boylston. In the Bigelow family in early nineteenth-century Boylston, both situations occurred. Andrew Bigelow had eight sons; he gave one his time, allowed another to buy his time, and apparently enjoyed the labor of his remaining six sons on his farm and in his mechanical pursuits. Barry Levy, *Town Born*, 263–72; *Centennial Celebration of the Incorporation of the Town of Boylston*, 118–21.

12. Thompson, *Customs in Common*, 467–531; Stewart, "Skimmington in the Middle and New England Colonies."

13. The civic ecology that limited individual striving is detailed in Innes, *Creating the Commonwealth*. The term is introduced on p. 16; discussion of the tension between industrious enterprise and self-regarding acquisitiveness, and the constraint of the latter, follows. On communal responsibility and the limits on individual striving, see esp. chap. 4.

14. Bushman, "Markets and Composite Farms," 365–66.

15. Thompson, "The Moral Economy of the English Crowd in the Eighteenth Century," *Customs in Common*.

16. Diary of Simon Davis, July 4, 1797, BHS. See also Bogin, "Petitioning and the New Moral Economy of Post-Revolutionary America," 398.

17. In 1800, Aaron White was in the top decile for wealth in Boylston; in 1796, Simon Davis was in the fourth decile. Boylston Tax Assessments, BHS.

18. For a compelling narrative of agrarian family values in colonial and early republic New England, see Shalhope, *A Tale of New England*.

19. See Wrightson, "Part One: Enduring Structures," in *English Society, 1580–1680*.

20. Nylander, "Our Great Family," in *Our Own Snug Fireside*, 20–53.

21. U.S. Population Census for Boylston, 1800.

22. Thomas White and Mary White Davis, "Recollections from Uncle Thomas White and Aunt Mary White Davis," private collection of Vernon Woodworth, Dover, Mass.

23. Demos, *A Little Commonwealth*, 107–8.

24. This claim runs counter to Barry Levy's assertion that towns interfered regularly with

family life in order to protect the value of labor. Children were removed from families or nuclear units were split up in Boylston only when they were poor charges or if they were deemed unruly or ill governed. Barry Levy, *Town Born*, 42–50.

25. Patriarchal family government died slowly in the frontier communities of New England and upstate New York. Ryan, *Cradle of the Middle Class*, 32. See also Shammas, "Anglo-American Household Government in Comparative Perspective."

26. Diary of Simon Davis, March 23, 1798; April 6, 1798; February 28, 1799, BHS.

27. Ryan, *Cradle of the Middle Class*, 31.

28. Ibid., 43.

29. The Federal Direct Tax List of 1798 reveals that two-thirds of houses in Worcester County were single story. On dwelling appearance, see Larkin, "From 'Country Mediocrity' to 'Rural Improvement.'" See also Hood and Izard, "Two Examples of Marginal Architecture in Rural Worcester County"; Stachiw and Small, "Tradition and Transformation."

30. Dupuis, *Boylston Taverns*, 20–21. Assumption for the tavern's interior based on Abbott Lowell Cummings, *The Framed Houses of Massachusetts Bay*; and Hubka, *Big House, Little House, Back House, Barn*.

31. The most notable difference was in the size and quantity of clothing. Compare selected inventories for Boylstonians of comparable age who died between 1800 and 1815: John Whipple, among the town's wealthiest residents, died at age fifty-eight with $386 worth of personal estate (household possessions); Oliver Dakin, of middling means, died at the same age with $491 worth of personal estate; while Timothy Temple, age sixty-two and among the town's poorest residents, died with $44 of personal estate. It was land, not household possessions, that distinguished wealth: Whipple had $1638, Dakin, $964, and Temple only $158 in real estate. Worcester County Probate Records, MA.

32. Davenport, *Brief Historical Sketch of Boylston*, 16.

33. See, for example, Diary of Simon Davis, February 6, 1798, Simon Davis Collection, BHS; Nylander, *Our Own Snug Fireside*, 222; Larkin, *Reshaping of Everyday Life*, 263.

34. See, for example, the poem that Oliver Sawyer copied into his schoolbook, OSV.

35. Jefferson famously offered this observation in his *Notes on the State of Virginia*, Query 19, "Manufactures," 274–75. For a discussion of farming versus the artifice of manufactures, mines, and forges, see Stilgoe, *Common Landscape of America*, 267.

36. Kulikoff, *From British Peasants to Colonial American Farmers*, prologue. See Bushman, "Massachusetts Farmers and the Revolution." Zakim discusses the agrarian ethos and the "indivisible bond that tied freedom to property and undergirded independence" in "The Business Clerk as Social Revolutionary," 565–66.

37. Onuf, *Jefferson's Empire*.

38. Massachusetts Valuation of 1784 for Shrewsbury, Massachusetts State House Library, Boston, Mass.; Massachusetts Valuation of 1801 for Boylston, typescript, OSV.

39. Pierce, *Peirce Genealogy*, 101–2.

40. For a detailed explanation of this ecological system, see Donahue, *The Great Meadow*, chap. 7.

41. See appendix C, table C-1.

42. The 1784 Massachusetts Valuation is for Districts 2, 3, and 4 of the town of Shrewsbury; these districts comprised the "North Precinct" that became Boylston in 1786. Massachusetts State House Library, Boston, Mass.

43. Kulikoff, *From British Peasant to Colonial American Farmers*, 216–26.

44. Historians have estimated that at an absolute minimum, the average family needed one dairy cow, one head of cattle for beef, one to two oxen for draft work, one to two swine, several sheep for wool, two tons of hay as winter feed for grazing livestock, and thirty bushels of grain. Mean farm holdings in Boylston easily met those requirements. Minimum requirements for average family maintenance are drawn from Merchant, *Ecological Revolutions*, 176–84.

45. [Worcester Agricultural Society], *Forty-Seventh Annual Report*, 66. This is an inclusive list of members since founding.

46. Ulrich, "A Friendly Neighbor," along with *Good Wives* and *A Midwife's Tale*.

47. See Diary of Mary White, February 1, 1806, UD: "Mr. White bought 65 lbs of flax for me." See also Diary of Simon Davis, March 1, 1798, BHS: "450 wt flax arriv'd from Newfane, Vermont." Probates with "widow's portions" included a ten pound flax allowance through the first quarter of the nineteenth century. See, for example, the will of David Hastings Sr. (wealth decile 3), Docket 28057, 57:211, or the will of Jonathan Bond Sr. (wealth decile 1), Docket 06188, 25:371, Worcester County Probate Records, MA.

48. Notes in the Store Ledger of Simon Davis, May 13, 1805, Simon Davis Collection, BHS.

49. On neighborly trade, see Ulrich, *Midwife's Tale*, 84–87; and Pruitt, "Self-Sufficiency and the Agricultural Economy."

50. Account Book of Aaron White, 1802–4, Aaron White Store Ledgers, BHS. For comparison, see Nathanial and Thomas Allen, Pre-Revolutionary Account Books, American Antiquarian Society, as quoted in Howard S. Russell, *A Long, Deep Furrow*, 144. See also Brooke, *Heart of the Commonwealth*, 274.

51. The Massachusetts Valuation of 1784 for Shrewsbury North Precinct (which would become Boylston two years later) lists an average of four milch cows and five neat cattle per household. If these cattle had been evenly distributed (which they were not), then every household would have been able to send three to four cattle a year to market, along with a little dairy. Massachusetts State House Library, Boston, Mass.

52. Rev. Peter Whitney as quoted in George L. Wright, *History of Worcester County*, 893.

53. *Centennial Celebration of the Incorporation of the Town of Boylston*, 21, 34–35; Davenport, *Brief Historical Sketch of Boylston*, 16.

54. See Thomas White and Mary White Davis, "Recollections from Uncle Thomas White and Aunt Mary White Davis," private collection of Vernon Woodworth, Dover, Mass.

55. Diary of Mary White, December 24, 1805; January 18, March 5, June 4, December 30, 1806; January 12, 21, February 10, 24, 27, March 7, September 21, 1807, UD.

56. On neighborliness in early modern English society, see Wrightson, *English Society*, 51–57; Ulrich "A Friendly Neighbor."

57. Davenport, *Brief Historical Sketch of Boylston*, 11–12. Davenport lists fifteen seed families who could trace their ancestry to the Great Migration and were "in some other degree related to each other." Another Boylston historian added, "most of them . . . [were] cousins, or in

some other degree, related to each other." Noonan, *Educational History of Boylston*, 65. See also Smith, "All in Some Degree Related to Each Other."

58. Kulikoff, *From British Peasants to Colonial American Farmers*, 219–23.

59. Larkin, "Accounting for Change," esp. 11–13.

60. Clark, "Household Economy, Market Exchange, and the Rise of Capitalism," 175; Kelleher, "The Debit Economy of 1830s New England."

61. Based on my study of all Boylston probate inventories from 1786 to 1800. On sharing the tools of dairying, see Ulrich, "A Friendly Neighbor," 395. Regarding flax production, Russell maintains that Worcester County towns, including Boylston, were strong linen production centers. Mary's diary for 1805–7 includes entries for processing flax and for both putting prepared flax out to be spun and spinning at home. Howard S. Russell, *A Long, Deep Furrow*, 164; Thomas White and Mary White Davis, "Recollections from Uncle Thomas White and Aunt Mary White Davis," private collection of Vernon Woodworth, Dover, Mass., 14; Diary of Mary White, 1805–7, UD.

62. Ulrich, *Good Wives*, 51–52.

63. Diary of Simon Davis, May 19, 1796, BHS.

64. Diary of Mary White, March 23, 1805, UD.

65. Ulrich, *Good Wives*, chap. 7; also *A Midwife's Tale*, esp. 183–89.

66. Diary of Simon Davis, September 24, 25, 1796, BHS.

67. Ibid., December 10, 1796, BHS.

68. Probate Account of Aaron Flagg, Docket 21102, 73:129, Worcester County Probate Records, MA.

69. Diary of Aaron White Jr., July 1819, MHS: "I remained at my father's house some time . . . but constantly refused, as I always have done in times past, to visit the neighbors, which conduct has always given my Father no small trouble."

70. Ulrich, *Midwife's Tale*, 90–93.

71. Tamar Farlin to Mrs. Partridge of Boylston, August 16, 1820, BHS.

72. The Thoreau quote is from "Solitude" in *Walden*. On "living thickly" in Concord, see Gross, "Quiet War with the State," 14.

73. Ezra Ripley, as quoted by Gross, "Quiet War with the State," 14.

74. Thomas White and Mary White Davis, "Recollections from Uncle Thomas White and Aunt Mary White Davis," private collection of Vernon Woodworth, Dover, Mass.

75. Diary of Mary White, June 16, 1806, UD.

76. Simon Davis to Persis Seaver, May 27, 1809, BHS.

77. Miller, *The New England Mind*, chap. 13.

78. Elazar, "The Political Theory of Covenant," 23.

79. Hall, *Worlds of Wonder*, 150–51.

80. That document has been lost, but the covenant their parent congregation in Shrewsbury wrote twenty years earlier survives. See Dupuis, *A Sword in My Hand*, 36; Ward, *History of the Town of Shrewsbury*, 118.

81. "Election to membership was thus a seal of one's moral acceptability to the community." Gross, *Minutemen and their World*, 23.

82. Molly Whittemore's case is referenced in Account Book of Rev. Ebenezer Morse (Mss A 1658), September 2, 5, and 9, 1759, R. Stanton Avery Special Collections, www.AmericanAncestors.org, NEHGS.

83. See the Shrewsbury Covenant of 1723, Ward, *History of Shrewsbury*, 118.

84. Maynard's case is referenced in Account Book of Rev. Ebenezer Morse (Mss A 1658), November 26, December 3, 1742; November 29, 1743, R. Stanton Avery Special Collections, www. AmericanAncestors.org, NEHGS. His confession is recorded in ibid., December 7, 1743.

85. Even the minister did not escape. See Dupuis, *Sword in My Hand*, 65–77.

86. Diary of Simon Davis, February 9, 1797, BHS.

87. Ibid., March 6, 1797, BHS.

88. Simon Davis refers to church sentiment in discussing a paper circulated "for the purpose of ascertaining *the mind* of the Parish." Ibid., January 3, 1797, BHS.

89. See 1792 floor and gallery seating plan for the Boylston meetinghouse, Boylston Manuscripts Collection, BHS.

90. Winthrop, "A Model of Christian Charity," 282.

91. Bushman, *From Puritan to Yankee*, 159.

92. Diary of Simon Davis, June 16, 1797, BHS.

93. Thomas White and Mary White Davis, "Recollections from Uncle Thomas White and Aunt Mary White Davis," 9, private collection of Vernon Woodworth, Dover, Mass.

94. Davenport, *Brief Historical Sketch of Boylston*, 13.

95. Dupuis, *Sword in My Hand*, 155.

96. Davenport, *Brief Historical Sketch of Boylston*, 24.

97. Diary of Simon Davis, May 25, 1796, BHS.

98. On the scruples of some over taking communion, see Hall, *Worlds of Wonders, Days of Judgment*, 161.

99. The North Parish was an "Old Light" church that accepted the Half-Way Covenant. Dupuis, *A Sword in My Hand*, 66, 83. On baptisms, see 70–71.

100. Rev. Eleazar Fairbanks was a 1775 graduate of the Calvinist Baptist Brown University. George L. Wright, "Boylston's Church History."

101. Brooke, *Heart of the Commonwealth*, 239.

102. Sanford, *Two Sermons*, 29–30.

103. Brooke, *Heart of the Commonwealth*, 239, 261.

104. Joseph S. Wood, *New England Village*, 52–70. On dispersed village settlement, see Jaffee, *People of the Wachusett*, 8, 14, 16, 123.

105. Stilgoe, *Common Landscape*, 49. The early buildings around Boylston's common are described by George L. Wright, "Boylston," 892. The historiography of corporately held versus private property is discussed in Allan Greer, "Commons and Enclosure," 365–66.

106. Barry Levy, *Town Born*, 39–42, 89–110. Levy believes restrictions on entering towns were intended to protect the value of local labor. While that may have been a consequence of warning out and deportation, town fathers' demonstrated concern was with protecting landowners from the tax burden of supporting the poor. Gross, *Minutemen and Their World*, 90, 228 n. 45.

107. New England town meeting records documented the concern for determining an indigent's town of birth and used the term "belongs to" to indicate nativity. Mary White used the same term to indicate the nativity of some traveling strangers who passed through Boylston. See, for example, Diary of Mary White, August 6, 1834, OSV: "A Mr. Freeman & his wife called here. . . . He *belonged* at New York, Lawrence County."

108. Elazar, "The Principles and Traditions Underlying State Constitutions," 15. Elazar points out that the Massachusetts state constitution of 1780 formalized covenant relationship as the basis of the body politic; many towns had written town covenants (in addition to congregational covenants) as the basis of their local government throughout the colonial period.

109. Elazar, "The Political Theory of Covenant," 4–6.

110. Barry Levy, *Town Born*, 37–42.

111. Ibid., 42–50.

112. In 1800, there were 151 male polls listed in Boylston Tax Assessment, BHS. Birthplace can be established for 131, or 87 percent. Of those, nearly half were born in Boylston, a quarter were born in a local Worcester County town, and a quarter were born in another Massachusetts town. None were born outside of Massachusetts. It is possible that some of the twenty polls whose nativity could not be determined were from more distant locations. See appendix A for description of Boylston prosopography.

113. U.S. Population Census, 1800. For Boylston, 56 percent of the population was under twenty-one years of age; only 15 percent was forty-five or older.

114. Gini coefficient for total property in Boylston in 1800 was 0.61; total physical wealth for New England on the eve of the Revolution was 0.64; for Boston in 1860 it was 0.94. (A higher number indicates greater inequality.) Only in frontier areas did the coefficient drop below 0.5. Anderson, *A People's Army*, 36–37; Larkin, "Rural Life in the North," 1212.

115. Between 1790 and 1800, the mean debt ratio (ratio of total debts to total assets) in probated estates of Boylston males was 0.24, slightly less than the 0.27 that Alice Hanson Jones found for all Americans on the eve of the Revolutionary War. The analysis of probate accounts reveals that nearly all creditors were fellow Boylstonians. Before 1810, no estate was liquidated for debt.

116. The population of Boylston in 1800 was 1050, 44 percent of whom were age twenty-one or over, so that there were approximately 231 males of age; the Boylston Tax Assessment for 1800 lists 151 male polls, or 66 percent of the of-age male population.

117. On the debate over the decline of deference, see Gross, "The Impudent Historian," 92–97. See also Alan Taylor, *William Cooper's Town*, 13–14, 156–57, 170–76.

118. From 1790 until 1800, Boylston's selectmen had an average tax decile of 1.57, while treasurers and clerks averaged 1.31. Deciles (1 = high, 10 = low) based on Boylston's 1800 tax assessment. From 1800 to 1809, the moderators, selectmen, assessors, and representatives to general court (the most important elected positions) had an average tax decile of 1.72; their average age was forty-three. Boylston Tax Assessments, BHS.

119. Brooke, *Heart of the Commonwealth*, 13.

120. Gross, *The Transcendentalists and Their World*, 5. Also Gross, "Squire Dickenson and Squire Hoar," 5, 17.

121. George L. Wright, "Boylston," 890.

122. Gross, "Squire Dickenson and Squire Hoar," 17.

123. Brooke, *Heart of the Commonwealth*, 239, 252, 257, 261. For "natural aristocracy," see the correspondence of Jefferson and Adams, specifically Jefferson's letter of October 28, 1813, and Adams's of November 15, 1813. Cappon, *The Adams-Jefferson Letters*.

124. George L. Wright, "Boylston," 887.

125. Brooke, *Heart of the Commonwealth*, 241–42.

126. Ibid., 280.

127. Burton, *The District School as It Was*; Noonan, *Educational History of Boylston*, 1–7.

128. See Burton, *The District School as It Was*. Barry Levy maintains that schools in colonial Massachusetts were consciously employed by towns as instruments to break the will of youth and discipline them to be productive laborers. Although brutal discipline exercised to keep order may have had the effect of producing better laborers, I have not found any evidence of school committees articulating any *intention* other than keeping rowdy youth from disrupting classroom order.

129. Parks, "Roads and Travel in New England"; and Underwood "Working the Roads," in *Quabbin: The Story of a Small Town*, 118–19. Mary White recorded instances of broken axels and overturned wagons from bad roads in Boylston.

130. Larkin, "Gathering Places."

131. Diary of Simon Davis, August 17, 1796 and March 6, 1797, BHS.

132. Thomas White and Mary Davis White, "Recollections from Uncle Thomas White and Aunt Mary White Davis," private collection of Vernon Woodworth, Dover, Mass.

133. On Shays's Rebellion, see Robert J. Taylor, *Western Massachusetts in the Revolution*; Szatmary *Shays' Rebellion*; Gross, *In Debt to Shays*; Richards, *Shays's Rebellion*; Gross, "A Yankee Rebellion?"

134. Suffolk Court Files, Worcester, September 1787, no. 155325, as cited in Noble, *A Few Notes on the Shays Rebellion*, 15–16.

135. Boylston receipts record payments to a total of thirteen townsmen "for Servisses Dun in Supressing the Late Rebellion in the westward Counties," May 4 and May 10, 1787. The original receipts are in the collection of the Boylston Historical Society; their transcription is available in *Centennial Celebration of the Incorporation of the Town of Boylston*, 99.

136. Brooke, *Heart of the Commonwealth*, 190.

137. I am grateful to Professor Leonard Richards for sharing this with me. Richards located Temple's indictment in the Suffolk Court records. Personal electronic correspondence, May 24, 2012.

138. See appendix D, table D-1.

139. Diary of Simon Davis, April 1, 1799, BHS.

140. Brooke, *Heart of the Commonwealth*, 262.

141. Gross finds the same constraint of class and community on the force of partisan conflicts in early republic Concord. *The Transcendentalists and Their World*, chap. 1, p. 12.

142. Brooke, *Heart of the Commonwealth*, 238.

143. Ibid., 273.

144. Diary of Simon Davis, July 5, 1798, BHS.

145. Petition of James Longley, Robert Andrews, and Aaron White, Agents for the town of Boylston, May 26, 1807, transcribed and printed in Lovell, *A Sketch of the Life of Major Ezra Beaman*, 18–20.

146. See *Pittsfield* (Mass.) *Sun*, September 17, 1840, 1, Newsbank, which lists former distinguished Federalists who had embraced Whiggery and names "Aaron White of Boylston" as one of the prominent actors in both parties.

147. Diary of Aaron White Jr., July 4, 1817, MHS.

148. Dupuis, *The Boylston Sketch Book*, 35–49.

149. For example, when Mary White put out flax to townswomen to spin, she recorded their first and last names and affixed the title of "Mr." to their husbands, but a member of the Bondsman family was simply "Moses' wife," without the familiar first name or the honorific. Diary of Mary White, May 14, 1805, UD.

150. Petition inserted into Boylston's Annual Town Meeting Warrant, April 21, 1798, as quoted in Dupuis, *History of Boylston, 1786–1886*, 18.

151. George L. Wright, *Names of Places*, 2–3.

152. Dupuis, *The Boylston Sketch Book*, 14–23. In some versions of the story, the body was buried and exhumed.

153. Ibid., 38.

154. Sarah was reputedly the daughter of a Native mother and an enslaved black father. See George L. Wright, *Names of Places*, 27–28.

155. Wright gives the fullest description of Sarah Boston in an unpublished paper, "Tramps & other Peculiar Characters," in the collection of the Boylston Historical Society. See also Tritsch, "Documenting Hassanamesit Woods."

156. George L. Wright, *Names of Places*, 28.

157. Tritsch, "Documenting Hassanamesit Woods."

158. Diary of Aaron White Jr., October 2, 1820, MHS.

159. Dupuis, *The Boylston Sketch Book*, 45.

160. Ibid., 42.

161. Ibid.

Chapter 2

1. William White to Charles White, April 27, 1841, OSV.

2. Diary of Mary White, March 2, 1829, OSV.

3. Sanford, *Two Sermons*, 52.

4. Diary of Mary White, March 1, 1830, OSV.

5. Sanford, *Two Sermons*, 28–29. Under Fairbanks, the congregation had revoked the Half-Way Covenant. On the relationship between New Light enthusiasm and Federalist strongholds in Worcester County, see Brooke, *Heart of the Commonwealth*, 239, 261.

6. George L. Wright, "Boylston" 897; Flagg, "Boylston," 314; *Centennial Celebration of the Incorporation of the Town of Boylston*, 63.

7. Sanford, *Two Sermons*, 45.

8. Cotton, *Causes and Effects of Female Regard to Christ* (emphasis added).

9. Cayton, "Who Were the Evangelicals?" 86–87.

10. Gross, "Doctor Ripley's Church," 9–11, discusses this conflict in Concord.

11. Gross, "Faith in the Boardinghouse," 3.

12. "Spiritual aristocracy" is a term used by Gross, *The Transcendentalists and Their World*, chap. 2, p. 12.

13. Cayton, "Who Were the Evangelicals?" 86–90.

14. On the Baptist church in Boylston, see George L. Wright, "Boylston," 897; Dupuis, *History of Boylston, 1786–1886*, 31–32; for the 1814 council, see Sanford, *Two Sermons*, 44.

15. Sanford, *Two Sermons*, 4.

16. Davis, *The Half Century*, "Unitarianism," 345–54.

17. Appleby, *Inheriting the Revolution*, 236; Butler, *Awash in a Sea of Faith*, 274–80; and Daniel Walker Howe, *What Hath God Wrought*, 211–22. See also Gross and Kelley, "An Age of Print?"

18. Cayton, *Who Were the Evangelicals*, 87–88. Morse's tract was *A Review of American Unitarianism* (Boston: Samuel T. Armstrong, 1815).

19. Channing, *A Letter to the Rev. Samuel C. Thatcher*.

20. Constitution, Boylston Female Society for the Aid of Foreign Missions Records, Church Archives, First Congregational Church of Boylston, Mass.

21. For the forty-one women who signed the constitution, age could be determined for thirty-two, mean wealth decile of head of household for thirty-five, and marital status for thirty-two. The mean age was thirty-eight, mean wealth decile was 3.1 (1 = high), and two-thirds were married. In addition, 61 percent of the women shared a surname, and presumably a family relationship, with someone else in the society.

22. It is not always possible to match the women, who signed the constitution with their first names, to later heads of household that can be identified with a church. Of those thirteen who could be matched, eleven were associated with conservative Congregational or Baptist households and two with Unitarian households; the rest were not official members of a church or could not be linked with a head of household.

23. Minute Book, January 8, 1816, Boylston Female Society for the Aid of Foreign Missions Records, Church Archives, First Congregational Church of Boylston, Mass.

24. Puffer, *The Widow's Mite*.

25. Cotton, *Causes and Effects of Female Regard to Christ*, 16–17.

26. Ibid., preface.

27. Boylan, "Evangelical Womanhood in the Nineteenth Century."

28. On the Concert of Prayer, see Davis, *The Half Century*, 299–300. The tactics of evangelism had long transatlantic history. See, for example, Gould, "Prelude: The Christianizing of British America."

29. Comly, *Life and Religious Labors of John Comly*, 278.

30. Rev. Samuel Russell, *Review of a pamphlet*, 5.

31. Ibid.

32. For other ministerial machinations, see Butler, *Awash in a Sea of Faith*, 274.

33. Doctor Todd of Pittsfield described Russell: "I have seen him in situations peculiarly trying, and yet I never have heard him make a severe or unkind remark about any man." Sanford, *Two Sermons*, 49. On pulpit exchange, see Gross, *Transcendentalists and Their World*, chap. 3, pp. 4–5.

34. Sanford, *Two Sermons*, 47.

35. Rev. Samuel Russell, *Review of a pamphlet*, 4.

36. In 1831, "100 out of 193 polls in the town pay [taxes] to the Congregational Society, or 'first parish.' The other 93 are divided betwixt the other three societies [Unitarian, Universalist, and Baptist], except eight or ten, who have united themselves with religious societies in other towns." However, very shortly the Unitarians and Universalists united, and the Baptists dissolved their meeting, presumably to rejoin the conservative Congregational society. Davenport, *Brief Historical Sketch of Boylston*, 28.

37. Sellers, *Market Revolution*, 30.

38. Cayton, "Who Were the Evangelicals?" 92–93.

39. Ibid., 85. Cayton is referring to Sellers's famous assessment of evangelicals as "stressed rural Yankees." Sellers, *Market Revolution*, 214

40. Sellers, *Market Revolution*, 30.

41. To study characteristics of Boylstonians by religious affiliation during this era, I created a religious membership database detailing household belonging, gender, age at conversion, household wealth, and household geographic location by church membership, 1812–43. The sources for that database were:

> Congregationalists: A Congregational heads-of-household list from 1843 as well as the Records of the First Congregational Church of Boylston, BHS; those mentioned as church members or converts by Mary White, years 1827–43; those identified as Congregationalists in the Boylston Historical Series.
>
> Unitarians: A listing of the members of the Unitarian congregation, 1830, compiled by Boylston historian George L. Wright from an 1836 congregational tax list and recorded in Dupuis, *The History of Boylston, 1786–1886*, 53.
>
> Baptists: Boylston and Shrewsbury Baptist Church Records, 1812–37, manuscript, OSV.
>
> Heads of household and geographic location identified from an 1830 town map listing all resident household heads, Manuscripts Collection, BHS. Heads of household are placed in the denomination to which their membership is known closest to the year 1830.
>
> Economic decile from Boylston Tax Assessments, 1810–50, BHS.

42. Of those Boylston heads-of-household for whom church affiliation is known, 35 percent were Congregational, 43 percent were Unitarian/Universalist, and 22 percent were Baptist (some of whom later returned to the Congregational Church after it separated from the Unitarians in 1833). If we consider all heads of household, about a quarter were Congregational, a third were Unitarian, a sixth were Baptist, and a quarter were unaffiliated. See Boylston Religious Affiliation Database, note 41.

43. Boylston's Unitarians were more likely to leave town than the Congregationalists. The subset of the population that were church members is a sample biased toward those who have made a commitment to a community and thus are less likely to move; even so, 64 percent of Boylston Unitarians during the town's crisis were still present or had an heir that was present in Boylston in 1850, where 78 percent of the Congregationalists remained.

44. Many of the Boylstonian dissenters were apparently sympathetic to more radical Universalist, rather than Unitarian, teachings. At first, it was itinerant Universalists whom Mary most frequently reported preaching in town. In 1831, Matthew Davenport reported that the town's two nonorthodox congregations were Baptist and *Universalist*. The two ministers who followed Cotton in leading the Unitarians also had Universalist connections. This distinction is key as the Universalists tended to be poorer, more radical, and more rural— and more common in rural northern Worcester County. See the unpublished paper of George Wright, "The Unitarians of Boylston," in the collection of the Boylston Historical Society; Dupuis, *The History of Boylston, 1786–1886*, 52–53. On Universalism in northern Worcester County, see Larkin, "Episodes from Daily Life."

45. Obituary of Aaron White Jr., *Webster (Mass.) Times*, December 3, 1886, Harvard College Library Clipping Sheet, Harvard University Biographical Files (HUG 300), HU, courtesy of Harvard University Archives.

46. Diary of Aaron White Jr., July 1819, MHS.

47. Sanford, *Two Sermons*, 47–48.

48. A study of social visits received and paid by the White family in 1836 by religious denomination reveals that they received 66 percent of their visits from Congregationalists, 8 percent from Unitarians, and 26 percent from unaffiliated families (N = 210). They paid 80 percent of their visits to Congregationalists, 13 percent to Unitarians (mostly their immediate neighbors, the Cottons), and 7 percent to unaffiliated families (N = 100). See Diary of Mary White, 1836, OSV.

49. The mean and median tax decile of men elected as selectman, town clerk, and representative to general court from Boylston decline noticeably in the contentious 1830s and 1840s. Between 1800 and 1830, the mean tax decile hovered consistently around 1.65 (1 = highest, 10 = lowest decile), and the median was always 1.0, an indication of deference to wealth. During the 1830s and 1840s, the mean rose to 2.6, the median to 2.0, likely reflecting a the role that religion and reform were playing in diluting deference to wealth alone. See Boylston Tax Assessments, BHS.

50. See, for example, Mary White's entry for February 22, 1830, reporting that her husband had hosted a meeting that evening to plan a slate of officials for the upcoming town meeting.

51. Conditions at town meeting were reported by witnesses in the ensuing court case.

52. Rev. Samuel Russell, *Review of a Pamphlet*, 3.

53. Howe's position in Boylston is reviewed in Dupuis, *History of Boylston, 1786–1886*, 62–63. Howe's activity at town meeting is recorded in the Boylston Town Clerk's Record Book, 1815–35, BHS.

54. John Howe, *Trial of the Action in Favor of the Rev. Samuel Russell*, 5.

55. Ibid., 8.

56. Ibid., 7.

57. Ibid., 6, 8, 14–15.

58. Sanford, *Two Sermons*, 55.

59. Ibid., 48. In six years of evangelical work, Russell added more to the church rolls by profession than his predecessor had done in twenty-eight years.

60. On the extraordinary agency of noninstitutionalized religion in this era, see Butler, *Awash in a Sea of Faith*, chap. 8.

61. Diary of Barnabas Davis, December 27, 1829; July 3, 1831, OSV.

62. Davis, *The Half Century*, 355.

63. Shiels, "The Scope of the Second Great Awakening," 234–35.

64. Gross, *The Transcendentalists and Their World*, chap. 3, p. 6.

65. Mary White to Charles White, November 18, 1838, OSV.

66. Diary of Mary White, January 24, 1830, OSV.

67. See, for example, the work of Rev. Asahel Nettleton, *Sermons from the Second Great Awakening*.

68. Mary White to Charles White, March 13, 1837; March 6, 1839, OSV.

69. Ibid., March 9, 1840, OSV.

70. Religious converts in Boylston Congregational Church, 1830–39, were 42 percent male, 58 percent female, with a mean age of 29.8 years and a median age of 24.0 years. The mean family wealth decile (for head of household) was 3.5 (1 = high, 10 = low). Two-thirds of converts converted with another family member, while one-half of converts had a family member already in the church. See Diary of Mary White, 1830–39, OSV, and appendix A.

71. Graff, *Conflicting Paths*, 117.

72. Cott, "Young Women in the Second Great Awakening"; Shiels, "The Scope of the Second Great Awakening," 232.

73. Kett, "Adolescence and Youth," 290.

74. On "maternal evangelism," see Ryan, "A Woman's Awakening," esp. 616–23.

75. Diary of Mary White, June 17, 1828, OSV.

76. Ibid., March 19, 1834, OSV. Mary also read *The Mother's Magazine*; see her diary for January 22, 1841.

77. Mary White to Charles White, March 9, 1840, OSV.

78. Most death records, even when suicide is the known cause, avoid making that designation. Mention of these seven suicides comes from the diaries of Mary White and of Barnabas Davis. Jack Larkin notes that there is an interesting though difficult-to-document link between revivals and suicides. He believes that the intense emotions produced by revival fever are likely related to suicidal behavior. Larkin, "Episodes from Daily Life."

79. Bell, *We Shall Be No More*. In addition to religious enthusiasm, Bell claims rising rates of suicide can be attributed to intemperance, debt, gambling, and dueling and can be interpreted either as acts of self-empowerment or of dispossession and submission to despair.

80. Marc Harris, "The People of Concord," 122–24.

81. *Reports Relating to the State Lunatic Hospital at Worcester*, 45–49.

82. Appleby, *Inheriting the Revolution*, 187.

83. Kraybill, *The Riddle of Amish Culture*, 36–37.

84. Gross, *Transcendentalists and Their World*, chap. 3, p. 6.

85. Ibid., chap. 3, p. 27.

86. See Boylan, "Evangelical Womanhood in the Nineteenth Century," esp. 62–71.

87. There is no record of any male voluntary association being formed in Boylston between 1812 and 1830, when they founded a temperance society.

88. Daniel Walker Howe, *What Hath God Wrought*, 175.

89. Mary White to Charles White, March 22, 1840, OSV.

90. All of these female organizations are mentioned in Mary's diary. Most were formed during the peak of the 1826–32 revival.

91. Cott, "Young Women in the Second Great Awakening," 21–22.

92. Diary of Mary White, February 16, 24, March 2, 1843, OSV. Boylan discusses the intimate relationships formed between evangelical women. Boylan, "Evangelical Womanhood," 69–71.

93. Dupuis, *History of Boylston, 1786–1886*, 70.

94. Davenport, *Brief Historical Sketch of Boylston*, 28. Reverend Sanford reported that in 1834 there were 148 church *members* (not polls). Sanford, *Two Sermons*, 56.

95. An Act to Incorporate the First Unitarian Congregational Society in Boylston. Approved by the Governor, February 21, 1834. *Laws of the Commonwealth of Massachusetts*.

96. Diary of Mary White, April 13, 1834, OSV.

97. George L. Wright, "Boylston's Church History."

98. Sanford, *Two Sermons*, 53.

99. Boylston Town Clerk's Record Book, November 9, 1835, BHS.

100. The long story of struggle over church property is recorded in the Town Meeting Minutes, 1835–43, Boylston Town Clerk's Record Book, BHS.

101. Sanford, *Two Sermons*, 58.

102. Town Meeting Minutes, March and November 1839, Boylston Town Clerk's Record Book, BHS.

103. Town Meeting Minutes, February 1843, Boylston Town Clerk's Record Book, BHS.

104. Sanford, *Two Sermons*, 59.

105. Appleby, *Inheriting the Revolution*, 183–84, 236; Daniel Walker Howe, *What Hath God Wrought*, 188–93; Butler, *Awash in a Sea of Faith*, 257.

106. Sanford, *Two Sermons*, 56. He overstated the case for toleration; there was intense anti-Romanism, as well as distrust of Mormons, Millerites, Shakers, and other sects, as evidenced in Mary's diary.

Chapter 3

1. Tom Kelleher (curator, OSV), conversation with the author, February 17, 2010.

2. See Baker and White, "Impact of Changing Plow Technology."

3. Francis White to Charles White, January 16, 1840, OSV.

4. See Henretta, "Families and Farms"; Rothenberg, "The Market and the Massachusetts Farmer"; Rothenberg, *From Market-Places to a Market Economy*; Clark, "Household Economy,

Market Exchange, and the Rise of Capitalism," or Clark, *Roots of Rural Capitalism*; Bushman, "Markets and Composite Farms."

5. Davenport, *Brief Historical Sketch of Boylston*, 15–16.

6. Ibid., 16.

7. Ibid. See also *Documents Relative to the Manufacturers in the United States*, 482.

8. George L. Wright, "Boylston," 887.

9. Brooke, *Heart of the Commonwealth*, 291–303.

10. See, for example, Diary of Mary White, July 31, 1837, OSV.

11. Caroline White to Charles White, March 18, 1837, OSV.

12. On garden produce, see Kimenker, "The Concord Farmer," 166–67.

13. Account Book of Joseph Flagg, 1827–46, OSV, exhibits yearly entries for a broad range of his farm's grains, vegetables, meat, diary, and wood products.

14. Analysis of Flagg's accounts, 1827–46, shows three-quarters of all his transactions were with other Boylstonians; a third of all his trades were with his closest neighboring family. See also the Account Book of Willard Andrews of Boylston, 1839–46, Manuscripts Collection, BHS.

15. Vickers, "Competency and Competition," 7; Bushman, "Markets and Composite Farms," 367; Clark, "Household Economy, Market Exchange, and the Rise of Capitalism," 172–77.

16. This demographic pressure has been well documented for colonial New England, beginning with Greven's aptly named *Four Generations*. Boylston reached critical population density by 1820; population did not rise again until the Civil War era. On population density in agrarian New England, see Anderson, *A People's Army*, 36–37. For Boylston's population, see Dupuis, *History of Boylston, 1786–1886*, 23; and the U.S. Population Census, 1810, 1820, 1830, 1840, 1850, and 1860.

17. A study of all probate records for Boylston males from the time of the town's founding in 1786 through 1850 reveals that the proportion of impartible estate divisions (home farm left to one son) declined steadily by decade, from a high of two-thirds in the 1780s to merely one-fifth by the 1840s. See All Male Boylston Probates with Distributions, 1786–1850, Worcester County Probate Records, MA.

18. The ratio of debts to assets for Boylston males who died between 1810 and 1850 and left complete probate administration accounts rose consistently over the period from 0.23 in the 1810s to 0.37 in the 1820s, 0.38 in the 1830s, and 0.41 in the 1840s. See Worcester County Probate Records, MA.

19. Larkin, *Reshaping of Everyday Life*, 224. See also Frederic J. Wood, *The Turnpikes of New England*; and Parks, "Roads and Travel in New England."

20. For marketmen in Worcester County, see Baker and Izard, "New England Farmers and the Marketplace," 36–38.

21. Parks, "Roads and Travel in New England."

22. Ibid.

23. Kelleher, "The Blackstone Canal."

24. Diary of Mary White, October 8, 1828, OSV.

25. Kelleher, "The Blackstone Canal."

26. Diary of Mary White, November 18, 19, 1834, OSV.

27. Hazen, *The Panorama of Professions and Trades*, preface.

28. *Cultivator* (June 1854): 175, as cited in Zakim, "The Business Clerk as Social Revolutionary," 569.

29. Van Tassel, "The Yeoman Becomes a Country Bumpkin."

30. Horace Bushnell, "The Age of Homespun," 398.

31. Jonathan Wheeler to Elisabeth Davenport, Grafton, July 22, 1830, Fruitlands Museum, Harvard, Mass.

32. Francis White to Charles White, July 25, 1840, OSV.

33. Borish, "Weighing Women's Work."

34. Mr. French's Address, *The New England Farmer; a Monthly Journal* (December 1852), as cited in Sutton, "From Farmhouse to Factory."

35. Seward, "Prejudice Against Farming," *New England Farmer; A Monthly Journal* (January 1853): 46. As quoted in Sutton, "From Farmhouse to Factory," 19.

36. Sutton, "From Farmhouse to Factory," 18–19.

37. Davenport, *Brief Historical Sketch of Boylston*, 15.

38. Colman, "An Address Delivered before the Massachusetts Agricultural Society," 2.

39. Larkin, "Accounting for Change," 17.

40. Davenport, *Brief Historical Sketch of Boylston*, 16.

41. This change is obvious in comparing Mary's diary entries on her household work in 1807 and 1827. By the 1820s she went to Worcester to purchase her linen sheetings, tablecloths, and dress goods, items previously produced at home or locally.

42. On rising household consumption, see Bushman, *Refinement of America*, chap. 8; and Jaffee, *A New Nation of Goods*.

43. Donahue, *The Great Meadow*, 228; Clark, "Household Economy, Market Exchange, and the Rise of Capitalism." See also Clark, *The Roots of Rural Capitalism*, chap. 5; Baker and Izard, "New England Farmers and the Marketplace," 43.

44. Of the 292 males born in Boylston 1786–1820 who survived to maturity, 75 percent (N = 219) emigrated, and 25 percent (N = 73) remained in town. See Boylston-Born Cohort Database in appendix A.

45. Flagg, "Boylston," 311; Davenport, *Brief Historical Sketch of Boylston*, 15. Out-migration can be confirmed by a diachronic study of Boylston's tax lists. When adjusted for mortality, about a third of Boylston's taxpayers left town by the end of each five-year period. This trend rose over the period from 1820 to 1835 and peaked between 1830 and 1835.

46. See appendix B, table B-1.

47. Ibid.

48. Mean tax decile of 2.71; 71 percent of those who left home to pursue farming relocated in another Worcester County town.

49. See appendix B, table B-2.

50. Aaron White Sr. to Charles White, October 10, 1837, OSV.

51. Ibid., September 12, 1838, OSV.

52. Ibid., July 26, 1838, OSV.

53. Ibid., July 26, 1838, OSV.

54. Ibid., March 19, 1839; February 1, 1837; July 13, 1836, OSV.

55. Ibid., June 27, 1841, OSV.

56. Mary White to Charles White, July 26, 1841, OSV.

57. Three-quarters of all sons who remained in town had fathers in the upper half of assessed wealth.

58. For sixty-six of the seventy-one sons who persisted in Boylston, the father's tax decile at age fifty can be determined. This allows us to determine the mean wealth decile of these fathers at approximately the age a son would be deciding to stay or to leave town. The mean tax decile for fathers of persisters is 3.79 (one = high). The mean tax decile for all men aged fifty to sixty in 1830 was 4.27.

59. Four-fifths of all taxpayers in the top quintile remained in Boylston. Eighty-nine percent of the men who reached their fortieth birthday in Boylston stayed in town for the rest of their lives. Two-thirds of all persisters in the 1820 to 1840 period were men born in town (an increase from 50 percent in the previous twenty-year period). See appendix B, table B-3.

60. The proportion of the Boylston male population aged sixteen and under fell dramatically between 1800 and 1840, while the proportion over forty-five rose dramatically. The proportion of young men between sixteen and twenty-five also rose. This is consistent with an out-migration of young families, an influx of transient young male workers, and an overall aging of established mature farmers and the elderly. See appendix B, table B-4.

61. This is the thesis of Opal's *Beyond the Farm*.

62. This is another form of the larger process of rationalization that has sometimes been considered modernization. Evangelical and Enlightenment ideas briefly joined forces, marrying Christian Perfectionism with doctrines of temporal and material progress.

63. Vickers, "Competency and Competition," 7. See also Bushman, "Markets and Composite Farms."

64. Henretta, "Families and Farms"; Rothenberg, "The Market and Massachusetts Farmers"; Clark, "Household Economy, Market Exchange, and the Rise of Capitalism"; Vickers, "Competency and Competition"; Bushman, "Markets and Composite Farms."

65. Atack, Bateman, and Parker, "The Farm, the Farmer, and the Market," 270–72.

66. This rationalization of farming is another aspect of that transformation that some scholars previously termed modernization. For a similar process in Concord, see Gross, "Lonesome in Eden," 5.

67. See the example of Dr. Josiah Bartlett of Concord. Gross, "'The Most Estimable Place in All the World,'" 3–4.

68. Davenport, *Brief Historical Sketch of Boylston*, 16 (emphasis in original).

69. Kimenker, "The Concord Farmer," 189.

70. Lowell, "Brighton Cattle Show Reports," 275.

71. Diary of Mary White, February 19, 1829; June 2, 1835, OSV. Rotating clover with tillage "fixes nitrogen from air, brings potassium and phosphorous from subsoil by deep, foraging roots." Liming clover helped clover restore soil fertility. Donahue, "'Skinning the Land,'" 18. Mary did not indicate *where* on his farm Aaron used the casks of lime.

72. Donahue, *The Great Meadow*, 207.

73. Diary of Mary White, March 16, 1830, OSV.

74. Kimenker, "The Concord Farmer," 178–79

75. Brian Donahue, "The Forests and Fields of Concord," 35; Kimenker, "The Concord Farmer," 178–79; See Atack, Bateman, and Parker, "The Farm, the Farmer, and the Market," 268–70. For technology and changes in farming, see also McClelland, *Sowing Modernity*.

76. No farm account book survives for White. However diary and letter references from 1827 to 1843 provide evidence of farm production. White sent about 150 bushels of corn to market, in addition to what he grew for his family. He grew around sixty bushels of oats, fifty of which he sent to market. He harvested approximately twenty-five to thirty bushels of rye and eighteen bushels of wheat per year, all apparently for home use. He raised up to 114 bushels of potatoes a year but mentioned selling only in small quantities of less than twenty bushels. He sent from eleven to twenty-six barrels of apples a year to market, along with several hogsheads of vinegar. He usually sent a calf and two pigs to market, while trading a fatted cow or two and his fattened oxen to men in neighboring Shrewsbury and Northborough. Mary churned or had her girls churn, pack, and send to market butter in quantities as small as a few pounds up to batches of forty-five pounds. Fowl were killed, plucked, and shipped in quantities ranging from six to eighteen.

77. Aaron White to Charles White, March 19, 1839, OSV.

78. Of thirty-three diary entries referring to trades outside of Boylston, two-thirds were for market trips to Boston, six were trips to Worcester, and the rest were scattered trades in the neighboring towns of Shrewsbury and Northborough. Only one trade was recorded outside Worcester County.

79. This information comes from collected references in the diary and letters of the White family. The Eager place yielded upland hay, grains, and apples and pastured some livestock; the Fuller place yielded upland hay and oats.

80. Inequality in the distribution of wealth, as measured by Gini coefficient, rose consistently between 1800 and 1850 in Boylston. Total property Gini coefficient rose from 0.61 in 1800 to 0.66 in 1830, 0.68 in 1840, and 0.71 in 1850. Real property Gini coefficient rose equally dramatically and consistently, from 0.66 in 1800 to 0.74 in 1850. See Tax Assessments of Male Residents of Boylston, 1800, 1820, 1830, 1840, and 1850, Boylston Tax Assessments, BHS. (No assessment survives for 1810.) To compare with Concord, Massachusetts, see Kimenker, "The Concord Farmer," 143–44. The proportion of Boylston taxpayers with no real property rose from about a quarter in 1820 to half in 1845; the proportion with no property at all rose from 11 percent in 1820 to 38 percent in 1845. Boylston Tax Assessments, 1815–45, BHS.

81. See appendix C, table C-2.

82. Atack, Bateman, and Parker, "The Farm, the Farmer, and the Market," 253–58.

83. Will and Partition of Real Estate for Benjamin Flagg, Docket 21133, 42:624–25, 43:241–48, Worcester County Probate Records, MA. See also George Wright, manuscript notes in "Flagg Family Papers" file, BHS.

84. A quarter of all Flagg's trades were with his closest neighboring family, the Brewers. We can determine the residence of 95 of the 106 people with whom Flagg traded. Of those, 70 percent lived in Boylston. Boylston trades amounted to 78 percent of the total, and 64 percent

of the value. This pattern of heavy trading with close neighbors was characteristic of social and economic networks of farmers' accounts.

85. Of the 963 entries for which a month is indicated, 330 fall in April, May, or June.

86. Flagg's debtors took over a year on average to make payment; some debts were left on his book for a decade or longer.

87. Diary of Mary White, August 17, 1837, OSV.

88. Sale of wood, grains, hay, and livestock products account for about half of the value of Flagg's trades; the labor/use of his self, sons, animals, or tools, along with the rent from his house and interest from his money, made up another third. The rest were miscellaneous debits for garden and orchard produce, tending livestock, and providing lumber and supplies to the town for public buildings, etc.

89. Flagg sold large quantities of corn, wood, oats, and cider to Worcester taverners and storekeepers. He hauled most goods to market in Shrewsbury but also traveled to Worcester and eight Worcester County mill towns.

90. Baker and Izard, "New England Farmers and the Marketplace," 42–46.

91. On Worcester County farmers adjusting prices to market rates, see Larkin, "Accounting for Change," 4. On Massachusetts farmers, see Rothenberg, "The Market and Massachusetts Farmers"; and Rothenberg, *From Market-Places to a Market Economy*.

92. For a comparison of Flagg's corn and potato prices with the Rothenberg Price Index, see appendix C, chart C-3.

93. "April 3, 1843, Agreement maid between Flagg and Brigham & Ball." He repeated the cow-rental arrangement with "Mr. Newton" the following week. Notes in Flagg Family Papers, BHS, record that the massive oak beams in the barn on the farm of Joseph Flagg were "timbers taken from the second meetinghouse when that structure was taken down."

94. J. M. Smith, Franklin County, Mass., 1865, quoted in Donahue, "'Skinning the Land,'" 14.

95. Raup, "The View from John Sanderson's Farm," 4. See appendix C, table C-4.

96. See appendix C, table C-5.

97. George Wright, manuscript notes in "Flagg Family Papers" file, BHS.

98. Donahue, "'Skinning the Land,'" 27–28.

99. See note 104.

100. For Boylston's marketable surpluses, see appendix C, table C-6.

101. Vickers, *Farmers and Fishermen*, 66, 82–83.

102. This transition is likely related to the maturation of Massachusetts farming communities. Anderson documents these conditions in *A People' Army*, chap. 2. Kimenker claims that hiring labor beyond family was rare before 1800 in Concord, Mass. "The Concord Farmer," 182.

103. Larkin, "'Labor Is the Great Thing in Farming,'" 204–16.

104. Caroline White to Charles White, March 18, 1837, OSV.

105. With three-quarters of Boylston's youth out-migrating, population fell from a high of 902 in 1820 to 797 in 1850. See U.S. Population Census, 1820–50. However, during the same 1820–50 period, the number of *polls* rose from 198 to 237. See Boylston Tax Assessments, BHS. A decline in total population with a rise in taxpayers likely indicates that out-migrating fami-

lies with children (counted as population but not as taxpayers) were being replaced by young, single men of taxpaying age. The high male sex ratio in Boylston during the 1830s and 1840s is also a likely indication of predominantly male in-migration. The male-to-female sex ratio in Boylston rose from 0.97 in 1820 to 1.025 in 1830 and 1.015 in 1840 before falling back to a more normal 0.996 in 1850. See U.S. Population Census, 1800–1840.

106. A study of the in-migrants on Boylston's tax list (those nonlocal men who appeared on a tax list for the first time), reveals that these were increasingly younger men; they were also increasingly poorer and from farther away. See appendix B, tables B-4, B-5, B-6.

107. Boylston historian William Dupuis claims that the first Irish immigrants began to arrive in Boylston in 1835 (likely migrating north after finishing work on the Blackstone Canal). DuPuis, *Strangers and Pilgrims*, 2:1 and appendix I.

108. Diary of Mary White, March 28, 1836; December 9, 1839, OSV.

109. Ibid., July 20, 1837, OSV.

110. "Imposter," *Salem Gazette* 8, no. 32 (April 20, 1830): 1, Newsbank.

111. Larkin, "'Labor Is the Great Thing in Farming,'" 219.

112. Caroline White to Charles White, n.d. (ca. 1837–40), OSV.

113. Larkin, "'Labor Is the Great Thing in Farming,'" 225.

114. There were exceptions to this for haying season. Mr. Bush and Mr. Abbot, among Boylston's most prosperous residents, lent a hand at this time of year.

115. Larkin, "'Labor Is the Great Thing in Farming,'" 202–3.

116. Ibid., 217. Sawtell's story is nearly identical to that of another laborer, John A. Woods, who rented and worked for Flagg for several years in the late 1830s. Woods labored for a quarter century in Boylston and never accumulated property.

117. Izard found similar results in her study of the Ward family female helps. "The Ward Family and their 'Helps,'" 76–81.

118. Ibid., 85–86.

119. Caroline White to Charles White, n.d. (ca. May 1838), OSV.

120. On the back leaf of her diary, Mary recorded Mrs. Simpson's wage for a day's laundering: thirty-three cents, about a third of a man's daily wage for farm work.

121. In 1800, 102 of 163 taxpayers were from the twenty founding families listed earlier; in 1850, 79 of the 259 taxpayers were from those same families.

122. See appendix C, table C-7.

123. This is based on a study of all Boylston probate inventories that specified farm tools, 1820–40, Worcester County Probate Records, MA. Gross confirms similar holdings in Concord. "Culture and Cultivation," 52.

124. See Baker and Izard, "New England Farmers and the Marketplace," 35.

125. Town Meeting Minutes, Boylston Town Clerk's Record Book, BHS.

126. Gross, "Culture and Cultivation," 1–54.

127. Ibid., 51; Gross, "'That Terrible Thoreau,'" 193.

128. Larkin, "'Labor Is the Great Thing in Farming,'" 222–26.

129. Lasser, "The Domestic Balance of Power," 5–6.

130. Gross, "Culture and Cultivation," 51.

131. Lasser, "The Domestic Balance of Power," 5–6.

132. Caroline White to Charles White, January 6, 1839, OSV.

133. Larkin, "Accounting for Change," 22, 25. Myron Stachiw's study of a Worcester County blacksmithing account book documents this shift from long-term credit accounts to cash during the 1840s. Stachiw, "Tradition and Transformation."

134. Paper assets (notes, book accounts, cash) as a proportion of total personal estate in all Boylston male probates with complete inventories rose dramatically after 1820, from 0.11 in the 1820s to 0.46 in the 1830s and 0.78 in the 1840s. Boylston probates, Worcester County Probate Records, MA.

135. Aaron White to Charles White, January 16, 1838, OSV.

136. Caroline White to Charles White, March 18, 1837, OSV.

137. The percent of Boylston estates auctioned in whole or part to settle debt rose steadily after 1810, from a low of 17 percent to 21 percent in the 1820s, 46 percent in the financially troubled 1830s, and 32 percent in the 1840s. See all Boylston probates with complete renderings of debts and assets, Worcester County Probate Records, MA. Donahue also notes an increase in loss of property to debt suits, vendue at death, and foreclosures between 1825 and 1850 in Concord, *The Great Meadow*, 222.

138. Caroline White to Charles White, March 18, 1837, OSV.

139. Halttunen, *Confidence Men and Painted Women*.

140. Aaron White to Charles White, August 10, 1840, OSV.

141. Ibid., January 14, 1837, OSV.

Chapter 4

1. Shalhope, *A Tale of New England*, chap. 1, relates such a struggle between a father's sense of familial/farm obligation and his son's personal desires and sensibilities.

2. Some of the material in this section was previously published in Fuhrer, "The Druggist's Apprentice." On rural youth in the city, see Halttunen, *Confidence Men and Painted Women*, esp. preface and chap. 1.

3. Demos, *Past, Present, and Personal*, 102.

4. Kulikoff, "The Progress of Inequality in Revolutionary Boston," 385.

5. For the Henshaw and Ward druggist dynasties, see Trask, *Brief Memoir of Andrew Henshaw Ward*.

6. Aaron White to Charles White, March 3, 1841, OSV.

7. Rorabaugh, *The Craft Apprentice*, esp. chaps. 2, 3, 5; and Paul E. Johnson, *Shopkeeper's Millennium*.

8. William White to Charles White, August 24, 1836, OSV.

9. Mary White to Charles White, July 28, 1836, OSV.

10. Aaron White to Charles White, August 10, 1836, OSV.

11. Quoted in Luskey, "Jumping Counters in White Collars," 184. On writing facility as a measure of productivity, see Zakim, "The Business Clerk as Social Revolutionary," 580.

12. Luskey, "Jumping Counters in White Collars," 173.

13. Halttunen, *Confidence Men and Painted Women*, 33–43.

14. One first-year apprentice complained, "Everything there is to perform that is heavy— I have to do it. But I shall not too soon be discouraged. I am sure that clerks in the first year . . . have to work harder than any other time." Zakim, "The Business Clerk as Social Revolutionary," 578.

15. The apothecary sold powders, dyestuffs, essences, oils, paints, and commodities of any sort that required mixing, measuring, or portioning out.

16. Aaron White to Charles White, March 19, 1839. Charles had begun his preparation for these duties by reading the professional's tome, *The Counting House Assistant*.

17. Journal of Charles White, March 30, 1840, OSV.

18. Aaron White to Charles White, March 23, 1841, OSV.

19. Journal of Charles White, March 26, 1841, OSV.

20. See Aaron White to Charles White, June 1, 1836, OSV.

21. The year Charles started his apprenticeship the popular press was abuzz with a sensational sex-and-death story involving a New York clerk and a prostitute. See Cohen, *The Murder of Helen Jewett*.

22. Caroline White to Charles White, January 26, 1839, OSV.

23. Mary White to Charles White, June 13, 1837, OSV.

24. Caroline White to Charles White, April 5, 1841, OSV.

25. Mary White to Charles White, June 28, 1837, OSV.

26. Gambler, "Tarnished Labor."

27. William White to Charles White, April 12, 1837, OSV.

28. Diary of Charles White, July 27, 1839, OSV.

29. Aaron White to Charles White, June 1, 1836, OSV. For the contemporary rhetoric of molding character, see Augst, "Composing the Moral Senses."

30. For examples of the internalized rhetoric of character formation, see Journal of David Clapp, May 13, 1822, AAS.

31. *Worcester City Directory*, 1844, AAS.

32. Boylston Vital Records, BHS; FamilySearch.org (Mormon Family Records), https://familysearch.org/.

33. On the craft of shoemaking in the preindustrial age, see Thomson, *The Path to Mechanized Shoe Production*, part 1; Blewett, *We Will Rise in Our Might*, part 1; and Dawley, *Class and Community*, chaps. 1, 2.

34. Worcester County Land Records, 206:643, WORC.

35. Boylston Vital Records and Boylston Tax Assessments 1800, 1820, 1825, and 1830, BHS. The Crossman family was in the seventh decile in 1800, dropped to the ninth decile in 1820, and rebounded to the sixth decile in 1830 and 1835 as Caleb came of age. Boylston Tax Assessments, BHS.

36. Brooke, *Heart of the Commonwealth*, 299.

37. Worcester County Land Records, 214:562, WORC.

38. Diary of Mary White, July 20, 1828, OSV.

39. Abishai Crossman's name appears on Boylston's Unitarian church documents and peti-

tions. See Petition of April 3, 1837, submitted to Wm. Moore, Chairman of the Board of Select-men, transcribed in the Hiram Harlow Collection, bk. 46, p. 44, BHS. See also Dupuis, *History of Boylston, 1786–1886*, 53.

40. Boylston Congregational Church Records, Sept. 1834; Feb. 14, 1837, BHS.

41. Smith v Crossman, March, 1840, suit for debt, 92:210, Worcester County Court of Common Pleas Records, MA.

42. Caroline White to Charles White, June 14, 1836, OSV; Fenno's advertisements appear in the *(Worcester) Massachusetts Spy*, 1822–24.

43. Worcester County Land Records, 306:480, 308:124, WORC. The 1835 land transactions list Caleb's occupation as cordwainer. Caroline White to Charles White, December 20, 1836, OSV; George L. Wright, "Boylston's Church History," BHS.

44. George L. Wright, "Boylston's Church History," BHS. See also the "Remarks of Henry Brigham," in *The Centennial Celebration of the Incorporation of the Town of Boylston*, 4.

45. Caleb Crossman to the Selectmen of Boylston, Fond du Lac, Wisconsin, November 1855, Boylston Manuscripts Collection, BHS. An 1856 Worcester County deed lists Crossman as a teacher and a resident of Toledo, Ohio. Worcester County Land Records, 568:10, 579:593, WORC. Crossman lived in Van Wert, Ohio, from 1867 to his death in 1889. Martin, *A Complete Genealogy of the Descendants of Matthew Smith*, 46.

46. U.S. Population Census, 1880.

47. Caleb Crossman to the Selectmen of Boylston, November 1855, Bolyston Overseers of the Poor Records, BHS.

48. Caleb Crossman to Centennial Committee, *Centennial Celebration of the Town of Boylston*, 90.

49. Martin, *A Complete Genealogy of the Descendants of Matthew Smith*, 46.

50. Schenck and Rann, "History of Corydon Township."

51. In 1820, he tried to expand his holdings by purchasing forty-four acres in neighboring Rutland, but within a year the property was mortgaged, and after two years, he was forced to sell the heavily indebted land back to its original owner. Shortly afterward, Isaac Hooper sold the whole of his Oakham estate of one hundred improved acres for $1,000. He did not purchase any other property. Hooper was only in his fifties at the time he sold his farm, and his young son only twelve, so it is unlikely that he was retiring or passing the land on to the next generation. Worcester County Land Records, 220:267, 220:271, 229:273, 229:273, WORC.

52. Ibid., 288:64.

53. Diary of Mary White, July 31, 1832; September 12, 1837, OSV.

54. On straw braiding, see Diary of Mary White, April 8, 1831; June 29, 1836, OSV.

55. See a typical round of evangelical visiting in Diary of Mary White, June 5, 1837, OSV: "I called at Mrs. Abbott's Mrs. Stratton's and Mrs. Hastings. Mrs. Hasting went with me to Mr. Tilton's. Mrs. Sanford and Mrs. Abbot and Miss Hooper and Mrs. Whipple and Mrs. Sal Bigelow and her mother, a Mrs. Parker [there]. Had an interesting meeting."

56. White, "Counting the Cost of Faith," 19–20.

57. Grimshaw, *Paths of Duty*, 6. Grimshaw is quoting an 1836 missionary memoir.

58. Ibid., 6–12.

59. Ibid, 9.

60. Diary of Mary White, September 19, 1832, OSV.

61. Fletcher and Young, *Amherst College Biographical Record*, "Class of 1829," 51–52.

62. Ibid.

63. Schenck and Rann, "History of Corydon Township."

64. Ibid.

65. Ibid.

66. Diary of Mary White, November 2, 1837, OSV.

67. Gilbert Rockwood to Henry R. Schoolcraft, August 1, 1845, in Schoolcraft, *Notes on the Iroquois*, 250–51. See a contrasting interpretation in which the Seneca institute their own reforms, Wallace, *The Death and Rebirth of the Seneca*.

68. Daughter Mary would also accompany her husband west as a missionary bride.

69. Benjamin Houghton Sr. was in the second decile of assessed wealth in Boylston for most of his adult life; he was repeatedly elected selectman during the 1820s. Town officers can be found in Dupuis, *History of Boylston, 1786–1886*, appendix I. Houghton family history is given in Noonan, *Educational History of Boylston*, 60–61.

70. "Houghton Family Reunion," *Worcester Spy*, 1901, newspaper clipping, BHS.

71. Information on Benjamin Houghton's estate comes from the following Worcester County Land Records, WORC: grantee: 314:367, 381:85, 339:151; grantor mortgage: 318:663, 333:281, 381:195; grantor deed: 337:449, 410:94, 332:468, 430:641.

72. For Lucy Ann's bridal portion, Aaron purchased a bedstead, featherbed, bureaus and a looking glass, tables and chairs, all necessary crockery, iron, tin, and kitchen items—and a cow; Mary supervised the production of all household linens, bed ticks, blankets, coverlets, comforters, quilts, carpets, bonnets, shoes, and seven new gowns, including one of crepe and one of silk. It was very much the same marriage portion they would provide for their own daughter, Eliza, the following year. Diary of Mary White, January–September 1832, OSV.

73. Diary of Mary White, September 20, 1832, OSV.

74. Worcester County Land Records, 314:367, 337:449, WORC. For Houghton's new house, see Mary White Jr. to Charles White, June 21, 1836, OSV. The value of the house is based on the sale of the land and house two years after its completion for $1,200.

75. Worcester County Land Records, 332:468, WORC.

76. Ibid., 337:449.

77. References to Houghton's renting come from the letters and diary of Mary White, who noted her niece's many "removes." See Diary of Mary White, August 1839; March 1841, OSV.

78. Mary White to Charles White, March 6, 1839; Diary of Mary White, May 22, 1839, OSV. On the humble status of shoe binding, see Vickers, "Competency and Competition," 10; Brooke, *Heart of the Commonwealth*, 296. See also Blewett, *We Will Rise in Our Might*, 2–25.

79. Worcester County Land Records, 381:85, 381:195, WORC. The occupation of the man who held the mortgage, George Maynard, is taken from the U.S. Population Census of 1850.

80. Diary of Mary White, March 1846, OSV. Sandy Hill was a mill village on the Hudson River near Troy that was incorporated in 1810. 1860 *Gazetteer*, provided by the Research

Library of the New York Historical Society, New York, N.Y. See also "Instructive and Interesting History of 'Squire' Aaron White," *Transcript*, March 19, 1889, clipping sheet for Aaron White Jr., Class of 1817, Harvard University Biographical Files, HU, courtesy of Harvard University Archives.

81. Benjamin Houghton to Deacon Henry Brigham of Boylston, Sandy Hill, New York, 1846, Hiram Harlow Collection, BHS.

82. The Houghtons' return is recorded in the diary of Mary White. Benjamin Houghton was listed as a carpenter with no estate in the 1850 U.S. Population Census for Boylston. In early 1851 the family moved to Ashland.

83. Ashland transformed from a town of ten-footer shoe shops to an industrial shoe center just at the time of Houghton's arrival. Higley, "Ashland," 550–54.

84. Obituary of Lucy Ann White Houghton, untitled and undated newspaper clipping in the files of the Ashland Historical Society.

85. Account Book of Joseph Flagg, p. 36, OSV.

86. Francis White to Charles White, August 30, 1842, OSV.

87. In Concord in 1818, a good farm laborer could expect to earn $120/year with board. Kimenker, "The Concord Farmer," 184.

88. Francis White to Charles White, August 30, 1842, OSV.

89. *Worcester Telegram*, February 11, 1907, newspaper clipping, BHS.

90. See documents relating to this property transaction in the Flagg Family Papers, BHS.

91. *Worcester Telegram*, February 11, 1907, newspaper clipping, BHS.

92. Untitled, undated newspaper clipping in "Obituary News Clippings" files, BHS.

93. Crane, *Historic Homes and Institutions*, 533.

94. Caroline White to Charles White, "Summer's Eve," 1837, OSV.

95. Ibid., August 19, 1839, OSV.

96. Aaron White to Charles White, August 15, 1837, OSV.

97. Caroline White to Charles White, February 17, 1840; Aaron White Sr. to Charles White, March 1, 1840, OSV.

98. See, for example, Aaron White to Charles White, January 4, 1841, OSV.

99. Caroline White to Charles White, June 14, 1836, OSV.

100. Ibid., Wednesday, May 1837, OSV.

101. Ibid., "Wed. morn.," May 1837, OSV.

102. Ibid., "Last Sabbath in May," 1839, OSV.

103. Ibid., June 3, 1839, OSV.

104. Diary of Mary White, May 11, October 27, 1843, OSV.

105. Francis White to Charles White, August 30, 1842, OSV.

106. Diary of Mary White, March 7, 1843, OSV.

107. Caroline White to Charles White, July 5, 1838, OSV.

108. Blewett, "Women Shoeworkers and Domestic Ideology," 426–27.

109. Caroline White to Charles White, July 19, 1841, OSV.

110. On the place of shoe binding in women's daily farmwork, see Blewett, *We Will Rise*

in Our Might, chap. 1. On women's pay for shoe work, see Blewett, "Women Shoeworkers," 405–7. On the number of women in Worcester County engaged in shoe outwork, see Larkin, "Women in the Workplace," 3–4.

111. Caroline White to Charles White, April 5, 1841, OSV.

112. See Chambers-Schiller, *Liberty, a Better Husband,* for discussion of the growing number of women who chose to remain single during this period in order to lead active, purposeful lives in multiple spheres.

113. Gross relates similar self-striving goals for Emerson's generation in Concord, Mass. "Young Men and Women of Fairest Promise."

Chapter 5

1. Merchant, *Ecological Revolutions,* 137–43.

2. The Thomas family farm was part of the land set off to West Boylston. Hamilton, *The History of West Boylston,* 41–42.

3. Jaffee, "The Village Enlightenment in New England."

4. Davenport, *Brief Historical Sketch of Boylston,* 18. On the emerging aesthetic for rural New England villages, see Gross, *Transcendentalists and Their World,* chap. 4, 12–15.

5. The Murdock family lived in that section of Boylston that became West Boylston. Hamilton, *The History of West Boylston,* 42–43.

6. On the transformative effect of expanded print and communication, see Daniel Walker Howe, *What God Hath Wrought,* chaps. 6, 16; Gross and Kelley, *An Extensive Republic.*

7. Francis White to Charles White, Worcester, January 16, 1840, OSV.

8. Davenport, *Brief Historical Sketch of Boylston,* 18.

9. Walters, *American Reformers,* 206–10; Daniel Walker Howe, *What Hath God Wrought,* 449–55.

10. Noonan, *Educational History of Boylston,* 10–11.

11. Ibid., 10.

12. Caroline White to Charles White, January 6, 1840, OSV.

13. For examples of these copybooks, see Oliver Sawyer's schoolbook, 1811, OSV; and Phineas Ball's schoolbook, 1837–38, Boylston Manuscripts Collection, BHS.

14. See Phineas Ball's schoolbook, Boylston Manuscripts Collection, BHS.

15. Pierpont, *The American First Class Book,* 3.

16. Noah Webster's *American Spelling Book* was also secular. However, it was written in the 1780s, before the great sectarian divide or Webster's own conversion to Calvinism. This text was a product of early nation making, asserting the superiority of uniquely American speech over corrupt British antecedents. Although it promoted civic over religious influence in schooling, it was not intended as an apology for Unitarian ethical curriculum. See Joseph J. Ellis, *After the Revolution,* chap. 6. By 1828, Webster considered education "useless without the Bible."

17. Bidwell, "The Moral Significance of the Common School," 53.

18. More than three-quarters of those elected to school-committee positions between 1825

and 1840 were members of a town church, far higher than the 50 percent average for the town. Half of the elected were Unitarians, half orthodox, revealing the struggle for sectarian domination. Boylston Town Clerk's Record Book, BHS.

19. The first line is from the *New England Primer*, a Puritan catechism of mankind's inherent sinfulness, divine punishment, and the inevitability of death. The second line, from Phineas Ball's schoolbook, Boylston Manuscripts Collection, BHS, reflects Unitarianism's general embrace of moral principles for the progressive improvement of individual and society.

20. Bidwell compared schooling in communities that were "morally-integrated," morally pluralist, and morally conflicted or polarized. Towns that are morally polarized and in the process of losing their moral integration will battle to produce conforming sentiments and to assert control over socialization of the next generation. Bidwell, "The Moral Significance of the Common School."

21. See, for example, the Indenture of Samuel Stone, who was "to be taught to read, write, and cipher, so far as is attainable by causing him to attend the town school in his school district at least eight weeks in every year during the term with suitable books and stationery." Town Meeting Minutes, 1826, Boylston Town Clerk's Record Book, BHS.

22. Petition of Benjamin Houghton to Town Meeting, March 21, 1836, Boylston Town Clerk's Record Book, BHS.

23. Town Meeting Minutes, March 1830 and January 1831, Boylston Town Clerk's Record Book, BHS.

24. Bourne, *The History of the Surplus Revenue of 1837*, appendix III. See also "Orders drawn on the Treasurer by the Selectmen," 1837, Boylston Town Clerk's Record Book, BHS.

25. Scott, "The Popular Lecture," 795. See also Watkinson, "Useful Knowledge?" 351–52.

26. Noonan, *The Educational History of Boylston*, 8–9.

27. This observation was made by the Boylston School Committee in 1842. School Committee Report citied in Noonan, *The Educational History of Boylston*, 11.

28. Caroline White to Charles White, January 26, 1839; Francis White to Charles White, January 17, 1838, OSV.

29. Aaron White to Charles White, May 1, 1838, OSV.

30. Bushman, *The Refinement of America*, 215–16.

31. Elizabeth White Conant to Charles White, November 14, 1836, OSV.

32. Mary White (sister) to Charles White, June 19, 1838, OSV.

33. Caroline White to Charles White, n.d. (no. 1.17); December 20, 1836; n.d. (no. 1.24); November 11, 1839, OSV.

34. Bushman, *The Refinement of America*, 217.

35. Caroline White to Charles White, July 19, 1839, OSV.

36. See Diary of Mary White, December 1832, 1834, OSV.

37. Kelley, "Reading Women/Women Reading," 419–23. See also Kelley, *Learning to Stand and Speak*, chap. 4.

38. See Gross and Kelley, "An Age of Print?"; Larkin, "The Merriams of Brookfield," 66–73; Daniel Walker Howe, *What Hath God Wrought*, 626–36.

39. Gross and Kelley, "An Age of Print?"

40. Gross, "Books, Nationalism, and History."

41. William White to Charles White, January 2, 1838, OSV (emphasis added).

42. Ibid., August 11, 1836, OSV.

43. Ibid.

44. Caroline White to Charles White, August 16, 18[40?], OSV.

45. White family daughters attended the Reading Society on a regular basis in 1827, 1828, 1829, and 1830, then again in 1832. The society appears to have disbanded in 1832, following the departure of Reverend Russell, suggesting a sectarian element to its membership.

46. Kelley, "Reading Women/Women Reading," 401–24. On self-fashioning through engagement with texts, Kelley cites Renaissance scholar Stephen Greenblatt, 403.

47. Richard D. Brown, *Knowledge Is Power*, 294.

48. Diary mention of lyceum lectures begins in 1830. As the decade progressed, the speakers were more frequently traveling professional lecturers unknown to Mary White. The lyceum was defined as a "mutual education association" by Josiah Holbrook in the 1820s. Boylstonian Matthew Davenport referred to the town's "mutual system of instruction" in 1831. Vern Wagner, "The Lecture Lyceum and the Problem of Controversy," 122; Davenport, *Brief Historical Sketch of Boylston*, 18. On the lyceum movement, see Watkinson, "Useful Knowledge?" and Bode, *The American Lyceum*.

49. Bode, *The American Lyceum*, 13.

50. Vern Wagner, "The Lecture Lyceum and the Problem of Controversy," 121.

51. Diary of Mary White, May 24, 1843, OSV.

52. Scott, "The Popular Lecture," 806.

53. Mary noted lyceum attendance by her children, friends, and live-in hired help.

54. Scott, "The Popular Lecture," 800–809.

55. Gross, "Lonesome in Eden," 8–9.

56. Davenport, *Brief Historical Sketch of Boylston*, 18.

57. Noonan, *Educational History of Boylston*, 11.

58. Opal, "Exciting Emulation," 448.

59. Tolley and Beadie, "Symposium: Reappraisals of the Academy Movement"; see also Sizer, "The Academies: An Interpretation."

60. See, for example, the acts of incorporation of New Salem Academy, 1795, and New Ipswich Academy, 1789. *History of the Connecticut Valley in Massachusetts*, 670; and Augustus A. Gould, *History of New Ipswich*, 200.

61. Tolley, "The Rise of Academies," 230–33.

62. This list is drawn from the curricula of schools attended by the White family children during the 1820s and 1830s, including the catalogues and histories of Leicester Academy (Washburn, *Historical Sketches of the Town of Leicester*, 22–24); Middlebury Seminary (Swift, *History of the Town of Middlebury*, 391–98); New Ipswich (N.H.) Academy, from Article II of the Constitution as cited in Augustus A. Gould, *History of New Ipswich*, 200, and the *Catalogue of New Ispwich Academy, 1830*; and Norton (Mass.) Academy, *Catalogue of the Officers and Members of Wheaton Female Seminary at Norton*, 8–9.

63. As quoted in Opal, "Exciting Emulation," 469.

64. Tolley and Beadie, "Symposium," 216.

65. This argument is from Opal, "Exciting Emulation."

66. "Life or Biography of Silas Fenton," 139–40, as quoted in Opal, "Exciting Emulation, 466.

67. Only third-born son Davis, who decided early on a career in tanning and leather sales, did not choose to attend a private academy. The other children attended Leicester Academy in Worcester County; New Salem Academy in Franklin County; Brookfield Seminary in Worcester County; Middlebury Seminary and Academy in Vermont; Phillips Academy in Andover, Mass.; Doctor Wardell's [Female] School, also in Andover; New Ipswich Academy in New Ipswich, N.H.; Norton Academy (also known as the Wheaton Female Seminary) in Norton, Mass.; the Baptist Seminary in Worcester; and the Baptist Manual Training School in Worcester.

68. Kett, *Rites of Passage*, 19; Beadie, "Academy Students in the Mid-Nineteenth Century," 253.

69. Firstborn Aaron was sent to Harvard; fifth-born William attended Williams and Brown. See "Instructive and Interesting History of 'Squire Aaron White," *Webster (Mass.) Times*, December 8, 1886, Harvard College Library Clipping Sheet, Harvard University Biographical Files (HUG 300), HU, courtesy of Harvard University Archives.

70. Mary White to Charles White, March 1, 1841, OSV.

71. The nine young women from Boylston were all, with one exception, from families in the third tax decile or higher.

72. Beadie, "Academy Students," 255–56.

73. Ibid., 255.

74. As quoted in Bushman, *Refinement of America*, 300.

75. Nash, "Cultivating the Powers of Human Beings." See also Kelley, *Learning to Stand and Speak*, chap. 3.

76. *Catalogue of the Officers and Members of Wheaton Female Seminary*.

77. On education for active citizenship, see Kelley, *Learning to Stand and Speak*, chap. 1.

78. William White to Charles White, March 19, 1838, W. J. White Collection, Archives and Special Collections, WC.

79. Text copied by Mindy Lamson from the *Rural Repository*, September 19, 1835, in Mindy Lamson's book, ca. 1836, Boylston Manuscripts Collection, BHS. The editors of the *Repository* indicated that the verses were from the pen of James Montgomery.

80. Aaron White to Charles White, October 10, 1837; Caroline White to Charles White, late 1839, OSV.

81. Mary White (mother) to Charles White, February 5, 1838; February 6, 1839; July 16, 1839; April 6, 1840, OSV.

82. Aaron White to Charles White, August 10, 1840, OSV.

83. Caroline White to Charles White, December 20, 1836, OSV.

84. Ibid., October 25, 1838, OSV.

85. Ibid., November 11, 1839, OSV.

86. Ibid., n.d. (ca. 1840, no. 1.15), OSV.

87. William White to Charles White, May 9, 1837, OSV.

88. Elizabeth White Conant to Charles White, March 25, 1839, OSV.

89. William White to Charles White, March 19, 1839, W. J. White Collection, Archives and Special Collections, WC.

90. Francis White to Charles White, August 30, 1840, OSV.

91. Aaron White to Charles White, June 27, 1841, OSV.

92. Sellers, *Market Revolution*, 366. See also Jaffee, "The Village Enlightenment in New England."

Chapter 6

1. Daniel Walker Howe, *What Hath God Wrought*, 244. For the literature of improvement, see Howe's notes to chap. 7.

2. Koschnik, *"Let a Common Interest Bind Us Together"*; Neem, *Creating a Nation of Joiners*; Daniel Walker Howe, "Religion and Politics," 126.

3. The historiography of antebellum reform is extensive. Major studies include Walters, *American Reformers*; and Mintz, *Moralists and Modernizers*. See also Sellers, *Market Revolution*; Daniel Walker Howe, *What Hath God Wrought*; and Appleby, *Inheriting the Revolution*. For women's role in antebellum reform, see Ginzberg, *Women and the Work of Benevolence*. For temperance, see Rorabaugh, *The Alcoholic Republic*; and Hampel, *Temperance and Prohibition in Massachusetts*; for health, see Nissenbaum, *Sex, Diet, and Debility in Jacksonian America*; for institutional uplift, see Rothman, *The Discovery of the Asylum*. See also Gross, "Giving in America." The literature of antislavery reform will be covered in a later chapter.

4. On the role of expanded communications, see Gross and Kelley, "Spreading the Word in Print," in *An Extensive Republic*; Daniel Walker Howe, *What Hath God Wrought*, 5–7, 690–98.

5. Tocqueville, *Democracy in America*, vol. 2, bk. 2, chap. 5, 106–10. On social capital, see Putnam, *Bowling Alone*.

6. Diary of Mary White, August 16, 1838, OSV.

7. Rorabaugh, *The Alcoholic Republic*, 194–200.

8. Aaron White Store Ledgers, 1802–4, BHS.

9. Diary of Simon Davis, July 13, 14, 1798, BHS.

10. Hampel, *Temperance and Prohibition*, 1; Rorabaugh, *The Alcoholic Republic*, chap. 1; Daniel Walker Howe, *What Hath God Wrought*, 167–68.

11. Hampel reviews the earlier historiography of temperance, *Temperance and Prohibition*, 2–3. On the various reasons for change in attitude toward drink, see Hampel, *Temperance and Prohibition*, 12–13; Appleby, "Personal Roots," 142–43; Paul E. Johnson, *Shopkeepers' Millennium*; Dannenbaum, *Drink and Disorder*.

12. On the origins of temperance in Massachusetts, see Hampel, *Temperance and Prohibition*, chap. 2.

13. Rorabaugh, *The Alcoholic Republic*, 190–93.

14. Diary of Mary White, September 8, 1830, OSV.

15. Mary White to Charles White, May 19, 1838, OSV.

16. Tocqueville, *Democracy in America*, vol. 2, bk. 2, chap. 4, 102–5.

17. Diary of Mary White, February 26, 1833, OSV.

18. Letter from Boylston Temperance Society, September 2, 1833, Massachusetts Society for the Suppression of Intemperance Collection, 1833, folder 2, AAS.

19. Boylston Congregational Church Collection, January 14, 1832, BHS.

20. Ibid., October 12, 1833.

21. Ibid., December 29, 1835.

22. Davis, *The Half Century*, 137–40; Hampel, *Temperance and Prohibition*, 46–51.

23. Diary of Mary White, December 15, 1835, OSV.

24. Ibid., May 19, 1835, OSV.

25. Hampel, *Temperance and Prohibition*, chap. 3.

26. Appleby, "Personal Roots," 142–48. Appleby also reviews the historiography of temperance motivations. See also Rorabaugh, *The Alcoholic Republic*, 202–22.

27. Samuel G. Reed of No. Brookfield to Fanny L. Tilton, April 9, 1832, Boylston Vital Records, BHS. The first temperance wedding in Boylston at which coffee was served instead of wine.

28. On children in temperance and temperance paraphernalia, see Hampel, *Temperance and Prohibition*, 92.

29. Carson, *Rum and Reform*, 16–17.

30. Diary of Mary White, July 4, 1842, OSV.

31. Ibid., June 27, 1843, OSV.

32. Hampel, *Temperance and Prohibition*, 90.

33. Diary of Mary White, May 4, 1842, OSV.

34. From "A Recollection of Sturbridge, Mass.," excerpted in Old Sturbridge Village Museum Education Department, "Reform: Temperance," 1.

35. Hampel, *Temperance and Prohibition*, 34, 52–53.

36. Diary of Aaron White Jr., November 15, 1834; October 21, 1835; January 6, 1837, MHS.

37. Hampel, *Temperance and Prohibition*, 53

38. Rorabaugh, *Alcoholic Republic*, 205.

39. Davenport, *Brief Historical Sketch of Boylston*, 16.

40. American Temperance Society, *Sixth Annual Report of the American Temperance Society*, 50.

41. Mary White to Charles White, February 20, 1838, OSV.

42. William White to Charles White, April 27, 1841, OSV.

43. Hampel, *Temperance and Prohibition*, 65–69.

44. As quoted in ibid., 62.

45. See Election Results, April 25, 1835, and April 2, 1838, Boylston Town Clerk's Record Book, BHS. In the first election, one set of three candidates received 84 percent of the vote. In the second election, one slate received 43 percent while the other received 47 percent. These were not party affiliations, Hampel claims, but represented pro- and antitemperance views. Hampel, *Temperance and Prohibition*, 65–69.

46. Hampel, *Temperance and Prohibition*, 79.

47. Davis, *The Half Century*, 138.

48. Brooke, *Heart of the Commonwealth*, 357–58.

49. Collins, "Speech Delivered at the First Public Meeting of the British and Foreign Temperance Society," 1.

50. Hampel, *Temperance and Prohibition*, 61–62.

51. "Reform: Temperance," 1978, resource packet edited by the Museum Education Department, Old Sturbridge Village.

52. Carson, *Rum and Reform*, 15; Hyde Park Historical Society, "Striped Pig."

53. The Dedham muster was held September 11, 1838; news of the Striped Pig Exhibition appeared by September 9 in the *Boston Gazette, Boston Centennial, New Bedford Mercury,* and *Rhode Island Republican*. By October 4, the story had been carried by papers in Maine, New Hampshire, and New Orleans. By November 14, 1838, the *New Orleans Daily Picayune* reported that the story was known in the Far West and in London. The story had certainly traveled to London by October of 1839, when it appeared in the *London Quarterly Review.*

54. See, for example, the broadside "Striped Pig Party: Liberal Meeting," in Rare Book and Special Collections Division, Printed Ephemera Collection, Portfolio 56, folder 36, LOC, which advertised that all opposed to the new license law, "without reference to political parties," should meet in the Springfield (Mass.) town hall on October 26, 1838. See also Notice in the *Farmers' Cabinet* (Amherst, N.H.), September 28, 1838, 3.

55. According to an editorial in the *Virginia Free Press* (Charlestown, W.Va.), June 27, 1839, Issue 22.

56. Both Striped Pig newspapers are at the AAS.

57. Song sheet, "Dedham muster, or, Striped pig. Tune—King and Countryman. Sold, by L. Deming, at the sign of the barber's pole, No. 61, Hanover Street, Boston, and at Middlebury, Vt.," n.d., Song Sheet Collection, Rare Book and Special Collections Division, LOC; broadside, "The Striped Pig: As Sung by Mr. Wills at the Tremont Theatre with great applause, the only correct one published," Printed Ephemera Collection, portfolio 56, folder 27, Rare Book and Special Collections Division, LOC.

58. Aaron White to Charles White, March 3, 1840, OSV.

59. Diary of Mary White, March 2, 1840, OSV.

60. On swine and the commons, see Steinberg, "Down to Earth," 811; Bellesiles, *Revolutionary Outlaws*, 63.

61. Jack Larkin, electronic correspondence with the author, October 31, 2011.

62. See Town Meeting Minutes, 1815–43, Boylston Town Clerk's Record Books, BHS.

63. See, for example, Wittmann, "Menageries and Markets."

64. See Potter, *Pyg*.

65. Lithograph, "La Piganino," http://www.porkopolis.org/art-museum/artist-index/piganino/ (February 2013). See also Tatham, *The Lure of the Striped Pig*, 43–44.

66. [Anonymous], *A History of the Striped Pig*, 8.

67. Caroline White to Charles White, January 26, 1839, OSV.

68. In the 1839 election for governor, Boylston cast 59 percent of its votes for Everett, 41 percent for Morton. On temperance in the 1838 and 1839 elections, see Hampel, *Temperance and Prohibition*, chap. 6.

69. Appleby, "Personal Roots," 154.

70. Altschuler and Blumin, "Limits of Political Engagement in Antebellum America," 879.

71. Levy, "A Moment with Jonathan Levy," 17. See also Levy, *Freaks of Fortune*; Murphy, "'Doomed . . . to Eat the Bread of Dependency'?"

72. See Thornton, "A 'Great Machine.'"

73. Probate of Aaron White, 64166, Worcester County Probate Records, MA.

74. Diary of Mary White, March 29, April 10, 1832, OSV.

75. Diary of Simon Davis, November 7, 1796, BHS.

76. The earliest law on legal settlement and eligibility for receipt of aid dates to 1639; the law was revised in 1655 to make it more difficult for strangers to join any settlement without consent of the inhabitants. John Cummings, "Poor-Laws of Massachusetts and New York," 22–24.

77. Ibid., 35–36.

78. For the literature of poor relief and poor reform in this era, see Mintz, *Moralists and Modernizers*, 82–85; Walters, *American Reformers*, 173–79; Rothman, *Discovery of the Asylum*, 155–79; Herdon, *Unwanted Americans*; Conrad E. Wright, *Transformation of Charity*.

79. Diary of Mary White, June 4 and October 28, 1836, OSV.

80. Quincy, *Massachusetts Committee on Pauper Laws*; David Wagner, *The Poorhouse*, 7–8.

81. This is less than the Worcester County average of 2 percent per year. Old Sturbridge Village Museum Education Department, "Reform: Poverty."

82. The terms were repeated at each annual meeting. Boylston Town Clerk's Record Books, BHS.

83. Boylston Town Clerk's Record Books, 1830–40, BHS.

84. On attitudes toward poverty, see Rothman, *Discovery of the Asylum*, 155–79.

85. From a low of $300 in 1825, the annual town budget for poor expenses rose steadily to a high of $1,000 in 1840. Boylston Town Clerk's Record Books, 1835–40, BHS.

86. Boylston Town Clerk's Record Book, February 1842, and entry for the death of Abigail Butler, May 5, 1843, Boylston Vital Records, BHS. See also Probate of Abigail Butler, Petition for Guardianship, Docket 09465, 239:515, Worcester County Probate Records, MA.

87. Suit of Ezra Goodale (by Pierce & Davenport) v Knight, March 1840, 92:64, Worcester County Court of Common Pleas Records, MA.

88. Wagner, *The Poorhouse*, 41–48; Rothman, *Discovery of the Asylum*, 161–74; Old Sturbridge Village Museum Education Department, "Reform: Poverty."

89. David Wagner, *The Poorhouse*, 4.

90. Quincy, *Massachusetts Committee on Pauper Laws*, 1–9.

91. Rothman, *Discovery of the Asylum*, 180.

92. The rules of Boylston's early poorhouse do not survive. However, the historian of neighboring Harvard noted that in 1825 the town's Poor Farm had fourteen rules regulating behavior, a breach of which would result in solitary confinement upon bread and water for twelve to forty-eight hours. Nourse, *History of the Town of Harvard*. The rules of neighboring Worcester's workhouse also survive, Wagner, *The Poorhouse*, 47.

93. David Wagner, *The Poorhouse*, 46.

94. Dupuis, *History of Boylston, 1786–1886*, 74.

95. Ward, "History of the Town of Shrewsbury," 22–24.

96. Wagner, *The Poorhouse*, 41–48.

97. Ward, "History of the Town of Shrewsbury," 22–24.

98. Boylston Town Clerk's Record Book, 1820, BHS.

99. "That of all causes of pauperism, intemperance, in the use of spirituous liquors, is the most powerful and universal." Quincy, *Report of the Committee for the Consideration of Pauper Laws of the Commonwealth of Massachusetts*, 17, 31. There is no evidence that any of those in Boylston poor relief in the 1820s or 1830s was a drunkard.

100. Dupuis, *History of Boylston, 1786–1886*, 75–76.

101. In the first published report of the poor farm in 1851–52, the average age of the eight inmates was seventy-one. Boylston Overseers of the Poor Records, BHS.

102. Gross makes a similar argument for Concord in "Giving in America," 31.

103. On insanity in America, see Grob, *The State and the Mentally Ill*; Rothman, *The Discovery of the Asylum*; Grob, *Mental Institutions in America*; and Jimenez, "Madness in Early American History." See also Grob, *The Mad Among Us*, chaps. 1–4.

104. Jimenez, "Madness in Early American History," 9.

105. Ibid., 34.

106. Grob, *The State and the Mentally Ill*, 5.

107. On the process of "distemperature," see Jimenez, "Madness in Early American History," 28.

108. Ibid., 27.

109. Mary White to Charles White, January 28, June 27, 1838; March 6, 1839, OSV.

110. Caroline White to Charles White, October 25, 1838, OSV.

111. Ibid., n.d. (ca. 1840), OSV (cataloged in the file of Mary Avery White Jr., Accession Number 1990.64.1.6.).

112. Jimenez, "Madness in Early American History," 31–34; Grob, *The State and the Mentally Ill*, 7–16.

113. Jimenez, "Madness in Early American History," 35.

114. Rev. Jedidiah Morse, in an 1801 Discourse before the Humane Society of the Commonwealth of Massachusetts, as quoted in M. A. Dewolfe Howe, *The Humane Society of the Commonwealth of Massachusetts*, 199–200. A similar observation is made by contemporary Davis, *The Half Century*, 115.

115. Jimenez, "Madness in Early American History," 36.

116. *Reports Relating to the State Lunatic Hospital at Worcester*, 4–5.

117. Davis, *The Half Century*, 115.

118. Blunt, *Childish Things*, 36–37.

119. Americans in the 1830s believed that the incidence of insanity in their society was increasing. This may, however, speak more to public awareness of and concern for the presence of disorderly people than to an actual increase in mental illness. Rothman, *The Discovery of the Asylum*, 110.

120. Grob, *The State and the Mentally Ill,* 26–27, report (requested February 23, 1829 by Horace Mann) submitted to the Massachusetts House of Representatives, February 13, 1830.

121. Grob, *The State and the Mentally Ill,* chap. 3.

122. Woodward, *Tenth Annual Report*; also quoted in Grob, in *The State and the Mentally Ill,* 55.

123. The most common causes of admission for insanity at the Worcester Insane Asylum in 1833 were intemperance (24 percent), bodily infirmity (16 percent), religious fanaticism/ enthusiasm (10 percent), family troubles (7 percent), failure in business/loss of property (7 percent), disappointed hopes or affections (6 percent), sexual excess (5 percent), miscellaneous (5 percent), and unknown (20 percent). Males were 60 percent and females 40 percent of the total. Personally culpable behaviors (intemperance, sexual excess, use of tobacco, excessive study, and fanaticism, which were twice as prevalent among men as among women, were 41 percent of the total admissions. *Reports Relating to the State Lunatic Hospital at Worcester,* 45–49.

124. The Massachusetts Mental Health Department denied access to Mary Ann Abbot's files. However, the asylum's 1838 annual report indicates diagnosis by sex, age, and date of admission, making it possible to identify the diagnosis for Mary Ann Abbot. "Date of Admission: September 8, 1837. Present Age: 42. Sex: Female. Marital Status—Single." See Patient Number 632, "Fifth Annual Report of the Trustees of the State Lunatic Hospital in Worcester," in *Reports Relating to the State Lunatic Hospital at Worcester,* 29.

125. Culbertson, *Cincinnati Lancet-Clinic,* 274

126. Compare to the "moral treatment" of Vermont farmer Hiram Harwood, 1838–39 in Shalhope, *A Tale of New England,* 222–41.

127. Grob discusses Woodward's treatments, *The State and the Mentally Ill,* 62–66.

128. Ibid., 36.

129. Diary of Mary White, September 23, 1837, OSV.

130. Mary White to Charles White, September 24, 1837, OSV.

131. Patient Number 632, "Fifth Annual Report of the Trustees of the State Lunatic Hospital in Worcester," in *Reports Relating to the State Lunatic Hospital at Worcester,* 29.

132. Grob documents the cost of maintaining an inmate at the Worcester Asylum in the 1830s at $2.50 per week. Grob, *The State and the Mentally Ill,* 87.

133. As Grob notes, "His claims concerning the curability of insanity received widespread attention and played an important role in setting into motion . . . the cult of curability." Ibid., 74.

134. "Third Annual Report of the Trustees of the State Lunatic Hospital in Worcester," (1835), *Reports Relating to the State Lunatic Hospital at Worcester,* 35.

Chapter 7

1. Diary of Mary White, January 12, 1838, OSV.

2. Burton's talks were later published as *White Slavery: A New Emancipation Cause.*

3. Burton, *White Slavery,* quotes from 116, 141, 104.

4. Ibid., 184.

5. Rice, "Making Way for the Machine."

6. Poe, "Maelzel's Chess Player." See also Wimsatt, "Poe and the Chess Automaton."

7. Burton, *White Slavery*, 143–44.

8. Ibid., 132–33.

9. Ibid., 185.

10. Diary of Mary White, January 19, 1838, OSV.

11. Formisano argues that Federalist/Jeffersonian contests in early republic Massachusetts failed to produce enduring partisan institutions, as party organization and influence were too inchoate and immature to function as an effective political system, and popular sentiment still believed partisan ideologies were injurious to the common good. Rather, this generation was more influenced by a candidate's personality and apparent fidelity to the principles and myths of the Revolution. Formisano, *Transformation of Political Culture*.

12. James Monroe, First Inaugural Address, March 4, 1817. Federalism held out longest in New England, but anti-British sentiment during and following the War of 1812 eclipsed Federalist sympathies and spelled the end of the party's power.

13. Formisano argues that the reason for this separation in Massachusetts lay in technological advances in communication and transportation that allowed for better party organization, the diverging interests of an economically developing nation, and the passing of the party-phobic revolutionary generation. Formisano, *Transformation of Political Culture*.

14. Bancroft, *History of the United States*; Turner, "The Significance of the Section in American History"; Schlesinger, *The Age of Jackson*; Benson, *The Concept of Jacksonian Democracy*; Hofstadter, *The Idea of a Party System*; Formisano, *The Transformation of Political Culture*; Pessen, *Jacksonian America*; Remini, *The Jacksonian Era*; Watson, *Liberty and Power*; Sellers, *The Market Revolution*; Feller, *The Jacksonian Promise*; Wilentz, *The Rise of American Democracy*; Daniel Walker Howe, *What Hath God Wrought*.

15. McGerr, *The Decline of Popular Politics*, 13–14. See also Gienapp, "'Politics Seem to Enter into Everything.'" For an opposing view and an analysis of the popular investment in politics in this era, see Altschuler and Blumin, "Limits of Political Engagement in Antebellum America"; and Jean H. Baker, "Politics, Paradigms, and Public Culture."

16. Capt. Aaron Whitney of Harvard was painted in 1841 reading the *Boston Statesmen*, one of the foremost Democratic newspapers of its time. My thanks to Judy Warner and Susan Lee of the Harvard Historical Society, Harvard, Massachusetts, for this information.

17. Daniel Walker Howe, "Religion and Politics."

18. Feller, "Politics and Society," 158.

19. In addition to works noted above, see Kohl, *The Politics of Individualism*; and Daniel Walker Howe, *The Political Culture of American Whigs*.

20. Feller, "Politics and Society," 152–53. Howe echoes the thought that Democrats prized "freedom from," while Whigs prized "freedom to." Daniel Walker Howe, "Religion and Politics," 132.

21. This question has been long debated, with distinctions based on region, economic class,

profession, religion, ethnicity, aspirations, or other ethnocultural factors. For a review of these views through 1990, see Feller, "Politics and Society."

22. Brooke, *Heart of the Commonwealth*, 310–12, 353–60.

23. Formisano cast Massachusetts Whigs and Democrats in a center-and-periphery context; Democrats were those cultural, religious, political, or economic outsiders resisting the hegemony of the dominant center. For his definition of Center-Periphery (drawn from political science models), see Formisano, *Transformation of Political Culture*, 6.

24. Ibid., 313–19.

25. Huston, "Economic History"; see also Howe, "Religion and Politics," 133, who compares the Democrats to the party "of the ethnocultural periphery."

26. Schlesinger, *The Age of Jackson*, 146–48.

27. Ibid., 190–209.

28. Ibid., 145–65.

29. See appendix D, table D-1. Note the rise in turnout—and solid Federalist consensus—during the War of 1812. See also Brooke, *Heart of the Commonwealth*, sect. 3.

30. It is important to note that partisan passions are revealed not so much by lopsided voting results as by *turnout* in combination with vote. For example, in 1829, Boylston saw a one-time spurt in Democratic votes for governor, but they came at a time when interest in politics was so low in Boylston, as across Worcester County, that barely a quarter of eligible voters bothered to cast a ballot. See appendix D, table D-1. See also Brooke, *Heart of the Commonwealth*, 325–26.

31. See appendix D, table D-1.

32. Boylston sent no delegates to the state's Anti-Masonic conventions. See *An Abstract of the Proceedings of the Anti-Masonic State Convention of Massachusetts*.

33. See appendix D, table D-1.

34. Brooke, *Heart of the Commonwealth*, 311.

35. See appendix D, table D-2.

36. Town Meeting Minutes, Boylston Town Clerk's Record Book, April 9, 1821, BHS.

37. Ibid., November 11, 1833, BHS.

38. In this, Boylston was in line with the rest of Worcester County. See Brooke, *Heart of the Commonwealth*, 314.

39. Ibid., 310–11.

40. See appendix D, table D-1.

41. Jean H. Baker, *Affairs of Party*; for an opposing view, see Altschuler and Blumin, "Limits of Political Engagement in Antebellum America." For evangelism and popular politics, see Daniel Walker Howe, "Religion and Politics."

42. Daniel Walker Howe, "Religion and Politics," 125; Gross, "Print and the Public Sphere," 258.

43. Diary of Mary White, August 31, 1840; September 9, 1840; October 29, 1840; November 6, 1840, OVS.

44. Ibid., October 10, 1843, OSV.

45. Caroline White to Charles White, November 11, 1839, OSV.

46. Diary of Aaron White Jr., March 24, 25, April 4–11, 14, 15, May 13, June 1, August 27, 1835; April 20, 21, November 14, 1836; June 22, August 28, 29, 30, September 8, 1837; January 3, March 10, May 2, September 18, October 16, 1838; January 16, February 19, June 1, 3, 13, August 20, 27, 28, 1839; March 28, April 4, 13, 15, 16, June 17, August 25, September 1, 14, 21, October 3, 5, 7, 10, 17, 20, 24, 31, November 4, 9, 1840; February 6, March 4, 1841, MHS. Diary volume from March 1841 to 1844 is missing.

47. Brooke, *Heart of the Commonwealth*, 354.

48. Worcester County Whig Records, Massachusetts Collection, 1629–1869, box 6, folder 3, AAS.

49. Diary of Mary White, August 31, November 6, 1840, OSV.

50. Ibid., June 17, 1840, OSV; Whig Party Papers, Whig State Convention, 1840, Letters of Delegates' Appointments, Massachusetts Collection, 1629–1869, box 6, folder 5, AAS.

51. One of the most useful tools in identifying Boylston's Whigs is an 1834 Worcester County petition to support the Second Bank of the United States. As John Brooke has shown, the 6,000 men on this list provide a reliable source of Whig support. The database of Boylston Whigs is drawn from this list (limited to men who remained in town and were present on the 1840 tax list) as well as records of county temperance advocates and Whig Party records at the American Antiquarian Society. The Democratic database was constructed using Boylston men who did not sign the petition, remained in town, and were present on the 1840 tax list, supplemented with reference to "Loco Focos" in Mary's diary. This is clearly a less reliable database, as it includes those 25 percent of eligible voters who cast *no* vote in 1840. However, it is safe to assume that men in the top four wealth deciles in this group were likely voters, and so a likely indication of Democratic support. Brooke, *Heart of the Commonwealth*, 331 n. 35; "Proceedings of Citizens of the County of Worcester, Massachusetts, In Relation to the Currency." Printed in the United States Congress, *House Documents, 1833–34*, 23rd Cong., 1st sess., vol. 3, no. 176, pp. 1–43; Massachusetts Society for the Suppression of Intemperance Collection, 1833, folder 2, AAS; Massachusetts Collection, 1629–1869, box 6, folders 2, 3, 5 and box 7, folder 6, AAS; Diary of Mary White, October 10, 1843, OSV.

52. The sixty-six men who were identified as Whigs in 1840 had an average wealth decile of 3.86, as compared to 5.88 for the potential Democrats. However, the Democrats dataset, being "all Non-Whigs," includes that 25 percent of taxpaying adult white males who did not bother to vote, likely poor and young men, and so biases the Democrat's wealth downward. If we assume that all nonvoters were also non-Whigs, and exclude the poorest quarter of the non-Whig dataset, the average wealth decile for potential Democrats rises slightly to 4.60.

53. Printed letter to every town, "Private and Confidential, Boston, July 15, 1844," Massachusetts Collection, 1629–1869, box 7, folder 6, Whig Party Papers, AAS.

54. John T. Cotton to Stephen Salisbury, Esq., Chairman of the Worcester County Whig Committee, November 4, 1844, Massachusetts Collection, 1629–1869, box 7, folder 6, Whig Party Papers, AAS.

55. Massachusetts Collection, 1629–1869, box 6, folder 4, AAS.

56. Diary of Aaron White Jr., April 16, May 28, 1840, MHS.

57. This is the argument of Kohl, *The Politics of Individualism*.

58. Livermore, *An Historical Research*, 119–20.

59. For the early republic's deeply ingrained fear of violence, especially in the wake of the French Revolution, see Cleaves, *The Reign of Terror in America*.

60. Gross, "Squire Dickenson and Squire Hoar," esp. 17.

61. Ibid. See, for example, 12.

62. See note 51.

63. "The Identity of the Old Hartford Convention Federalists with the Modern Whig Harrison Party, Carefully Illustrated," *Pittsfield (Mass.) Sun* 41, no. 2087 (September 17, 1840): 1. (reprinted from the *Boston Post*).

64. Gross, "Quiet War with the State," 15. See also "The Machine-Readable Transcendentalists" and "'That Terrible Thoreau.'"

65. Gross notes that persistent attachment to kin led Emerson, "in counterreaction, to assert so vehemently the absolute independence of the self." "The Machine-Readable Transcendentalists," 512.

66. Gross, "Quiet War with the State," discusses individual sovereignty. The quote is from 3.

67. The obituary of Aaron White Jr. draws special notice to the opposing political views of father and son. "His father, Aaron White Sr., was a leading man in town affairs. . . . In the days of Federalism and Democracy, he was a staunch Federalist and in this respect unlike his son, Aaron Jr., who early took up with the democratic party and adhered to it to the last." *Webster (Mass.) Times*, December 3, 1886, Harvard College Library Clipping Sheet, Harvard University Biographical Files (HUG 300), HU, courtesy of Harvard University Archives.

68. Diary of Aaron White Jr., May 1, 1815, MHS.

69. Ibid., March 31, June 14, June 25, 1817, MHS.

70. Ibid., October 23, 1818, MHS.

71. Ibid., Thanksgiving 1821, MHS.

72. Ibid., 1821–23, MHS.

73. *Providence (R.I.) Patriot* 27, no. 6 (January 21, 1829): 1, Newsbank. At a meeting of stockholders, Aaron White was elected a director and named cashier. Entry for "Aaron White," in Windham County, Connecticut History, http:www.Ancestry.com. See also Joseph Avery White to Wm. H. Tillinghast, May 26, 1886, HUG 300, box 1064, folder: White, Aaron, Harvard University Biographical Files, HU, courtesy of Harvard University Archives.

74. Aaron White Jr. to William White, cited in "The Minutes of the Christian Convention, Held at Aurora, Ill., October 31st and November 1, 1867," in *Pamphlets: Religious, Miscellaneous*, 29–31.

75. Brooke, *Heart of the Commonwealth*, 322, 328. See also Gross, "Commemorating Concord."

76. Diary of Aaron White Jr., December 14, 16, 1834; February 24, 1835; April 20, 1836; June 21, July 10, 1837; January 7, June 17, 18, 21, 24, 1839; January 18, 19, 1841, MHS. See also *Newport (R.I.) Mercury*, September 17, 1831, and *Rhode Island American*, February 24, 1832, both of

which report on White's election as representative to Anti-Masonic statewide conventions in those years, and *Newport (R.I.) Mercury*, February 28, 1832, which notes his appointment as secretary of the Rhode Island Anti-Masonic Convention.

77. Brooke, *Heart of the Commonwealth*, 340.

78. Thornton, "A 'Great Machine,'" 567–97.

79. Caroline White to Charles White, Wednesday, May 1837, OSV.

80. Diary of Aaron White Jr., May 16, 1837, MHS.

81. Wilentz, *Rise of American Democracy*, 205–11.

82. For historiography on the Bank War sympathetic to the Democrats, see Schlesinger, *Age of Jackson*, 74–131; Sellers, *Market Revolution*, 321–26; and Wilentz, *Rise of American Democracy*, 207–11, 218–21, 227–32. For accounts sympathetic to Whigs, see Daniel Walker Howe, *What Hath God Wrought*, 373–86.

83. Lepler, "Pictures of Panic."

84. On the "public good" justifications given for chartering these banks, see Bodenhorn, *State Banking in Early America*, 78; on New England's early banking practices, see ibid., chap. 4.

85. Temin, *Engines of Enterprise*, 150–51. See Lamoreaux, *Insider Lending*, for banks operating to raise capital for their directors' industrial investment.

86. Brooke, *Heart of the Commonwealth*, 305.

87. Towers, "Bank Fraud in the Age of Mob Violence."

88. Perkins, "Rise and Fall of Relationship Banking"; Lamoreaux, *Insider Lending*.

89. Perkins, "Rise and Fall of Relationship Banking." See also Towers, "Bank Fraud in the Age of Mob Violence."

90. *Evening Post*, March 3, 1804, as cited by Greenberg, *Advocating the Man*, 55.

91. Massachusetts, 94:6, R. G. Dun & Company Credit Report Volumes, 1840–95, Baker Library Historical Collections, Harvard Business School, HU.

92. Thornton, "A 'Great Machine.'"

93. Towers, "Bank Fraud in the Age of Mob Violence."

94. Mihm, *A Nation of Counterfeiters*, 12.

95. Ibid., 1–3. Other recent studies of paper money in the early American republic include Anthony, *Paper Money Men*; Sandage, *Born Losers*; Kamensky, *The Exchange Artist*.

96. Mihm, *A Nation of Counterfeiters*, 3. See also Rothbard, *History of Money and Banking*, 78–79.

97. Rothbard, *History of Money and Banking*, 78–79. See also Mihm, *A Nation of Counterfeiters*, 5.

98. Mihm, *A Nation of Counterfeiters*, 8.

99. Ibid., 4–9, 286–89.

100. Greenberg, *Advocating the Man*, 56–57.

101. Obituary of Aaron White Jr., *Webster (Mass.) Times*, December 3, 1886, Harvard College Library Clipping Sheet, Harvard University Biographical Files (HUG 300), HU, courtesy of Harvard University Archives.

102. Diary of Aaron White Jr., August 14, 1838, MHS.

103. Ibid., July 13, 1835; May 12, 1837; March 7, 12, 1838, MHS.

104. On the panic of 1837, see Rothbard, *History of Money and Banking*, 97–100; Daniel Walker Howe, *What Hath God Wrought*, 501–5; Sellers, *Market Revolution*, 353–55.

105. Aaron White Sr. to Charles White, January 16, 1838, OSV.

106. Fenner Brown, Aaron White Jr., et al., "To the Hon. General Assembly of the State of Rhode Island," 1839, broadside memorial, OSV. Aaron White's diary states that he authored this document and presented it to Brown and the others for approval and support. White authored resolutions concerning banks during the panic of 1837 and another during the follow-up panic of 1839. See Diary of Aaron White Jr., June 5, 1837, October 24, 1839, MHS.

107. Diary of Aaron White Jr., October 11, 1839, MHS.

108. So he declared on his self-composed gravestone epitaph.

109. Williamson, *American Suffrage*, 3–7.

110. Ibid., 77, 92. The war itself produced suffrage reforms in only six states.

111. Chaput and DeSimone, "Strange Bedfellows."

112. Dennison, "The Dorr War and Political Questions," 35–38

113. Testimony of Aaron White Jr., *Rhode Island—Interference of the Executive.*

114. The story of Rhode Island suffrage is told in Williamson, *American Suffrage*, as well as Coleman, *The Transformation of Rhode Island*, and more recently in Formisano, *For the People.*

115. Williamson, *American Suffrage*, 243–44.

116. Goodell, "Rights and Wrongs of Rhode Island," 20. Goodell was a supporter of Dorr's cause.

117. These words are from the Declaration of Independence but are not included in the Constitution. See Fritz, "America's Unknown Constitutional World."

118. Goodell, "Rights and Wrongs of Rhode Island," 45.

119. Bicknell, *The History of the State of Rhode Island*, 793.

120. Gettleman, *The Dorr Rebellion*, 38–39; Formisano, *For the People*, 164–65.

121. Bowen, "The Recent Contest in Rhode Island," 23.

122. Aaron's suffrage activities during this time are documented in his diary. See entries for December 15, 1840; January 20, January 29, February 12, April 17, July 4, August 7, and August 14, 1841. See also his testimony before Congress as records in *Rhode Island—Interference of the Executive*, 277–78, where he reported that he "was frequently invited to address suffrage meetings."

123. Testimony of Aaron White Jr., *Rhode Island—Interference of the Executive*, 277–78.

124. *New England Historical and Genealogical Register*, 7:139; Fischer, *Paul Revere's Ride*, 97 n. 17; Bicknell, *History of the State of Rhode Island*, 782.

125. Gettleman, *The Dorr Rebellion*, 12–17; Goodell, "Rights and Wrongs of Rhode Island," 5, 34; Formisano, *For the People*, 163.

126. Williamson, *American Suffrage*, 247–48.

127. For Aaron White's personal reflections on Dorr's character, see the letters of Aaron White Jr. to Walter Snow Burgess, esp. December 28, 29, 30, 1844; January 20, 1845; and December 29, 1854, Digital Online Library, BU.

128. "Examination of Timothy Hoskins, William Simons, & Others," *New York Spectator* (New York, N.Y.), August 17, 1842, reprinted from the *Providence (R.I.) Journal,* Newsbank.

129. Fritz, *American Sovereigns*, chap. 8; Conley, *Democracy in Decline*, part 4; Gettleman, *The Dorr Rebellion*, chaps. 2, 3.

130. Fritz, *American Sovereigns*, 147.

131. Goodell, "Right and Wrongs of Rhode Island, 58.

132. Conley, *Democracy in Decline*, 317.

133. "Nine Lawyers' Opinion" was written by Samuel Y. Atwell, Joseph K. Angell, Thomas F. Carpenter, David Daniels, Thomas W. Dorr, Levi C. Eaton, John P. Knowles, Dutee J. Pearce, and Aaron White Jr. This excerpt is cited from Bicknell, *The History of the State of Rhode Island*, 795. The essay was also printed as a pamphlet in 1880 as "The Right of the People of Rhode Island to Form a Constitution: The Nine Lawyers' Opinion," *Rhode Island Historical Tracts*, no. 11. The debate is discussed at length in Gettleman, *The Dorr Rebellion*, 63–70.

134. Sullivan and Lydia Dorr to Thomas W. Dorr, April 8, 1842, box 4, folder 5, Dorr Papers.

135. Thomas W. Dorr to Aaron White Jr., Providence, April 19, 1842, box 4, folder 7, Dorr Papers.

136. Bowen, "The Recent Contest in Rhode Island," 33.

137. Ibid., 33–36.

138. Thomas W. Dorr to Aaron White Jr., New York, May 12, 1842, box 4, folder 11, Dorr Papers.

139. Aaron White Jr. to Thomas W. Dorr, Woonsocket, May 15, 1842, box 4, folder 13, Dorr Papers.

140. Ibid., May 25, 1842, box 4, folder 15, Dorr Papers.

141. Bowen, "The Recent Contest in Rhode Island, 38.

142. [Curtis] writing as "A Citizen of Massachusetts," *The Merits of Thomas W. Dorr*, 33. See also testimony of Aaron White Jr., *Rhode Island—Interference of the Executive*, 281–82.

143. It is not known if Dorr actually stayed with Thomas White while in New York. However, Dorr did direct Aaron White Jr. to send letters by private hand, addressed to Thomas White in New York. See Thomas W. Dorr to Aaron White Jr., New York, June 1, 1842, box 4, folder 17, Dorr Papers.

144. The deduction of Dorr's whereabouts immediately after the failed arsenal attack is based on Dorr's letter dated Woonsocket, May 19, 1842, box 4, folder 14; White's letter of May 25, 1842, relating the flight to New York, box 4, folder 15; and Dorr's response of May 27, 1842, box 4, folder 15, Dorr Papers.

145. See Thomas W. Dorr to Aaron White Jr., May 27, 1842, box 4, folder 15, Dorr Papers, in which he directs that "our friends who wish information concerning suffrage affairs in Rhode Island to communicate with *you*." White responded, "It is understood that while you are gone I take care of your Chair, which supposition furnished me with no small labor in answering inquiries, giving advice, etc. . . . I expect to be arrested, but I know of no possible crime they can lay to my charge, except that of being a 'pestilent fellow.'" Aaron White Jr. to Thomas W. Dorr, Woonsocket, June 5–8, 1842, box 4, folder 17, Dorr Papers.

146. Diary of Mary White, May 21, June 8, 1842, OSV.

147. Aaron White Jr. to Thomas W. Dorr, June 1, 1842, box 4, folder 17, Dorr Papers.

148. Ibid., June 5, 1842, box 4, folder 17, Dorr Papers.

149. Testimony of Aaron White Jr., *Rhode Island—Interference of the Executive*, 278.

150. Although White repeatedly insisted that the General Assembly *must* meet, he also repeatedly insisted "as for any idea of making any attempt to establish the People's Constitution by force of arms at present you must abandon it entirely." See Aaron White to Thomas Dorr, June 12, 1842, box 4, folder 18; June 18, 1842, box 4, folder 20; June 26, 1842, box 4, folder 20, Dorr Papers.

151. Aaron White Jr. to Thomas W. Dorr, June 5, 1842, box 4, folder 17, Dorr Papers.

152. Ibid., June 12, 1842, box 4, folder 18, Dorr Papers.

153. Formisano, *For the People*, 169–70.

154. "Private Examination of Chas. W. Carter," *New York Spectator* (New York, N.Y.), Wednesday, August 17, 1842; reprinted from *Providence (R.I.) Journal,* Newsbank.

155. See *North American and Daily Advertiser* (Philadelphia, Pa.), no. 1017 (July 1, 1842): col. 7, Infotrac. This time Dorr fled north, to sanctuary with sympathizers in northern New Hampshire. Aaron White once again assisted him in reaching asylum. See *New York Spectator* (New York, N.Y.), Wednesday, August 17, 1842, Infotrac. See also Aaron White Jr.'s obituary in *Webster (Mass.) Times*, December 3, 1886, Harvard College Library Clipping Sheet, Harvard University Biographical Files (HUG 300), HU, courtesy of Harvard University Archives: "Esquire White became an ardent adherent of Governor Dorr, personally and politically, and chief advisor in all matters, touching political subjects and the personal affairs of his friend the Governor, aiding him after the Chepachet affair, including the pursuit of his foes, to a safe retreat to the mountains of New Hampshire."

156. Testimony of Aaron White Jr., *Rhode Island—Interference of the Executive*, 79–81.

157. *North American and Daily Advertiser* (Philadelphia, Pa.), no. 1017 (July 1, 1842): col. 7, Infotrac. On Sullivan Dorr's treatment, see Goodell, *Rights and Wrongs of Rhode Island*, 64–65.

158. Testimony of Aaron White Jr., *Rhode Island—Interference of the Executive*, 280–81.

159. Goodell, "Rights and Wrongs of Rhode Island, 70.

160. Aaron White Jr. to Thomas W. Dorr, New Boston, March 7, 1843, box 7, folder 4, Dorr Papers.

161. On Aaron's flight to Connecticut, see Aaron White Jr. to Thomas Dorr, September 1, 1842, Dorr Papers. See also Shapardson, "The 'Old Square'—Aaron White of Quinebaug Conn. Secretary under Governor Dorr," and article in the Quinebaug Historical Society Leaflets, 2, no. 24, private collection of Linda Branniff. I am grateful to Linda Branniff of Quinebaug, Connecticut, for bringing this article to my attention.

162. Diary of Mary White, July 26, 30, August 8, 13, 1842, OSV.

163. See Aaron White Jr. to Thomas W. Dorr, New Boston, Conn., September 1, 1842, Dorr Papers; also testimony of Aaron White Jr., *Rhode Island—Interference of the Executive*, 283.

164. Aaron White Jr. to Walter Snow Burgess, January 20, 1845, Digital Online Library, BU.

165. The arguments that went before the Supreme Court were twofold: first, that the Law and Order party, having no legitimacy after the ratification of the People's Constitution, had no right to declare martial law and thus committed unlawful breaking and entering during

their warrantless home searches; second, that President John Tyler, by sending Federal troops to support Law and Order forces in Newport and by failing to send troops to support the People's Constitution party, had failed to execute the Republican Guarantee Clause (ensuring that lawful republican government be respected and upheld). For a discussion of these cases, see Conley, *Democracy in Decline*, 361–65.

166. Aaron White to Thomas W. Dorr, June 5–8, 1842, box 4, folder 17, Dorr Papers.

167. Gross, "Young Men and Women of Fairest Promise," 15. The Transcendentalists would also have agreed with Aaron's definition of the heroic. See Gross, "Quiet War with the State," 16.

168. Shalhope, "Review: The Radicalism of Thomas Dorr," 386–88.

169. Aaron White Jr. to Thomas W. Dorr, New Boston, Conn., April 17, 1843, box 7, folder 8, Dorr Papers.

170. Aaron White Jr. to Walter Snow Burgess, Washington, D.C., January 20, 1845, Digital Online Library, BU.

171. Schlesinger, *The Age of Jackson*, 505.

Chapter 8

1. *Liberator*, August 4, 1837, as quoted by Sterling, *Ahead of Her Time*, 35.

2. Mary White to Charles White, June 2, 1840, OSV. Portions of this chapter were previously published in Fuhrer, "'We All have Something to Do.'"

3. Sterns, "Reform Periodicals and Female Reformers," 683; Ginzberg, "'Moral Suasion Is Moral Balderdash,'" 607. On Grace and Job Martyn, see Ginzberg, *Women and the Work of Benevolence*, 113–14.

4. Boylan, "Timid Girls, Venerable Widows, and Dignified Matrons," 790.

5. Caroline White to Charles White, December 20, 1836, OSV.

6. Diary of Mary White, December 23, 1836, OSV.

7. Mary White to Charles White, February 20, 1838, OSV.

8. Slaves, of course, resisted slavery from its beginning. For antislavery historiography, see Huston, "The Experiential Basis of Northern Antislavery Impulse," esp. 610–18. For a more recent synthesis of scholarship, see Newman, *The Transformation of American Abolitionism*; on the Garrisonian years, see Walters, *The Antislavery Appeal*. For the post-1840 rise of political abolitionism, see Laurie, *Beyond Garrison*.

9. Walters, *The Antislavery Appeal*, vii.

10. Mintz, *Moralists and Modernizers*, 128.

11. Mary White to Charles White, May 1839, OSV.

12. Boylston Female Antislavery Society, Constitution, Boylston Manuscripts Collection, BHS.

13. Oshantz, *Slavery and Sin*.

14. Gross, "Helen Thoreau's Antislavery Scrapbook," 109.

15. On female motivations for antislavery, see Jeffrey, *The Great Silent Army of Abolitionism*, 36–41.

16. Thomas White and Mary White Davis, "Recollections from Uncle Thomas White and Aunt Mary White Davis," private collection of Vernon Woodworth, Dover, Mass.

17. Average black population in Worcester County ranged between 1 and 1.5 percent between 1790 and 1850. "Interpretive Sourcebook on African Americans."

18. Izard, "Guy Scott of Sturbridge," 10–11. For more recent work on race and slavery in New England, see Lemire, *Black Walden*; and Melish, *Disowning Slavery*.

19. Reiss, "P. T. Barnum, Joice Heth, and Antebellum Spectacles of Race," esp. 84–85. See also Reiss, *The Showman and the Slave*.

20. Reiss, *The Showman and the Slave*, 69, 160.

21. Reiss, "P. T. Barnum, Joice Heth, and Antebellum Spectacles of Race," 95.

22. Diary of Mary White, September 2, 1835, OSV.

23. Radical Garrisonians embraced the equality of souls. See Dudden, *Fighting Chance*, 5. The Grimké sisters also adopted the doctrine of the equality of souls.

24. Jeffrey, *Great Silent Army of Abolitionism*, 3.

25. Anti-abolition mobs rioted in New York City in 1833 and 1834, in Philadelphia in 1835 and 1838, and in Boston in 1835. See Richards, *Gentlemen of Property and Standing*.

26. Jeffrey, *Great Silent Army of Abolitionism*, 3, 49–52.

27. This number is based on Mary White's 1840 history of the Boylston Female Anti-Slavery Society (BFASS), BHS. Gross found similar triumph over religious difference in the antislavery efforts of Concord. Gross, "Helen Thoreau's Antislavery Scrapbook," 110–11.

28. Forty-eight women contributed in some way to antislavery in Boylston between 1836 and 1842 (combined original and ultraist societies). Characteristics, where known, are as follows:

>Marital status (known for 45 of 48): married, 47 percent; single, 42 percent; widowed, 11 percent
>Household wealth (known for 38 of 48): mean tax decile (1 = high), 3.3
>Church affiliation: Congregational, 23 percent; Unitarian, 33 percent; unchurched or unknown, 44 percent
>Age (known for 40 of 48): mean age, 37.4; median age, 35; modal age, 35.

See Record Book of the Boylston Female Antislavery Society, Boylston Manuscripts Collection, BHS; Diary of Mary White and White family letters, OSV.

29. Mary's social network was determined by compiling a record of visits paid and received in 1836. Diary of Mary White, 1836, OSV.

30. More than three-quarters of the members whose taxable household wealth could be determined were in the top three deciles.

31. Those who were active abolitionists represented less than a tenth of Boylston's females over the age of sixteen. Twenty women were active participants in the society, though, as Mary often lamented, most meetings brought together only a handful of faithful servants.

32. See Jeffrey, *Great Silent Army of Abolitionism*, 42–43.

33. Record Book, Boylston Female Antislavery Society (BFASS), BHS.

34. With lyrics by Garrison, this song was set to the tune of "Auld Lang Syne," by Jairus

Lincoln. Lincoln, *Anti-Slavery Melodies*, 70–71. Mary hosted Jairus Lincoln; it is probable the BFASS hymns included his work.

35. Jeffrey, *Great Silent Army of Abolitionism*, 22–23.

36. Hannah S. P. Cotton to "Mrs. Chapman," October 27, 1839, Antislavery Collection, BPL, courtesy of the Trustees of the Boston Public Library/Rare Books.

37. Wm. L. Garrison, *Liberator*, January 2, 1837, 3, as reproduced in "Women, Anti-Slavery and the Constitution in Rural New England: A Sourcebook for Interpretation," 2 vols., edited by Lynn Manring and Jack Larket, n.d., OSV, reporting on the recent Boston Antislavery Fair.

38. See, for example, the pincushion, board with stencil illustration on fabric, ca. 1835, in the Friends Historical Library Collection of Swarthmore College, Swarthmore, Pa.

39. Garrison described items at the Boston Ladies' Antislavery Fair in *Liberator*, January 2, 1837, 3.

40. "Pastoral Letter of the General Association of Massachusetts to the Congregational Churches Under Their Care," July 28, 1837. On the Grimké sisters, see Lerner, *Grimké Sisters from South Carolina*; the Pastoral Letter is discussed on 132–33.

41. Diary of Mary White, October 2, 3, 1837, OSV.

42. For example, see ibid., September 9, 1837; October 4, 1839, OSV.

43. Ibid., November 18, 1843, OSV.

44. Drake, as quoted in Jeffrey, *Great Silent Army of Abolitionism*, 126.

45. Jeffrey, *Great Silent Army of Abolitionism*, 126. Even Garrison reassured members of the Boston Female Antislavery Society that they were "not called upon to decide that you will make bosom friends of colored females, or invite them into your parlor or eat or drink with them, or walk with them in the streets." Garrison to Boston Female Antislavery Society, April 1834, MHS, as cited in Jeffrey *Great Silent Army of Abolitionism*, 45.

46. Caroline White to Charles White, December 20, 1836, OSV.

47. *American Anti-Slavery Almanac for 1840*, 49.

48. References to the *Emancipator, Cradle of Liberty, Liberty Bell*, and *Slavery As It Is* are from the BFASS records, BHS. Mary refers to reading the *Liberator* in a letter to Charles dated June 9, 1840, OSV.

49. Jeffrey, *Great Silent Army of Abolitionism*, 108–26.

50. Hannah S. P. Cotton of the Boylston Female Antislavery Society to Mrs. Maria Weston Chapman, October 27, 1839, Antislavery Collection, BPL.

51. Resolution of the Female Antislavery Society of Boylston, October 16, 1839 and Mary White to Maria Weston Chapman, March 16, 1840, Antislavery Collection, BPL.

52. Jeffrey, *Great Silent Army of Abolitionism*, 60.

53. See, for example, Mary White to Mrs. Chapman, October 16, 1839, Antislavery Collection, BPL: "Voted that the above resolutions be printed in the antislavery newspapers."

54. The address is transcribed in full in Stanton, *History of Woman Suffrage*, 339–40.

55. Harriet Peck of Kent County, R.I., in 1836, as cited in Van Broekhoven, "Let Your Names Be Enrolled," in *Abolitionist Sisterhood*, 188.

56. Mary White to Mrs. Chapman, March 16, 1840, Antislavery Collection, BPL.

57. Jeffrey provides examples in *Great Silent Army of Abolitionism*, 89–92.

58. *Liberator*, August 4, 1837, as quoted by Sterling, *Ahead of Her Time*, 35.

59. Harriet Hale of Providence, R.I., February, 1841, as quoted in *Abolitionist Sisterhood*, 190.

60. Mary's letters to her Boston-based son, Charles, include requests for petition forms; see, for example, letters of July 28 and August 19, 1839, OSV.

61. The eight antislavery petitions sent to Congress from Boylston in 1837–38 include the following: 1. Submitted under the name of Harriet Sanford on January 4, 1838, signed by 197 women to abolish slavery and the slave trade in Washington, D.C.; 2. Submitted by Wm. H. Sanford on February 5, 1838, signed by 71 men and 93 women to abolish slavery and the slave trade in Washington, D.C; 3. Submitted by Wm. H. Sanford on February 5, 1838, signed by 70 men and 94 women to abolish slavery and the slave trade in the United States; 4. Submitted by Wm. H. Sanford on February 5, 1838, signed by 74 men and 94 women against admission of proslave territories to the Union; 5. Submitted by Wm. H. Sanford on February 5, 1838, signed by 70 men and 97 women against admission of proslave states to the Union; 6. Submitted by Wm. H. Sanford on February 5, 1838, signed by 72 men against annexation of Texas to the Union; 7. Submitted by Harriet Sanford on 2/5/1838 signed by 94 women against annexation of Texas to the Union; 8. Submitted by Harriet Sanford on December 18, 1838, signed by 124 women to abolish slavery and the slave trade in Washington, D.C., and against admission of proslave states to the Union. See Manring and Larkin, "Women, Anti-Slavery, and the Constitution." I made additions using copies of original petitions from NA. The petitions were noted in issues of the *Massachusetts Spy* dated September 20, 1837; January 1, 1838; February 14, 1838; and December 26, 1838. Note that Mary White's diary refers to antislavery petitioning through 1842, indicating that there were more Boylston women's petitions than noted here.

62. I am grateful to independent scholar Diana M. Smith, who recovered these petitions from NA and shared her copies with me.

63. Petition of the Women of Boylston, Massachusetts, to Congress, box 34 of the Library of Congress box 123, Twenty-fifth Congress of the United States, NA. Though the petition was not pre-printed, the women of Boylston copied the verbiage of the Boston Female Anti-Slavery Society, published in their Annual Report for 1836, *Right and Wrong in Boston in 1836*.

64. No more than one-third of the males over twenty-one years of age could be induced to sign an antislavery petition, whereas well over half of the women put their names down on most petitions. Robert Gross found the same discrepancy in male-female signers in Concord, Mass., where two-thirds of the women signed, compared only a quarter of the men. See "Helen Thoreau's Antislavery Scrapbook," 108. No more than 35 percent of Boylston men over the age of twenty-one signed an antislavery petition; 85 percent of Boylston adult females signed a petition.

65. Previous research indicated that Boylston had no male antislavery society. See Manring and Larkin, "Women, Anti-Slavery, and the Constitution." However, recent digitization of the *Liberator* has made a more thorough search possible. On May 14, 1836, the *Liberator* recorded that Boylston sent thirty men to the New England Anti-Slavery Convention. Most of these men were young, and virtually all were Congregationalists. On April 20, 1838, the *Liberator* reported that Boylston had a male antislavery society with *140 members*, William Sanford, Presi-

dent. This seems highly inflated, as Sanford could never gather more than seventy-four male signatures for Boylston antislavery petitions. Mary White never mentions any meetings held or work performed by the male society. The male society kept no record of work, made no donations, and sent no delegates to convention; in comparison, the West Boylston male antislavery society did all of the above. By 1840, the Boylston male society, like the Female society, had split upon sectarian lines. The nine remaining members of the "old" male organization, as recorded in the *Liberator*, April 3, 1840, were predominantly older, poorer, and Unitarian.

66. Mary's diary specifically mentions antislavery petitions being carried by herself, her daughters Mary and Caroline, and their Congregationalist friend Lucy Goodenow. See Diary of Mary White, June 30, July 14, 1837; October 16, 1838; November 5, 1839; November 13, 16, December 9, 1840; November 1, 1841; December 15, 1842, OSV.

67. Gross describes the local Whig male elite in Concord as also being firmly opposed to abolition work, refusing to join the anti-slavery society or sign petitions. Gross, "Helen Thoreau's Antislavery Scrapbook," 110.

68. Half of the women and nearly two-thirds of the men were in their twenties or thirties, far exceeding the proportion of the population in this age bracket on the 1840 U.S. census.

69. Alternatively, it could merely indicate that young people were more likely to embrace reform than their elders.

70. Journal of Samuel Fisher, November 2, 1837, Northborough Historical Society. I am grateful to Northborough historian Robert Ellis for sharing this information with me. Ellis believes the reference is to Mary White. Ellis, *Northborough in the Civil War*, 22. Mary's sister, Nancy Avery White, lived in nearby Westborough, and may also have been the speaker. Neither women mentioned speaking in her diary. Diary of Nancy Avery White, White-Forbes Collection, Octavo VI, vol. 6, AAS.

71. On the Grimké sisters, see Lerner, *The Grimké Sisters from South Carolina*.

72. "Pastoral Letter of the General Association of Massachusetts to the Churches under their Care," *Liberator*, August 11, 1837, as reproduced in "Women, Anti-Slavery and the Constitution in Rural New England: A Sourcebook for Interpretation," 2 vols., edited by Lynn Manring and Jack Larket, n.d., OSV.

73. On this schism, see Wyatt-Brown, *Lewis Tappan and the Evangelical War Against Slavery*, chap. 10; Walters, *Antislavery Appeal*, chap. 1; Debra Gold Hansen, "The Boston Female Antislavery Society and the Limits of Gender Politics," in Yellin and Van Horne, *Abolitionist Sisterhood*.

74. For images of such bed quilts, see Bassett, *Massachusetts Quilts*, chap. 10.

75. Deborah Chapman to Anne Chapman, New Bedford, February 29, 1840, Antislavery Collection, BPL (emphasis added).

76. Mary White to Mrs. Chapman, December 2, 1839, Antislavery Collection, BPL.

77. Ibid., March 16, 1840, Antislavery Collection, BPL.

78. Ibid., December 2, 1839, Antislavery Collection, BPL.

79. Ibid., March 16, 1840, Antislavery Collection, BPL.

80. Mary White was chosen president, the wife of the new Unitarian minister was elected vice president, and the daughter of the old Unitarian minister was elected secretary/treasurer.

81. Mary White to Mrs. Chapman, March 16, 1840, Antislavery Collection, BPL.

82. Diary of Mary White, July 6, 1842, OSV.

83. Mary White to Mrs. Chapman, December 11, 1842, Antislavery Collection, BPL.

84. Mary generally referred to the new Female Benevolent Society as the "antislavery sewing circle"; it met at the vestry of the Congregational church. She referred to the work of her "old organization" as the "Antislavery Meeting," which met at the town hall.

85. Congregational Church–based female antislavery societies after 1839 usually focused on the "Canada Mission," visiting, supporting, and educating local blacks, and eliminating or reducing racism. See Jeffrey, *Great Silent Army of Abolitionism*, 160.

86. Mary also noted attending lectures on and by fugitive slaves; she oversaw appraisal and packing of sewn items to be shipped to Canada, possibly assisted fugitives on their way to freedom, and nursed free blacks who settled locally. Diary of Mary White, October 26, 1843; February 12, April 2, 1844; July 4, August 4, 1848, OSV.

87. This shift to general benevolence and moral reform follows other "new organization" groups in the Boston area. See Hansen in Yellin and Van Horne, *Abolitionist Sisterhood*, 59.

88. Records of the Congregational Church of Boylston, February 15, 1843, Boylston Manuscripts Collection, BHS.

89. Diary of Mary White, April 6, 1848, OSV.

90. Ibid., July 4, 1847, OSV.

91. "Worcester County would lead the state in votes for the Liberty Party between 1841 and 1847, reaching 14 percent of the total vote." Brooke, *Heart of the Commonwealth*, 368.

92. David C. Murdock to S. Salisbury, Esq., November 4, 1844, Massachusetts Collection, 1629–1869, box 7, folder 6, Whig Party Papers, AAS.

93. Brooke, *Heart of the Commonwealth*, 361.

94. Diary of Mary White, September 14, 1848, OSV.

95. Ibid., April 6, 1843, OSV.

96. Ibid., April 8, 1847, OSV.

97. See appendix D, tables D-1, D-2.

98. For Free Soil activism in Worcester County, see Brooke, *Heart of the Commonwealth*, 375–83.

99. Petition of Calvin Barker et al., of Millbury against the Gag-Rule, as quoted in Brooke, *Heart of the Commonwealth*, 378.

100. Brooke, *Heart of the Commonwealth*, 378–79.

101. The resolution was adopted at the Free Soil Convention held at Worcester, June 28, 1848. George Allen is identified as the author of the resolution in ibid., 371.

102. William White to Charles White, September 22, 1839, OSV.

103. Jeffrey, *Great Silent Army of Abolitionism*, 52.

Conclusion

1. Sears, *Days of Delusion*. The letters collected by Sears reveal strong Millerite response in Worcester County.

2. Diary of Mary White, January 17, 24, March 8, 9, 10, 26, 1843, OSV.

3. Dupuis, *Lives Thus Spent*, 39.

4. Historians debate the degree of fanaticism of Miller's followers. For a comment on the debate, see Craig and Housley, "Communications," 315–18.

5. They were Samuel, Lucy, and Johanna Flagg. Dupuis, *History of Boylston, 1786–1886*, 55.

6. As quoted by Gross, "Commemorating Concord."

7. Rev. A. P. Marvin, "Response," in *Centennial Celebration of the Incorporation of the Town of Boylston*, 72–73.

8. George L. Wright, "Boylston," 894.

9. Mary White to Charles White, June 2, 1840, OSV.

10. Article on Aaron White Jr., *Daily Inter Ocean* (Chicago, Ill.), March 31, 1889. See also Shapardson, "The Old Square—Aaron White of Quinebaug Conn."

11. Obituary of Aaron White, *Webster (Mass.) Times*, December 3, 1886, Harvard College Library Clipping Sheet, Harvard University Biographical Files (HUG 300), HU, courtesy of Harvard University Archives.

12. Larned, *Historic Gleanings in Windham County*, 165.

13. George L. Wright, address, November 13, 1929, BHS.

14. "M.S.W.," *Boston Recorder*, n.d., clipping, White Family Collection, OSV.

15. DuPuis, *History of Boylston, 1786–1886*, 42.

BIBLIOGRAPHY

Archives

American Antiquarian Society, Worcester, Mass.
  Massachusetts Collection, 1629–1869
  Massachusetts Society for the Suppression of Intemperance Collection
  "A New Nation Votes: American Election Returns, 1787–1825"
  White-Forbes Collection
Ashland Historical Society, Ashland, Mass.
  Newspaper Clipping Collection
Boston Public Library, Boston, Mass.
  Antislavery Collection, Rare Books and Manuscripts
Boylston Historical Society, Boylston, Mass.
  Boylston Antislavery Society Collection
  Boylston Congregational Church Collection
  Boylston Manuscripts Collection
  Boylston Overseers of the Poor Records
  Boylston Tax Assessments
  Boylston Town Clerk's Record Books
  Boylston Vital Records
  Correspondence Collection
  Simon Davis Collection
  Flagg Family Papers
  Hiram Harlow Collection
  Newspaper Clippings Collection
  Aaron White Store Ledgers
  George Wright Collection
Brown University, Providence, R.I.
  Center for Digital Scholarship, Digital Online Collection
  Dorr Correspondence, Thomas Wilson Dorr Papers, 1826–45, Rider Collection, John Hay
      Library
Collections of Old Sturbridge Village, Old Sturbridge Village Research Library, Sturbridge,
      Mass.
  Boylston and Shrewsbury Baptist Church Records, 1812–37, manuscript
  Fenner Brown, Aaron White Jr. et al., "To the Hon. General Assembly of the State of
      Rhode Island at Their Session to Be Holden on the Last Monday in October, 1839,"
      broadside memorial
  Barnabas Davis Diary
  Joseph Flagg Account Book

Oliver Sawyer Schoolbook, Manuscript Collection
U.S. Census for Population, Agriculture and Manufacturing, 1801–50, microfilm
    White Family Collection
First Congregational Church of Boylston, Mass.
    Boylston Female Benevolent Society Records, Church Archives
    Boylston Female Society for the Aid of Foreign Missions Records, Church Archives
Fruitlands Museum, Harvard, Mass.
    Davenport-Wheeler Collection
Harvard University, Cambridge, Mass.
    Harvard University Biographical Files, ca. 1700– , Harvard University Archives
    R. G. Dun & Company Credit Report Volumes, 1840–95, Baker Library Historical
        Collections, Harvard Business School
Infotrac, 19th Century U.S. Newspapers, Online Database   ·
Library of Congress, Washington, D.C.
    Music Division
    Rare Book and Special Collections Division
        Printed Ephemera Collection
        Song Sheet Collection
Massachusetts Archives, Boston, Mass.
    Worcester County Court of Common Pleas Records
    Worcester County Probate Records
Massachusetts Historical Society, Boston, Mass.
    Aaron White Jr. Diaries, 1815–80, manuscript
Massachusetts State House Library, Boston, Mass.
    Massachusetts Valuation of 1784, microfilm
National Archives, Washington, D.C.
    Antislavery Petitions from the Citizens of Boylston to the United States Congress
New England Historic Genealogical Society, Boston, Mass.
    Account Book of Rev. Ebenezer Morse (Mss A 1658), R. Stanton Avery Special Collections,
        www.AmericanAncestors.org (including Boylston [North Parish Shrewsbury]
        Church Records, 1742–75)
Newsbank, America's Historical Newspapers Collection, Early American Newspapers, Series I,
    1690–1876
Northborough Historical Society, Northborough, Mass.
    Samuel Fisher Journals, Manuscript Collections
Private collection of Linda Branniff, Dudley, Mass.
    Quinabaug Historical Society Leaflets Collection
Private collection of Vernon Woodworth and Molly Scott Evans, Dover, Mass.
    Thomas White and Mary White Davis, "Recollections from Uncle Thomas White and Aunt
        Mary White Davis, My Great Uncle and Great Aunt," transcript
University of Delaware Special Collections, Newark, Del.
    Diary of Mary White, 1805–7, 1827–35 (2 vols.), Diaries, Journals, and Ship's Logs
        Collection, University of Delaware Library
Williams College, Williamstown, Mass.
    W. J. White Collection, Archives and Special Collections

Worcester County Registry of Deeds, Worcester, Mass.
  Worcester County Land Records

Published Primary Sources

Abbott, John S. C. *The Mother at Home: Or The Principles of Maternal Duty, Familiarly Described*. 1833. Reprint, Solid Ground Christian Books, 2005.

American Temperance Society. *Sixth Annual Report of the American Temperance Society, Presented at the Meeting in New York, May 1833*. Boston: Seth Bliss, 1833.

An Abstract of the Proceedings of the Anti-Masonic State Convention of Massachusetts: held in Faneuil Hall, Boston, Dec. 30 and 31, 1829 and Jan. 1, 1830. Boston: John Marsh, 1830.

[Anonymous]. *A History of the Striped Pig*. Boston: Whipple and Damrell, 1838.

Bancroft, George. *History of the United States of America, from the Discovery of the American Continent*. Boston: Little, Brown, and Company, 1854–78.

Bourne, Edward Gaylord. *The History of the Surplus Revenue of 1837; Being an Account of Its Origin, Its Distribution Among the States, and the Uses to Which it was Applied*. New York: G. P. Putnam's Sons, 1885.

Bowen, Francis. "The Recent Contest in Rhode Island." *North American Review* 58, no. 123 (April 1844). Reprinted separately as pamphlet, Boston: Otis, Broaders, and Company, 1844. Page numbers from pamphlet edition.

Burton, Warren. *The District School as It Was and Other Writings*. Boston: Press of T. R. Marvin, 1852.

———. *White Slavery: A New Emancipation Cause, Presented to the People of the United States*. Worcester: M. D. Phillips, 1839.

Bushnell, Horace. "The Age of Homespun: Secular Sermon delivered at the Centennial Celebration of Litchfield County, August 14th, 1851." Reprinted in *Work and Play*. New York: Scribner and Sons, 1881.

Catalogue of New Ispwich Academy, 1830. New Ipswich, N.H.

Catalogue of the Officers and Members of Wheaton Female Seminary at Norton, MS [sic] for the Year Ending Oct. 20, 1840. Boston: Crocker & Brewster, Printers, 1840.

Centennial Celebration of the Incorporation of the Town of Boylston, Massachusetts. August 17, 1886. Worcester: Press of Sanford & Davis, 1887.

Channing, William Ellery. *A Letter to the Rev. Samuel C. Thatcher on the Aspersions Contained in a Late Number of the Panoplist, on the Ministers of Boston and the Vicinity*. Boston: Wells and Lilly, 1815.

Child, Lydia Maria, and David Child, eds. *The American Antislavery Almanac for 1840*. American Almanac Collection, Library of Congress. New York and Boston: Published for the American Anti-Slavery Society, 1839–40. Collins, William. "Speech Delivered at the First Public Meeting of the British and Foreign Temperance Society." *Temperance Society Record* (Glasgow, Scotland) 2, no. 18 (November 1831): 1.

Colman, Henry. "An Address Delivered before the Massachusetts Agricultural Society at the Brighton Cattle Show, October 17th, 1821." *Massachusetts Agricultural Repository and Journal* 7 (January 1822). Boston: Wells and Lilly, 1822.

Comly, John. *Journal of the Life and Religious Labors of John Comly, Late of Byberry Pennsylvania*. Philadelphia: Published by his children, T. Ellwood Chapman, 1853.

Cotton, Ward. *Causes and Effects of Female Regard to Christ: Illustrated in a Sermon Delivered Before the Female Society in Boylston For the Aid of Foreign Missions, At Their Request, October 1, 1816.* Worcester: William Manning, Printer, 1817.

Culbertson, J. C., M.D., ed. *The Cincinnati Lancet-Clinic, a Weekly Journal of Medicine and Surgery,* n.s., 16. Cincinnati: Dr. J. C. Culberson, 1886.

[Curtis, George Ticknor]. *The Merits of Thomas W. Dorr and George Bancroft as They Are Politically Connected.* Boston: Printed by John H. Eastburn, 1844.

Davenport, Matthew. *A Brief Historical Sketch of the Town of Boylston; in the County of Worcester; From Its First Settlement to the Present Time.* Lancaster, Mass.: Carter, Andrews and Company, 1831.

Davis, Emerson. *The Half Century: Or, a History of the Changes That Have Taken Place, and Events That Have Transpired, Chiefly in the United States, between 1800 and 1850.* Boston: Tappan & Whittemore, 1851.

Documents Relative to the Manufactures in the United States (also known as the McLane Report). U.S. Treasury, 1832.

Emerson, Ralph Waldo. *The Collected Works of Ralph Waldo Emerson.* Edited by Robert Spiller et al. Cambridge, Mass: Harvard University Press, 1971.

Flagg, Augustus. "Boylston." In *History of Worcester County, Massachusetts, Embracing a Comprehensive History of the County from Its First Settlement to the Present Time, with a History and Description of Its Cities and Towns,* vol. 1, edited by Abijah Perkins Marvin. Boston: C. R. Jewett & Co., 1879.

Goodell, William. "Rights and Wrongs of Rhode Island." *Christian Investigator,* no. 8 (September 1842). Whitesboro, N.Y.: Press of the Oneida Institute.

Gould, Augustus A. *History of New Ipswich: From Its First Grant in 1736 to the Present Time.* Boston: Gould and Lincoln, 1852.

Harlow, William. "Historical Sketch of the Town of Shrewsbury." In D. Hamilton Hurd, *History of Worcester County Massachusetts,* 2 vols. Philadelphia: J. W. Lewis & Co., 1889.

Harrington, Henry F. "The Village Death Bell." In *Ladies Companion and Literary Expositor,* edited by William W. Snowden, 12. New York: W. W. Snowden, 1840.

Hazen, Edward. *The Panorama of Professions and Trades; or Every Man's Book.* Philadelphia: Uriah Hunt and Sons, 1836.

Higley, George T. "Ashland." In *History of Middlesex County, Massachusetts,* edited by D. Hamilton Hurd. Philadelphia: J. W. Lewis & Co., 1890.

History of the Connecticut Valley of Massachusetts with Illustrations and Biographical Sketches of Some of Its Prominent Men and Pioneers. Vol. 2. Philadelphia: Louis H. Everts, 1879.

Howe, John. *Trial of the Action in Favor of the Rev. Samuel Russell of Boylston against John Howe of Boylston for Defamation At the Supreme Judicial Court, Holden at Worcester, April a.d. 1831.* Worcester: Spooner and Church, Printers, 1831.

Hyde Park Historical Society. "Striped Pig." *Hyde Park Historical Record* 2, no. 3 (October 1892): 44–53.

Jefferson, Thomas. *Notes on the State of Virginia.* London: John Stockdale, 1787.

Larned, Ellen Douglas. *Historic Gleanings in Windham County, Connecticut.* Providence: Preston and Rounds Co., 1899.

Laws and Liberties of Massachusetts. Reprinted from the 1648 edition in the Henry E.

Huntington Library, with an introduction by Max Farrand. Cambridge: Harvard University Press, 1929.

Laws of the Commonwealth of Massachusetts Passed at the Several Sessions of the General Court, Beginning Jan. 1834, and Ending April, 1836. Vol. 13. Boston: Dutton and Wentworth, 1836.

Lincoln, Jairus. *Anti-Slavery Melodies: For the Friends of Freedom*. Hingham: Elijah B. Gill, 1843.

Lincoln, William. *History of Worcester, Massachusetts from its Earliest Settlement to September 1836 with Various Notices Relating to the History of Worcester County*. Worcester: Published by Charles Hersey, Henry J. Howland Printer, 1862.

Livermore, George. *An Historical Research Respecting the Opinions of the Founders of the Republic on Negroes as Slaves, as Citizens, and as Soldiers*. Boston: John Wilson & Son, 1862.

Lovell, Albert A. *A Sketch of the Life of Major Ezra Beaman, together with Documents of Public Interest*. Worcester: F. P. Rice, 1882.

Lowell, John. "Brighton Cattle Show Reports." In *American Farmer* 8.1, no. 35 (November 17, 1826): 275.

————. "Remarks on the Agriculture of Massachusetts." *Massachusetts Society for Promoting Agriculture Journal* 5 (July 1819): 317–59.

Martin, Sophia Smith. *A Complete Genealogy of the Descendants of Matthew Smith of East Haddam, Conn. with Mention of his Ancestors, 1637–1890*. Rutland: Vt.: The Tuttle Company, 1890.

Monroe, James. "First Inaugural Address, Tuesday, March 4, 1817." In *U.S. Presidential Inaugural Addresses*. ReadHowYouWant.com, 2007.

New England Historical and Genealogical Register. 1853.

Nourse, Henry S. *History of the Town of Harvard, Massachusetts, 1732–1893*. Harvard: W. J. Coulter for Warren Hapgood, 1894.

Pamphlets: Religious, Miscellaneous. Vol. 3. Ann Arbor: University of Michigan, 1874.

Pierce, Frederick Clifton. *Peirce Genealogy: Being the Record of the Posterity of John Pers, an Early Inhabitant of Watertown, in New England, with Notes on the History of Other Families of Peirce, Pierce, Pearce, etc*. Worcester: Press of Chas. Hamilton, 1880.

Pierpont, John. *The American First Class Book*. Boston: Hilliard, Gray, Little and Wilkins, 1826.

Poe, Edgar Allan. "Maelzel's Chess Player." *Southern Literary Messenger* 2 (April 1836): 318–26.

"Proceedings of Citizens of the County of Worcester, Massachusetts, in Relation to the Currency." In U.S. Congress, *House Documents, 1833–34*, 23rd Cong., 1st sess., vol. 3, no. 176.

Puffer, Reuben. *The Widow's Mite: A Sermon Delivered at Boylston, Before the Boylston Female Society for the Aid of Foreign Missions, Jan. 8, 1816*. Worcester: William Manning, 1816.

Quincy, Josiah. *Report of the Committee for the Consideration of Pauper Laws of the Commonwealth of Massachusetts*. Boston: Russell and Gardner, 1821.

Reports and Other Documents Relating to the State Lunatic Hospital at Worcester, Mass. Printed by order of the Senate. Boston: Dutton and Wentworth, Printers to the State, 1837.

Rhode Island—Interference of the Executive in the affairs of June 7, 1844. Read, and postponed till the first Monday in December next. Submitted by Mr. Burke (also known as *Burke's Report*]. 28th Cong., 1st Sess. House of Representatives #546. Washington, D. C.: Blair & Rives, 1844.

Russell, Rev. Samuel. *Review of a pamphlet entitled "Trial of the action in favor of the Rev.*

Samuel Russell of Boylston against John Howe of Boylston, for defamation at the Supreme Judicial Court, holden at Worcester, April, a.d. 1831. Boston: Peirce and Parker, 1831.

Sanford, William H. *The Years of Many Generations Considered: Two Sermons, Preached in Boylston, Massachusetts, October 17 and 25, 1852, Giving A History of the Congregational Church and Ministry in Said Town and also Embracing Many Facts Relating to the First Settlers of Said Place*. Worcester: C. Buckingham Webb, 1853.

Schenck, J. S., and W. S. Rann. "History of Corydon Township." In *History of Warren County*. Syracuse: D. Mason, 1887. http://www.pa-roots.com/index.php/warren- county/172-history-of-warren-county/378-history-of-warren-county-chapter-49 (February 2013).

Schoolcraft, Henry Rowe. *Notes on the Iroquois: or, Contributions to American History, Antiquities, and General Ethnology of Western New York*. New York: Bartlett and Welford, 1846.

Stanton, Elizabeth Cady, Susan B. Anthony, and Matilda Joslyn Gage, eds. *History of Woman Suffrage. Vol. 1, 1848–1861*. 2d ed. Rochester, N.Y.: Charles Mann, 1889.

Swift, Samuel. *History of the Town of Middlebury in the County of Addison, Vermont*. Middlebury, Vt.: A. H. Copeland, 1859.

Tocqueville, Alexis de. *Democracy in America*. Vols. 1(1835) and 2 (1840). New York: Vintage Classics, 1990.

Trask, William Blake. *Brief Memoir of Andrew Henshaw Ward*. Albany: J. Munsell, 1863.

Ward, Andrew H. "History of the Town of Shrewsbury." *Worcester Magazine and Historical Journal* 2 (May 1826): 22–24.

———. *History of the Town of Shrewsbury, Massachusetts, from Its Settlement in 1717 to 1829*. Boston: Samuel G. Drake, 1847.

Washburn, Emory. *Historical Sketches of the Town of Leicester, Massachusetts*. Boston: John Wilson and Son, 1860.

Winthrop, John. "A Model of Christian Charity" (1630). In *Winthrop Papers*, vol. 2. Boston: Massachusetts Historical Society, 1929–47.

Woodward, Dr. Samuel. *Tenth Annual Report of the Trustees of the State Lunatic Asylum at Worcester, Massachusetts, Dec. 1842*.

[Worcester Agricultural Society]. *Forty-Seventh Annual Report. Transactions of the Worcester Agricultural Society for the Year 1865; Together with the By-Laws and List of Members of the Society, Revised and Corrected*. Worcester, Mass.: Printed by Chas. Hamilton, 1865.

Worcester City Directory. 1844. Collections of the American Antiquarian Society, Worcester, Mass.

Wright, George L. "Boylston." In *History of Worcester County, Massachusetts, with Biographical Sketches of Many of Its Pioneers and Prominent Men*, edited by D. Hamilton Hurd, 885–902. Philadelphia: J. W. Lewis & Co., 1889.

———. "Boylston's Church History." http://www.boylstonhistory.org/glw-church.htm (February 2013).

———. *Names of Places*. Boylston Historical Series, vol. 1. Boylston, Mass.: Boylston Historical Commission, 1980.

———. "Tramps and Other Peculiar Characters." Unpublished paper in the collection of the Boylston Historical Society.

Secondary Sources

Altschuler, Glenn C., and Stuart M. Blumin. "Limits of Political Engagement in Antebellum America: A New Look at the Golden Age of Participatory Democracy." *Journal of American History* 84, no. 3 (December 1997): 855–885.

Anderson, Fred. *A People's Army: Massachusetts Soldiers and Society in the Seven Years' War*. Chapel Hill: University of North Carolina Press, 1984.

Anthony, David. *Paper Money Men: Commerce, Manhood, and the Sensational Public Sphere in Antebellum America*. Columbus: Ohio State University Press, 2009.

Appleby, Joyce. *Capitalism and a New Social Order: The Republican Vision of the 1790s*. New York: New York University Press, 1984.

———. *Inheriting the Revolution: The First Generation of Americans*. Cambridge: Harvard University Press, 2000.

———. "Modernization Theory and the Formation of Modern Social Theories in England and America." *Comparative Studies in Society and History* 20, no. 2 (April 1978): 259–85.

———. "The Personal Roots of the First American Temperance Movement." *Proceedings of the American Philosophical Society* 141, no. 2 (June 1997): 141–59.

Archer, Melanie, and Judith R. Blau. "Class Formation in Nineteenth-Century America: The Case of the Middle Class." *Annual Review of Sociology* 19 (1993): 17–41.

Armitage, David. *Ideological Origins of the British Empire*. Cambridge: Cambridge University Press, 2000.

Atack, Jeremy, Fred Bateman, and William N. Parker. "The Farm, the Farmer, and the Market" and "Northern Agriculture and the Westward Movement" in *The Cambridge Economic History of the United States*, edited by Stanley L. Engerman and Robert E. Gallman. Cambridge: Cambridge University Press, 2000.

Augst, Thomas. "Composing the Moral Senses: Emerson and the Politics of Character in Nineteenth-Century America." *Political Theory* 27, no. 1 (February 1999): 85–120.

Bailyn, Bernard. *The Ideological Origins of the American Revolution*. Cambridge: Harvard University Press, 1967.

Baker, Andrew, and Frank G. White. "The Impact of Changing Plow Technology in Rural New England in the Early Nineteenth Century." Unpublished paper, January 1990. Old Sturbridge Village Research Library, Sturbridge, Mass. http://resources.osv.org/explore_learn/document_viewer.php?DocID=715 (June 2013).

Baker, Andrew H., and Holly V. Izard. "New England Farmers and the Marketplace, 1780–1865: A Case Study." *Agricultural History* 65, no. 3 (Summer 1991): 29–52.

Baker, Jean H. *Affairs of Party: The Political Culture of Northern Democrats in the Mid-Nineteenth Century*. Ithaca: Cornell University Press, 1983.

———. "Politics, Paradigms, and Public Culture." *Journal of American History* 84, no. 3 (December 1997): 894–99.

Banner, Lois W. "Religious Benevolence as Social Control: A Critique of an Interpretation." *Journal of American History* 60, no. 1 (June 1973): 423–44.

Barron, Hal S. *Those Who Stayed Behind: Rural Society in Nineteenth Century New England*. Cambridge: Cambridge University Press, 1984.

Bassett, Lynne Z, ed. *Massachusetts Quilts: Our Common Wealth*. Lebanon, N.H.: University Press of New England, 2009.

Beadie, Nancy. "Academy Students in the Mid-Nineteenth Century: Social Geography, Demography, and the Culture of Academy Attendance." *History of Education Quarterly* 41, no. 2 (Summer 2001): 251–62.

Bell, Richard. *We Shall Be No More: Suicide and Self-Government in the Newly United States.* Cambridge: Harvard University Press, 2012.

Bellesiles, Michael A. *Revolutionary Outlaws: Ethan Allen and the Struggle for Independence on the Early American Frontier.* Charlottesville: University Press of Virginia, 1995.

Bender, Thomas. *Community and Social Change in America.* Baltimore: Johns Hopkins University Press, 1978.

Benes, Peter, ed. *Wonders of the Invisible World, 1600–1900.* Dublin Seminar for New England Folklife Annual Proceedings, 1992. Boston: Boston University Press, 1993.

Benson, Lee. *The Concept of Jacksonian Democracy: New York as a Test Case.* Princeton: Princeton University Press, 1961.

Bicknell, Thomas Williams. *The History of the State of Rhode Island and Providence Plantations.* Vol. 2. New York: American Historical Society, 1920.

Bidwell, Charles E. "The Moral Significance of the Common School." *History of Education Quarterly* 6, no. 3 (Autumn, 1966): 50–91.

Blewett, Mary H. *We Will Rise in Our Might: Workingwomen's Voices from Nineteenth-Century New England.* Ithaca: Cornell University Press, 1991.

———. "Women Shoeworkers and Domestic Ideology: Rural Outwork in Early Nineteenth-Century Essex County." *New England Quarterly* 60, no. 3 (September 1987): 403–28.

Blumin, Stuart M. "The Hypothesis of Middle-Class Formation in Nineteenth-Century America: A Critique and Some Proposals." *American Historical Review* 90, no. 2 (April 1985): 299–338.

Blunt, Susan Baker. *Childish Things: The Reminiscence of Susan Baker Blunt.* Edited by Francis Mason. Grantham, N.H.: Thompson & Rutter, 1988.

Bode, Carl. *The American Lyceum: Town Meeting of the Mind.* New York: Oxford University Press, 1956.

Bodenhorn, Howard. *State Banking in Early America: A New Economic History.* New York: Oxford University Press, 2003.

Bogin, Ruth. "Petitioning and the New Moral Economy of Post-Revolutionary America." *William and Mary Quarterly* 45, no. 3 (July 1988): 392–425.

Borish, Linda. "Weighing Women's Work: Artifact and Ideology in Farm Women's Well-Being, 1820–1870." Unpublished paper. Old Sturbridge Village Research Library, Sturbridge, Mass.

Boydston, Jeanne. *Home and Work: Housework, Wages, and the Ideology of Labor in the Early Republic.* New York: Oxford University Press, 1990.

Boylan, Anne M. "Evangelical Womanhood in the Nineteenth Century: The Role of Women in Sunday Schools." *Feminist Studies* 4, no. 3 (October 1978): 62–80.

———. "Timid Girls, Venerable Widows, and Dignified Matrons: Life Cycle Patterns Among Organized Women in New York and Boston, 1797–1840." *American Quarterly* 38, no. 5 (Winter 1986): 779–97.

Breen, T. H. *The Marketplace of Revolution: How Consumer Politics Shaped American Independence.* New York: Oxford University Press, 2004.

Brooke, John L. *The Heart of the Commonwealth: Society and Political Culture in Worcester County, Massachusetts, 1713–1861*. Amherst: University of Massachusetts Press, 1989.

Brown, Christopher Leslie. *Moral Capital: Foundations of British Abolitionism*. Chapel Hill: University of North Carolina Press, 2006.

Brown, Richard D. "The Emergence of Urban Society in Rural Massachusetts, 1760–1820." *Journal of American History* 61, no. 1 (June 1974): 29–51.

———. *Knowledge Is Power: The Diffusion of Information in Early America, 1700–1865*. New York: Oxford University Press, 1989.

———. *Modernization: The Transformation of American Life, 1600–1865*. New York: Hill and Wang, 1976.

———. "Modernization and the Modern Personality in Early America, 1600–1865: A Sketch of a Synthesis." *Journal of Interdisciplinary History* 2, no. 3 (Winter 1972): 201–28.

Bushman, Richard L. *From Puritan to Yankee: Character and the Social Order in Connecticut, 1690–1765*. Cambridge: Harvard University Press, 1967.

———. "Markets and Composite Farms in Early America." *William and Mary Quarterly* 55, no. 3 (July 1998): 351–74.

———. "Massachusetts Farmers and the Revolution." In *Society, Freedom, and Conscience: The Coming of the Revolution in Virginia, Massachusetts and New York*, edited by Richard M. Jellison, 77–124. New York: W. W. Norton & Company, 1976.

———. *The Refinement of America: Persons, Houses, Cities*. New York: Vintage Books, 1992.

Butler, Jon. *Awash in a Sea of Faith: Christianizing the American People*. Cambridge: Harvard University Press, 1990.

Cappon, Lester J., ed. *The Adams-Jefferson Letters: The Complete Correspondence between Thomas Jefferson and Abigail and John Adams*. 2 vols. Chapel Hill: University of North Carolina Press, 1959.

Carson, Gerald. *Rum and Reform in Old New England*. Sturbridge, Mass.: Old Sturbridge Village, 1966.

Cates, James A. "Facing Away: Mental Health Treatment with the Old Order Amish." *American Journal of Psychotherapy* 59, no. 4 (2005): 371–83.

Cayton, Mary Kupiec. "Who Were the Evangelicals? Conservative and Liberal Identity in the Unitarian Controversy in Boston, 1804–1844." *Journal of Social History* 31, no. 1 (Autumn 1997): 85–107.

Chambers-Schiller, Lee Virginia. *Liberty, a Better Husband: Single Women in America: The Generations of 1780–1840*. New Haven: Yale University Press, 1984.

Chaput, Erik J., and Russell J. DeSimone. "Strange Bedfellows: The Politics of Race in Antebellum Rhode Island." *Common-Place* 10, no. 2 (January 2010). http://www.common-place.org/vol-10/no-02/chaput-desimone/ (February 2013).

Clark, Christopher. "Household Economy, Market Exchange, and the Rise of Capitalism in the Connecticut Valley, 1800–1860." *Journal of Social History* 13, no. 2 (Winter 1979): 169–89.

———. *The Roots of Rural Capitalism: Western Massachusetts, 1780–1860*. Ithaca: Cornell University Press, 1990.

———. "The View from the Farmhouse: Rural Lives in the Early Republic." *Journal of the Early Republic* 24, no. 2 (Summer 2004): 198–207.

Cleaves, Rachel Hope. *The Reign of Terror in America: Visions of Violence from Anti-Jacobinism to Antislavery*. New York: Cambridge University Press, 2009.

Cohen, Patricia Cline. *The Murder of Helen Jewett: The Life and Death of a Prostitute in Nineteenth-Century New York*. New York: Alfred Knopf, 1998.

Coleman, Peter J. *The Transformation of Rhode Island, 1790–1860*. Providence: Brown University Press, 1963.

Conley, Patrick T. *Democracy in Decline: Rhode Island's Constitutional Development, 1776–1841*. Providence: Rhode Island Historical Society, 1977.

Cott, Nancy F. *The Bonds of Womanhood: "Woman's Sphere" in New England, 1780–1835*. New Haven: Yale University Press, 1977.

———. "Young Women in the Second Great Awakening in New England." *Feminist Studies* 2, no. 1/2 (Autumn 1975): 15–29.

Craig, Lee A., Barry Goodwin, and Thomas Grennes. "The Effect of Mechanical Refrigeration on Nutrition in the United States." *Social Science History* 28, no. 2 (Summer 2004): 325–36.

Craig, Robert F., and Kathleen Housley. "Communications." *New England Quarterly* 62, no. 2 (June 1989): 315–18.

Crane, Ellery Bicknell, ed. *Historic Homes and Institutions and Genealogical and Personal Memoirs of Worcester County Massachusetts with a History of Worcester Society of Antiquity*. Vol. 1. New York: The Lewis Publishing Company, 1907.

Cronon, William. *Changes in the Land: Indians, Colonists, and the Ecology of New England*. New York: Hill and Wang, 1983.

Cummings, Abbott Lowell. *The Framed Houses of Massachusetts Bay, 1625–1725*. Cambridge: Harvard University Press, 1979.

Cummings, John. "Poor-Laws of Massachusetts and New York: With Appendices Containing the United States Immigration and Contract Laws." *Publications of the American Economic Association* 10, no. 4 (July 1895): 15–135.

Danhof, Clarence H. *Changes in Agriculture: The Northern United States, 1820–1870*. Cambridge: Harvard University Press, 1969.

Dannenbaum, Jed. *Drink and Disorder: Temperance Reform in Cincinnati from the Washingtonian Revival to the WCTU*. Urbana: University of Illinois Press, 1984.

Dawley, Alan. *Class and Community: The Industrial Revolution in Lynn*. Cambridge: Harvard University Press, 1976.

Demos, John. *A Little Commonwealth: Family Life in Plymouth Colony*. New York: Oxford University Press, 1970.

———. *Past, Present, and Personal: The Family and the Life Course in American History*. New York: Oxford University Press, 1986.

Demos, John, and Virginia Demos. "Adolescence in Historical Perspective." *Journal of Marriage and the Family* 31, no. 4 (November 1969): 632–38.

Dennison, George M. "The Dorr War and Political Questions." In *The 1979 Yearbook of the Supreme Court Historical Society Publications*, edited by William F. Swindler, 45–62. Washington, D.C.: Supreme Court Historical Society, 1978.

Donahue, Brian. "The Forests and Fields of Concord: An Ecological History, 1750–1850." In *Concord: A Social History*, edited by David Hackett Fisher. Waltham, Mass.: Brandeis University, 1983.

————. *The Great Meadow: Farmers and the Land in Colonial Concord*. New Haven: Yale University Press, 2004.

————. "'Skinning the Land': Economic Growth and the Ecology of Farming in 19th Century Massachusetts." Unpublished paper, Brandeis University, October 1980.

Dublin, Thomas. "Rural Putting Out Work in Early Nineteenth-Century New England: Women and the Transition to Capitalism in the Countryside." *New England Quarterly* 64, no. 4 (December 1991): 531–73.

————. *Transforming Women's Work: New England Lives in the Industrial Revolution*. Ithaca: Cornell University Press, 1994.

————. *Women at Work: The Transformation of Work and Community in Lowell, Mass., 1826–1860*. New York: Columbia University Press, 1979.

Dudden, Faye E. *Fighting Chance: The Struggle Over Women Suffrage and Black Suffrage in Reconstruction America*. New York: Oxford University Press, 2011.

Dupuis, William O. *Boylston: Images of America*. Charleston, S.C.: Acadia Press, 2001.

————. *Boylston in the Revolutionary War*. Boylston Historical Series, vol. 10. Boylston, Mass.: Boylston Historical Commission, 1979.

————. *The Boylston Reader*. Boylston, Mass.: Old Pot Publication, Boylston Historical Society, 1997.

————. *The Boylston Sketch Book*. Boylston Historical Series, vol. 11. Boylston, Mass.: Boylston Historical Commission, 1978.

————. *Boylston's Minutemen*. Boylston Historical Series, vol. 9. Boylston, Mass.: Boylston Historical Commission, 1980.

————. *Boylston Taverns*. Boylston Historical Series, vol. 8. Boylston, Mass.: Boylston Historical Commission, 1980.

————. *Historical Sites of Boylston*. Boylston Historical Series, vol. 7. Boylston, Mass.: Boylston Historical Commission, 1980.

————. *History of Boylston, 1742–1786*. Boylston Historical Series, vol. 4. Boylston, Mass.: Boylston Historical Commission, 1980.

————. *History of Boylston, 1786–1886*. Boylston Historical Series, vol. 12. Boylston, Mass.: Boylston Historical Commission, 1978.

————. *Index to the Historical Series*. Boylston Historical Series, vol. 14. Boylston, Mass.: Boylston Historical Commission, 1980.

————. *Lives Thus Spent*. Boylston, Mass.: The Fuller Foundation, 1981.

————. *Strangers and Pilgrims*. 2 vols. Boylston, Mass.: Boylston Historical Commission, 1982.

————. *A Sword in My Hand: The Life of Rev. Dr. Ebenezer Morse of Boylston, Massachusetts*. Published by the author, 1992.

Elazar, Daniel J. "The Political Theory of Covenant: Biblical Origins and Modern Developments." *Publius* 10, no. 4 (Autumn 1980): 3–30.

————. "The Principles and Traditions Underlying State Constitutions." *Publius* 12, no. 1 (Winter 1982): 11–25.

Ellis, Joseph J. *After the Revolution: Profiles in Early American Culture*. New York: W. W. Norton, 1979.

Ellis, Robert P. *Northborough in the Civil War: Citizen Soldiering and Sacrifice*. Charleston, S.C.: The History Press, 2007.

Feller, Daniel. *The Jacksonian Promise: America, 1815–1840*. Baltimore: Johns Hopkins University Press, 1995.

———. "Politics and Society: Toward a Jacksonian Synthesis." *Journal of the Early Republic* 10 (Summer 1990): 135–61.

Fischer, David Hackett, ed. *Concord: A Social History*. Waltham, Mass.: Brandeis University, 1983.

———. *Paul Revere's Ride*. New York: Oxford University Press, 1994.

Fletcher, Robert S., and Malcolm O. Young, eds. *Amherst College Biographical Record of the Graduates and Non-Graduates, 1821–1921*. Centennial ed. Amherst: Published by the College, 1927.

Formisano, Ronald P. *For the People: American Populist Movements from the Revolution to the 1850s*. Chapel Hill: University of North Carolina Press, 2008.

———. *The Transformation of Political Culture: Massachusetts Parties, 1790s-1840s*. New York: Oxford University Press, 1983.

French, Norman H. *Sawyer's Mills*. Boylston Historical Series, vol. 3. Boylston, Mass.: Boylston Historical Commission, 1980.

Fritz, Christian G. *American Sovereigns: The People and America's Constitutional Tradition Before the Civil War*. Cambridge: Cambridge University Press, 2008.

———. "America's Unknown Constitutional World." *Common-Place* (October 2008). http://www.common-place.org/pasley/?page_id=491 (February 2013).

Fuhrer, Mary Babson. "The Druggist's Apprentice: A Diary of Coming of Age in Antebellum Boston." In *In Our Own Words: New England Diaries, 1600 to the Present*, Dublin Seminar for New England Folk Life Annual Proceedings 2006/2007, 39:160–73. Boston: Boston University Press, 2009.

———. *Letters from the "Old Home Place": Anxieties and Aspirations in Rural New England, 1836–1843*. Boylston, Mass.: Old Pot Publications, 1997.

———. "'We All have Something to Do in the Cause of Freeing the Slave': The Abolition Work of Mary White." In *Women's Work in New England, 1620–1920*, Dublin Seminar for New England Folk Life Annual Proceedings 2001, 26:109–25. Boston: Boston University Press, 2001.

Gambler, Wendy. "Tarnished Labor: The Home, the Market, and the Boardinghouse in Antebellum America." *Journal of the Early Republic* 22, no. 2 (Summer 2002): 177–204.

Gettleman, Marvin E. *The Dorr Rebellion: A Study in American Radicalism, 1833–1849*. New York: Random House, 1973.

Gienapp, William E. "'Politics Seem to Enter into Everything': Political Culture in the North." In *Essays on American Antebellum Politics, 1840–1860*. Edited by Stephen E. Maizlish and John J. Kushma. College Station: Texas A&M University, 1982.

Gilmore, William. *Reading Becomes a Necessity of Life: Material Culture in Rural New England, 1780–1835*. Knoxville: University of Tennessee Press, 1989.

Ginzberg, Lori D. "'Moral Suasion Is Moral Balderdash': Women, Politics, and Social Activism in the 1850s." *Journal of American History* 73, no. 3 (December 1986): 601–22.

———. *Women and the Work of Benevolence: Morality, Politics, and Class in the 19th-Century United States*. New Haven: Yale University Press, 1990.

Gould, Eliga H. *The Persistence of Empire: British Political Culture in the Age of the American Revolution*. Chapel Hill: University of North Carolina Press, 2000.

———. "Prelude: The Christianizing of British America." In *Missions and Empire*, edited by Norman Etherington. Oxford: Oxford University Press, 2008.

Graff, Harvey J. *Conflicting Paths: Growing Up in America*. Cambridge: Harvard University Press, 1995.

Greenberg, Joshua R. *Advocating the Man: Masculinity, Organized Labor, and the Household in New York, 1800–1840*. New York: Columbia University Press, 2006. http://www.guteneberg-e.org/greenberg (February 2013).

Greene, Jack P. *Pursuits of Happiness: The Social Development of Early Modern British Colonies and the Formation of American Culture*. Chapel Hill: University of North Carolina Press, 1988.

Greer, Allan. "Commons and Enclosure in the Colonization of North America." *American Historical Review* 117, no. 2 (April 2012): 365–86.

Greven, Philip F., Jr. *Four Generations: Population, Land, and Family in Colonial Andover, Massachusetts*. Ithaca, N.Y.: Cornell University Press, 1970.

Griffin, Clifford S. "Religious Benevolence as Social Control, 1815–1860." *Mississippi Valley Historical Review* 44, no. 3 (December 1957): 423–44.

———. *Their Brothers' Keepers: Moral Stewardship in the United States, 1800–1865*. New Brunswick, N.J.: Rutgers University Press, 1960.

Grimshaw, Patricia. *Paths of Duty: American Missionary Wives in Nineteenth Century Hawaii*. Honolulu: University of Hawaii Press, 1989.

Grob, Gerald N. *The Mad Among Us: A History of the Care of America's Mentally Ill*. New York: The Free Press, 1994.

———. "Review: *The Discovery of the Asylum Social Order and Disorder in the New Republic*, by David J. Rothman." *Political Science Quarterly* 87, no. 2 (June 1972): 325–26.

———. *The State and the Mentally Ill: A History of Worcester State Hospital in Massachusetts, 1830–2920*. Chapel Hill: University of North Carolina Press, 1966.

Gross, Robert A. "Books, Nationalism, and History." *Papers of the Bibliographical Society of Canada* (September 22, 1998): 107–23.

———. "Commemorating Concord." *Common-Place* 4, no. 1 (October 2003). http://www.common-place.org/vol-04/no-01/gross/ (February 2013).

———. "Culture and Cultivation: Agriculture and Society in Thoreau's Concord." *Journal of American History* 69, no. 1 (June 1982): 42–61.

———. "Doctor Ripley's Church": Congregational Life in Concord, Massachusetts, 1778–1841." *Journal of Unitarian Universalist History* 33 (2009–10): 1–37.

———. "Faith in the Boardinghouse: New Views of Thoreau Family Religion." *Thoreau Society Bulletin* 250 (Winter 2005): 1–5.

———. "Giving in America: From Charity to Philanthropy." In *Charity, Philanthropy, and Civility in American History*, edited by Lawrence J. Friedman and Mark D. McGarvie, 19–48. Cambridge: Cambridge University Press, 2003.

———. "Helen Thoreau's Antislavery Scrapbook." *Yale Review* 100, no. 1 (January 2012): 103–20.

———. "The Impudent Historian: Challenging Deference in Early America." *Journal of American History* 85, no. 1 (June 1998): 92–97.

———. "Lonesome in Eden: Dickinson, Thoreau, and the Problem of Community in Nineteenth-Century New England." *Canadian Review of American Studies* 14, no. 1 (Spring 1983): 1–17.

———. "The Machine-Readable Transcendentalists: Cultural History on the Computer." *American Quarterly* 42, no. 3 (September 1989): 501–21.

———. *The Minutemen and their World*. New York: Hill and Wang, 1976.

———. "'The Most Estimable Place in All the World': A Debate on Progress in Nineteenth-Century Concord." *Studies in the American Renaissance* (1978): 1–15.

———. "Print and the Public Sphere in Early America." In *The State of U.S. History*, edited by Melvyn Stokes, 245–64. New York: Berg Press, 2002.

———. "Quiet War with the State: Henry David Thoreau and Civil Disobedience." *Yale Review* 93, no. 4 (October 2005): 1–17.

———. "Squire Dickenson and Squire Hoar." *Proceedings of the Massachusetts Historical Society*, 3rd ser., 101 (1989): 1–23.

———. "'That Terrible Thoreau': Concord and Its Hermit." In *A Historical Guide to Henry David Thoreau*, edited by William E. Cain, 181–241. New York: Oxford University Press, 2000.

———. "Transcendentalism and Urbanism: Concord, Boston, and the Wider World." *Journal of American Studies* 18, no. 3 (December 1984): 361–81.

———. *The Transcendentalists and Their World* (forthcoming).

———. "A Yankee Rebellion? The Regulators, New England and the New Nation." *New England Quarterly* 82, no. 1 (March 2009): 112–35.

———. "Young Men and Women of Fairest Promise: Transcendentalism in Concord." *Concord Saunterer* 2, no. 1 (Fall 1994): 5–18.

———, ed. *In Debt to Shays: The Bicentennial of an Agrarian Rebellion*. Publications of the Colonial Society of Massachusetts and Historic Deerfield, vol. 65. Charlottesville: University of Virginia Press, 1993.

Gross, Robert A., and Mary Kelley. "An Age of Print? The History of the Book and the New Nation." *Common-Place* 11, no. 4 (July 2011). http://www.common- place.org/vol-11/no-04/author/ (February 2013).

Gross, Robert A., and Mary Kelley, eds. *An Extensive Republic: Print, Culture, and Society in the New Nation, 1790–1840*. Vol. 2 of *History of the Book in America*. Chapel Hill: University of North Carolina Press, 2010.

Hahn, Steven, and Jonathan Prude. *The Countryside in the Age of Capitalist Transformation: Essays in the Social History of Rural America*. Chapel Hill: University of North Carolina Press, 1985.

Hall, David D. *Worlds of Wonder, Days of Judgment: Popular Religious Belief in Early New England*. Cambridge: Harvard University Press, 1989.

Halttunen, Karen. *Confidence Men and Painted Women: A Study of Middle-Class Culture in America, 1830–1870*. New Haven: Yale University Press, 1982.

Hamilton, Helen Maxwell. *The History of West Boylston*. West Boylston, Mass.: West Boylston Historical Society, 2000.

Hammond, Bray. *Banks and Politics in America, from the Revolution to the Civil War*. Princeton: Princeton University Press, 1957.

Hampel, Robert L. *Temperance and Prohibition in Massachusetts, 1813–1852*. Ann Arbor: University of Michigan Research Press, 1982.

Harris, Marc. "The People of Concord: A Demographic History, 1750–1850." In *Concord: A Social History*, edited by David Hackett Fisher. Waltham, Mass.: Brandeis University, 1983.

Harris, Tim. *London Crowds in the Reign of Charles II: Propaganda and Politics from the Restoration until the Exclusion Crisis*. Cambridge: Cambridge University Press, 1987.

Hazen, Craig James. *The Village Enlightenment in America: Popular Religion and Science in the Nineteenth Century*. Urbana: University of Illinois Press, 2000.

Herdon, Ruth Wallis. *Unwanted Americans: Living on the Margin in Early New England*. Philadelphia: University of Pennsylvania Press, 2001.

Henretta, Michael. "Families and Farms: *Mentalité* in Preindustrial America." *William and Mary Quarterly* 35, no. 1 (January 1978): 3–32.

———. "Review: The Morphology of New England Society in the Colonial Period." *Journal of Interdisciplinary History* 2, no. 2 (Autumn 1971): 379–98.

Heyrman, Christine Leigh. *Southern Cross: The Beginnings of the Bible Belt*. Chapel Hill: University of North Carolina Press, 1997.

Hofstadter, Richard. *The Idea of a Party System: The Rise of Legitimate Opposition in the United States, 1780–1840*. Berkeley: University of California Press, 1969.

Hogan, David. "Modes of Discipline: Affective Individualism and Pedagogical Reform in New England, 1820–1850." *American Journal of Education* 99, no. 1 (November 1990): 1–56.

Hood, J. Edward, and Holly V. Izard. "Two Examples of Marginal Architecture in Rural Worcester County: Identifying and Documenting the Homes of New England's Marginalized Peoples." Unpublished paper presented at the Annual Meeting of the Society for American Archaeology in Chicago, March 25, 1999. http://resources.osv.org/explore_learn/document_viewer.php?DocID=770 (June 2013).

Hostetler, John. *Amish Society*. 4th ed. Baltimore: Johns Hopkins University Press, 1993.

Howe, Daniel Walker. *The Political Culture of American Whigs*. Chicago: University of Chicago Press, 1979.

———. "Religion and Politics in the Antebellum North." In *Religion and American Politics: From the Colonial Period to the Present*, 2d ed., edited by Mark A. Noll and Luke E. Harlow. New York: Oxford University Press, 2007: 121–43.

———. *What God Hath Wrought: The Transformation of America, 1815–1848*. New York: Oxford University Press, 2007.

Howe, M. A. Dewolfe, ed. *The Humane Society of the Commonwealth of Massachusetts: An Historical Review, 1785–1916*. Boston: The Humane Society, 1918.

Hubka, Thomas C. *Big House, Little House, Back House, Barn: The Connected Farm Buildings of New England*. Lebanon, N.H.: University Press of New England, 1984.

Hurd, Henry M., ed. *The Institutional Care of the Insane in the United States and Canada*. Baltimore: Johns Hopkins University Press, 1917.

Huston, James. "Economic History." H-SHEAR Forum on Daniel Walker Howe's *What Hath God Wrought*, October 27, 2008. http://h-net.msu.edu/cgi-bin/logbrowse.pl?trx=vx&list=h-shear&month=0810&week=d&msg=xC7PayA4egDoXIRVNPkdcA&user=&pw= (June 2013).

Huston, James L. "The Experiential Basis of Northern Antislavery Impulse." *Journal of Southern History* 56, no. 4 (November 1990): 609–40.

Hutton, Patrick H. "The History of Mentalities: The New Map of Cultural History." *History and Theory* 20, no. 2 (October 1981): 237–59.

Innes, Stephen. *Creating the Commonwealth: The Economic Culture of Puritan New England*. New York: W. W. Norton & Company, 1995.

"Interpretive Sourcebook on African Americans in Rural New England." Unpublished study, 1990. Old Sturbridge Village Research Department, Sturbridge, Mass.

Isaac, Rhys. *The Transformation of Virginia, 1740–1790*. Chapel Hill: University of North Carolina Press, 1982.

Izard, Holly. "Guy Scott of Sturbridge: Exploring Cultural Diversity." *Old Sturbridge Visitor* (Winter 1994): 10–11.

———. "The Ward Family and their 'Helps': Domestic Work, Workers, and Relationships on a New England Farm, 1787–1866." *Proceedings of the American Antiquarian Society* 103, no. 1 (1993): 61–90.

Jaffee, David. *A New Nation of Goods: The Material Culture of Early America*. Philadelphia: University of Pennsylvania Press, 2010.

———. *People of the Wachusett: Greater New England in History and Memory, 1630–1860*. Ithaca: Cornell University Press, 1999.

———. "The Village Enlightenment in New England, 1760–1820." *William and Mary Quarterly* 47, no. 3 (July 1990): 327–46.

Jedrey, Christopher M. *The World of John Cleaveland: Family and Community in Eighteenth Century New England*. New York: W. W. Norton & Company, 1979.

Jeffrey, Julie Roy. *The Great Silent Army of Abolitionism: Ordinary Women in the Antislavery Movement*. Chapel Hill: University of North Carolina Press, 1998.

Jellison, Richard M., ed. *Society, Freedom, and Conscience: The American Revolution in Virginia, Massachusetts, and New York*. With essays by Jack P. Greene, Richard L. Bushman, Michael Kammen. New York: Norton, 1976.

Jimenez, Mary Ann. "Madness in Early American History: Insanity in Massachusetts from 1700 to 1830." *Journal of Social History* 20, no. 1 (Autumn 1986): 25–44.

Johnson, Curtis D. *Redeeming America: Evangelicals and the Road to the Civil War*. Chicago: Ivan Dee, 1993.

———. "Supply-side and Demand-side Revivalism? Evaluating the Social Influences on New York State Evangelism in the 1830s." *Social Science History* 19, no. 1 (Spring 1995): 1–30.

Johnson, Paul E. *A Shopkeeper's Millennium: Society and Revivals in Rochester, New York, 1815–1837*. New York: Hill and Wang, 1978.

Juster, Susan M., and Maris A. Vinovskis. "Changing Perspectives on the American Family in the Past." *Annual Review of Sociology* 13 (1987): 193–216.

Kamensky, Jane. *The Exchange Artist: A Tale of High-Flying Speculation and American's First Banking Collapse*. New York: Penguin, 2008.

Katz, Michael. *The Irony of Early School Reform: Educational Innovation in Early Nineteenth-Century Massachusetts*. Cambridge: Harvard University Press, 1969.

Kelleher, Tom. "The Blackstone Canal: Artery to the Heart of the Commonwealth." Unpublished research paper, 1997. Old Sturbridge Village Research Library, Sturbridge, Mass. http://resources.osv.org/explore_learn/document_viewer.php?DocID=1928 (June 2013).

———. "The Debit Economy of 1830s New England." Unpublished study. Old Sturbridge Village Research Library, Sturbridge, Mass. http://www.teachushistory.org/detocqueville-visit-united-states/articles/debit- economy-1830s-new-england (February 2013).

Kelley, Mary. *Learning to Stand and Speak: Women, Education, and Public Life in America's Republic*. Chapel Hill: University of North Carolina Press, 2006.

———. "Reading Women/Women Reading: The Making of Learned Women in Antebellum America." *Journal of American History* 83, no. 2 (September 1996): 401–24.

Kelly, Catherine E. *In the New England Fashion: Reshaping Women's Lives in the Nineteenth Century*. Ithaca: Cornell University Press, 1999.

Kelsey, Darwin P. "Early New England Farm Crops: Flax." Unpublished paper, 1980. Old Sturbridge Village Research Library, Sturbridge, Mass.

Kerber, Linda K. *Women of the Republic: Intellect and Ideology in Revolutionary America*. Chapel Hill: University of North Carolina Press, 1980.

Kett, Joseph F. "Adolescence and Youth in Nineteenth-Century America." *Journal of Interdisciplinary History* 2, no. 2 (Autumn, 1971): 283–98.

———. *Rites of Passage: Adolescence in America 1790 to the Present*. New York: Basic Books, 1977.

Kimenker, James. "The Concord Farmer: An Economic History." In *Concord: A Social History*, edited by David Hackett Fischer. Waltham, Mass.: Brandeis University, 1983.

Kohl, Lawrence Frederick. "The Concept of Social Control and the History of Jacksonian America." *Journal of the Early Republic* 5, no. 1 (Spring 1985): 21–34.

———. *The Politics of Individualism: Parties and the American Character in the Jacksonian Era*. New York: Oxford University Press, 1989.

Koschnik, Albrecht. *"Let a Common Interest Bind Us Together": Associations, Partisanship and Culture in Philadelphia, 1775–1840*. Charlottesville: University of Virginia Press, 2007.

Kraybill, Donald. *The Riddle of Amish Culture*. Rev. ed. Baltimore: Johns Hopkins University Press, 2001.

Kraybill, Donald B., and Marc B. Olshan, eds. *The Amish Struggle with Modernity*. Hanover, N.H.: University Press of New England, 1994.

Kulikoff, Allan. *The Agrarian Origins of American Capitalism*. Charlottesville: University of Virginia Press, 1992.

———. *From British Peasants to Colonial American Farmers*. Chapel Hill: University of North Carolina Press, 2000.

———. "The Progress of Inequality in Revolutionary Boston." *William and Mary Quarterly* 28, no. 3 (July 1971): 375–412.

———. "The Transition to Capitalism in Rural America." *William and Mary Quarterly* 46, no. 1 (January 1989): 120–44.

Lamoreaux, Naomi R. *Insider Lending: Banks, Personal Connections, and Economic Development in Industrial New England*. New York: Cambridge University Press, 1994.

Lampi, Philip J. "First Democracy Project: A New Nation Votes." Database of American Election Returns, 1787–1825. American Antiquarian Society, Worcester, Mass. http://elections.lib.tufts.edu/ (June 2013).

Larkin, Jack. "Accounting for Change: Exchange in the Rural Economy of Central New England." Unpublished paper. Old Sturbridge Village Research Library, Sturbridge, Mass.

———. "Episodes from Daily Life: 'The Life and Writings of Minerva Mayo by herself,' an Exercise in Microhistory." Unpublished paper presented as the Kidger Academic Award talk to the New England History Teachers' Association, March 1999. Old Sturbridge Village Research Library, Sturbridge, Mass.

———. "From 'Country Mediocrity' to 'Rural Improvement': Transforming the Slovenly Countryside in Central Massachusetts." Unpublished paper. Old Sturbridge Village Research Library, Sturbridge, Mass.

———. "Gathering Places." *Old Sturbridge Village Visitor*. Sturbridge, Mass., 1981.

———. "'Labor Is the Great Thing in Farming': The Farm Laborers of the Ward Family of Shrewsbury, Massachusetts, 1787–1860." *Proceedings of the American Antiquarian Society* 99, no. 1 (1989): 201–15.

———. "The Merriams of Brookfield: Printing in the Economy and Culture of Rural Massachusetts in the Early Nineteenth Century." *Proceedings of the American Antiquarian Society* 96, pt. 1 (April 1986): 39–69.

———. *The Reshaping of Everyday Life, 1790–1840*. New York: Harper & Row, 1988.

———. "Rural Life in the North." In *Encyclopedia of American Society History*, edited by Mary Kupiec Cayton, Elliott J. Gorrn, and Peter W. Williams, 2:1219. New York: Charles Scribner's Sons, 1993.

———. "Women in the Workplace: Rural New England in the Early Nineteenth Century." Unpublished paper, 1982. Old Sturbridge Village Research Library, Sturbridge, Mass.

Larson, Andrew. "Men of Small Property: Harry Franco and Henry Ward Beecher in the Ante-Bellum Market." *Common-Place* 10, no. 4 (July 2010). http://www.common-place.org/vol-10/no-04/lawson/ (February 2013).

Laslett, Peter. *The World We Have Lost: England Before the Industrial Age*. 3rd ed. New York: Charles Scribner's Sons, 1984.

Lasser, Carol. "The Domestic Balance of Power: Relations Between Mistress and Maid in Nineteenth-Century New England." *Labor History* 28, no. 1 (Winter 1987): 5–22.

Laurie, Bruce. *Artisans into Workers: Labor in Nineteenth-Century America*. New York: The Noonday Press, 1989.

———. *Beyond Garrison: Antislavery and Social Reform*. Cambridge: Cambridge University Press, 2005.

Lemire, Elise. *Black Walden: Slavery and Its Aftermath in Concord, Massachusetts*. Philadelphia: University of Pennsylvania Press, 2009.

Lepler, Jessica. "Pictures of Panic: Constructing Hard Times in Words and Images." *Common-Place* 10, no. 3 (April 2010). http://www.common-place.org/vol- 10/no-03/lepler/.

Lerner, Gerda. *The Grimké Sisters from South Carolina: Pioneers for Women's Rights and Abolition*. Boston: Houghton Mifflin, 1967.

Levy, Barry. *Town Born: The Political Economy of New England from Its Founding to the Revolution*. Philadelphia: University of Pennsylvania Press, 2009.

Levy, Jonathan. *Freaks of Fortune: The Emerging World of Capitalism and Risk in America*. Cambridge: Harvard University Press, 2012.

———. "A Moment with Jonathan Levy, on Capitalism." *Princeton Alumni Weekly* 112, no. 3 (October 26, 2011).

Lockridge, Kenneth A. *A New England Town: The First Hundred Years*. Enlarged ed. New York: W. W. Norton & Company, 1985.

Lovett, Robert W. "Squire Rantoul and His Drug Store, 1796–1824." *Bulletin of the Business Historical Society* 25, no. 2. (June 1951): 99–114.

Lubken, Deborah. "Joyful Ringing, Solemn Tolling: Methods and Meanings of Early American Tower Bells." *William and Mary Quarterly* 69, no. 4 (October 2012): 823–42.

Luskey, Brian P. "Jumping Counters in White Collars: Manliness, Respectability and Work in the Antebellum City." *Journal of the Early Republic* 26, no. 2 (Summer 2006): 173–219.

MacFarlane, Alan. *The Origins of English Individualism.* Oxford: Basil Blackwell, 1978.

Mackall, Joe. *Plain Secrets: An Outsider among the Amish.* Boston: Beacon Press, 2007.

Main, Gloria L. *Peoples of a Spacious Land: Families and Cultures in Colonial New England.* Cambridge: Harvard University Press, 2001.

Maizlish, Stephen E., and John J. Kushma, eds. *Essays on American Antebellum Politics, 1840–1860.* College Station: Texas A&M University, 1982.

Manring, Lynn, and Jack Larkin. "Women, Anti-Slavery, and the Constitution in Rural New England: A Sourcebook for Interpretation." Unpublished study. Old Sturbridge Village Research Library, Sturbridge, Mass.

Margo, Robert A., and Georgia C. Villaflor. "The Growth of Wages in Antebellum America: New Evidence." *Journal of Economic History* 47, no. 4 (December 1987): 873–95.

McClelland, Peter D. *Sowing Modernity: America's First Agricultural Revolution.* Ithaca: Cornell University Press, 1997.

McCrossen, Alexis. "The Sound and Look of Time: Bells and Clocks in Philadelphia." *Common-Place* 13, no. 1 (October 2012). http:/www.common-place.org/vol-13/no-01/mccrossen (February 2013).

McCusker, John J., and Russell R. Menard. *Economy of British America, 1607–1789.* Chapel Hill: University of North Carolina Press, 1991.

McGerr, Michael E. *The Decline of Popular Politics: The American North, 1865–1928.* New York: Oxford University Press, 1986.

Melish, Joanne Pope. *Disowning Slavery: Gradual Emancipation and "Race" in New England, 1780–1860.* Ithaca: Cornell University Press, 1998.

Merchant, Carolyn. *Ecological Revolutions: Nature, Gender, and Science in New England.* Chapel Hill: University of North Carolina Press, 1989.

Merrill, Michael D. "Cash Is Good to Eat: Self-Sufficiency and Exchange in the Rural Economy of the United States." *Radical History Review* 3 (1977): 42–71.

Mihm, Stephen. *A Nation of Counterfeiters: Capitalists, Con Men, and the Making of the United States.* Cambridge: Harvard University Press, 2007.

Miller, Perry. "The Marrow of Puritan Divinity." In *Errand into the Wilderness*, 48–98. Cambridge: Harvard University Press, 1956.

———. *The New England Mind: The Seventeenth Century.* 1939. Reprint, Cambridge: Harvard University Press, 1983.

Mintz, Steven. *Moralists and Modernizers: America's Pre-Civil War Reformers.* Baltimore: Johns Hopkins University Press, 1995.

Morgan, Rev. John Ellsworth. *Historical Review of the First Congregational Church, Boylston, Massachusetts.* Boylston: First Congregational Church Committee, 1943.

Murphy, Sharon Ann. "'Doomed . . . to Eat the Bread of Dependency'? Insuring the Middle-Class against Hard Times." *Common-Place* 10, no. 3 (April 2010). http://www.common-place.org/vol-10/no-03/murphy/ (February 2013).

Murrin, John. "No Awakening, No Revolution? More Counter Factual Speculation." *Reviews in American History* 11, no. 2 (June 1983): 161–71.

Nash, Margaret A. "Cultivating the Powers of Human Beings: Gendered Perspectives on

Curricula and Pedagogy in Academies of the New Republic." *History of Education Quarterly* 41, no. 2 (Summer 2001): 239–50.

Neem, Johann N. *Creating a Nation of Joiners: Democracy and Civil Society in Early National Massachusetts*. Cambridge: Harvard University Press, 2008.

———. "The Elusive Common Good: Religion and Civil Society in Massachusetts, 1780–1833." *Journal of the Early Republic* 24, no. 3 (Autumn 2004): 381–417.

Newman, Richard S. *The Transformation of American Abolitionism: Fighting Slavery in the Early Republic*. Chapel Hill: University of North Carolina Press, 2002.

Nissenbaum, Stephen. *Sex, Diet, and Debility in Jacksonian America: Sylvester Graham and Health Reform*. Chicago: The Dorsey Press, 1980.

Noble, John. *A Few Notes on the Shays Rebellion*. Worcester, Mass.: Reprinted from the *PAAS*, Press of C. Hamilton, 1903.

Noonan, William C. *Educational History of Boylston*. Boylston Historical Series, vol. 6. Boylston, Mass.: Boylston Historical Commission, 1980.

Nylander, Jane C. *Our Own Snug Fireside: Images of the New England Home, 1760–1860*. New York: Alfred A. Knopf, 1993.

Old Sturbridge Village Museum Education Department, ed. "Reform: Poverty." Sturbridge, Mass.: Old Sturbridge Village, 1979.

———. "Reform: Temperance." Sturbridge, Mass.: Old Sturbridge Village, 1978.

Onuf, Peter S. *Jefferson's Empire: The Language of American Nationhood*. Charlottesville: University of Virginia Press, 2000.

Opal, J. M. *Beyond the Farm: National Ambitions in Rural New England*. Philadelphia: University of Pennsylvania Press, 2008.

———. "Exciting Emulation: Academies and the Transformation of the Rural North, 1780s-1820s." *Journal of American History* 91, no. 2 (September 2004): 445–70.

Oshantz, Molly. *Slavery and Sin: The Fight against Slavery and the Rise of Liberal Protestantism*. New York: Oxford University Press, 2012.

Osterud, Nancy Grey. *Bonds of Community: The Lives of Farm Women in Nineteenth-Century New York*. Ithaca: Cornell University Press, 1991.

Parks, Roger N. "Roads and Travel in New England, 1790–1840." Sturbridge, Mass.: Old Sturbridge Village Booklet Series, 1965.

Perkins, Edwin. "The Rise and Fall of Relationship Banking." *Common-Place* 9, no. 2 (January 2009). http://www.common-place.org/vol-09/no-02/talk/ (February 2013).

Pessen, Edward. *Jacksonian America: Society, Personality, and Politics*. Rev. ed. Chicago: University of Illinois Press, 1985.

Pope, Charles Henry, and Thomas Hooper. *Hooper Genealogy*. Boston: Published by Charles H. Pope, 1908.

Potter, Russell. *Pyg: The Memoirs of Toby, the Learned Pig*. New York: Penguin Books, 2012.

Prude, Jonathan. *The Coming of Industrial Order: Town and Factory Life in Rural Massachusetts, 1810–1860*. New York: Cambridge University Press, 1983.

Pruitt, Betty Hobbs. "Self-Sufficiency and the Agricultural Economy of Eighteenth-Century Massachusetts." *William and Mary Quarterly* 41, no. 3 (July 1984): 334–64.

Putnam, Robert D. *Bowling Alone: The Collapse and Revival of American Community*. New York: Simon and Schuster, 2000.

Raup, Hugh M. "The View from John Sanderson's Farm: A Perspective for the Use of the Land." *Forest History* 10, no. 1 (April 1966): 2–11.

Reiss, Benjamin. "P. T. Barnum, Joice Heth, and Antebellum Spectacles of Race." *American Quarterly* 51, no. 1 (March 1999): 78–107.

———. *The Showman and the Slave: Race, Death, and Memory in Barnum's America.* Cambridge: Harvard University Press, 2001.

Remini, Robert V. *The Jacksonian Era.* 2nd ed. Wheeling, Ill.: Harlan Davidson, 1997.

Rice, Stephen P. "Making Way for the Machine: Maelzel's Automaton Chess-Player and Antebellum American Culture." *Proceedings of the Massachusetts Historical Society* 3rd ser., 106 (1994): 1–16.

Richards, Leonard L. *Gentlemen of Property and Standing: Anti-Abolition Mobs in Jacksonian America.* New York: Oxford University Press, 1970.

———. *Shays's Rebellion: The American Revolution's Final Battle.* Philadelphia: University of Pennsylvania Press, 2002.

Roediger, David R. *The Wages of Whiteness: Race and the Making of the American Working Class.* Rev. ed. London: Verso, 2007.

Rorabaugh, W. J. *The Alcoholic Republic: An American Tradition.* New York: Oxford University Press, 1979.

———. *The Craft Apprentice: From Franklin to the Machine Age in America.* New York: Oxford University Press, 1986.

Rothbard, Murray N. *A History of Money and Banking in the United States: The Colonial Era to World War II.* Auburn, Ala.: Ludwig von Mises Institute, 2002.

Rothenberg, Winifred Barr. *From Market-Places to a Market Economy: The Transformation of Rural Massachusetts, 1750–1850.* Chicago: University of Chicago Press, 1992.

———. "The Market and the Massachusetts Farmer, 1750–1850." *Journal of Economic History* 41 (1981): 283–314.

Rothman, David. *The Discovery of the Asylum: Order and Disorder in the New Republic.* Rev. ed. Boston: Little Brown, 2006.

Rude, George. *The Crowd in History: A Study of Popular Disturbances in France and England, 1730–1848.* 1964. Reprint, London: Serif, 2005.

Ruggles, Steven. "The Transformation of American Family Structure." *American Historical Review* 99, no. 1 (February 1994): 103–28.

Russell, Howard S. *A Long, Deep Furrow: Three Centuries of Farming in New England.* Abridged ed. Hanover, N.H.: University Press of New England, 1982.

Rutman, Darrett B. "Assessing the Little Communities of Early America." *William and Mary Quarterly* 43, no. 2 (April 1986): 164–78.

Ryan, Mary P. *Cradle of the Middle Class: The Family in Oneida County, New York, 1790–1865.* Cambridge: Cambridge University Press, 1981.

———. "A Woman's Awakening: Evangelical Religion and the Families of Utica, New York, 1800–1840." *American Quarterly* 3, no. 5 (Winter 1978): 602–23.

Sandage, Scott. *Born Losers: A History of Failure in America.* Cambridge: Harvard University Press, 2005.

Scott, Donald M. "The Popular Lecture and the Creation of a Public in Mid-Nineteenth Century America." *Journal of American History* 66, no. 4 (March 1980): 791–809.

Schlesinger, Arthur M., Jr. *The Age of Jackson*. Boston: Little, Brown & Company, 1945.

Sears, Clara Endicott. *Days of Delusion: A Strange Bit of History*. Boston: Houghton Mifflin Co., 1924.

Sellers, Charles. *The Market Revolution: Jacksonian America, 1815–1846*. New York: Oxford University Press, 1991.

Shalhope, Robert E. "Review: The Radicalism of Thomas Dorr." *Reviews in American History* 2, no. 3 (September 1974): 383–89.

———. *A Tale of New England: The Diaries of Hiram Harwood, Vermont Farmer, 1810–1837*. Baltimore: Johns Hopkins University Press, 2003.

———. "Toward a Republican Synthesis: The Emergence of an Understanding of Republicanism in American Historiography." *William and Mary Quarterly* 29, no. 1 (January 1972): 49–80.

Shammas, Carole. "Anglo-American Household Government in Comparative Perspective." *William and Mary Quarterly* 52, no. 1 (January 1995): 104–44.

———. "How Self-Sufficient Was Early America?" *Journal of Interdisciplinary History* 13, no. 2 (Autumn 1982): 247–72.

Shapardson, Laura E. "The Old Square—Aaron White of Quinebaug, Conn. Secretary Under Gov. Dorr." Paper read at a meeting of the Quinabaug Historical Society, November 29, 1909. Quinabaug Historical Society Leaflets, 2, no. 24. Quinebaug, Conn.

Shiels, Richard D. "The Scope of the Second Great Awakening: Andover, Massachusetts as a Case Study." *Journal of the Early Republic* 5, no. 2 (Summer 1985): 223–46.

Showalter, Rev. Dr. Douglas K. "The Early Days." Massachusetts Conference United Church of Christ, 2003. http://www.macucc.org/about-us/vig1.htm.

Simpson, Alan. *Puritanism in Old and New England*. Chicago: University of Chicago Press, 1955.

Sizer, Theodore R. "The Academies: An Interpretation." In *The Age of the Academies*, 1–48. New York: Teachers College, Columbia University, 1964.

Smith, Daniel Scott. "All in Some Degree Related to Each Other: A Demographic and Comparative Resolution of the Anomaly of New England Kinship." *American Historical Review* 94, no. 1 (February 1989): 44–79.

———. "Parental Power and Marriage Patterns: An Analysis of Historical Trends in Hingham, Massachusetts." *Journal of Marriage and Family* 35, no. 3 (August 1973): 419–28.

Spiegel, Alix. "One Man Tackles Psychotherapy for the Amish." Transcript of radio interview with Dr. James A. Cates, with Michele Norrris. *NPR: All Things Considered*, March 18, 2009. http://www.npr.org/templates/story/story.php?storyId=102053475.

Stachiw, Myron O. "Tradition and Transformation: Emerson Bixby and the Social, Material and Economic World of Barre Four Corners." Unpublished paper presented at the 1988 annual meeting of the Society for Historians of the Early American Republic, July 22, 1988. Old Sturbridge Village Research Library, Sturbridge, Mass.

Stachiw, Myron, and Nora Pat Small. "Tradition and Transformation: Rural Society and Architectural Change in Nineteenth-Century Central Massachusetts." In *Perspectives in Vernacular Architecture* 3 (1989): 135–48.

Steinberg, Ted. "Down to Earth: Nature, Agency, and Power in History." *American Historical Review* 107, no. 3 (June 2002): 798–820.

Sterling, Dorothy. *Ahead of Her Time: Abbey Kelley and the Politics of Antislavery*. New York: W. W. Norton & Company, 1991.

Sterns, Bertha-Monica. "Reform Periodicals and Female Reformers, 1830–1860." *American Historical Review* 37, no. 4 (July 1932): 678–99.

Stewart, Steven J. "Skimmington in the Middle and New England Colonies." In *Riot and Revelry in Early America*, edited by William Pencak, Matthew Dennis, and Simon P. Newman, 41–86. University Park: Pennsylvania State University Press, 2002.

Stilgoe, John R. *Common Landscape of America, 1580–1845*. New Haven: Yale University Press, 1982.

Stoll, Steven. *Larding the Lean Earth: Soil and Society in Nineteenth-Century America*. New York: Hill and Wang, 2002.

Stone, Lawrence. *The Family, Sex and Marriage in England, 1500–1800*. Abridged paperback ed. New York: Harper and Row, 1979.

Sutton, Sarah Campbell. "From Farmhouse to Factory: Dairy Centralization in Worcester County, Massachusetts." Unpublished paper, Brandeis University, 2008.

Szatmary, David P. *Shays' Rebellion: The Making of an Agrarian Insurrection*. Amherst: University of Massachusetts Press, 1980.

Tatham, David. *The Lure of the Striped Pig: The Illustration of Popular Music in America, 1820–1870*. Barre, Mass.: The Imprint Society, 1973.

Taylor, Alan. "The Early Republic's Supernatural Economy: Treasure Seeking in the American Northeast, 1780–1830." *American Quarterly* 38, no. 1 (Spring 1986): 6–34.

———. *William Cooper's Town: Power and Persuasion on the Frontier of the Early American Republic*. New York: Vintage Books, 1995.

Taylor, George Rogers. *The Transportation Revolution, 1815–1860*. Economic History of the United States, vol. 4. Armonk, N.Y.: M. E. Sharpe, 1977.

Taylor, Robert J. *Western Massachusetts in the Revolution*. Providence: Brown University Press, 1954.

Temin, Peter, ed. *Engines of Enterprise: An Economic History of New England*. Cambridge: Harvard University Press, 2000.

Thirsk, Joan, ed. *The Agrarian History of England and Wales, 1640–1750*. Regional Farming Systems, vol. 5. Cambridge: Cambridge University Press, 1984.

Thomas, Keith. *Religion and the Decline of Magic*. New York: Oxford University Press, 1997.

Thompson, E. P. *Customs in Common: Studies in Traditional Popular Culture*. New York: The New Press, 1993.

———. "The Moral Economy of the English Crowd in the Eighteenth Century." *Past and Present* 50 (1971): 76–136.

Thomson, Ross. *The Path to Mechanized Shoe Production in the United States*. Chapel Hill: University of North Carolina Press, 1989.

Thornton, Tamara Plakins. "Between Generations: Boston Agricultural Reform and the Aging of New England, 1815–1830." *New England Quarterly* 59, no. 2 (June 1986): 189–211.

———. "A 'Great Machine' or a 'Beast of Prey': A Boston Corporation and Its Rural Debtors in an Age of Capitalist Transformation." *Journal of the Early Republic* 27, no. 4 (Winter 2007): 567–97.

Tolley, Kim. "The Rise of Academies: Continuity or Change?" *History of Education Quarterly* 41, no. 2 (Summer 2001): 225–39.

Tolley, Kim, and Nancy Beadie. "Symposium: Reappraisals of the Academy Movement." *Higher Education Quarterly* 41, no. 2 (Summer 2001): 216–24.

Tonnies, Ferdinand. *Community and Society, Gemeinschaft und Gesellschaft*. Translated by Charles P. Loomis. 1887. Reprint, Mineola, N.Y.: Dover Publications, 2011.

Towers, Frank. "Bank Fraud in the Age of Mob Violence." Review of Robert E. Shalhope, *The Baltimore Bank Riot: Political Upheaval in Antebellum Maryland*. Published on H-Net for H-SHEAR, May 2010. http://h-net.msu.edu/cgi-bin/logbrowse.pl?trx=vx&list= h-slavery&month=1005&week=b&msg=TSlKykakGZnCZoEA7KtSmA&user=&pw= (June 2013).

Tritsch, Electa Kane. "Documenting Hassanamesit Woods: Its History and Cultural Resources." Oakfield Research for the Hassanamesit Woods Management Committee, November 2006.

Turner, Frederick Jackson. *The Rise of the New West, 1819–1829*. New York: Harper & Brothers, 1906.

———. "The Significance of the Section in American History." *Wisconsin Magazine of History* 8, no. 3 (March 1925): 255–80.

Tyler, Alice Felt. *Freedom's Ferment: Phases in American Social History to 1860*. Minneapolis: University of Minnesota Press, 1944.

Ulrich, Laurel T. *The Age of Homespun: Objects and Stories in the Creation of an American Myth*. New York: Alfred A. Knopf, 2001.

———. "A Friendly Neighbor: Social Dimensions of Daily Work in Northern Colonial New England." *Feminist Studies* 6, no. 2 (Summer 1980): 392–405.

———. *Good Wives: Image and Reality in the Lives of Women in Northern New England, 1650–1750*. New York: Vintage Books, 1991.

———. *A Midwife's Tale: The Life of Martha Ballard, Based on Her Diary, 1785–1812*. New York: Alfred A. Knopf, 1991.

Underwood, Francis W. *Quabbin: The Story of a Small Town with Outlooks on Puritan Life*. 1893. Reprint, Northeastern University Press, 1986.

Van Tassel, Kristin. "Nineteenth-Century American Antebellum Literature: The Yeoman Becomes a Country Bumpkin." *American Studies* 43, no. 1 (Spring 2002): 51–73.

Vickers, Daniel. "Competency and Competition: Economic Culture in Early America." *William and Mary Quarterly* 47, no. 1 (January 1990): 3–29.

———. *Farmers and Fishermen: Two Centuries of Work in Essex County, Massachusetts, 1630–1850*. Chapel Hill: University of North Carolina Press, 1994.

Wagner, David. *The Poorhouse: America's Forgotten Institution*. Lanham, Md.: Rowman & Littlefield Publishers, 2005.

Wagner, Vern. "The Lecture Lyceum and the Problem of Controversy." *Journal of the History of Ideas* 15, no. 1 (January 1954): 119–35.

Wallace, Anthony F. C. *The Death and Rebirth of the Seneca*. New York: Alfred A. Knopf, 1970.

———. *Rockdale: The Growth of an American Village in the Early Industrial Revolution*. New York: W. W. Norton & Company, 1978.

Walters, Ronald G. *American Reformers, 1815–1860*. New York: Hill and Wang, 1978.

———. *The Antislavery Appeal: American Abolitionism after 1830*. New York: W. W. Norton & Company, 1978.

Waters, John J. "The Traditional World of New England Peasants: A View from Seventeenth-Century Barnstable." *New England Historical and Genealogical Register* 130, no. 1 (1976): 3–21.

Watkinson, James D. "Useful Knowledge? Concepts, Values, and Access in American Education, 1776–1840." *Higher Education Quarterly* 30, no. 3 (Autumn 1990): 351–70.

Watson, Harry L. *Liberty and Power: The Politics of Jacksonian America*. New York: Noonday Press, 1990.

Weir, David A. *Early New England: A Covenanted Society*. Grand Rapids, Mich.: William B. Eerdmans Publishing Company, 2005.

Welter, Barbara. "The Cult of True Womanhood, 1820–1860." *American Quarterly* 18, no. 2 (Summer 1966): 151–74.

White, Ann. "Counting the Cost of Faith: America's Early Female Missionaries." *Church History* 57, no. 1 (March 1988): 19–30.

Wiebe, Richard H. *The Opening of American Society: From the Adoption of the Constitution to the Eve of Disunion*. New York: Alfred A. Knopf, 1984.

———. *The Search for Order, 1877–1920*. New York: Hill and Wang, 1967.

Wilentz, Sean. *The Rise of American Democracy: Jefferson to Jackson*. Abridged college ed. New York: W. W. Norton & Company, 2009.

Williamson, Chilton. *American Suffrage: From Property to Democracy, 1760–1860*. Princeton: Princeton University Press, 1960.

Wimsatt, W. K., Jr. "Poe and the Chess Automaton." *American Literature* 11, no. 2 (May 1939): 138–51.

Wittmann, Mattew. "Menageries and Markets: The Zoological Institute Tours of Jacksonian America." *Common-Place* 12, no. 1 (October, 2011). http://www.common-place.org/vol-12/no-01/lessons/ (February 2013).

Wood, Frederic J. *The Turnpikes of New England and Evolution of the Same through England, Virginia and Maryland*. Boston: Marshall Jones Company, 1919.

Wood, Gordon S. *The Radicalism of the American Revolution*. 1991. Reprint, New York: First Vintage Books Edition, 1993.

Wood, Joseph S. *The New England Village*. Baltimore: Johns Hopkins University Press, 1997.

Wright, Conrad E. *The Transformation of Charity in Post-Revolutionary New England*. Boston: Northeastern University Press, 1992.

Wrightson, Keith. *English Society, 1580–1680*. New Brunswick, N.J.: Rutgers University Press, 1982.

Wyatt-Brown, Bertram. *Lewis Tappan and the Evangelical War Against Slavery*. Baton Rouge: Louisiana State University Press, 1997.

Yellin, Jean Fagan, and John C. Van Horne, eds. *The Abolitionist Sisterhood: Women's Political Culture in Antebellum America*. Ithaca: Cornell University Press, 1994.

Zakim, Michael. "The Business Clerk as Social Revolutionary; or, a Labor History of the Nonproducing Classes." *Journal of the Early Republic* 26, no. 4 (Winter 2006): 563–603.

Zuckerman, Michael. *Peaceable Kingdoms: New England Towns in the Eighteenth Century*. New York: Alfred A. Knopf, 1970.

INDEX

Abbot, Jason, 23–27 passim, 41, 52, 82, 175, 178, 182–85, 249, 288 (n. 114)

Abbot, Mary, 23–27 passim, 51, 66, 68, 178, 182–85, 236, 249, 291 (n. 55)

Abbot, Mary Ann, 178, 182–84, 303 (n. 124)

Abolition. *See* Antislavery

Academies, rural, 112–20 passim, 126, 142–51, 246, 296 (nn. 60, 62), 297 (n. 67)

Account books, 25–26, 77, 100, 247, 287 (n. 84), 289 (n. 133); account book of Aaron White, 22, 286 (n. 76); account book of Joseph Flagg, 90, 293 (n. 85)

Agricultural societies, 21, 87, 272 (n. 45)

Alcohol, 152, 155–68; as cause of poverty, 172, 175–76, 302 (n. 99); as cause of insanity or suicide, 182, 281 (n. 79), 303 (n. 123). *See also* Temperance

Almanacs, 28, 126

Ambition, 9–10, 14, 23, 103, 133, 135, 153; economic, 75, 86, 118; for personal betterment, 103, 111, 119, 143–44, 247

American Revolution, 4, 11, 200, 215–16, 243; rhetoric of, 9, 11, 13, 36; promises of, 11, 13; and social order in Boylston, 31–32, 33, 36, 39, 48, 153, 191; heritage of, 103; ideals of, 189–91, 199, 200, 203, 211, 212, 215–16, 221, 241

Amish, 68

Anti-Masonry, 192, 205, 214, 305 (n. 32), 308 (n. 7)

Antislavery, 155, 214, 223–44

The Anti-Slavery Almanac, 232

Anxiety, 5, 16, 101, 180, 184; religious, 65, 66, 246; economic, 101, 103, 200, 204, 208; parental, 102–7 passim, 128, 150, 218

Apprentices, 64, 84–85, 104–9, 111, 139, 204, 290 (nn. 14, 21)

Assets: land as asset, 35; church, 70–71; aptitude as asset, 84, 101; paper, 100; capital, 110; real and personal property, 111, 172, 178, 275 (n. 15); bank, 209. *See also* Capital

Associations: voluntary, 8, 48, 282 (n. 87); evangelical, 51–54, 67, 69–70; educational, 126, 143, 296 (n. 48); reform, 152–55, 156–63, 167–68; and political affiliation,

185, 189, 191, 194; antislavery, 224–26, 228–40, 242–44, 314 (n. 45)

Asylums, lunatic, 181–85, 246, 303 (nn. 123, 124, 132, 134)

Authority: customary, 1, 66, 139, 168, 184, 194; patriarchal, 5, 16, 95, 115, 143, 176; political, 12, 13, 19, 214, 216; hierarchal, 12, 32; gentry-led cultural, 13, 31, 36, 126, 150, 153; religious, 33, 48, 66, 72; in shaping moral values in school, 128, 132, 134–35; vested in self, 154, 203, 239

Autonomy, 5, 156, 200, 202, 203, 223. *See also* Freedom; Independence; Liberty; Self-determination; Self-mastery; Self-reliance

Avery, Mary Allen, 179–80

Bancroft, George, 191, 203, 215

Bank notes, 100, 191, 208–12

Banks, 88, 100, 169, 190, 191, 197, 201, 205, 206–12

Baptists, 50, 56, 57, 160, 190, 197, 236, 274 (n. 100), 278 (nn. 14, 22), 279 (nn. 36, 41, 42), 280 (n. 44), 297 (n. 67)

Barnum, P. T., 227

Belonging: communal, 3, 9, 10, 48, 247; corporate, 12–14, 49, 58, 71; farm family, 17, 279 (n. 41); neighborhood, 24, 28; covenant, 29; church, 32–34; town, 34–35, 275 (n. 107); and exclusion, 42–44; and voluntary churches, 69; and self-cultivation, 127, 150; and voluntary societies, 157; political, 213, 215; and self-ownership, 247

Blacks: in Boylston, 42–44, 249, 277 (n. 154), 313 (n. 17); and political belonging, 213, 215; Boylstonian conceptions of, 226–27; and antislavery, 232, 237, 243, 247, 317 (nn. 85, 86)

Blackstone River Canal, 79, 205, 288 (n. 107)

Bliss, Asher, 113–15

Boardinghouses, 66, 107–8, 117

Bonds: social, 2, 103; of affection, 9, 119, 127; of localism, 9, 173; of family, 15–16, 101, 119, 150; communal, 28, 44, 185; neighborly, 28, 90, 101, 187; of volunteer

345

activism, 157; of faith, 54; of religious fellowship, 69; with land, 89, 271 (n. 36); of intellect, 127; of schoolmates, 147–48; political, 198; of antislavery work, 228–40, 242. *See also* Obligations

Bondsman family, 42–44, 226, 227, 277 (n. 149)

Boston, Mass.: travel to and from, 7, 78, 79; as marketplace, 19, 22, 23, 78–79, 84, 87, 88; as cosmopolitan center, 50, 82; as destination for White children, 64, 74, 78, 83, 85, 121; connections to, 69–70, 82, 224; as place to shop, 82; as destination for Boylston sons, 83; and challenges of urban life for country youth, 104–8; and antislavery contacts, 223, 224, 229, 238, 242

Boston, Sarah, 43–44

Boston Female Antislavery Society, 229, 230, 233–34, 237, 238, 242–314 (n. 45)

Boylston Female Antislavery Society, 224–26, 228–40, 242–44, 314 (n. 45)

Boylston Maternal Association, 67, 155

Boylston Moral Reform Society, 69, 155

Boylston Temperance Society, 155, 156–61, 167–68

Burton, Warren, 186–88, 195, 196, 199

Bush, Jotham, 23, 27, 36, 201, 288 (n. 114)

Bush, Mary, 26, 27, 51, 68

Butler, Abigail, 172, 178, 301 (n. 86)

Calvinism, 29, 48–62 passim, 131, 144, 202, 225, 294 (n. 16); and covenant, 29–30; and corporate belonging, 29–30, 144; New Light, 33, 48, 50, 277 (n. 5); Old Light, 33, 274 (n. 99)

Canals, 7, 50, 70, 76, 78–80, 82, 88, 190, 204, 205, 288 (n. 107)

Capital: family strategies for accumulating, 14, 19, 22–23, 85, 108; land as, 18; and shoemaking, 76, 110; social, 154, 298 (n. 5); and corporations, 169, 206; and banks, 206, 308 (n. 85)

Cash: scarcity of, 24, 38, 77, 208; cash value of farm products, 25; wages, 38, 97, 124; transactions, 77, 90–92, 289 (nn. 133, 134); need for, 78–79, 83, 89; pursuit of, 97, 100, 124; as transformative, 100–101, 104, 247

Catholicism, 94, 213

Chapman, Maria, 232–34, 238, 239, 242, 314 (nn. 36, 50, 51, 53, 56), 316 (n. 76), 317 (nn. 81, 83)

Character: of yeomen, 19, 81; personal, 60, 106, 115, 117, 146, 200, 208, 215, 221, 309

(n. 127); formation of, 108–9, 131, 142, 145, 290 (nn. 29, 30); shaped through reading, 128, 131, 135, 138–40; flawed, 171, 172, 176, 177, 183

Charter Party, 212–21

Church, 4, 5, 8, 9, 10, 46–73, 251 (n. 3); established state ("Standing Order"), 8, 9, 55, 194, 223; covenanted, 11, 14, 39; as corporate entity, 12, 31; seating, 13, 42; discipline, 14, 30–31, 110; and social order, 14, 39, 50; orthodox Congregational, 14, 50–51, 55–58, 70–72, 249; attendance, 16; belonging, 30, 32–34, 49; admission to, 30, 33; exclusion from, 42; liberalism and Unitarian, 49–51, 55–57, 70–72; and discord, 58–61; revivals, 61–63; disestablishment, 70–72, 154, 193–94; choir, 109, 111, 117; and temperance, 110, 157–58, 159, 160, 166; and school curriculum, 131–32; membership and political affiliation, 190, 193, 197, 201; dissenting churches, 191; membership and antislavery, 228, 235, 237–38, 239, 240; and Millerism, 245

Civil War, 149, 247, 249, 283 (n. 16)

Class, 56–58, 98, 128, 147, 195, 206, 214, 235, 242, 250, 268 (n. 18), 276 (n. 141), 304 (n. 21); privileged, 56, 57, 99, 191, 206, 211; middle, 81, 86, 97, 108, 125, 128, 137, 141–42, 145, 151, 166, 168, 176, 185, 189–90, 191, 217, 221, 226; of landless laborers, 94, 145, 168; white-collar, 104–9, 221; of urban youth, 107; working (mechanics, artisans, operatives), 107, 140, 212; of rural poor, 170–77

Clerk, shop, 79–81, 104–9, 136

Cold Water Army, 159, 160. *See also* Temperance

Colleges: Harvard College, 16, 31, 48, 58, 203, 204, 215; Amherst College, 114; Williams College, 136, 297 (n. 69); preparation for college, 142–43; White family offspring and college, 145, 204, 249; Mt. Holyoke College, 146, 249; Brown College, 297 (n. 69)

Comfortable subsistence, 19, 92, 118

Common good: and covenant, 34–35; as goal of gentry authority, 36, 189, 246; customary defense of, 39; as customary, 45, 75; undermined by religious sectarianism, 48; challenged by voluntary association, 51, 75, 154, 168; undermined by competition, 144; undermined by partisan politics, 202, 216, 304 (n. 11);

and bank policies, 208; eclipsed by plural interests, 246

Communication: improvements in, 6, 7, 294 (n. 6), 298 (n. 4); and pamphlets, 50, 53, 65, 154, 164, 198, 310 (n. 133); and family, 149–50; and politics, 198, 304 (n. 13); and localism, 173. *See also* Newspapers; Printing; Tracts

Competence, economic, 19, 23, 80, 83, 100, 107, 109–10, 119, 133

Competition: and need for land, 12, 23; and markets, 77, 110, 132; and education, 133, 143–44; and partisan politics, 189, 194, 195; and demise of common good, 246

Concert of prayer, 54, 278 (n. 28)

Congregationalism: and orthodoxy, 14; and covenant relationship, 37, 39, 275 (n. 108); and conflicts with liberalism, 48, 49–61 passim, 131–32, 280 (n. 48); and evangelicalism, 61–70, 278 (n. 22), 281 (n. 70); as Standing Order, 72, 194, 201; and reform, 155–58; and political affiliation, 193–94, 197; and antislavery, 224–25, 228, 235, 237–39, 295 (n. 18), 313 (n. 28), 315 (n. 65), 316 (n. 66), 317 (nn. 84, 85); characteristics of, 279 (nn. 36, 41), 280 (n. 43). *See also* Calvinism; Church

Consensus: as customary ideal, 12–13, 141, 194; and covenant, 30, 55; in town government, 37, 41; Federalist, 39, 59, 191, 192, 305 (n. 29); challenged by religious sectarianism, 49, 55, 132, 194; challenged by social reform, 154, 155; on Free Soil, 242

Constitutions: Massachusetts Constitution, 34, 194, 275 (n. 108); U.S. Constitution, 39, 42, 207, 213, 309 (n. 117); of voluntary associations, 51–52, 158, 278 (nn. 20, 21, 22), 312 (n. 12); Rhode Island Constitution, 213–21, 311–12 (nn. 150, 165)

Constitutional Party of Rhode Island, 213–21, 311 (n. 150). *See also* Dorr, Thomas W.; Suffrage

Conventions: Hartford Convention, 41, 307 (n. 63); temperance, 158, 159; political, 189, 191, 195, 196, 197, 198–99; Anti-Masonic, 205, 305 (n. 32), 308 (n. 76); Rhode Island constitutional convention, 213–15; antislavery, 220, 224, 230, 233, 236, 242, 315 (n. 65); Free Soil Convention, 317 (n. 101)

Conversion, religious, 33, 49, 62–70, 72, 132, 153, 183, 240, 279 (n. 41), 294 (n. 16)

Cooperation, neighborly, 13, 25, 157, 247

Corporate sensibility, 9, 12–14, 17, 28–45 passim, 243, 246, 247, 269 (n. 4), 274 (n. 105); and religion, 47, 49, 57, 66, 68, 70, 71, 72, 126; and private education, 143, 144; and voluntary societies, 157; and politics, 191, 194, 202, 216

Corporations: town, 40–41; religious, 71, 88; financial, 88, 169–70, 189–91, 195, 207, 212; educational, 144; for improvement, 153

Cotton, Hannah Sophia, 185, 233, 314 (nn. 36, 50)

Cotton, John, 198, 202, 306 (n. 54)

Cotton, Sally, 136, 239

Cotton, Ward, 23, 27, 33, 48–51, 52–56, 62, 72, 120, 123, 132, 193, 280 (nn. 44, 48)

Cousinhood, 24, 98, 173

Covenant, 11, 14, 29–41 passim, 44, 47–72 passim, 246, 269 (n. 4), 273 (n. 80), 274 (n. 83), 275 (n. 108)

Credit, 23; store accounts, 22, 86, 93, 124, 163; long-term farm accounts, 24–25, 86, 90, 98, 100, 109, 169, 275 (n. 115), 289 (n. 133); from financial institutions, 121, 169, 206–11, 246

Crossman, Abijah, 10, 23, 27, 96, 109–12, 113, 117, 164–68, 176, 249, 290 (nn. 35, 39), 291 (n. 41)

Crossman, Caleb, 109–12, 119, 124, 158, 176, 291 (nn. 45, 47, 48)

Curriculum, 129–32, 135, 146, 294 (n. 16)

Davenport, Matthew, 76, 146, 280 (n. 44), 296 (n. 48)

Davis, Simon, 14–40 passim, 99, 156, 170, 270 (n. 17), 274 (n. 88)

Death, 1, 18–19, 130, 147, 295 (n. 19); as providence, 26, 29, 183; of Sophia Whitney, 42, 44; and autopsy, 43, 227; of Samuel Russell, 70; of Caleb Crossman, 112, 291 (n. 45); hoped-for reunion after, 147–48; insurance in event of, 169–70; of Mary Allen Avery, 179–80; of Mary Ann Abbot, 183–84; of Aaron White Sr., 248; of Aaron White Jr., 249; of Mary White, 250. *See also* Suicide

Debt: neighborly account books, 20, 24–26, 90, 287 (n. 86); from acquiring land, 35, 78, 89; suits for, 60, 111; loss of farms to, 101, 291 (n. 51); from speculation, 121; as cause of insanity, 182, 281 (n. 79); as political issue, 190; banks and, 208–10; at probate, 275 (n. 115), 283 (n. 18), 289 (n. 137)

Federalism, 191–92, 304 (n. 12), 307 (n. 67); and gentry, 7, 39–40, 153; and consensus, 39, 59, 191–93, 305 (n. 29); and social order, 39, 153, 191–92, 200; and corporatism, 39–40; and politics, 39–42, 188, 191–93, 201, 204, 277 (n. 146), 304 (nn. 11, 12), 307 (n. 67); and religion, 277 (n. 5)

Female benevolence, 51–54, 66–70, 228–32, 242–43

Fifteen Gallon Law, 162–68

Flagg, Joseph, 89–93, 94, 95, 96, 100, 158, 170, 247, 283 (n. 14), 286 (n. 84), 287 (nn. 86, 88, 89, 92, 93), 288 (n. 116)

Flagg, Levi Lincoln, 94, 118–19, 122, 127, 147, 196, 249

Folk belief, 11, 28, 126

Freedom, 11–12, 42, 43, 45, 154, 189, 199, 218, 223, 271 (n. 36), 304 (n. 20); of conscience, 51, 154, 166; of self-determination, 85, 101, 140, 186, 246; from family obligations, 118; and self-control, 156; from imposed social norms, 163; economic, 177; from slavery, 223–44. *See also* Autonomy; Independence; Liberty

Freehold, 8, 19, 39, 81–82, 212–13

Freemasonry, 192, 205

Free Soil Party, 241–42, 317 (nn. 98, 101)

French Revolution, 37, 200, 218, 307 (n. 59)

Gag rule, 234, 236, 241

Garrison, William Lloyd, 224–25, 229, 230, 238, 312 (n. 8), 313 (nn. 23, 34), 314 (nn. 39, 45)

Gentility: pursuit of, 6–7, 8, 12, 83, 109, 111; middle-class female ideals of, 81, 120; through schooling, 135–47 passim; lampooning of, 166–67, 248. *See also* Refinement

Gentry, 7, 9; and improvement, 21, 37, 116, 153, 166; and social order, 32–33, 36–37, 39, 48, 142, 153, 191, 240; as Federalist elite, 39; deference to, 39–40, 60, 126; and orthodoxy, 48, 57; landed identity of, 101; and education, 135, 143–45; and corporations, 169, 207–8; and privilege, 200, 202; obligations of, 200–201. *See also* Squirearchy

Gough, John, 168

Grimké, Sarah and Angelina, 230–32, 236, 313 (n. 25), 314 (n. 40), 316 (n. 71)

Hartford Convention, 41

Harvard, Mass., 2, 152, 301 (n. 92), 304 (n. 16)

Harvard College, 16, 31, 48–49, 58, 204, 215, 297 (n. 69)

Heth, Joice, 227

Hierarchies, 12, 31, 32, 39, 68, 103, 127, 153, 203, 244

Holden, Mass., 15–16, 155

Hooper family, 112–15, 291 (nn. 51, 55)

Hopedale, Mass., 185

Houghton, Benjamin, Jr., 115–17, 124, 292 (nn. 74, 77), 293 (n. 82)

Houghton, Benjamin, Sr., 21, 63, 116, 133, 292 (nn. 69, 71)

Howe, John, 1–2, 21, 59–61, 70–71, 132, 242, 249, 280 (n. 53)

Immigrants, 94–95, 98, 107, 128, 173, 212–13, 247, 288 (n. 107)

Improvement, 4–5, 9, 12, 14, 75, 86, 101, 246, 295 (n. 19), 298 (n. 1); social, 7, 36–37, 152–85 passim; in transportation, 7, 78–80, 92, 99; in farming, 21–23, 74, 86–89, 118–19; material, 82–83; as self-striving, 86; personal, 104, 122, 226, 246; through education, 126–51 passim; and Whigs, 189, 200–201, 212. *See also* Reform

Independence: from social bonds, 2, 45, 103; from obligations of family farming, 6, 103; through land-owning, 8, 11, 19, 100, 190, 203, 249, 271 (n. 36); and civic obligation, 39; and cash, 97; from social norms, 103, 202–3; as self-determination, 108, 125, 156, 159, 174, 202–3, 307 (n. 65); as economic self-support, 109, 117, 119, 123–24, 141, 177, 211; from tyranny of concentrated power, 191, 192, 202–3, 211–12; from slavery, 223–44. *See also* Autonomy; Freedom; Liberty

Indians. *See* Native Americans

Individualism, 8–10, 12–13, 23, 28, 45, 197, 199, 203, 223, 243, 246–47; and religion, 36, 48, 49, 64, 68, 72–73; and personal striving, 86, 103–25, 144; and reading, 140; and self-cultivation, 151; and voluntary association, 152–53, 157, 159

Industry, 6–7, 76, 79–80, 128, 174, 185, 213, 235; textile, 79–80, 117, 179, 193, 201, 205, 210, 235; shoe-making, 85, 109–11, 117, 290 (n. 33), 293 (n. 83); and class, 128, 192, 202, 212; and capital, 169, 207–8, 308 (n. 85); and Whigs, 189

Insanity: and religious enthusiasm, 67; and study, 143; and alcohol, 156; and reform, 177–85
Insurance: community as, 13, 168; insurance companies, 168–70
Interdependence, 9, 119; covenant, 14, 35, 68; neighborly, 77, 98–99, 143, 150, 170, 185, 270 (n. 9); and hired help, 97; generational, 148; and insurance, 173
Irish, 94–95, 107, 247, 248, 249, 288 (n. 107)

Jackson, Andrew, 121, 134, 192, 207; era of, 188–89, 268 (nn. 9, 10), 269 (nn. 21, 22); Democrats, 189–91

Kinship. *See* Families
Knowledge: traditional agrarian, 21, 87; pursuit of, 119, 126–51 passim, 167, 244; democratized, 126–27, 143; and betterment, 132, 133–34, 135–36, 140–42, 144; professional, 184–85

Labor: factory, 6, 84, 117; of evangelical womanhood, 68–69; choices in, 80–81, 83–85; urban white-collar, 80–81, 104–9, 111; and wages, 93–97, 99–100; outwork, 110, 117, 124; school teaching, 123; at poor farm, 174; in lunatic asylum, 183; and liberal Democrats, 191, 202, 208; and suffrage in Rhode Island, 212–13, 221; and Free Soil, 241–42. *See also* Farm labor
Landholding: and civic identity, 8, 19, 80, 81–82, 84, 89, 117; and franchise, 35, 214
Landlessness, 94, 195, 212–14
Law and Order Party. *See* Charter Party
Law of 1838. *See* Fifteen Gallon Law
Lectures, 8, 64, 108, 135; lyceum, 140–42, 151, 296 (n. 48); temperance, 154–59; political, 186–88, 196; antislavery, 224, 230–42 passim, 317 (n. 86)
Letter-writing, 137–38
Liberty, 2, 5, 7, 9, 11, 36, 45, 79, 117, 153, 163, 174, 189–222 passim; as self-control, 156; as economic self-sufficiency, 177; and slavery, 223–44 passim. *See also* Autonomy; Freedom; Independence
Liberty Party, 240–41
License Law. *See* Fifteen Gallon Law
Lincoln, Levi, 192, 234, 236
Liquor. *See* Alcohol; Temperance
Loco Focos. *See* Democratic Party
Log Cabin campaign, 198–99, 214
Lyceums, 140–42, 151, 296 (n. 48)

Maelzel, Johann, 187, 223
Mann, Horace, 131, 132, 134, 181
Marketers, 74, 78–79, 84, 88–89, 90
Market Revolution, 6, 83, 268 (n. 12)
Markets, 11, 13; local marketplaces, 22–23; distant marketplaces, 23, 79–80, 90, 110, 118, 246; marketing firms, 90, 91, 118; producing for, 90–93; vicissitudes of, 91, 103; capital, 206. *See also* Farming: and markets
Martyn, Grace Smith, 224, 312 (n. 3)
Martyn, Job, 224, 312 (n. 3)
Massachusetts State Board of Education, 131, 134
Massachusetts Temperance Union, 158
Meadows, 19–20, 90, 92, 166
Meetinghouses: as signifying social order, 31–32, 34, 39, 46–47, 226, 274 (n. 89); as source of dispute, 40, 48, 55, 58, 70–72; proximity to, 40, 57; deconstruction of, 71–72, 91, 287 (n. 93); as contested sectarian space, 141, 157
Middle class: gentility, 81, 125, 137; manhood, 86, 226; domestic ideals, 97, 185; respectability, 108, 128, 142, 189–90, 191; and private academies, 145; among Dorrite supporters, 214, 217; and antislavery, 225–26
Migration, 83–86; and transience, 93–95, 97–100. *See also* Immigrants; Mobility, geographic
Militia, 14, 34, 44, 107; and antitemperance, 163; Dorrite, 219
Mill: villages, 76, 80, 90, 92, 93, 117, 287 (n. 89), 292 (n. 80); textile, 112, 117, 201, 205
Millennialism, 63, 153, 245
Millerites, 245
Missionary work, 51–52, 54, 66, 69, 70, 85, 113–15, 155, 248
Mobility, geographic, 251, 253; with improved transportation, 79; consequences of, 98–99, 153, 172–73
Morse, Ebenezer, 32, 33, 274 (nn. 82, 84)
Mortgages, 78, 81, 169, 176–77, 291 (n. 51); mortgage of Benjamin Houghton Jr., 116–17, 292 (nn. 71, 79); from commercial bank, 208–9
Morton, Marcus, 168, 194, 300 (n. 68)
Murdock, David C., 127, 139, 151, 240, 294 (n. 5)
Music: rough, 14; and sociability, 24, 27, 109; church, 30, 33, 109, 111, 117, 166, 183; as profession, 111; town performances of, 116;

as ornamental art, 143; and reform, 152, 159; and politics, 198–99, 215; and black stereotypes, 227

National Republican Party, 188, 192–93, 200–201, 206–7

Native Americans, 43–44, 69–70, 85, 113–15, 155, 226, 248

Natural aristocracy, 37, 200–201, 276 (n. 123)

Neighbors: and belonging, 9, 13–14; neighborliness, 14, 26–28, 108, 120; and mutual obligations, 20, 74, 77; as trading partners, 20–23, 24–26, 35, 77, 86–89, 90, 93; and neighborhood, 23–28, 34; and kin, 24; and religious strife, 58–59; and hired help, 93–94, 95–96; and changing relations, 98–100, 246; and risk management, 168–70; and welfare provision, 170–71, 174, 177, 184–85; and political strife, 221–22

Newspapers, 137; and religious sectarianism, 50–51, 70; and cosmopolitanism, 121; and reform, 154, 164, 300 (n. 56); and politics, 188, 195, 198, 205, 210, 304 (n. 16); and antislavery, 233, 236, 314 (n. 53)

Obligations: of town membership, 34–35, 38, 173, 185; of squirearchy, 36–37, 38–39, 202–3; of converted Christians, 69, 190; to improve, 87, 119, 152–53; transformed by cash, 100–101, 104; neighborly, 100–101, 108, 120, 169, 244; family, 112, 119, 148–51, 202, 289 (n. 1); of town toward members, 129, 133, 170–73; and alcohol, 156. See also Bonds; Interdependence; Neighbors

Orchards, 19, 20, 77, 84, 152, 202, 287 (n. 88)

Outwork: as alternative employment, 97; straw braiding, 97, 113, 124, 291 (n. 54); shoe binding, 110–11, 292 (n. 78), 293 (n. 110), 294 (n. 110)

Panic of 1819, 204, 208

Panic of 1837, 91, 111, 116, 121, 174, 176–77, 197, 207, 210–11, 229, 309 (nn. 104, 106)

Paper money. See Bank notes

Pastures, 19–20, 23, 90–92, 109, 166, 286 (n. 79)

Patriarchy. See Families: and patriarchy

Paupers. See Poor relief; Poverty

Penmanship, 105, 136–37, 138, 143

People's Constitution of Rhode Island, 214–21

People's Convention of 1841 (R.I.), 214–15

Petitions, 2, 36, 40–41, 42, 59, 133; temperance, 152, 154, 162–63, 167–68;

petition for poor farm, 174–75; political, 196–97, 201, 214, 306 (n. 51); antislavery, 223, 226, 229, 233–36, 239–41, 242, 243, 315 (nn. 60, 61, 63, 64, 65), 316 (nn. 66, 67)

Pluralism, 8–10; and religious orthodoxy, 50–51, 61, 72; and economic change, 98–100; and reform, 157; and politics, 195, 202, 222

Politics: partisan, 7, 59, 186–99, 207; Striped Pig Party, 164–68; suffrage, 213–21. See also Anti-Masonry; Democratic Party; Free Soil Party; Liberty Party; National Republican Party; Whig Party

Poor farms, 173–77, 249, 301 (n. 92), 302 (n. 101)

Poor relief, 9, 35, 37, 170–77, 185, 301 (nn. 78, 85)

Popular sovereignty, 212–21. See also Dorr, Thomas W.

Poverty, 31, 117, 170–77, 178, 246; and landless laborers, 94–96, 97, 288 (n. 106); and growing inequality in distribution of wealth, 98–99, 271 (n. 31); and diverging interests, 99; as consequence of intemperance, 156, 172, 175, 301 (n. 84), 302 (n. 99); and pigs, 166–67. See also Poor relief

Pratt, Jeremiah, 177–78

Printing: and spreading of ideas, 50, 126, 138–39, 142, 154, 268 (n. 7), 294 (n. 6), 298 (n. 4); of schoolbooks, 130; of paper money, 209

Privilege: of gentry elite, 7, 36–37, 57–58, 200, 202; and private education, 143, 151; distrust of, 191, 195–215 passim

Production, household. See Farm products

Productivity, farming, 79, 87–89

Professions: as competence, 8, 22; and elevated status, 37, 57; growth in, 80, 83–84, 85, 104; and education, 101, 111, 135, 136–37, 145, 290 (n. 16); and medical treatment, 184–85; and support for Thomas Dorr, 213–15, 221

Profit orientation in farming, 86–93

Providence, R.I., 7, 78, 79, 82, 83, 100, 121, 204, 214–19 passim, 227, 234

Providences, 3, 12, 14, 26, 28, 29, 41, 168, 173, 177, 183. See also Fate; Risk management

Quincy Report, 173–74, 176

Race, 42–44, 223, 226–27, 236, 313 (n. 18). See also Blacks; Native Americans

Railroads, 70, 76, 78, 79, 92, 190, 205

Rationalism: and religion, 56–57; in farming,

hard money, 206–7; and banking, 208–12 passim, 308 (n. 82); and antislavery, 235, 240–41, 316 (n. 67)

White, Aaron, Jr., 16, 28, 58, 161, 248–49, 307 (n. 73); and politics, 196, 199–221, 307 (n. 67), 309 (nn. 106, 122, 127), 310 (nn. 133, 143, 145), 311 (nn. 150, 155, 161); and antislavery, 236

White, Aaron, Sr.: as storekeeper, 22–23; as neighbor, 23–26; as squire, 36–37, 270 (n. 17); in civic service, 41, 76; and farming, 82, 86–89, 99; and family sensitivities, 84–85, 101–2, 148–51; and hired help, 93–94, 96, 118; and economic anxiety, 100–101, 104, 105, 106, 211; aspirations for sons, 136–37; and temperance, 156, 161–62, 164–66; and investments, 169–70; and politics, 200–202, 219–20, 307 (n. 67); and banks, 206–9; and antislavery, 235–36, 240, 242

White, Caroline, 76, 92–115 passim, 119–24, 178, 248, 249; and efforts to earn money, 97, 100, 123–24; and teaching, 97, 129–30; and domestic work, 120; and education, 120, 135, 145–46; and family sensitivities, 149–50; on temperance, 167–68; and grandmother's dementia, 179; political views, 196, 206; and antislavery, 224, 245, 316 (n. 66)

White, Elizabeth, 97, 119, 120, 123, 137, 140, 149

White, Francis, 74–75, 81, 85, 93, 96, 101, 118, 122, 195, 248; and schooling, 127–28, 135–36, 144–45, 150

White, Isaac Davis, 65, 85, 147, 148, 149, 248

White, Joseph Avery, 15, 26, 65, 85, 106, 148, 149, 150, 161–62, 248

White, Mary: diary record of, 3–4, 267 (n. 5); family of, 15–16; and seasonal rhythms, 18–19, 20–22; and reproduction, 22–23; and production, 23, 76–77, 120, 273 (n. 64), 292 (n. 72); and neighborliness, 23–28; and religious beliefs, 29–30, 50, 58;

and evangelical activism, 47–70 passim, 281 (n. 76); and Russell controversy, 60; and marketing, 78–79, 92, 286 (n. 76); and travel, 79–80; and consumption, 82–83, 284 (n. 41); anti-Catholicism, 94; and Irish immigrants, 95; and hired help, 96–97, 100, 288 (n. 12); and temperance, 154–55, 157–58, 159–62, 166–67; and politics, 186, 188, 193, 195–96, 199; and Dorr Rebellion, 218; and antislavery, 223–44, 313 (nn. 27, 29, 31), 314 (nn. 34, 48), 315 (nn. 60, 61), 316 (nn. 65, 66, 70, 80), 317 (nn. 84, 86); later years, 250–51

White, Mary (daughter of Mary and Aaron), 97, 120, 137, 248

White, Samuel Charles: conversion of, 64–66; urban apprenticeship of, 82, 84–85, 104–9, 290 (nn. 16, 21), 315 (n. 60); profession of, 109, 248; education of, 135–37, 139

White, Thomas, 23, 29, 81, 85, 96, 148, 149, 150, 218, 220, 248

White, William, 46, 72, 148, 248, 297 (n. 69); on conversion, 65; as missionary, 85; advice to Charles, 104, 108, 139, 149–50; and writing school, 136–37; on intemperance, 162; on antislavery, 243

Whitney, Sophia Martyn, 42, 44

Woodlots, 18, 19–20, 21, 25, 90, 91, 92, 95

Woodward, Samuel B., 181–84, 303 (n. 127)

Woonsocket Falls, R.I., 161, 196, 205–6, 214, 218, 219, 310 (n. 144)

Worcester, Mass., 40, 44, 70, 74–92 passim, 108–23 passim, 155–84 passim, 186, 196, 197, 198, 205, 233, 240, 242, 286 (n. 78), 287 (n. 89), 297 (n. 67), 301 (n. 92), 317 (n. 101)

Worcester Lunatic Asylum, 181–85

Working Men's Party, 221

Yeomen: identity of, 8, 80, 84, 145; independent status of, 19–20, 117. *See also* Farming